Silent Features

A collection of essays on fifteen feature-length silent films and two silent serial features. The aims of the collection are threefold: to provide detailed accounts of a wide array of films produced between the early 1910s and the early 1930s; to focus principally on films that may be well-known but that have rarely been discussed in detail; and hence to appeal to those interested in film style and its history.

> "Silent Features is a unique and an important contribution to the general field of film studies, but particularly to the serious study of silent films. ... The authors are all specialists in their subjects, and all are remarkably (and thankfully) jargon-free. Each essay is highly readable, informative, and whenever possible illustrated with frame stills. For each film, readers are given relevant cultural and historical information, an appropriate business background, and a cinematic definition of visual style, generic context, and narrative structure. ... Neale has contributed an excellent introductory essay addressing the issues of "feature" film definition, acting styles, international comparisons, and the general progression of cinema throughout the decades represented."
>
> *Professor Jeanine Basinger, Wesleyan University*

Steve Neale is Emeritus Professor of Film Studies at the University of Exeter, and Academic Director of the Bill Douglas Centre for the History of Cinema and Popular Culture.

Exeter Studies in Film History

Series Editors: **Richard Maltby,** Professor of Screen Studies, Flinders University
Steve Neale, Professor of Film Studies, University of Exeter

Parallel Tracks: The Railroad and Silent Cinema, Lynne Kirby (1997)

The World According to Hollywood, 1918–1939, Ruth Vasey (1997)

'Film Europe' and 'Film America': Cinema, Commerce and Cultural Exchange 1920–1939, edited by Andrew Higson and Richard Maltby (1999)

A Paul Rotha Reader, edited by Duncan Petrie and Robert Kruger (1999)

A Chorus of Raspberries: British Film Comedy 1929–1939, David Sutton (2000)

The Great Art of Light and Shadow: Archaeology of the Cinema, Laurent Mannoni (2000)

Popular Filmgoing in 1930s Britain: A Choice of Pleasures, John Sedgwick (2000)

Alternative Empires: European Modernist Cinemas and Cultures of Imperialism, Martin Stollery (2000)

Hollywood, Westerns and the 1930s: The Lost Trail, Peter Stanfield (2001)

Young and Innocent? The Cinema in Britain 1896–1930, ed. Andrew Higson (2002)

Legitimate Cinema: Theatre Stars in Silent British Films 1908–1918, Jon Burrows (2003)

The Big Show: British Cinema Culture in the Great War (1914–1918), Michael Hammond (2006)

Multimedia Histories: From the Magic Lantern to the Internet, edited by James Lyons and John Plunkett (2007)

Going to the Movies: Hollywood and the Social Experience of Cinema, edited by Richard Maltby, Melvyn Stokes and Robert C. Allen (2007)

Alternative Film Culture in Inter-War Britain, Jamie Sexton (2008)

Marketing Modernity: Victorian Popular Shows and Early Cinema, Joe Kember (2009)

British Cinema and Middlebrow Culture in the Interwar Years, Lawrence Napper (2009)

Reading the Cinematograph: The Cinema in British Short Fiction 1896–1912, edited by Andrew Shail (2010)

Charles Urban: Pioneering the Non-fiction Film in Britain and America, 1897–1925, Luke McKernan (2013)

Cecil Hepworth and the Rise of the British Film Industry 1899–1911, Simon Brown (2016)

The Appreciation of Film: The Postwar Film Society Movement and Film Culture in Britain, Richard L. MacDonald (2016)

The Lost Jungle: Cliffhanger Action and Hollywood Serials of the 1930s and 1940s, Guy Barefoot (2016)

Celluloid War Memorials: The British Instructional Films Company and the Memory of the Great War, Mark Connelly (2017)

UEP also publishes the celebrated five-volume series looking at the early years of English cinema, *The Beginnings of the Cinema in England*, by John Barnes.

Silent Features

*The Development of Silent Feature Films
1914–1934*

edited by
Steve Neale

UNIVERSITY
of
EXETER
PRESS

First published in 2018 by
University of Exeter Press
Reed Hall, Streatham Drive
Exeter EX4 4QR
www.exeterpress.co.uk

© 2018 Steve Neale and the individual contributors

The right of Steve Neale and the individual contributors to be identified as authors of this work has been asserted by them in accordance with the Copyright, Designs and Patents Act 1988.

British Library Cataloguing in Publication Data
A catalogue record for this book is available from the British Library.

Hardback ISBN 978 0 85989 289 6
Paperback ISBN 978 0 85989 291 9

Cover image: still from *Lady Windermere's Fan* (1925), Chapter 8

Typeset in Adobe Caslon Pro
by Forewords, Oxford

This book is dedicated to all devotees, scholars and students of silent cinema

Contents

Acknowledgements ix

Notes on Contributors x

Introduction 1
Steve Neale

1 *Germinal* (1913) 14
    Ben Brewster

2 *Assunta Spina* (1915) 32
    Lea Jacobs

3 *L'Enfant de Paris* (1913) 48
    Heather Heckman

4 *The Wishing Ring* (1914) 60
    Rebecca Genauer

5 *The Phantom Carriage (Körkarlen)* (1921) 73
    John Gibbs and Douglas Pye

6 *Dr Mabuse, der Spieler (Dr Mabuse, the Gambler)* (1922) 91
    Steve Neale

7 *Lazybones* (1925) 110
    Scott Higgins

8 *Lady Windermere's Fan* (1925) 131
    Steve Neale

9 *The Strong Man* (1926) 144
    Joe Kember

10 *Miss Mend* (1926) 162
    Vincent Bohlinger

11	*Wings* (1927) Sara Ross	176
12	*Palais de Danse* (1928) Martin Shingler	193
13	*Piccadilly* (1929) Jon Burrows	205
14	*The Kiss* (1929) Patrick Keating	221
15	*Love and Duty (Lian'ai yu yiwu)* (1931) Anne Kerlan	232
16	*I Was Born, But... (Umarete wa mita keredo)* (1932) Alex Clayton	243
17	*Street Without End (Kagiri naki hodo)* (1934) Lisa Dombrowski	253
Notes		274
Bibliography		310
Index		323

Acknowledgements

I would like first of all to thank Simon Baker, Richard Maltby and University of Exeter Press for their support. In addition, I would like to thank Ben Brewster and Lea Jacobs for agreeing to rework their online article on acting, Chris Grosvenor for compiling the index, Scott Higgins and Lisa Dombrowski for all their help, and all the other contributors to this book for their patience. Last but not least, love and thanks go to Karen Edwards, who supported me throughout and who helped me through a computer crisis of epic proportions.

S.N.

Notes on Contributors

Vincent Bohlinger is Associate Professor and Director of Film Studies at Rhode Island College. His primary interests are in Soviet cinema, and he is a regular contributor to *Studies in Russian and Soviet Cinema* and *KinoKultura*. He is currently working on a book on Soviet film style from the late 1920s to the mid-1930s and co-editing a collection of essays on movie stars in Russian/Soviet cinema.

Ben Brewster was editor of *Screen* and taught Film Studies at the University of Kent before becoming Assistant Director of the Wisconsin Center for Film and Theater Research in Madison, Wisconsin. He is the co-author of *Theatre to Cinema* (1996) and has contributed articles on early cinema to *Screen*, *Cinema Journal*, *Film History*, *Cinema & Cie* and a number of essay collections.

Jon Burrows is an Associate Professor in the Department of Film and Television Studies, University of Warwick. He is the author of *Legitimate Cinema* (2003) and *The British Cinema Boom, 1909–1914* (2017) and various essays and articles on the subject of silent British cinema.

Alex Clayton is Senior Lecturer in Film and Television at the University of Bristol. He is the author of *The Body in Hollywood Slapstick* (2007), co-editor of *The Language and Style of Film Criticism* (2011), and a member of the editorial board of *Movie: A Journal of Film Criticism*. He has published a range of essays on screen comedy, performance and aesthetics, and his next book is entitled *Funny How? Sketch Comedy and the Art of Humor* (forthcoming).

Lisa Dombrowski is Associate Professor of Film Studies at Wesleyan University. She is the author of *The Films of Samuel Fuller: If You Die, I'll Kill You!* (2008) and the editor of *Kazan Revisited* (2011), and has written for the *New York Times*, *Film Comment*, *Film Quarterly*, *Film History*, and the Criterion Collection.

Rebecca Genauer is a doctoral student at the University of Wisconsin–Madison, where she is undertaking research on William de Mille. She is also a contributor to *Films on Ice: Cinemas of the Arctic* (2015).

John Gibbs is Professor of Film at the University of Reading. He is a member of the editorial board of *Movie: a journal of film criticism* and the author of *Mise-en-Scène: Film Style and Interpretation* (2002), *Filmmakers' Choices* (2006) and *The Life of Mise-en-Scène: Visual Style and British Film Criticism, 1946–78* (2013). His collaborations with Douglas Pye include the collections *Style and Meaning* (2005) and *The Long Take: Critical Approaches* (2017), audiovisual essays on *Notorious* and *The Phantom Carriage* and coediting the series *Palgrave Close Readings in Film and Television*.

Heather Heckman is Director of Moving Image Research Collections at the University of South Carolina. She has contributed essays to *The American Archivist*, *The Moving Image* and *Colour and the Moving Image: History, Theory, Aesthetics, Archive* (2013).

Scott Higgins is Charles W. Fries Professor of Film Studies and Director of the College of Film and the Moving Image at Wesleyan University. His books include *Harnessing the Technicolor Rainbow* (2007), *Arnheim for Film and Media Studies* (2011), and *Matinee Melodrama* (2016). He has contributed to *Serial Narrative* (2017), *Behind the Silver Screen: Editing and Special Effects* (2016), and *The Ultimate Stallone Reader* (2014).

Lea Jacobs teaches film history and aesthetics in the Department of Communication Arts at the University of Wisconsin-Madison. She is the author of *The Wages of Sin: Censorship and the Fallen Woman Film* (1997), *The Decline of Sentiment: American Film in the 1920s* (2008), *Film Rhythm after Sound* (2015), and co-author of *Theatre to Cinema* (1998). She has also contributed articles to *Cinema Journal*, *Film History*, *Iris*, *Screen* and a number of other publications.

Patrick Keating is an Associate Professor in the Department of Communication at Trinity University in San Antonio. He is the author of *Hollywood Lighting from the Silent Era to Film Noir* (2010), the editor of *Cinematography* (2014), and a contributor to *The Classical Hollywood Reader* (2012).

Joe Kember is an Associate Professor in Film at the University of Exeter. He is the author of *Marketing Modernity: Victorian Popular Shows and Early Cinema* (2009), and a number of articles and essays in *Early Popular Visual Culture, The Velvet Light Trap, Visual Delights II* (2002) and *The Sounds of Early Cinema* (2012).

Anne Kerlan is a researcher at the Centre d'études sur la Chine moderne et contemporaine, a team of the UMR Chine Corée Japon (CNRS-EHESS, Paris). She is an historian of Chinese visual culture. In addition to co-editing and contributing to *Loin d'Hollywood? Cinématographies nationales et modèle Hollywoodien* (2013) she has published several articles and a book on a the history of a major Chinese studio, *Hollywood à Shanghai. L'épopée des studios Lianhua (1930–1948)* (2014).

Steve Neale is Emeritus Professor of Film Studies at the University of Exeter. He is the author of *Genre and Hollywood* (2000), co-author of *Epics, Spectacles and Blockbusters: A Hollywood History* (2010), editor of *The Classical Hollywood Reader* (2012), co-editor of *'Un-American' Hollywood: Politics and Film in the Blacklist Era* (2007) and *Widescreen Worldwide* (2010), and a contributor to *Film Moments: Criticism, Theory, History* (2010) and to *Film Studies* and *Movie*.

Douglas Pye is Senior Visiting Research Fellow in the Department of Film, Theatre and Television at the University of Reading. He is the author of *Movies and Tone* (2007), co-author of *100 Film Musicals* (2011), and co-editor of *The Long Take: Critical Approaches* (2017), *Style and Meaning* (2005) and *The Movie Book of the Western* (1996). He co-edits with John Gibbs the series *Palgrave Close Readings in Film and Television* and is a member of the editorial board of *Movie: a journal of film criticism*.

Sara Ross is an Associate Professor and the Director of Undergraduate Programs for the School of Communication and Media Arts at Sacred Heart University. Her research interests include late silent film, romantic comedy, and the development of female characters in Hollywood. She has published articles on these and other topics in *Aura, Camera Obscura, Film History, Modernism and Modernity*, and a number of anthologies.

NOTES ON CONTRIBUTORS

Martin Shingler is a Senior Lecturer in Radio and Film at the University of Sunderland. He is the author of *When Warners Brought Broadway to Hollywood, 1923–1939* (2018) and *Star Studies: A Critical Guide* (2012), co-author of *On-Air: Methods and Meanings of Radio* (1994) and *Melodrama: Genre, Style and Sensibility* (2004), and co-editor of the BFI Film Star book series.

Introduction

Steve Neale

Silent Features is a collection of essays on fifteen feature-length silent films and two silent serial features, their diverse stylistic, generic and structural characteristics, and the national, historical and industrial contexts from which they emerged. Arranged chronologically and illustrated wherever possible with frame stills, the aims of the collection are threefold: to provide detailed accounts of a wide array of films produced in a number of different countries between the early 1910s and the early 1930s; to focus either on films that are little known or on aspects of well-known films that have rarely been discussed in detail; and hence to appeal to those interested in various aspects of film style and its history. All but two of these films, *Palais de Danse* (1928) and *Love and Duty* (1931), are currently available on DVD, though it should be noted that, unlike the Bologna DVD version, the Kino DVD version of *Assunta Spina* (1915) is incomplete. Either way it is to be hoped that complete DVD or online copies of *Palais de Danse* and *Love and Duty* and other silent films will become available in the near future.

The term 'feature' derives from variety, vaudeville, and a number of other forms of live entertainment in the USA in the late 1800s and early 1900s. It was applied to a number of early films, some of them longer than average, such as boxing films and Passion Play productions, and some of them imports from France. But most were split-reel or single-reel in length, their status as features determined by their literary, biblical or historical content, by the use of tinting or toning (or both), or by the presence of a lecturer, singer or musician.[1] By the late 1900s and early 1910s, longer imports from Italy and France, most of them literary or historical in nature, most of them multi-reel in length and structure, and many of them accompanied by full-blown orchestras in large-scale theatres, helped prompt the advent of picture-palace cinemas and the eventual domination of feature-length films in the USA.² Feature-length productions, however, were not just the province of the West. Britain, Denmark, Germany, Russia and Sweden joined Italy and France in spreading the production of multi-reel features in Europe, China produced *A Couple in Trouble* and India *Raja Harischandra* (both of them four-reel films) in 1913, and the Nikkatsu company in Japan inaugurated the production of a monthly programme of 'three-to-four reel films at each of its studios' in or by 1914.³

Films from China and Japan will be discussed later on in this book. Its opening chapters, however, focus on European films, and more specifically on the topic of acting in *Germinal* (France, 1913) and *Assunta Spina* (Italy, 1915). These films derive from Naturalist or quasi-Naturalist sources (Emile Zola's novel and Salvatore di Giacomo's play, respectively). Yet both eschew Naturalist acting, which, as Ben Brewster and Lea Jacobs point out in their respective chapters, was a feature of the theatre in late 1800s but no longer the dominant acting style either in the theatre or in the cinema by the mid 1910s. Here, with the use of copious frame stills, Brewster and Jacobs take the opportunity not only to argue that 'pictorial acting' remained dominant in the 1910s, but to revise their own account of Naturalism and its influence in their book, *Theatre to Cinema*.⁴ Thus in his article on *Germinal*, Brewster notes Michel Marie's claim that the acting is 'astonishingly sober',⁵ but points out in detail that in what was a prestigious adaptation of naturalist novel was nevertheless marked by pictorial acting. Thus the scene in which Lantier comes out of hiding and enters the Maheus's house is 'organized by movements of the characters around the table, blocking and unblocking one another, and assuming greater prominence when closer to the camera than when further away'. And thus during the course of the film's closing scene, in which Lantier comes to the Maheus's house to say a last goodbye, Henry Krauss, who plays Lantier, acts out the words of an intertitle as a mime. Moreover, and in addition, the scene involves posing, 'not because it is a high point of action, but because it is an epilogue in which the moral—the significance of the events we have witnessed—is being presented'. In this way if, as Marie suggests, we witness the invention 'of a specifically cinematic direction of actors', then 'such a specific cinematic acting style arises not from the adaptation of naturalist acting techniques into the cinema but from a reduction in scale and emphasis of the pictorial styles of acting that the early cinema had taken over from the live theatre'.

Similar concerns are evident in the chapter by Lea Jacobs on *Assunta Spina*, which focuses largely on Francesca Bertini, an Italian actress who was first accorded 'diva' status in *Sangue bleu* (1914). In *Sangue bleu*,

Bertini plays an upper-class woman, and this gives her ample scope for graceful pictorial gestures and poses. But in *Assunta Spina* she plays a lower-class laundress, and this means not that pictorial gestures and poses are abandoned, but that decorum and elegance are played down. Thus in contrast to the graceful poses and gestures in *Sangue bleu*, those exchanged by Assunta and her jealous lover's mother in *Assunta Spina* are marked by violent lunges and 'uncouth' gestures. Although these are largely produced by the latter (thus leaving a measure of decorum for the star), the 'gestures of the principals themselves constitute the thrust and parry of the verbal argument. They are exploited for the expressiveness and are crucial to the rhythmic articulation of the scene, orchestrating the developing conflict in the way that a shot-reverse-shot interchange might in the sound cinema.' Similar principles govern the later scene in which Assunta converses with Funelli (Carlo Benedetti), a notary, in the lobby of the court-house. Here the principals conduct what Jacobs describes as 'gestural duet' punctuated by dialogue titles, 'evoking such complex ideas as feigned indifference, and a slightly mocking graciousness' from Benedetti that 'rank alongside Bertini's work as one of the high points of this style'.

If the chapters on *Germinal* and *Assunta Spina* are concerned with acting in the 1910s, the articles on *L'Enfant de Paris* (1913) and *The Wishing Ring: An Idyll of Old England* (1914) are more concerned with style and structure. *L'Enfant de Paris* was directed by Léonce Perret for Gaumont in France, *The Wishing Ring* by Maurice Tourneur for the World Film Corporation in New Jersey. Along with their striking 'contre-jour' lighting effects (in which characters are either filmed in shadowy silhouette against the sunlight visible through doors and windows or outdoors at dawn or twilight), these films are marked not only by experiments in style and structure but, in the case of *L'Enfant de Paris*, by a number of unusual production practices. As Heather Heckman points out in her discussion of *L'Enfant de Paris*, while Perret and cameraman Georges Specht generally adhered to Gaumont's slightly high-angled eye-level camera style when framing characters nearest to the camera, they shot their scenes in strict chronological order and routinely placed the camera in 'marginally different' positions when doing so, thus making the differences between these positions barely discernible—and thus generating over 240 set-ups in a film comprising 290 shots in total. *The Wishing Ring* is less eccentric. However, at a point prior to the formation of what has come to be called 'the 'classical Hollywood cinema', and hence to the aesthetic norms and production practices that governed most of its films in the late 1910s and early-mid 1920s,[6] the rise of the US feature film in the earlier part of the decade introduced 'new challenges and freedoms', as Rebecca Genauer points out in her essay. Thus, while *The Wishing Ring* looks to the theatre for its basis by adapting a contemporary stage play by Owen Davis, and while the film's structure 'is classical in some respects', the result is 'an atypical distribution of essential story events, an equally atypical assignment of character goals, and a marked effacement of conflict'.

The 1920s

By the late 1910s, the relative dominance of European feature films in the international market had been curtailed by the advent and effects of World War I. Although movie-going 'increased its dominating market position as the cheapest and most accessible mass entertainment', continental markets were fragmented, capital for feature-film production in a number of Europe countries was relatively scarce, and the presence and popularity of US films, already a growing feature of the pre-war market, was well and truly established by the time the war (and its immediate aftermath) had ended.[7] During the course of the war, Denmark and Sweden were both officially neutral but sympathetic to Germany and thus open to the German film market. Here they sought to maintain the success they had achieved with pioneering films, styles and genres, such as the former's risqué multi-reel melodramas, the latter's multi-reel literary adaptations, and the extent to which both were marked by what Brewster and Jacobs call 'The Pictorial Style'.[8] This style characterizes the multi-reel *Ingeborg Holm*, which was produced on the eve of the war in 1913, and directed by Victor Sjöström for Svenska Film in Sweden, and which is devoid of intra-scene edits.[9] But, as John Gibbs and Douglas Pye point out, and as is the case in other, later Sjöström features, editing of all kinds is as essential to *The Phantom Carriage* (*Körkarlen*) (1921) as its staging, framing, lighting and, in the case of *The Phantom Carriage*, its multiple exposure effects. One of a number of Swedish adaptations of the novels of Selma Lagerlöff, and one of four adaptations directed by Sjöström between 1917 and 1921, *The Phantom Carriage* is marked not just by a mix of natural and supernatural ingredients, but by an 'unusually elaborate temporal structure' and an equally elaborate orchestration of framings, looks and gestures. It is also marked by a recurrent use of doors and doorways, and an insistence on the extent to which the characters and their relationships (spiritual or earthly) are marked by isolation and obstruction. Only Edit (Astrid Holm) seems able connect with the violent and destructive David (Victor Sjöström). But her love for him is only reciprocated at the point at which she dies and is borne into the spirit world—and at which David also dies and is borne into the spirit world.

As Kristin Thompson and David Bordwell point out, 'the very success of the Swedish cinema abroad contributed to its decline. After about 1920, Svenska concentrated on expensive prestige productions designed for export', and the artistic success of the films directed by Sjöström and his compatriot Maurice Stiller prompted Hollywood to lure them away from Sweden.[10] Elsewhere in continental Europe, the 1920s was a period of considerable change. Italy sought to regain its international status, but its 'dependence on formulaic filmmaking' simply exacerbated the industry's problems, and France was no longer the international powerhouse it had been in the 1900s and early 1910s.[11] Amidst the decline of Pathé and Gaumont, the fragmentation of its production, distribution and exhibition sectors, and the increasing dominance of US films (and subsequent German ones as well), the latter's late-1910s and 1920s films were marked by a vibrant array of stylistic experiments, by a number of important trends and movements, and by the advent of a number of strands of critical and theoretical discourse.[12] Elsewhere, Russia became the Soviet Union following the Revolution of 1917, giving eventual rise to a major national film industry, while production in Britain began to shrink catastrophically as the dominance of Hollywood increased.

In Germany, a ban on the importation of foreign films (which was introduced by the German government in 1916) helped bolster domestic film production and led to an increase in the number of production companies. These developments continued after Germany's defeat at the end of World War I. The ban was not lifted until 31 December 1920, thus protecting the German market and facilitating recovery and growth in the war's immediate aftermath. As a result, the number of production companies increased (from 25 in 1914 to 130 by 1918 and over 300 by 1921), while a parallel 'trend toward mergers and larger companies' was inaugurated by the formation of Ufa (Universum Film Aktiengesellschaft) in 1917.[13] Nearly all the films produced by these companies have been either lost or ignored. Considerable attention has been paid, however, to the post-war historical spectaculars directed by Ernst Lubitsch, which were as successful in the USA and elsewhere as they were in Germany itself. Of the other late-1910s and early- to mid-1920s German films, only a handful of 'expressionist' films have been closely examined.[14] Alongside *Das Kabinett des Dr Caligari* (*The Cabinet of Dr Caligari*) (1919), *Genuine* (1920), *Schatten* (*Warning Shadows*) (1922), *Raskolnikov* (1923) and *Wachsfigurenkabinett* (*Waxworks*) (1924), *Dr Mabuse, der Spieler* (1922) is sometimes cited as an example. But even though it contains a jokey reference to expressionist painting, *Mabuse* is marked by few, if any, expressionist ingredients; rather, it is a much more obvious and interesting example of a two-part serial thriller featuring an almost superhuman villain, a dogged detective, a world-weary heroine, and a number of other vivid characters. Contributing to an established European trend towards serials with feature-length episodes (and to a cycle of two-part serial features in Germany itself), it is also an example of a tie-in, with instalments of the novel by Norbert Jacques published alongside the writing of the script by Thea von Harbou and director Fritz Lang. Although there are a number of important differences between the novel and the film, both contain episodes of murder, theft, gambling and kidnap, both use the trope of hypnosis to mark Mabuse's power, and both gave rise to a number of subsequent Mabuse films.

As Lea Jacobs has argued in her book, *The Decline of Sentiment*, the mid-1920s marked the advent of a shift in taste among journalists and reviewers of films in the USA, who 'began to criticize films on the grounds that they were cloying, foolishly optimistic, or too intent on achieving big dramatic effects'.[15] Leading to the emergence of a cycle of 'sophisticated comedies', naturalistic dramas, and male-oriented adventure films and war films, and to a decline in the production of what were increasingly perceived as over-didactic films of the sort that peppered the mid- to late 1910s and early 1920s, some of these comedies, dramas and war films, and some of the exceptions to them, are discussed in several contributions to this book. One of these exceptions is *Lazybones* (1925). As a sentimental melodrama directed by Frank Borzage, *Lazybones* appears initially to exemplify the type of film that reviewers and journalists were beginning to criticize. However, as Scott Higgins points out in his essay on the film, *Lazybones* is marked by a number of unusual features. The film's protagonist, Steve Tuttle (Buck Jones), simply drifts from situation to situation, apparently lacking any consistent goals. In lieu of what we might now term a 'classical Hollywood narrative' in which a central protagonist pursues goals, confronts and overcomes obstacles, and eventually attains his or her aims, Borzage segments his narrative and unifies his film around the repeated situation of the failed embrace. By so doing, he generates pathos in unusual ways, explores alternatives to conventional narrative structures, and tests the limits of Hollywood's (and Borzage's) melodramatics.

In contrast to *Lazybones*, *Lady Windermere's Fan* (1925) and its director Ernst Lubitsch were at the forefront of the trend towards sophisticated comedy. Lubitsch was a German émigré who had already directed *The Marriage Circle* and *Forbidden Paradise* (both 1924), and who went on to direct *So This is Paris* (1926), all of which were marked by 'sophisticated' ingredients and all of which were adaptations of stage plays. *Lady Windermere's Fan* was no exception. It was adapted from a play by Oscar Wilde, which was marked by Wilde's trademark verbal wit. Lubitsch, however, discarded Wilde's dialogue, made a number of alterations to the storyline, added a number of new scenes and sequences, and drew (in secret, it seems) on motifs from a British version produced by Ideal Films in 1916. He also filled his film with a dazzling array of glances, cutaways, poses and facial expressions, and with layers of irony that serve to expose the rigidities and double standards of upper-class life and the disappointments, frustrations and injustices experienced both by those who adhere to its rules and by those who transgress them.

As is well documented, Lubitsch was heavily influenced (as were other contributors to the sophisticated cycle) by *A Woman of Paris*, which had been produced and directed by Charlie Chaplin and released in 1923, and which pioneered a style marked less by melodramatic reactions and emphatic moral judgements than by inference, irony and wit.[16] Chaplin himself appears only fleetingly, and the style he pioneered here is in many ways an exception to that which marks his other feature films. Indeed, as is evident in *The Kid* (1921), *The Gold Rush* (1925) and *The Circus* (1928), Chaplin maintained and, if anything, increased his commitment to sentiment and pathos in the films in which he starred himself. To that extent, his 1920s films differ not only from those of Buster Keaton and Harold Lloyd, but from those of Harry Langdon, too. *The Strong Man* (1926) is one of a number of feature-length comedies that centres on Langdon's idiosyncratic persona and performance skills. Like Steve Tuttle in *Lazybones*, but to a much more extreme degree, the Langdon character lacks goals. Thus, as Joe Kember points out, humour emerges primarily from Langdon's 'mastery of gesture while at the same time nothing, besides Harry's bewilderment and failure to connect, seems to happen'. Unlike some of his earlier and later films, *The Strong Man* contains at least some conventional features—in this film Harry somehow ends up with a female partner—but its overall structure consists largely of extended passages of deliberately slow, opaquely motivated and weakly expressive performance. Frequently confronted 'with a face that failed, most of the time, to emote in a familiar or conventional manner', spectators find themselves involved in observing 'a series of difficult social interactions'. In this way, they—and we—are required 'to work hard if we wish to decipher Langdon's ineffectual communications'. The only other option is 'to avert our eyes' in a mixture of puzzlement, annoyance, embarrassment, and shame.

By the mid-1920s, the Soviet Union had eschewed the tragic dramas, tableau styles and unhappy endings that marked so many of Russia's pre-Revolutionary films and favoured imports, and instead promoted the production of newsreels, documentaries and feature films based overwhelmingly on the talents of its young directors and cameramen, and on various styles and theories of montage.[17] One of these directors was Boris Barnet, whose mid- to late 1920s films were heavily influenced by the theories and practices of Lev Kuleshov. Barnet, whose chosen genre was comedy, trained as an actor in Kuleshov's experimental workshop in Moscow. All his 1920s films were produced at Mezhrabpom, a studio that tended to favour popular genres, and made during the period of NEP (New Economic Policy), which was marked by the abandonment of War Communism and the introduction of a mixed economy. As Vincent Bohlinger explains in his essay on *Miss Mend* (*Мисс Менд*) (1926), Barnet's first film, which was co-directed by Barnet and Fedor Otsep, was evidence of a wary fascination with all things American and all things Hollywood, and it this fascination that lies at *Miss Mend*'s heart. Based on Marietta Shaginian's popular novel, *Miss Mend* is partly set in the USA and features characters with distinctly American-sounding names. It also replicates the plot conventions and genre tropes of American dime novels and serial-queen melodramas, combining these with liberal doses of comedy in feature-length episodes (four in all) that echo the structural characteristics of European serials such as *Fantômas* (1913–14) and *Les Vampires* (1915–16). Beginning with an overview of responses to *Miss Mend*, Bohlinger goes on to look in detail at various episodes in order to demonstrate the use of editing and the ways in which Soviet film-makers appropriated Western film-making strategies even as they sought to forge a new, better, and distinctively Soviet cinema.[18]

In the USA itself, the mid- to late 1920s were marked, as noted above, not just by the advent of sophisticated comedies, but by adventure films and war films too. These last were set in World War I and at least two of them, *The Big Parade* (1925) and *Wings* (1927), were produced and released as 'superspecials'—expensive, lengthy and prestigious films that were designed to be road-shown in select picture-palace venues at higher-than-average ticket prices for months and sometimes years.[19] Noting that *Wings* premiered at the Criterion Theater in New York on August 12 for what became a record-breaking run, and that showings of the film were accompanied not just by a live orchestra but also by a battery of live and pre-recorded sound effects, Sara Ross goes on to consider the film's spectacular sequences of aerial combat and the technologies that underpinned and enhanced them, and the ways in which these sequences dovetail with a plot involving 'friendship, rivalry, love and loss'. She also details William Wellman's involvement in the film as director, considers the moral contradictions associated with war (and with World War I in particular), and discusses the roles played by female characters (most notably Mary, played by Clara Bow) in a film that tends on the one hand to marginalize female characters, but on the other to celebrate their capacity for commitment, bravery, persistence and, in the film's heartbreaking penultimate sequence, maternal love and forgiveness.

Elsewhere, and despite the crises plaguing its history in the 1920s, the British film industry produced a variety of neglected but important films, as Christine Gledhill argues in her book, *Reframing British Cinema*.[20] One of these films was *Palais de Danse*, directed by Maurice Elvey in 1928. Martin Shingler's essay focuses in detail on a scene that occurs approximately forty-eight minutes into the film. A particular point of interest in this scene is the way in which a set of oppositions—male and female, youth and age, and working class and upper class—are articulated across a series of shots in which Lady King (Hilda Moore) realizes that she has been deceived by the man who she thinks is a European noble but who turns out to be a 'taxi dancer' at a Palais de Danse. This renders her previous treatment of a young female dancer (Mabel Poulton) hypocritical. But as a respectable married woman it also exposes her to blackmail, giving rise to a delicately articulated passage of poses, looks and gestures involving the use of the actors' bodies, eyes and hands.

A year after the production of *Palais de Danse*, a film called *Piccadilly* was produced at the Elstree studio complex owned by British International Pictures (BIP). However, unlike *Palais de Danse*, and as Jon Burrows points out in his essay, *Piccadilly* was an Anglo-German co-production financed by BIP and a partnership put together by the German director E.A. Dupont between the Berlin studio Gloria-Film and the Munich-based Emelka. As he also points out, *Piccadilly* was thus 'the product of "Film Europa", as the Germans called it', a federalized body designed to confront 'competition from Hollywood from a position of comparable economic strength' by sharing investments, increasing production budgets, exchanging 'ideas and creative personnel', and enabling 'European films to perform more effectively in a variety of different markets'.[21] Amidst the hybrid elements, marginal spaces, and international ingredients that marked many consequent co-productions, those in *Piccadilly* included a German director and a British screenwriter (the novelist Arnold Bennett), Anna May Wong, who was both Chinese and American and who had appeared in a number of Hollywood films and European co-productions, London settings that invited comparisons (and that forged narrative interactions) between the fashionable and upper-class West End (Piccadilly) and the mythologically criminal, immigrant and working-class East End (Limehouse). As Burrows explains, *Piccadilly* 'is effectively geared around an uncertainty principle, as protagonists regularly shift places with each other'. It features 'back-and-forth camera pans or tilts rather than conventional analytical editing', and these serve to 'link disparate spaces and people rather than compartmentalizing them'. In addition, images of 'cross-cultural influence abound', as Dupont enjoyed 'playing with the stock tropes of Limehouse'. 'Perhaps', as Burrows concludes, 'it was as a means of responding to the accusation that he was constitutionally incapable of understanding the true nature of Englishness that he highlighted its inevitable adulteration.'

Piccadilly was among the last silent British and West European feature films. Preceded by a number of abortive or commercially unsustainable systems, Warner Bros. and Western Electric, a subsidiary of the American Telephone & Telegraph company, had successfully pioneered a sound-on-disc system by the mid- to late 1920s in the USA, though it was largely displaced by sound-on-film systems when, in 1928, the five largest Hollywood production companies agreed to adopt a system devised by Western Electric, and when RKO and other rival companies continued to use or adopt alternative systems. In part because of the time lag between initiation, production and release, however, a considerable number of Hollywood films in the late 1920s were silent.[22] Although it was accompanied in a number of venues by 'disc-synchronised music',[23] *The Kiss* (1929), an MGM production which was directed by the Belgian-born Jacques Feyder and which starred the Swedish-born Greta Garbo, was one such film. As Patrick Keating notes in his essay on the film, *The Kiss* is notable for its creative handling of narration and its unusual style, which mixes art deco designs with flamboyant camera movements and elegant lighting. An extended exploration of the ideal of glamour, *The Kiss* uses a lying flashback and the self-consciously stylish decor to stress the inauthentic nature of its protagonist's lifestyle even as it hints that inauthenticity can perhaps be celebrated as a modern form of freedom.

The 1930s

By 1931, most Hollywood films were talkies and most European countries had converted to sound. However, as Thompson and Bordwell point out, sound 'spread through the world's theatres at an uneven pace. Some small countries, especially in eastern Europe and the Third World, produced no films, but their few theatres were wired relatively quickly', while 'silent screenings lingered on in some middle-size markets with small production sectors'.[24] In China, the Star Film Company and Unique Film Company 'invested heavily in sound technology and produced their first sound films in 1931', as Anne Kerlan points out in her essay on *Love and Duty* (*Lian 'ai yu yiwu*). But a deliberate decision was made by the recently-formed United Photoplay Service (UPS, otherwise known as the Lianhua Film Company or Lianhua yingye gongsi) to produce *Love and Duty*, its first feature-length production, as a silent film, in part because UPS and a number of other Chinese production companies wished to resist the further incursion of Western technologies and films, and to develop their own instead.[25]

Love and Duty was adapted from a novel by S. Horose, a Polish émigré who had been educated in France, who had married her Chinese husband in Paris, and who moved with him to China in or around 1911. In her novels, many of which were initially written in English or French then later translated into Chinese, she sought to explore the cultural differences between China and Europe and the effects of both Western and Chinese traditions on her female protagonists. In *Love and Duty*, she tells a heartbreaking story of romantic love, familial duty, forced marriage, scandalous elopement with her lover (a childhood sweetheart), her lover's abandonment of her when she gives birth to a baby girl, the subsequent adoption of the girl by her former husband, and her eventual suicide. Producer Zhu Shilin described the central issue in the novel as 'that of individual free choice', a 'very new question' in China, and the film focuses firmly on this issue and its particular implications for women even as it alters one or two details and plot points. Unlike the novel, the film mixes Chinese and Western ingredients, most of the latter derived from Hollywood films (some of which are directly alluded to or quoted), and it tends to soften or elide some of the harsher narrative detail. Its chief glory is the performance of Ruan Lingyu, who not only plays the film's central female character as a teenage girl and older woman, but who also plays her daughter.

The final contributions to this book are an essay by Alex Clayton on *I Was Born, But...* (*Umarete wa mita keredo*) (1932), directed by Ozu Yasujiro, and an essay by Lisa Dombrowski on *Street Without End* (*Kagiri naki hodo*) (1934), directed by Naruse Mikio. Both films were produced by Shochiku and shot at Shochiku's Kamata studio. As David Bordwell observes in his writings on Japanese cinema, Japanese films in the 1920s and early- to mid-1930s were marked by a proliferation of sub-genres and by what may well be the broadest array of styles, most of them founded on Hollywood continuity principles, in pre-World War II film history.[26] Following an earthquake in Tokyo in 1923, the film companies most affected built new and up-to-date studios and new and up-to-date theatres. The two major companies, Nikkatsu and Shochiku, were vertically integrated (owning production studios, distribution facilities and theatres), which meant that they could 'control and profit from American imports' as they 'and dozens of smaller studios pumped out 600 to 800 films a year'.[27] Part of a general trend towards all things modern, many Japanese films were marked by contemporary urban settings, fads and fashions, and by the presence of those US and European films that often helped to introduce them. Along the way, many pre-war traits and practices were discarded. Women were no longer portrayed by men, programmes of films were shortened, and the dominance of lengthy static shots began to abate. However, as Clayton points out, the *katsuben* or *benshi*, who commented on the action and who often spoke the characters' dialogue, strengthened their position. Becoming the equivalent of film stars, they exercised a hold that was not really broken until 1935, thus helping to delay the introduction of sound.[28]

Ozu's stylistic traits are well known. However, they were adopted, explored, adjusted and modified in a number of ways in the late 1920s and early 1930s, as Ozu, who eschewed the making of *jidai-geki* (historical films of one sort or another), sought instead to explore the parameters and genres of *gendai-geki* (films with contemporary settings). These included the 'salaryman' films, 'student' films, home dramas, female melodramas, *hahao mono* or mother films, 'hooligan' or street crook films, *keko eiga* or 'tendency' films, *shoshimin-geki* or films about the lower middle class, and comedies of all sorts, among them the *nonsansu* or 'nonsense' films. Although marked by *nonsansu* features, *I Was Born, But...* is unusually didactic, unusually full of literal and metaphorical lessons, and unusually preoccupied with status and power. Clayton suggests that the film's subtitle (*A Picture Book for Grown-Ups*) hints not just at lessons to be learned, but at 'the potential of silent film, specifically—the medium of successive soundless pictures—to renew and edify our vision'. This is particularly evident in the ways in which the framing of bodies and bodily deportment gives rise to pictorial patterns as 'the film repeatedly sets the bowing body against perpendicular lines'. These lines tend to mark the adult world even as 'round things: baseball caps, bread rolls, bike wheels, ball games' tend to mark that of the boys. Pecking orders criss-cross both domains. But, as Keiji (Sugawara Hideo) and Yoshi (Tatsuo Saito) begin to learn the rules of adult compromise and deference, they also acquire 'the resolve to self-determination which is the true break with childhood' too.

Naruse is probably less well known than Ozu. Responding to the polices promoted by Kido Shiro at Shochiku in the late 1920s and early- to mid-1930s, his films were marked by occasional *nonsansu* features, but were largely aimed at a growing market for female-centred films, and, as Dombrowski explains, *Street Without End* was his last Shochiku production. In a film built on parallels, and in a film marked by both comedy and drama, *Street Without End* explores the lives and loves of two young women, Sugiko (Shinobu Setsuko) and Kesako (Katori Chiyoku), who work in a cafe in Tokyo. Sugiko has the opportunity to marry her boyfriend and become a film actress, but she meets, marries, and eventually leaves a wealthy man (and his family) and returns to the cafe alone. Kesako, on the other hand, finds a job in the film industry, but eventually leaves it to marry her long-standing boyfriend. Full of contemporary urban imagery, quotes from motion pictures, and depictions of film-making, *Street Without End* is marked stylistically by what Bordwell has called 'piecemeal decoupage',[29] a style that facilitates the use of an array of devices in specific scenes and segments, but that also, in this case at least, 'encourages close attention to subjective cues, especially those regarding choice'. This is nowhere more evident than in the film's last shot, a shot that concludes this introduction and that ends by inviting us to ponder Sugiko's choices—and to wonder what they may now be.

1

Germinal (1913)

Ben Brewster

Germinal was directed by Albert Capellani and produced by the Société Cinématographique des Artistes et des Gens de Lettres (Artists' and Writers' Film Company), usually known as SCAGL. The latter was a subsidiary—really, a production unit and a release label—established in 1908 by Pathé Frères, the main French film producing and distributing company (indeed, the world's largest film company), in anticipation of competition from the newly founded Film d'Art in the production of artistically respectable films. Albert Capellani, who had started his career as an actor and then progressed to stage manager at the Alhambra Music Hall in Paris, before becoming a director for Pathé in 1905, was appointed artistic director of SCAGL on its foundation and, as an individual director, became its specialist in literary subjects, notably a series of Victor Hugo adaptations, including *Notre Dame de Paris* in 1911, *Les Misérables* in 1912 and *Quatre-vingt-treize*, which was shot in 1914, but only released, in a version completed by André Antoine, in 1921. *Germinal*, adapted from Émile Zola's 1885 novel, was shot in the winter and spring of 1913, with exteriors in Auchel, near Béthune, Pas-de-Calais, and released in November of the same year. At 165 minutes, it was a super-feature, and was the first film screened in Pathé's flagship house in Paris, the Omnia Pathé, as the sole item on the programme.[1]

Michel Marie has claimed that the acting in *Germinal* is 'astonishingly sober... very internalized, "under dramatized"... Capellani is inventing as we watch the specifically cinematic direction of the actor; this relies more on the body as a whole, on gait, on movements in the frame and on interactions between the characters than on the expressivity of gestures and looks'.[2] Although not directly a claim that the acting in Capellani's film is 'naturalistic' in the sense of the acting style promoted by the naturalist movement in the theatre (one variant of which was eventually codified as the Stanislavsky Method), Marie's opposition between an acting based on the 'expressivity of gestures and looks' (by the latter—'*regards*'—I think he must mean 'facial expressions') and one that is 'internalized' and 'under-dramatized' recalls Roberta Pearson's opposition between 'histrionic' and 'verisimilar' acting styles,[3] and certainly suggests that some such claim is in the background.

Indeed, an adaptation of *Germinal* has to deal in some way with the fact that the novel is one of the key texts of literary naturalism. Capellani had previously adapted Zola, notably a version of *L'Assommoir* in 1909,[4] but his most significant titles had been from high-class melodramatic authors (versions of *Les Deux orphélines*, 1909, from the 1874 play by d'Ennery and Cormon; *Le Courrier de Lyon*, 1911, from the 1850 play by Moreau, Siraudin and Delacourt; and *Les Mystères de Paris*, 1912, from the 1842 novel by Eugène Sue) and from romantics like Victor Hugo. Hugo's plays can be considered the epitome of a pictorial and situational drama, and in *Theatre to Cinema*, Lea Jacobs and I used a description by the Ibsenite William Archer of a scene in *Hernani* as an example of how changes in the dramatic situation during a scene could be conveyed by the actors posing together to form stage pictures, dissolving those poses and reposing to form other pictures.[5] This kind of acting is also found in Capellani's Hugo adaptations. Figures 1 and 2 are of two moments in a climactic scene in *Notre Dame de Paris*—the moment when Claude Frollo finds Esmeralda hiding in the cathedral and attempts to rape her, whereupon Quasimodo attacks and threatens to kill him, but Esmeralda orders Quasimodo to let him go. It is clear from these stills that the actors are moving from pose to pose, and grouping themselves to modulate the stage picture overall, in this case into tableaux, moments when all the actors are still.

Figure 1   Figure 2

There are reasons why the posing should be so emphatic in this example. First, the film is set in the Middle Ages, and everywhere period subjects were thought to require broader posing then contemporary ones (Roberta Pearson makes this point in discussing differences in the acting in different Griffith-directed Biograph films).[6] Secondly, Stacia Napierkowska, who plays Esmeralda, was a dancer before she was an actress, and always has broader gestures than other actors (not necessarily because dance typically had broader gestures, but rather, I suspect, because dancers could produce broad gestures and exaggerated poses without losing grace much more easily than non-dancers). Thirdly, Quasimodo is a hunchback, which imposed a set of stereotyped grotesque postures and movements, largely absolving Henry Krauss, the actor, from the requirement of grace. Finally, Claude Garry, playing Frollo, uses his tall stature and his monk's long robe to create a sinister figure, which then dramatically contrasts with the bent hunchback, establishing the terms in which moral contrasts between the characters could be portrayed in pose and gesture.

The acting in *Germinal* for much of the time is not like this, as Marie indicates. Moreover, as befits a naturalistic work, the film uses real settings in the industrial North of France—industrial exteriors (Figure 3), street scenes in miners' settlements (Figure 4) and industrial interiors (Figure 5)—and goes to some length to match those industrial interiors which are sets to the exteriors, to the point that I am not sure whether Figure 6 shows a real pithead or a set, though I incline to the latter. Also, the film has some naturalistic stereotypes—eating scenes, and in particular scenes where people eat standing up (Figure 7), or indeed, as we shall see later, lying on the ground. However, I hope to be able to demonstrate that the actors and director in *Germinal* have not started out from naturalistic principles and carried them through the film consistently (as we argued in *Theatre to Cinema* that Sjöström did in 1919 in *Ingmarssönerna—The Ingmarssons*)[7] so much as they have reduced the scale of the pictorial

Figure 3

Figure 4

Figure 5

Figure 6

Figure 7

posing and gesture that were thought appropriate to Hugo when the novel adapted is, instead, by Zola.

To make this demonstration, I will analyse and illustrate various scenes in the film,[8] but in the opposite order to that in which they appear there. This is because, generally speaking, climactic scenes occur later and typically contain broader gesture, so they show the pictorial acting traditions more clearly than the earlier scenes.[9]

In the closing scene of the film, Lantier comes to the Maheus' house to say a last goodbye. He finds no one there but Bonnemort (played by Marc Gérard) and the Maheus' baby.[10] Maheu's wife, La Maheude (played by Jeanne Cheirel), comes in, and he tells her he is leaving, then learns she is going down the mines as a haulage woman. As he approaches the house, Lantier, played by Henry Krauss,[11] pauses on the doorstep before entering (Figure 8). This pause could be realistically motivated, as he has caused disaster to the household, so might hesitate to meet its survivors, but it is clearly part of 'making an entrance' and his glance is fairly squarely to camera. There follows a title, translatable as 'The past and the future'. Inside the house (Figure 9), Bonnemort, now senile, is sitting to the left, while the baby's cradle is to the right. Lantier enters and tries to get Bonnemort to respond to a greeting, but fails (Figure 10). La Maheude

Figure 8

Figure 9

Figure 10

Figure 11

Figure 12

Figure 13

comes in and she and Lantier greet one another (Figure 11). He tells her he is leaving Montsou, and asks why she is dressed for the mine; she shows him the company's letter giving her a job (Figure 12). After an insert of the letter, she indicates her responsibilities—the senile Bonnemort and the infantile Estelle (Figure 13). She asks Lantier what he will do, and he indicates vague hopes of advancement with a gesture to the skies (Figure 14). She turns away and busies herself with her lunch things. So far, though I hope the posing is clear enough, it is not very marked. But

Figure 14

Figure 15

Figure 16

Figure 17

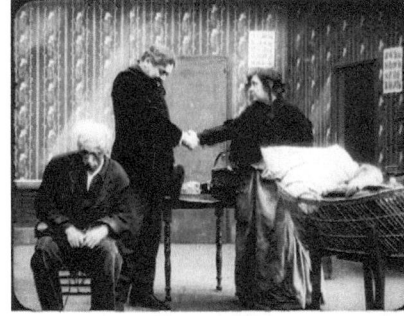
Figure 18

Figure 19

then Lantier comes to the front, points to Bonnemort and waves his right hand, indicating that the old man is done for (Figure 15), turns and pats the baby (Figure 16), then raises his right arm to the skies, indicating a hopeful future (Figure 17). La Maheude turns back towards him and they shake hands in farewell (Figure 18), then both stoop in grief (Figure 19). He looks significantly to camera (Figure 20), then re-exits.

In the middle part of the scene, Krauss acts out the words of the intertitle as a mime. This kind of mime, generally frowned on by contemporary

Figure 20   Figure 21

commentary, is found in less portentous contexts in the film. For example, one of the blacklegs running the gauntlet makes the child gesture—a hand held out palm down at waist level—to his assailants, miming 'I have to support my children'. However, as well as this mime, the scene involves posing, and in fact works by the two mobile actors moving from pose to pose. Posing is broad here not because it is a high point of the action, but because it is an epilogue in which the moral—the significance of the events we have witnessed—is being presented, and it leads naturally to the final scene (Figure 21), which follows Zola in linking the season and the landscape to the deliberately ambiguous idea of fecundity via the revolutionary name of one of the spring months, 'Germinal'.

The next example is the scene where Lantier comes out of hiding and goes to the Maheus' house, which is in mourning for Toussaint Maheu. Echoing his departure into hiding, when he escaped police at the front door by running out the back, he approaches the house via its back garden, pausing significantly on the threshold as he does in the final scene, just discussed (Figure 22). Inside the house the surviving adult family members, Catherine, Chaval, Zacharie, La Maheude and Bonnemort, are grouped round the central table. The scene that follows is organized by movements of the characters round the table, blocking and unblocking one another, and assuming greater prominence when closer to camera than when further away (the film uses the standard waist-high Pathé camera, which gives a greater sense of depth than a higher camera would). French actors seem to have been particularly adept at this kind of ensemble work, perhaps because it was emphasized by formal training at the Comédie française and the Odéon; actors with this training formed Film d'Art; similarly trained actors formed the Pathé and SCAGL stock companies; and their examples meant that this style prevailed in Pathé films more than in those of most Italian and American companies.

At the beginning of the scene, Zacharie (actor unknown) and Chaval (played by Jean Jacquinet) are standing rear centre. Catherine is sitting to the left of the table (Catherine is played by Sylvie).[12] La Maheude is sitting to its right, her head buried in her arms. Bonnemort is sitting midground right in a daze (Figure 23). The rear right door opens, and Lantier enters. Zacharie and Chaval turn to look at him, but the others do not react (Figure 24). He comes to stand immediately behind the table between Catherine and La Maheude. He looks down at Catherine, who turns to look up at him (Figure 25). She gets up and wearily retreats to rear left, joining Chaval, who has crossed past Zacharie to the left. La Maheude raises her head as Lantier turns to look at her. She starts as she recognizes the man who has brought ruin on her family (Figure 26). He makes a gentle gesture of condolence and apology. She reaches up and grabs him by the lapels. He grasps her hands (Figure 27) and gently pushes them down. She collapses weeping on the table. Catherine weeps into her apron, Chaval rear left glares at Lantier (Figure 28). Zacharie moves a little leftward, staring at Lantier. Chaval comes forward to stand between Lantier and Catherine. He looks Lantier up and down and laughs in a sinister way (Figure 29), then turns away, stopping as Catherine embraces Zacharie. Chaval goes to join them as the street door left opens, and two miners enter and hand Chaval a paper (Figure 30). There follows an insert of the leaflet announcing the meeting to discuss a return to work. The scene resumes, and the miners, Zacharie and Chaval exit left through the door. Catherine watches Lantier from rear left (Figure 31). She comes forward and opens the door, telling Lantier he must face the music (Figure 32). He exits left. Catherine closes the door (Figure 33).

Each actor runs through a series of poses representing his or her different, largely silent, responses to the situation: Lantier's regret and embarrassment; Catherine's resigned grief; Chaval's *Schadenfreude*; La Maheude's grief, anger at Lantier, then despairing resignation; Bonnemort's mental absence. The whole scene forms a series of pictures as these poses are entered, then broken as the actors move, reposing when they stop. Indeed, Chaval is only present for pictorial reasons, to add his 'voice' to the ensemble of attitudes. Realistically (i.e. in terms of realistic motivation), he is still the despised blackleg and abuser of the daughter of the family, and would not be welcome at a scene of mourning for a leader of the strike. Yet, despite the extreme emotion of the scene, the gestures are mostly quite small, with the one exception of Cheirel as La Maheude angrily grasping Krauss's lapels.

The next scene I wish to focus on is the confrontation between the strikers and the blacklegs at the pithead. After scenes of the blacklegs

Figure 22

Figure 23

Figure 24

Figure 25

Figure 26

Figure 27

desperately climbing the ladders out of the pit, an alternation is established between the pithead area (with the cages and the main shaft to the left) and the adjacent emergency shaft (off right in the pithead scenes). When the blacklegs begin to emerge from the top of the emergency shaft, Zacharie, Maheu (played by Mévisto, Sr) and Lantier leave the pithead for the emergency shaft. Zacharie, Maheu and Lantier run on left. Lantier starts grabbing blacklegs as they emerge from the shaft and hauling them off left. Chaval enters from the shaft, hiding his face in his hands. Maheu

GERMINAL (1913)

Figure 28

Figure 29

Figure 30

Figure 31

Figure 32

Figure 33

grabs him, pushes him to the right and begins to punch him, but Lantier intervenes, holding back the strikers, telling them 'This man is mine!' He grabs a short pickaxe from one of the strikers, throws it at Chaval's feet, takes another for himself and rolls up his sleeves for the combat (Figure 34). Chaval slowly bends down and picks up the axe. Catherine enters from behind the blacklegs now crowding the entrance to the shaft. She runs between Lantier and Chaval, facing Lantier and shielding Chaval with outstretched arms. Lantier gestures for her to get out of the way

Figure 34

Figure 35

Figure 36

Figure 37

(Figure 35). Instead, she leans forward and slaps him hard in the face (Figure 36). He staggers, then sobers up, throws down the axe and covers his face with his right hand, as Catherine leans back, stretching out her arms to protect Chaval. Tableau (Figure 37). Lantier tells the strikers 'That's enough!' They protest and he shouts them down. Maheu crosses to stand between Lantier and Catherine, and goes to hit them. Zacharie exits left. Lantier drags Maheu away and off left.

    Matched cut to the pithead as Lantier drags Maheu on right. Lantier shouts for quiet to the strikers and looks off right. Catherine enters right, hands on hips, defying the strikers. They subside (Figure 38). She shrugs, and walks slowly through them to midground centre. She stops and looks around. They are afraid to touch her. Lantier looks ashamed, takes his scarf from his pocket and ties it round his neck (Figure 39). Chaval enters right slowly, his head bowed, dragging his feet, in contrast to Catherine (Figure 40). The strikers shake their fists at him but move no nearer. He glares at Lantier (Figure 41), then follows Catherine through the crowd (one striker spits him in the face; he wipes off the spittle, but does not stop) and off rear centre. The strikers close the gap, leaving Zacharie, Maheu, Souvarine and Lantier across the front. They discuss what to

GERMINAL (1913)

Figure 38

Figure 39

Figure 40

Figure 41

do. Lantier says 'Let's go!', and leads the strikers in a march off front left, leaving Souvarine standing alone.

Once again, the scene, though a highly mobile one, is organized around a series of moments of relative stasis: when Lantier confronts Chaval with the pick; when Catherine prevents the fight by standing between the two men; when she sobers Lantier up by slapping him, then shields her husband with her arms; when she faces the wall of angry miners without flinching; when she turns as she moves through them, refusing to run; when Chaval stops to glare at Lantier (an action foreshadowing his perfidious denunciation of Lantier in the next scene). Sylvie's last turn before exiting is, indeed, a classic example of 'making an exit', even though the actual disappearance of the actress is postponed until Chaval has already entered, so diverting attention from it. Nevertheless, with the exception of the slap, the gestures are not large in scale, hands are not raised above shoulders. Moreover, the full scene is an edited sequence, with the two sides of an alternation linked by precise action matching the movements of members of the crowds of miners and blacklegs from the pithead to the top of the emergency shaft and back.

The final sequence—three shots—that I will examine is the moment

Figure 42

Figure 43

Figure 44

Figure 45

when Lantier first realizes that Catherine, whom he met in her work clothes and assumed was a boy, is in fact a young woman. He has been taken on that day as a *hercheur*, a haulage man, working with Catherine shovelling the coal hacked from the face by the cutters into trams (*herches* or *berlines*), which are then pushed to the pit bottom by child workers (*galibots*). Catherine has been much better at this work than Lantier throughout the morning, but then the team breaks for lunch. Catherine has brought her lunch from home, but Lantier, who had been walking all night, has none. The shot is preceded by a title translatable as 'In which Lantier realizes why Chaval was so eager to keep him away'. Chaval, jealous of Catherine, was unhappy that Maheu took on the outsider, and especially that Catherine was particularly welcoming of him; Chaval's attitude has mystified Lantier hitherto.

The scene is a mine gallery, with the face worked by Maheu's team just off left. To the right is one of the trams used by the team. Catherine is midground centre with a shovel. She puts a shovelful of coal onto the tram (Figure 42), then says it is lunchtime and throws down the shovel. Lantier, behind her, comes forward as she sits down on a rock front right (Figure 43). He picks up his scarf and puts it round his neck, and puts on

GERMINAL (1913)

Figure 46

Figure 47

Figure 48

Figure 49

his coat. Without getting up, Catherine gets her lunch bag from where it is hanging front right and opens it. She takes off the headscarf covering her hair and shakes it loose. Lantier sits down front left facing forward, his eyes still averted from Catherine (Figure 44). He takes off his helmet and headscarf, and rubs his head ruefully. He turns and looks towards Catherine, then freezes (Figure 45). She opens a sandwich, lifts her head to eat it and sees him staring at her (Figure 46). She lowers the sandwich to ask what is the matter (Figure 47). He laughs sheepishly and indicates her hair (Figure 48). She laughs incredulously and pulls a hank of her hair forward to show it to him (Figure 49). He expresses his bemusement. She ties her hair up in a bun and puts her headscarf on again. She takes a bite from her sandwich. He sits, arms on knees (he has no lunch). She notices, stops eating and asks does he not have anything to eat? He lowers his head and mutters that he will be all right. She holds the bitten sandwich out to him (Figure 50). He shakes his head and looks away. She looks at the bite, gestures that he naturally doesn't want to eat where she has bitten, and turns the sandwich round, holding the unbitten side out to him, laughing. He finally takes the sandwich, grinning. He bites into it ravenously (Figure 51). She gets down her bottle from where it was hanging front right and

Figure 50 | Figure 51

Figure 52 | Figure 53

Figure 54 | Figure 55

drinks from it. She offers it to him, he says 'Thank you', she wipes the mouth of the bottle and hands it to him. He is still chewing. She gets up and sits closer to him by the tram. He drinks (Figure 52), wipes the bottle mouth, then hands it back to her. She drinks, then offers it to him again. He says 'No', she recorks the bottle, then lies full length on her front, head to camera, and eats more of her sandwich. She asks him how he lost his former job (Figure 53). He gestures striking the supervisor. She expresses understanding. She gets to her knees and they talk (Figure 54).

GERMINAL (1913)

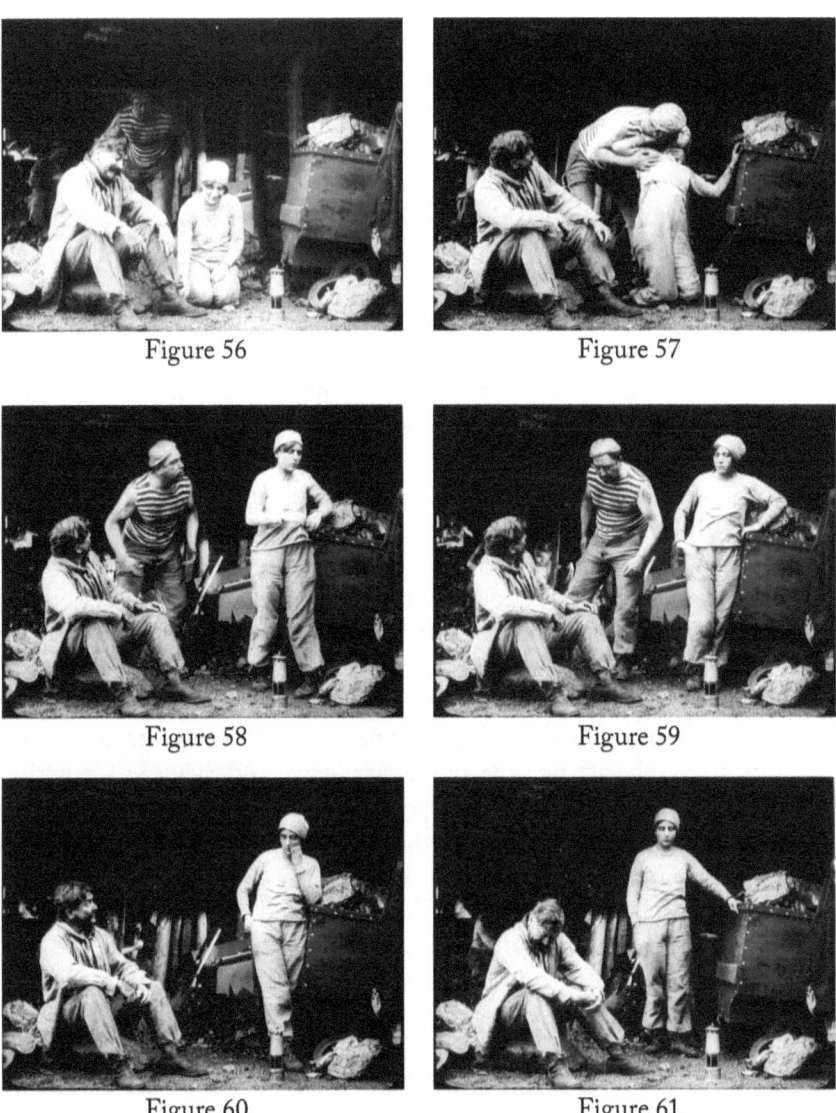

Figure 56

Figure 57

Figure 58

Figure 59

Figure 60

Figure 61

Cut to the nearby coal face. Maheu, Zacharie and Chaval are eating their lunch. Chaval listens, then turns, half rises and looks off right (Figure 55). Maheu asks what is the matter. Chaval says 'Oh nothing', and sits down again. He listens again, puts down his sandwich and shuts up Maheu's protestations. Pan right as he starts to the rear, hesitates a moment while a tram is pushed from rear right and off front right, then sets off to rear right.

Cut back to the setting of the previous scene. Lantier and Catherine are talking as at the end of that shot. Chaval enters rear left and comes to stand behind and between them, bent nearly double because of the low roof. He listens a moment (Figure 56), then comes forward, grabs Catherine and kisses her brutally on the mouth (Figure 57). She gets up and pushes him away, then stands looking sadly off front right (Figure 58). Chaval glares at Lantier (Figure 59), then re-exits rear left. Lantier looks at Catherine, asking, 'Is he your man?' She puts her hand to her mouth (Figure 60) and turns away without replying. He expresses wry sorrow, then looks down at his feet. She retreats slightly with no response (Figure 61).

Posing is much less evident in this scene, presumably one of the ones Marie was thinking of when he talked about 'internalization'. An important issue of character motivation is at stake. The novel depends for one of its main lines of action—its 'romance plot', though the phrase seems odd in connection with a novel by Zola—on Lantier and Catherine's mutual attraction and its lack of consummation until Catherine is in her death throes during the mine disaster. The long delay in the consummation, in particular, is weakly motivated in the novel, but the authorial commentary in a novel can explain and hence motivate almost any behaviour on the part of its characters. Drama and film have fewer means to provide character motivation, so the problem is more acute. This is partly solved by a plot change: the film makes Chaval Catherine's established sweetheart before the story starts; the acting of Jacquinet as Chaval and Sylvie as Catherine in the first scene in which they appear together makes it clear that the initiative comes from Chaval and that Catherine is reluctant, although the suit is favoured by her father. In the book, by contrast, the parents do not wish to lose a breadwinner in the family and are therefore strongly opposed to any match for Catherine, and the moment he kisses her in this scene is the first time that Chaval has more than hinted at an attraction to Catherine. Nevertheless, it is the scene I have just illustrated that most strongly motivates both Lantier's attraction and his diffidence (again, a plot compression in the film brings Lantier's realization that Catherine is a woman and Chaval's claim to sexual ownership of her into the same scene).

A 'naturalist' cast to the scene is given by its reliance on business: the work Catherine and Lantier do before the section illustrated; the preparations for lunch, including adjustments of dress; and the eating and drinking. This is emphasized by Catherine's 'unladylike' and hence ungraceful behaviour, making the actress roll on the floor and eat lying on her belly. Most of these resources fall to Sylvie, as Catherine is the one with the lunch, the hair and the sexual naivety to treat Lantier's mistake about her sex as a childish joke, and hence to romp uninhibitedly in his presence until the situation is brutally sexualized by Chaval, when she retreats into embarrassment, literally moving back in the frame away from Krauss. Krauss, by contrast, has to convey Lantier's two changes of attitude to Catherine—from the assumption that he is with a boy to his recognition of Catherine's sex and his aroused sexual interest in her, and to his disappointment and inhibition when he thinks she is already taken—while sitting on the ground with no possibilities of substantial movement and nothing to do except for his much briefer moments of eating the sandwich and drinking from the flask. Although there is some quasi-business, such as the mimed explanation of how he came to be tramping the roads, most of what has to be done is done by quite small changes in head and body position, a quite narrow range of smiles, frowns and blank looks, and makings and breakings of eye contact—looking at Catherine and looking away from her. This acting does indeed, in Marie's words, depend 'on the body as a whole . . . movements in the frame and . . . interactions between the characters', and on stance if not on gait (Marie's word, 'démarche', can mean either). Nevertheless, in making stills to illustrate the scene, it was not difficult to find the moments of stasis when Krauss was in effect posing (the moments for Sylvie were more difficult, because business like eating a sandwich is not stationary in the same way). This can be contrasted with an impressive scene which I cannot illustrate, because there are no poses in it. The fight between Chaval and Lantier in the streets of Montsou is a tour de force. In a single shot, Krauss and Jacquinet apparently hit each other, fall, turn over and over, wrestling in the dust, reach for and grab fallen knives, until Catherine intervenes to prevent Lantier from killing Chaval. The only thing in it that could be called a pose is a moment when Jacquinet jumps up with both feet off the ground, challenging Lantier (playing the villain, Jacquinet's posing is always more marked than Krauss's).[13] Otherwise, the fight is all business, and executing it is more a matter of choreography or acrobatics than of expression.[14] But the scene in which Lantier recognizes that Catherine is a woman is still orchestrated by movements from pose to pose, although the poses have become very unmarked and their expressive intent much less clear. If this is, as Marie suggests, the 'invention as we watch of a specifically cinematic direction of actors', then such a specifically cinematic acting style arises not from the adaptation of naturalistic acting techniques into the cinema but from a reduction in scale and emphasis of the pictorial styles of acting that the early cinema had taken over from the live theatre.

2

Assunta Spina (1915)

Lea Jacobs

In 1910, the owners of a Copenhagen movie house decided they could make more money if they showed longer films for longer runs. Since such films were not available in the market, they hired an actress trained at the Royal Danish Theatre and her husband as director, and made *Afgrunden* (*The Abyss*). The film was enormously successful, and not only in Denmark: in Germany it created a craze for the 'monopoly film' and made an international star of the then unknown actress, Asta Nielsen. Nielsen and her husband Urban Gad were lured away to work in Germany, producing such films for a new, international film market. This new market was particularly attractive for producers in countries such as Germany and Denmark, and later Italy, which were increasingly locked out of the international market for short films, which was dominated by France and the USA. Although the Italian features that were most successful in the USA and are best known today were classical epics (*Quo Vadis?*, *Cabiria*), the films that were most important in Europe drew directly on the model of Asta Nielsen's films: films centred on a female star and designed to give her the maximum scope to display her acting talents, films which rapidly came to be known in Italy as 'diva films'. (Although dictionaries usually give 'divo/a' as the word for film star, in this period the masculine form seems to have been rarely used.) One of these divas was Francesca Bertini.

Francesca Bertini had been a film actress long before she became associated with the diva tradition. First noted for her roles in films by Film d'Arte Italiana, the affiliate Pathé set up to make the kind of high-class short film pioneered by the French Film d'Art company but in scenic Italian backgrounds, she appeared in many kinds of parts until, with the feature *Sangue bleu* (Nino Oxilia, 1914), the Roman film company Celio promoted her as a diva. *Sangue bleu* borrows directly from the Nielsen example; indeed, the 'tango of death' that the heroine is forced to dance on a variety stage is almost an exact copy (with identically dressed cowboy partner) of the dance that Nielsen was forced to perform in *Afgrunden*. Perhaps characteristically different from the Danish film is the fact that, at the end of that dance, Elena stabs herself, whereas Nielsen's Magda stabs her lover. In addition, Elena is an upper-class woman divorced by her aristocratic husband who runs away with a famous actor, while Nielsen's Magda is a Copenhagen piano teacher who rejects marriage with the son of a country pastor to follow an itinerant circus artiste. Moreover, the Nielsen heroine is much more clearly following her own desire, one which leads her to reject the option of a respectable marriage, while the Bertini character is undone by the force of circumstances beyond her control: divorcing a husband who no longer loves her, she loses her daughter to him when she is falsely accused of having a lover. In general, the diva plays someone who belongs to, or joins, a cosmopolitan aristocracy, and she is more likely to be a passive victim than the active heroine typical of Nielsen's parts.

That such an ambience is not universal is demonstrated by one of Bertini's later feature roles, as a laundress, in *Assunta Spina* (Gustavo Serena for Caesar Film, Rome, 1915). Adapted from a Neapolitan dialect play by Salvatore di Giacomo that was first staged in 1909, the film is set very specifically in lower-class Naples, and the exteriors were indeed filmed in Naples.[1] Gian Piero Brunetta[2] suggests that the range of Bertini's roles, by contrast with that of other Italian divas, such as Lyda Borelli, implies that her acting can be described as 'naturalistic'. While the plot of *Assunta Spina* fits under the rubric of naturalism, and while the acting and staging of some scenes in the film also show the influence of naturalism, Bertini's technique (and, incidentally, that of Nielsen as well) is more reminiscent of Sarah Bernhardt than it is of Eleanora Duse, and the blocking and use of gesture in the film is largely governed by what Ben Brewster and I have discussed in terms of 'pictorialism' in acting.

The scene in *Sangue bleu*[3] in which Elena is forced to give up her daughter to her former husband may serve as a benchmark of a pictorial style. As is typical of this film, and of the Italian diva film in general, the set is quite deep, thus allowing for marked and prolonged entrances and exits (Figure 1).

At the beginning of the scene (Figure 2), Bertini is in the left foreground when a servant announces the Prince. She crosses to foreground right and the magistrate who oversees their divorce agreement approaches her

Figure 1

Figure 2

Figure 3

Figure 4

Figure 5

Figure 6

foreground centre, while the Prince (Angelo Gallina) remains in the left midground (Figure 3). She lifts her hands in an imploring gesture, then runs to the Prince and puts her arms around him in an appeal (Figure 4). Her importuning gesture and his subsequent rolling of the eyes are emphasized by a cut-in (Figure 5). After a cut back to long shot, Bertini turns from the Prince to the magistrate, imploring again with her hands folded and raised. The Prince takes this opportunity to exit midground

Figure 7

Figure 8

Figure 9

Figure 10

left (Figure 6). Turning and acknowledging his exit, Bertini moves a few paces away from the camera and extends her arms (Figure 7). The Prince re-enters carrying the girl, and Bertini takes the child from him and moves to the foreground, followed by the child's nurse. While embracing the child, Bertini gestures to the nurse to leave them. The nurse exits left, then re-enters and makes a more muted appeal to the Prince, standing in the midground. Finally, she approaches the mother and child in the foreground and gestures that they must go (Figure 8). Bertini stands and relinquishes the child to her, staggering to a chair front right and holding on to it for support (Figure 9). All exit through the rear door as she lowers her head in despair (see Figure 1, above). Although one might assume the scene would end there, it does not. Bertini slowly rises up, turning to the right, puts her hands to her cheeks in horror and runs to the rear door, posing in the doorway (Figure 10). After making another gesture with hands on head in despair, she turns and walks towards the camera, making a series of poses: elbows bent and hands on shoulders, then arms crossed (Figure 11); then arms unfolded and upraised as she hesitates a moment in her approach; then a quick run to the foreground, where a slight downward slope reveals a table, where she sits to write a letter to

Figure 11   Figure 12

the actor who will now take the place of her husband and beloved child (Figure 12).

One of the things that Ben Brewster and I argued in *Theatre to Cinema* is that the use of gesture in this kind of acting should not be understood simply as calling upon a lexicon, e.g. arms crossed with hands on shoulders 'means' despair, but rather, almost as it would in dance, it should be seen as elaborating and helping to orchestrate a given dramatic situation.[4] The mother's reaction to the loss of her child is highly stereotyped; in order to understand the scene, the spectator hardly needs the accumulation of gesture that Bertini employs to convey her grief. Indeed, at a narrational level, the accumulation of gesture would only be necessary if the scene were working counter to stereotype, if, for example, we needed to be informed that the mother was overjoyed at having the child taken off her hands. But what is at issue in Bertini's performance in *Sangue bleu* is not so much the conveyance of narrative information as the rhythmic articulation of the performance. In a scene largely devoid of editing, it is the timing and pacing of the gestures that move our attention from one actor to the next, from one entrance or exit to the next and from one phase of the action to the next. Even the running to the door at the end, which might seem a superfluous wallowing in sorrow, is in fact a strategy by which Bertini effects a transition between the moment in which Elena stands at the chair, head bent in sorrow, and the moment in which, desperate, she decides to write to the man she had, up to this point, carefully kept at a distance. An appreciation of this kind of acting involves not only an attention to the grace and aptness of the gestures employed, but also to how they mobilize the space of the set and exhaust the range of emotional possibilities of the situation. Rather than being 'read' for their meaning, they should be savoured like a jazz musician's improvisations on a well-known theme.

In *Theatre to Cinema* we suggested that naturalism marks a definitive break with the range of acting styles that employed gesture towards pictorial ends. The important feature of naturalist acting as it developed in the 1880s was not that it encouraged actors to approximate real life, or even some conventionalized notion of the real; rather, in their staging practices, the great naturalist directors and actors were willing to abandon not only graceful movement and gesture, but also highly emphatic and expressive gesture. In the naturalist theatre, incidental activity, stage business, became much more important than the telling gesture or pose as a way of organizing the actor's activity on stage. There are many well-known instances of the importance accorded to mundane stage business within the movement. For example, in the 1905 Moscow Art Theatre production of Ibsen's *Ghosts*, described by Frederick and Lise-Lone Marker,[5] Konstantin Stanislavsky staged the opening scene, in which exposition is provided by a conversation between Regine and her father the carpenter Engstrand, by having the carpenter on stage from the start of the act, busy fixing the lock on the garden door. Such activity bears some relation to character, but it is not designed to produce a pleasing composition, nor to epitomize an emotion or situation. Along with the highly elaborated use of stage business, the naturalist theatre of the 1880s fostered an 'underplayed', even opaque acting style. For example, the naturalist director Otto Brahm commented approvingly on the performance style of Rudolf Rittner, one of the actors hired when Brahm took over the administration of the Deutsches Theater in the 1890s:

> I had the impression of something which gained extraordinary clarity from its very insignificance: I saw him simply go out a door, nothing more. He had read a letter from his Musotte, and as he mulled it over, filled with its mournful tidings, he walked off, without any ceremony—I think I have never seen anything like it. Since our whole former style of acting required an appearance of volition, of careful attention to detail, the 'effective exit' was one of the weightiest requirements of this school. Every step was defended like the retreat from a battlefield, the actor holding every eye on himself until the last. The significance of Rittner's exit consisted in that he simply went out, adding nothing. This delighted me and in this little action I saw symbolized the whole revolution of our new method of presentation.[6]

Obviously, the last thing a diva can do is simply go out through a door; doors are for posing in, and the conventions of the diva film, even the set design and the articulation of space, are predicated on the actress

Figure 13   Figure 14

thinking up something new and intriguing to do on her way to that threshold.

As I have already noted, while there are some ways in which *Assunta Spina* appears to be inspired by naturalism, it seems to fall largely within the compass of pictorial acting and staging.[7] Even the location shooting, which would seem to be an outgrowth of *verismo*, actually works towards a spectacular use of landscape. Of course, it could be argued that, given the topography of the Bay of Naples, one would have to be a sorry cinematographer indeed not to achieve spectacular backgrounds, but even landlocked city scenes (such as Figure 13) seem to have been calculated in terms of their pictorial effect. Similarly, the wonderful set of Assunta's laundry (Figure 14) allows for the display of incidental business, here the women working inside as well as people loafing in the 'street' outside. But note that the set is structurally similar to that of Elena's residence in *Sangue bleu*, discussed above, and that it also allows for highly dramatic entrances and exits—a propensity that is underscored by the filmmaker's willingness to adopt different camera positions on the set for different scenes, varying the space according to situation and mood (this being one of the most striking differences between *Assunta Spina* and *Sangue bleu*).

The emphasis on working-class life does give rise to departures from the kinds of decorum and elegance with which the diva is usually associated. In one early scene, Michele has lunch with Assunta and her father, feeding his fiancée with his knife (Figure 15), and, even after Michele has put on his hat and coat in preparation for their departure, the couple continue eating and drinking (Figure 16), a gesture which in the context of Italy in the 1910s would probably have been considered much more uncouth than it does to the fast-food-wise consumers of today. Nonetheless, such instances of incidental activity decline precipitously after the opening, expository, sections of the film as Bertini relies increasingly on expressive gesture related to the dramatic situation.

ASSUNTA SPINA (1915)

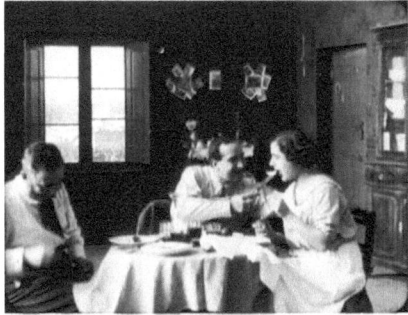

Figure 15

Figure 16

Figure 17

Figure 18

Thus, after Michele, having slashed Assunta's face in a jealous rage, has been put on trial for assault, Assunta is confronted in the lobby of the courthouse by Concetta, Michele's mother (Figure 17).[8] Concetta lunges forward violently at the sight of her enemy (Figure 18), complaining that Assunta has ruined her son's life. Concetta's gesture is matched by Bertini's forward movement (Figure 19). She then moves in to stand nose to nose with Concetta as she defends herself and turns to show her scarred face (Figure 20). But if Assunta is by no means simply passive, the most radical departures from lady-like decorum are assigned to Concetta, not the star. As her friends try to pull her back, Concetta spits at Assunta (Figure 21) and makes rude gestures (Figure 22). Throughout this interchange Bertini remains relatively still, only putting her hand to her brow at the end of it (Figure 23).

A measure of relative decorum is thus preserved for the star. Moreover, the uncouth gestures, while motivated as typical of working-class Neapolitans, are far from incidental movements that are simply there to typify a class or a social position. Note the blocking of the scene, with each of the antagonists supported by female attendants in two carefully posed groups, each of which reacts as an ensemble to the gestures of the

Figure 19 　　　　　　　　Figure 20

Figure 21 　　　　　　　　Figure 22

Figure 23

principals. The gestures of the principals themselves constitute the visual counterpart of the thrust and parry of verbal argument. They are exploited for their expressiveness and are crucial to the rhythmic articulation of the scene, orchestrating the developing conflict in the way that a shot reverse shot interchange might in the sound cinema.

A final example is from two scenes that also take place in the lobby of the courthouse. The first[9] seems quite naturalistic in its evocation of extraneous incident and activity, the second quite the opposite. The

ASSUNTA SPINA (1915)

Figure 24

Figure 25

Figure 26

Figure 27

courthouse lobby set is formed of three rear walls at oblique angles, with doors to the different court rooms in the left and centre ones and the building's exit through the right (Figure 24). There are two tables, one midground left, the other further back and to the right. Behind each table sits an usher (named Diodate Sgueglia and Aniello Torelli respectively in the play, unnamed in the film's titles). There is much incidental activity in the first view of this set. People of different social classes and professions come and go through the doors. A priest and others try to give papers to or get directions from Sgueglia. Two policemen enter front right, leading a man in prisoner's uniform, followed by his wife and child, whom he tries to talk to as the policemen try to hurry him forward. He is taken off into the rear left courtroom; his wife and child and various of his wife's friends are joined by the priest rear centre, where they talk together excitedly. Assunta enters with some of the laundresses and Michele is brought in. He tries to talk to Assunta but is taken off by the police through the rear centre doors.

In contrast with this emphasis on incidental activity is the scene which follows the sentencing of Michele. Assunta enters from the rear centre door, followed by three laundresses (Figure 25). Ernestina, one of the

Figure 28

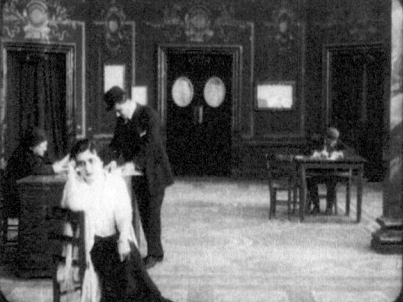
Figure 29

Figure 30

laundresses, gives her a chair. Funelli (Carlo Benedetti), at Sgueglia's table midground left, looks at Assunta curiously. It is just possible to see that Funelli asks Sgueglia who Assunta is, but this is largely blocked by Assunta and the laundresses in front of Sgueglia's table.

Just before the title, 'The sentence. Two years! Two years!', Bertini poses with her hand on her head (Figure 26). Bertini sits in the chair. The laundresses bend over her. Funelli is just visible continuing to look at her from Sgueglia's table (Figure 27). Bertini rises and reaches out to Michele as he is dragged by policemen on through the rear centre doors and then off front right (Figure 28).

Following the title 'Federico Funelli, a notary, is struck by Assunta', the lobby is inexplicably empty save for Funelli, Assunta and the two ushers. This permits a focus on the gestural duet about to be performed by the two principals. At first, Funelli seems to be ignoring Assunta (Figure 29). Then he approaches her (Figure 30). A dialogue title follows (many titles in *Assunta Spina*—at least, in the L'Immagine Ritrovata restoration—combine two or more speeches, without indication of the speakers, whose names, deducible from the surrounding images, I have added in square brackets).

ASSUNTA SPINA (1915)

Figure 31

Figure 32

> [Funelli]: 'Come, come, there's no point in distressing yourself like this.'
>
> [Assunta]: 'Suppose they send him to a gaol a long way away? How shall I get to see him?'

Funelli comes closer to Assunta, with his hands in his pockets and shrugging. She looks at him and begins to stand (Figure 31). Funelli leans back and puts his left thumb in his waistcoat armhole, then leans forward and wiggles his eyebrows (Figure 32). Dialogue titles follow, first:

> [Assunta]: 'And what must I do? Money? How much? I'll sell everything. Tell me! Speak!'

Then:

> [Funelli]: 'It is not a question of money . . . with you.'
> [Assunta]: 'Thanks very much!'

The poses interspersed with the dialogue titles refer to them, almost as if phrase by phrase. Bertini poses with raised hands, corresponding to the section of the title which reads 'What must I do?' (Figure 33). She reaches to her head and ears, indicating she will sell her jewellery. He responds with a gesture indicating 'I don't want money' (Figure 34). There is a belly-to-belly pose as he says '. . . with you' (Figure 35). To indicate Assunta's refusal, Bertini turns away from Funelli and wraps her shawl around herself (Figure 36). She reaches over and sets the chair between them with a plop, mirroring her ironic 'Thanks very much!' (Figure 37). She sits on the chair. He raises his arm in an 'OK!' gesture (Figure 38). She drops her head as he looks away (Figure 39). He turns to look at her again, gesturing with a sweep of his right hand. He goes to Sgueglia's table. She

Figure 33

Figure 34

Figure 35

Figure 36

Figure 37

Figure 38

moves her head from her right hand, with her right elbow resting on her knee, to her left hand, left elbow resting on the chair back (Figure 40).

Funelli exits and Assunta remains seated. Ernestina brings word that Michele is supposed to serve his time far from Naples, in Avellino. Funelli re-enters and observes the women talking (he is visible behind them). Bertini then raises her hands to her head in despair. She looks rear left, sees Funelli and shoos Ernestina off front right. She stands and moves the chair that she had previously interposed between them off to the left

ASSUNTA SPINA (1915)

Figure 39

Figure 40

Figure 41

with a decided gesture. Funelli pretends to ignore her and goes to the table rear right, his back to her. She stretches out her left arm to Funelli, calling him. He turns and points to his chest with his right hand, as if to say: 'Are you talking to me?' (Figure 41). Assunta glances at Sgueglia as Funelli saunters to front right. Satisfied Sgueglia will not hear, she grabs Funelli's right elbow with her left hand and whispers in his ear. Dialogue titles follow, first:

> [Assunta]: 'You told me Michele could stay here in Naples?'
> [Funelli]: 'Yes its true.'

Then:

> [Assunta]: 'Then I want him to stay in Naples!'
> [Funelli]: 'All right . . . but we should discuss this somewhere else.'

They negotiate. Assunta turns to look back before exiting (Figure 42). She exits front right, while Funelli stays to wink triumphantly at Sgueglia. He makes a gesture with right hand held high, palm down,

Figure 42 Figure 43

fingers extended—the conventional mime gesture for 'Caught!' (Figure 43). He exits front right.

The actors' gestures and poses in this scene do not seem substantially different from the use of gesture or attitude in other diva films of this period and are perfectly consonant with the pictorial style. Bertini's pose standing arm outstretched as the police take Michele away resembles her pose in *Sangue bleu* when the Prince exits to get his daughter. Her poses with head on hand while sitting in the chair resemble similar 'thinking' poses from other scenes in *Sangue bleu*, not to mention Borelli's similar use of a chair in *Ma l'amor mio non muore!* While we do not find an extended passage in which the diva is left alone to express her grief in gesture, as is common in the genre, the film does eliminate the supernumeraries in the later lobby scene, in contrast with the first, in order to call attention to the interchange between Bertini and Benedetti, a gestural interchange which has been carefully plotted to follow the course of the intertitles. Finally, Benedetti's gestures evoking such complex ideas as feigned indifference and a slightly mocking graciousness, as well as the final mark of triumph exchanged between the men, seem to us to rank alongside Bertini's work as one of the high points of this style.

Which brings us to a final speculation on the absence of the *divo* in the European cinema of the teens. As noted in *Theatre to Cinema*, naturalist acting in the sense of the abjuration of emphatic gesture, the kind of pared-down style celebrated by Otto Brahm, would have been a very big risk in the early feature cinema—at a point in film history in which filmmakers were just beginning to learn how to tell long and complex plots without the use of spoken language. In my view, it is not really attempted until the very late 1910s and early 1920s, once filmmakers have mastered the panoply of editing and staging devices that provide other means not only of telling stories, but of developing and heightening dramatic situations. The cinema remains wedded to pictorial acting techniques in the 1910s for very good reasons that are intrinsic to the development of the medium itself. However, as Jon Burrows has insightfully pointed out in a recent work on acting in the early British feature,[10] by this point in theatre history, pictorial styles had begun to seem old fashioned (even if some commentators bemoaned the 'anæmic' acting of the modern school, they thereby recognized the current taste for reduced styles). The many derogatory remarks about actors posing in the American and English film-industry trade press suggest that this discourse was making itself felt in the cinema (although it is not evident to us that this was the case in Italy), even while film actors continued to pose and obviously felt the need to pose. Perhaps the widespread social conventions that make it more acceptable for women to articulate emotions and to have recourse to expressive gesture made it easier for actresses to circumvent this particular conundrum. The diva may move her hands about her face, flutter about in her chair and strike tortuous attitudes in ways that no male film star—as opposed to a male character actor or a 'heavy', such as Benedetti playing Funelli in *Assunta Spina*—any longer dared to attempt. Hence, for example, Mario Bonnard's stiff and relatively wooden performance in contrast with Borelli's rapid alteration of posture and gesture in *Ma l'amor mio non muore!* The male equivalent of the diva is not the man who sighs and poses, but the stevedore who climbs sheer rock faces and dives off high cliffs—Maciste, who first appeared in the epic *Cabiria* (1914).

3

L'Enfant de Paris (1913)

Heather Heckman

L'Enfant de Paris, considered by many to be the first feature produced by France's Gaumont, was avidly rediscovered in the 1990s and early 2000s. French film scholars praised Léonce Perret's eye for pictorial beauty,[1] from his sumptuous on-location photography in the South of France to his penchant for mixing high-contrast lighting schemes with deep sets.[2] In an essay devoted to the 1993 Gaumont restoration of the film, Jean A. Gili wrote:

> A feature of great breadth, a well-structured scenario that holds the spectator in suspense as it walks the spectator through slums and bourgeois interiors from Paris to Nice, carefully crafted images shot by a camera operator inspired by the play of light, Léonce Perret's film incontestably belongs in a series of works that, on the eve of the First World War—1913 was also the year of *Fantômas* and *Germinal*—allowed French cinema to figure among the great providers of spectacles to inflame the imagination of audiences.[3]

But if *L'Enfant de Paris* is undoubtedly a document of the great talent of Léonce Perret—as well as, it should be noted, the great talents of Perret's stable of recurring performers and of his long-time cameraman/collaborator Georges Specht—it is also a document of working procedure in Perret's unit. In an era when production documentation is sparse, films often provide our only clues to the norms not just of style but of film practice. Indeed, *L'Enfant de Paris* leaves a trail of clues suggesting that Perret shot in sequence, even when the story he was telling practically cried out for the more efficient approach adopted by American film-makers as early as 1909.⁴

At the heart of Perret scholarship there has remained a mystery about editing. Perret's staging has been celebrated by François de la Bretèque, and by Lea Jacobs and Ben Brewster.⁵ But his editing has elicited more bemusement than awe.⁶ Georges Sadoul, in an attribution cited again and again by French scholars, credits Perret with an 'extremely refined cinematic vocabulary'. Yet Sadoul also concludes that 'Perret surpasses the Griffith of *Birth of a Nation* and demonstrates that French technique was superior to American technique, except in editing'.⁷ Laurent Le Forestier, in contrast, argues that Perret was an early adopter of many elements of continuity editing, including shot reverse shot.⁸ Richard Abel agrees that Perret's editing is in some way ahead of the continental curve: 'The explicit attention to characterization manifest in these latter cut-in close shots makes *L'Enfant de Paris* one of the French films to share in a development just then getting underway in American cinema.'⁹ Nevertheless, Abel, like Sadoul, hedges his bets, arguing that Perret innovated 'an alternative system of analytical editing to that which, in the American cinema, would later be called "classical"'.¹⁰

If these debates seem familiar in early cinema studies, Ben Brewster's careful study of Perret's second bona fide *long métrage*, *Le Roman d'un mousse* (1914), certainly stands out. Brewster evinces no small amount of awe at the climactic court room scene of *Le Roman d'un mousse*, which features sixteen unique camera set-ups by his count. Many of them he found almost imperceptible, and indeed he was able to come up with the count of sixteen only by comparing frame enlargements from the sequence side-by-side. Sixteen unique set-ups in a single sequence seems quite atypical for a European film from 1914, and for Brewster, at least, it is no surprise that Perret departed for America in 1916.¹¹ Yet there is a paradox that needs to be resolved: imperceptible changes in set-ups—however many there may be—are not part of the standard toolkit of continuity film-making and may even have been a violation of its emerging norms.

What was Perret up to? Was he working on a parallel system, as Abel suggests? Was he (or was Specht) an obsessive perfectionist, carefully attuned to the precise alignment of every framing? Or, are these minute variations about practice rather than style? *L'Enfant de Paris*, made a year earlier than *Le Roman d'un mousse* and in many ways a simpler work, constitutes an appealing test case.¹² *L'Enfant de Paris* was released on 17 September 1913 in Gaumont's flagship theatre, the Gaumont Palace. It ran as a full-length feature, with an intermission between a first part focused on the bourgeois orphan Marie-Laure (Suzanne Privat) and a second part focused on the lower class orphan Le Bosco (Maurice Lagrénée). Its total running time at 16 frames per second (and including intertitles and inserts) was approximately two hours. In the weeks that followed, it also circulated to smaller theatres in a serialized, five-part version, closer to the model of Perret's more famous colleague, Louis Feuillade.

The story the film tells is a simple one. It begins in the drawing room of the de Valen family, as the patriarch, Captain de Valen (Émile Keppens), learns he has been called away to serve in the colonies. He is killed in action and his wife (Jeanne Marie-Laurent) dies of grief, orphaning their young daughter Marie-Laure (the titular 'child of Paris'). After her uncle (Henri Duval) is also sent into combat, Marie-Laure is dispatched to boarding school, where she is bullied by teachers and fellow students alike. She runs away, only to be captured by the gangster Le Bachelier (Louis Leubas), who deposits her at the home of the drunkard Tiron (Marc Gérard), a home which, happily for Marie-Laure, is shared by the young and gentle-natured urchin Le Bosco. A year passes and her father, reported dead but apparently only missing in action, returns to France a hero. Le Bachelier recognizes an opportunity and tries to ransom his captive. When the police attempt to thwart his plot, Le Bachelier escapes with the girl *and* her father's money to Nice. Le Bosco, utterly enamoured of Marie-Laure, tracks the kidnapper and ultimately helps the police recover the child. As a reward, Captain de Valen adopts Le Bosco, and the little family of three is united in Nice la Belle.

Gaumont publicity announced that the film was 'in 46 tableaux'.[13] There are considerably more than forty-six shots in the film, but it is possible to arrive at this figure by counting the number of interior scenes. For example, we see the de Valen salon in a total of six discrete scenes over the course of the film's first act. Each one of these six scenes figures into the rough count of forty-six tableaux.[14] Moreover, each of the six scenes is taken from a marginally different camera position. For most viewers, myself included before this analysis, the majority of the displacements are so slight as to be imperceptible. In fact, the difference between set-ups 2 and 5 is so small that I could only detect it by holding a straight edge up to the screen while the video played, or with the aid of Photoshop software to manipulate digital stills (see Figure 1). The piano, which undergoes a drastic change between shots 2 and 3, supports the hypothesis that 2 and 5 are indeed separate set-ups. It appears that Perret and Specht never repeat a set-up in any of the six returns to the same basic view of the same basic salon space.

Perhaps surprisingly, this same principle seems to hold over the entire course of the film. I counted 290 shots in *L'Enfant de Paris*, a figure that

L'ENFANT DE PARIS (1913)

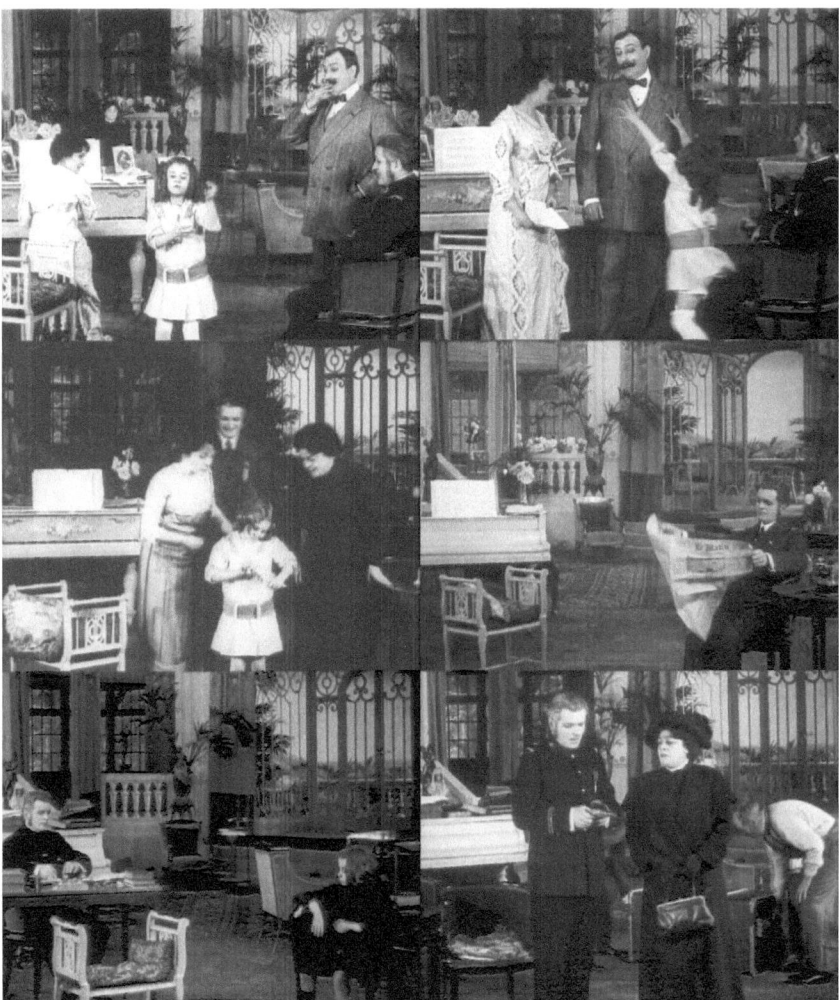

Figure 1

includes fifty inserts and cut-ins but no intertitles. Even if we remove the inserts and cut-ins, there is still a staggering mismatch between shots and tableaux. This is not because the same forty or so set-ups are repeated an average of six times, either: I counted 243 unique set-ups in a film with 290 shots.[15] Approximately eighty-three per cent of the shots in *L'Enfant de Paris*'s two-hour running time are set-ups that appear never to recur. Among the seventeen per cent of shots that do repeat, nearly all were broken by a single intervening shot, usually an insert, cut-in or POV (point of view), categories that had been accepted as standard interruptions in the tableaux style by many European directors.[16] This data supports the

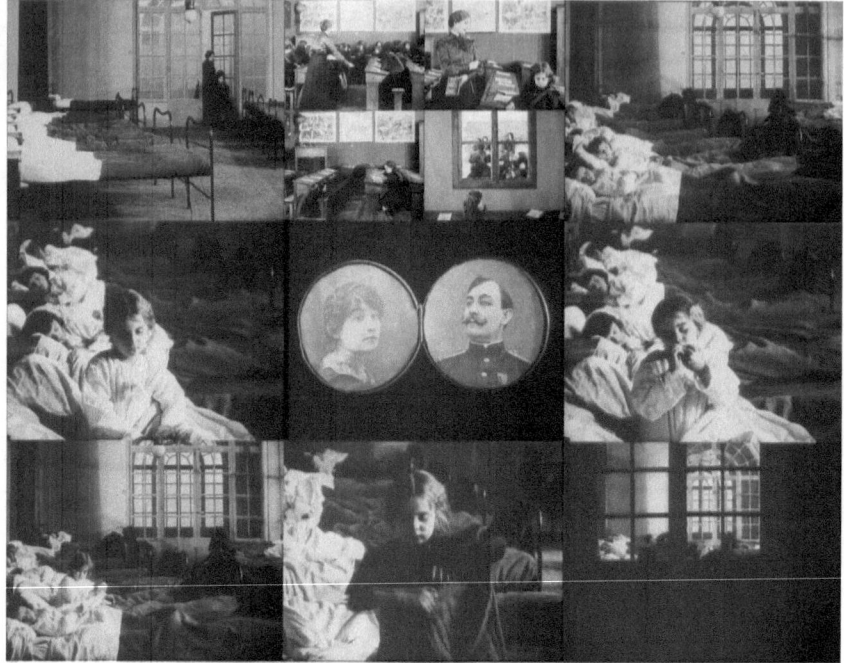

Figure 2

hypothesis that Perret's unit shot in sequence. It is literally incredible that, in a workflow that was determined by space and actor availability, Specht would have gone to the trouble of slightly displacing his camera to the left or right, or forward or back. Instead, it seems that Perret's workflows were determined by linear story logic.

Consider the example of Marie-Laure's boarding school break (see Figure 2). Her dormitory is initially presented in a long shot, with a line of identical beds receding into the background. The camera is positioned slightly to the left of centre and angled a shade to the right. The headmistress leads Marie-Laure down a hallway, visible through windows in the background, into the room through French doors in the right rear corner. Marie-Laure and the headmistress walk the entire length of the dormitory (from long shot to medium long shot), up to the bed in the left foreground. The older woman brusquely removes Marie-Laure's doll and hat, and bats away the child's outstretched hands. The headmistress exits out to the right foreground, only to re-enter to rip the sobbing girl's coat off and replace it with a black smock. The harrowing scene ends, and the two exit to the right together.

When the action returns to the same location later that night, however, the lighting has changed (the room is slightly dimmer) and the camera

L'ENFANT DE PARIS (1913)

has moved in (though, paradoxically, fewer beds are present in the *mise en scène*). Sitting on the second bed on the left, Marie-Laure sits up, looks skyward, takes her locket out, looks at it, closes it quickly and lays back down. From the right foreground, a woman passes to the French doors at the back, peers through the windows and exits through a door in the left background. Slowly, Marie-Laure sits up again. In an axial cut-in to medium shot, Marie-Laure looks directly into the lens, says something, sobs, looks down and kisses her locket. This action is followed by an insert of the open locket on a black background, displaying photos of Marie-Laure's deceased parents. After the insert, Perret cuts back to the same medium close-up as the girl wipes her eyes with her sheets, then he returns to the master shot as Marie-Laure begins to put her shoes on. This double insert structure, which is the only one of its kind in the film, appears to justify out-of-sequence shooting.

An intertitle, 'L'Evasion', briefly interrupts the images. In the following shot, Perret has returned to the same basic medium close-up configuration. This time, however, there is no insert structure to bracket the cut-in, and tellingly, the camera position has changed. The camera is at a somewhat lower position, and displaced slightly to the right (cutting off the heads of the sleeping girls frame left). Nothing in the action of the shots accounts for the camera displacements between our first and second views of the dormitory in long shot and of Marie-Laure in medium close-up. No actions take place at the edges of the frame that might account for a change in position or angle. No items of the *mise en scène* are meaningfully activated or suppressed. The changes smack of entropy rather than order.

Throughout the film, camera positions are determined, within a generous margin of error, by the French norm of 'fixity of viewpoint'.[17] Each of the two major French studios asserted its brand with a dominant, default camera position. At Pathé, a waist-height camera level was the norm. At Gaumont, the preferred height was eye level at a slight high angle.[18] This characteristic position was the default for all scenes (one could say that the camera position determined the view in French cinema of this period, rather than the reverse). At Gaumont, then, the characters closest to the camera were captured in a *plan français*: in the foreground, the bottom of the frame hit between knee and mid-shin.[19] Typically, a single space was filmed from this same viewpoint not just within a scene, but across the length of entire films. Perret's particular camera position of choice, as Brewster has suggested, is a *plan français* at a slightly oblique angle to the rear wall of the set. This was apparently a personal stylistic choice—an effort, perhaps, to differentiate himself from Feuillade's axial views whilst still adhering to house style.[20] The term 'fixity of viewpoint' captures the functional limitations of the approach. Directors at Gaumont rarely experimented with novel views of interior spaces, even if there was variation in the device they chose. Nor, at least in Perret's case, did they think of the viewpoint as truly fixed in space. There was no compelling reason to keep track of the precise position of the camera for any given scene, as long as the general approach to viewpoint was maintained.

Inserts and their cousins also conformed to fixity of viewpoint after a fashion. Like his peers, Perret dispensed with the subtle personal stylistic flourish that characterized his long-shot views, sticking almost religiously to direct frontal viewpoints for inserts and cut-ins. This, David Bordwell has argued, 'is the most conservative strategy for breaking down the scene, since it is least likely to disorient the audience'.[21] It is, in other words, a means of dissecting space that conforms to the fixed view. Although many historians want to celebrate Perret's analytical editing, he largely conforms to the norms of his period.[22] Even performance is harnessed to the guiding principle of frontality for enlarged views. When, for example, Le Bosco begins to track Marie-Laure and her menacing abductor, he presents each of his clues to the camera, taking care to highlight the narratively salient details.

But if inserts were often the functional equivalent of intertitles, cut-ins (and perhaps POVs) occupied an uncertain space. Inserts were, unquestionably, shots to be handled out of sequence as individual elements, rather than as units in a narrative chain. Cut-ins, like the first cut-in to medium close-up on Marie-Laure, were frequently treated in this same way. They were truly edited into the master shot, using a workflow that approaches the one that became dominant in film shooting because of its extraordinary efficiency (shoot separately and then, literally, cut in). But other cut-ins, like the second version of the Marie-Laure medium close-up, display the hallmarks of in-sequence shooting. Either they are themselves variants of previous views or the return to the master shot betrays a small camera displacement. There are too few of these variants to know for sure; perhaps they were merely retakes or coverage. Tantalizingly, though, they might be paradoxical evidence of emerging interest in analytical editing—or perhaps more accurately, analytical camera placement. Perhaps Perret was beginning to conceive of cut-ins as narrative units rather than elements outside the story, as functional equivalents of tableaux rather than intertitles.

There is something else that is surprising about the forty-six tableaux: there aren't more. By my count, interior long shots account for seventy-five shots. Inserts account for another fifty shots. That leaves 170 shots unaccounted for, in a film that was advertised as forty-six tableaux.

L'ENFANT DE PARIS (1913)

Perret's very long film, it seems, rather flummoxed Gaumont's publicity department. Their description, 'a film in 46 tableaux', might convey the impression that Perret attained feature length by stringing together a series of long-duration long shots. In fact, much of the running time's dilation is achieved by exterior action.

To silence the random noise of accidental camera displacement, we might instead dissect the film into 'views', asking not how many absolute set-ups there were, but instead how many equivalent set-ups there were. I counted 175, give or take,[23] for the whole film, including only eighteen tableaux-style interior long shots. There is, it must be conceded, a qualitative difference between the tableaux and the other shots. First, average duration is on the longer side for the tableaux. The de Valen salon tableaux that open the film average approximately one minute (intertitles and inserts excluded). In contrast, the exterior shots that follow Marie-Laure's escape at the end of the first serialized segment average only twenty seconds (intertitles and inserts excluded). There are also more frequent returns to the tableaux viewpoints. At the median (and excluding interruptions for inserts and intertitles), Perret returns to the same approximate set-up for interior long-shots twice; the median exterior view is repeated only once.

The fact that exteriors constitute the majority of the views in *L'Enfant de Paris* must nevertheless be significant. To some extent, Perret dilated his running time by stringing together tableaux. But he also drew upon a multiplicity of exterior views to draw out the action of his film to two full hours. What functions did those many exterior views serve? Many were luxuriously pictorial. When the action moves to Nice in the final acts of the film, Perret begins to pile on scenic views of the French coast. Le Bosco's hunt for Marie-Laure takes him through some of the most beautiful locations in the city, from the bustling downtown to the natural aperture framings of the tree-studded, glistening coast. There is some narrative logic here: Le Bosco is searching for Marie-Laure. But the excess of locations with seemingly no connection to Marie-Laure would seem to connect more meaningfully with the early tradition of exotic actuality films than with the emerging tradition of detective films.

Other exterior views might be labelled 'comings and goings', a norm of French cinema that Perret observed almost religiously.[24] Film-makers at France's largest studios included interstitial material between locations, showing characters' departures and/or arrivals (and sometimes even full trajectories). The practice originated at the beginning of the one-reel period, and seems to have continued into the early 1910s at both Pathé and Gaumont. Perret appears to have wholeheartedly adopted 'comings and goings', which are highly systematized in his films. Whenever a major character travels from one point to another, Perret includes a shot of either that character's departure or arrival (or sometimes both). In total, thirty-nine shots in the films might be counted as comings or goings. A long shot of a vehicle pulling through estate gates—filmed sometimes from inside, sometimes from outside the gate—marks displacement by car or carriage, for instance. For foot travel, two alternatives appear again and again in Perret's films. The first is a long shot of a building's exterior that captures the character's entrance or exit. However, Perret and his camera operator George seem to have preferred the second option (the notably more pictorial one), which appears with even greater frequency: the camera is placed inside a doorway, and shoots through the aperture of the doorway as the character enters or exits. Natural light from the exterior is the principal light source, creating a visually striking high-contrast composition, with a darkened foreground and a bright background. Perret liked this particular configuration so much that it persists in his films for a decade at least (1922's *L'Empire du diamant*, for example, features this set-up repeatedly).

The final major category of exterior shots is pursuit. Roughly thirty minutes of *L'Enfant de Paris* could be described as adhering to a loose chase structure, marking it as a central strategy to Perret's approach to long-form narrative. Throughout virtually all of these thirty minutes, Perret never really engages in cross-cutting, a device that was already well established across the Atlantic. Instead, Perret prefers to follow each performer's action through space, only then cutting back to another performer in a previously visited space. Even on location, Perret's unit appears to shoot in sequence.

For example, when Le Bachelier ransoms Marie-Laure, Perret shows Captain de Valen's car arriving on the Ile Ste Louis, with a distant view of the Hôtel de Ville in the background. De Valen steps down and walks towards the camera. In the next set-up (rotated roughly 90 degrees, if my memory of Paris geography holds), he lingers nervously on the *quai*, with a view of Notre Dame in the background. A man comes forward from the background, and exchanges what appear to be a few congenial words. Perret cuts back to de Valen's waiting car in front of the Hôtel de Ville, which has, in the meantime, crept up on the horizon. Nothing in frame accounts for the move, and with all three performers present, economy seems an unlikely motivating factor.

Consider, too, the way Le Bosco's investigation unrolls in the fourth reel.[25] First, the action follows Le Bachelier, as he escapes from the clutches of the police with Marie-Laure: The action begins in a long shot in a back room at the bar (shot 1, set-up 1). Le Bachelier uncovers a

L'ENFANT DE PARIS (1913)

trap door, and climbs down with his captive. Cut to a medium shot (shot 2, set-up 2) of their descent (ostensibly below the trap door), then to a medium long shot in a darkened room (shot 3, set-up 3). Le Bachelier and Marie-Laure emerge from obscurity at the back, and head towards the camera. Le Bachelier opens curtains to a window frame left. The camera is now located on the exterior of the building, rotated 90 degrees clockwise (shot 4, set-up 4). The composition is a masked, medium close-up of a small window covered by a grill. Le Bachelier forces the grill off. Perret returns inside to the medium long shot (shot 5, set-up 3). Le Bachelier seizes Marie-Laure and heads back to the window, at which point Perret cuts back to the medium close-up on the exterior (shot 6, set-up 4). Le Bachelier pushes Marie-Laure through the opening, then climbs out himself. The action moves to a long shot outside a modest shack (shot 7, set-up 5). Le Bachelier enters from the right foreground with Marie-Laure. The two enter the shack.

Inside the shack in medium long shot (shot 8, set-up 6), Le Bachelier looks over his left shoulder, presumably towards the door, and lays the child down. He takes off his jacket, puts on a robe and begins to tie a handkerchief around his neck. He walks left. Again, Perret moves the camera outside at a 90 degree angle for a medium close-up through a window (shot 9, set-up 7). Le Bachelier peers though a window. He ties the handkerchief around his neck. Back inside (shot 10, set-up 6), Le Bachelier loads clothes and the now struggling Marie-Laure into a laundry basket. He runs his hands through the pockets of his old overcoat and stuffs what he finds into his 'new' dressing coat. He puts on a hat, takes a cane and straps the basket to his back. Perret returns to a slightly different version of the exterior long shot (shot 11, set-up 7 or 5). Le Bachelier looks around, then begins to walk like an old man, turning the corner and exiting to the right foreground. The camera rotates 90 degrees clockwise to a path alongside the shack (shot 12, set-up 8). Le Bachelier walks down the path into the depth. At roughly centre frame, he stops, then scales the hill to his left, exiting frame right. He carries Marie-Laure through two more long shots, each street exteriors (shots 13 and 14, set-ups 9 and 10). The two exit together towards the camera in the left foreground.

At this point, Perret returns to the bar, where Le Bosco and Captain de Valen interact with the police. Thus, Le Bosco tracks Le Bachelier to the shack only after Le Bachelier's trajectory is complete. In a long shot at the bar (shot 15, set-up 11), Captain de Valen reassures Le Bosco. The police enter and talk to the Captain. The Captain gives Le Bosco his card.[26] Perret cuts in to an insert of the calling card (shot 16, set-up 12), then back to the long shot of the bar (shot 17, set-up 11). The scene clears out.

Only Le Bosco and a few policemen are left in frame. Le Bosco clenches his fists and brings them down through the air. He looks right and exits to the right foreground. An intertitle informs us that he has decided to conduct his own investigation. In a return to the master shot, Le Bosco re-enters and goes up the stairs to a door in the right midground.

Le Bosco enters a bare *chambre de bonne*, captured in a medium long shot (shot 18, set-up 13). He opens the skylight, shrugs and steps back down. He exits through the same door. Le Bosco enters the back room with the trap door from the left background (shot 19, set-up 14 or 1). Perret cuts in to a medium shot (shot 20, set-up 15) as Le Bosco runs a knife along the outline of the trap door and pulls up a lock of hair. He looks dead at the camera, holding the lock up for the audience to see. Then, he pounds the door with the knife and starts to pry it up. Cut back to the master shot of the back room (shot 21, set-up 14 or 1). Le Bosco opens the door, looks down at the stairs, starts, gets up and runs to the door in the left background. He stops and yells, swinging his arms violently as if he is cursing. He turns and goes down the trap door.

Perret skips over the medium shot that intervened with Le Bachelier and Marie-Laure, and goes right to a close variant of the room at the bottom of the stairs (shot 22, set-up 15 or 3). Le Bosco finds a hat, heads towards the light and climbs out of the window. In a variant on the medium close-up of the de-grated window (shot 23, set-up 16 or 4), Le Bosco climbs out. Things get a little strange here, as Le Bosco appears to circle around to the shack from the direction Le Bachelier left in. Le Bosco approaches from the side path (shot 24, set-up 17 or 8). He stops, points to the ground and bends over. In a cut-in to a medium close-up (shot 25, set-up 18), Le Bosco points to his clue: footprints in the mud. Back in the master shot, Le Bosco starts to follow the footprints (shot 26, set-up 17 or 8). He arrives at the shack (shot 27, set-up 18 or 5) and enters. Inside (shot 28, set-up 19 or 6), he finds Le Bachelier's coat and runs his hands through the pockets. Finding nothing, he drops the overcoat and picks up Le Bachelier's suit jacket. He removes a letter from its pocket. After the requisite cut-in (shot 29, set-up 20), Le Bosco hits the letter, looks up and turns to go (shot 30, set-up 19 or 6). Back outside the shack, he runs out of frame towards the right foreground, ending the third segment of the serialized cut (shot 31, set-up 20 or 5).

Although it is likely that the trajectories of Le Bachelier and Le Bosco overlap in the story time, they are separated in the plot. Each line of action runs onscreen in its entirety, despite the high potential for suspense (particularly because Le Bachelier appears to circle back towards the bar and Le Bosco appears to head to the shack from the direction Le Bachelier leaves it). Nor does Perret make use of the cross-cutting device in the film's other major chase sequences.[27] Shooting in sequence meant that Perret had to do all of the location work twice. But perhaps there is a way that separating the lines of action as he (and many of his Gallic colleagues) did obscured the potential efficiency of out-of-sequence shooting. Conversely, it is interesting to speculate that the vogue for cross-cutting might have contributed to the rise of out-of-sequence shooting in the USA. Moving immediately from one line of action in a single location could have laid bare some of the underlying efficiency of that approach.

In the end, the most plausible explanation for Perret's strangest editing habit is one that has very little to do with editing. It is most likely that he shot in sequence, adhering to theatre's much longer-established time-based artistic tradition. This solution was an obvious one, especially perhaps for Perret, who came out of the Comédie Française. A healthy margin of error between specific camera set-ups in recurring spaces points to a relatively loose approach to shooting. There is nothing to preclude careful recordkeeping and precision in camera placement when shooting in sequence—but Perret's unit, it seems, was not concerned with precision. The fact that the changes are invisible to most spectators makes the choice a rational one. After all, precision comes at a price in labour. In some cases, however, such as Le Bosco's pursuit of Le Bachelier, the apparently uncontrolled approach to shooting might have had a cost in narrative clarity. Was Le Bosco really tracking Le Bachelier from the opposite direction? Or did the unit lose track of their shooting coverage? Whatever the case, it is a blessing for the historian that Perret and his small crew were not concerned with precision, because it reveals a key aspect of their working process. With a little luck, the same method might be applied to other films of this period, telling us more about the diffusion of innovations in production workflows as running times began to grow during the fascinating transitional era.

4

The Wishing Ring (1914)

Rebecca Genauer

It has become commonplace to open any essay on Maurice Tourneur by bemoaning his absence from, or marginal place in, standard film histories. As Richard Koszarski and Richard Suchenski both note, the fact that Tourneur was widely celebrated as one of the finest and most artistically inclined directors in the 1910s makes his relative omission from subsequent historical discourse all the more inexplicable.[1] The standard account identifies Tourneur's inability and unwillingness to operate successfully within the confines of Hollywood's mode of production as the reason for his popular and critical decline. According to Suchenski, Tourneur began to declare his desire for artistic autonomy, and to criticize the constraints of the profit-driven star system, in and around 1918.[2] Jan-Christopher Horak argues that beyond flaunting the director's increasing disenchantment, Tourneur's polemical streak aligned with his idiosyncratic and often atavistic style—a style at odds with the developing classical system.[3] Either way, such was Tourneur's objection to the increasing industrialization of Hollywood that he eventually walked off set (and out of Hollywood) when Louis B. Mayer insisted that a producer be present during filming.[4]

Tourneur's hostility to the Hollywood mode of production and consequent departure for Europe are not unrelated to an equally interesting though less examined phenomenon: his emergence as an acclaimed filmmaker during the rise of the feature film in the USA. Given Tourneur's antipathy to the rationalization and standardization of film production, it is unsurprising that the director's early successes in his adopted country coincided with the development of the feature film. While the formation of classical Hollywood cinema in the late 1910s hinged on the coalescence of standardized production practices and modes of representation, the rise of the US feature film in the earlier part of the decade introduced new challenges and freedoms. This was a period in which narratives and modes of narration were subject to experimentation and debate as filmmakers were forced to reject the routine practices of the preceding single-reel and two-reel period while contending with the challenge of filling longer films with sufficient story material, distributing narrative information across five or more reels and articulating increasingly complex stories. Tourneur's five-reel feature film, *The Wishing Ring: An Idyll of Old England*, was a response to these developments.

When *The Wishing Ring* was released in November 1914, critics praised its fairytale charm, its slight but appealing story and its likeable performances. The film retains its charm today, but it is also, and perhaps not coincidentally, a fascinating artefact of the laxity inherent in this (and any other) transitional period. While Tourneur is usually acclaimed for his use of lighting (and especially his use of silhouettes), what is also salient in *The Wishing Ring* is the way in which he employs the increased length of the multi-reel feature to articulate a distinct and elaborative mode of narration, in which descriptive elements proliferate rather than drive the narrative forward. Thus while the film's structure is classical in some respects, Tourneur reduces many of its usual features. The result is an atypical distribution of essential story events, an equally atypical assignment of character goals and a marked effacement of conflict. Although these characteristics might have caused problems, Tourneur's visual style, which incorporates highly edited sequences as well as scenes consisting largely of long takes, evades these problems by enhancing the film's impression of diegetic completeness and narrative unity.

The Film and its Contexts

The Wishing Ring was Maurice Tourneur's third directorial effort for the World Film Corporation, which was based in Fort Lee, New Jersey. Having first been trained as a painter and having subsequently worked as a stage director under André Antoine in France, Tourneur went to the USA in 1914 with credentials that suited World Film's ethos and the artistic environment of Fort Lee. Many of the films produced by World and other Fort Lee companies were directed by high-profile European émigrés, among them Emile Chautard and Albert Capellani. World also specialized in feature-length adaptations of stage plays, particularly those produced on Broadway by William Brady or the Shuberts, both of whom had financial stakes in the company.[5] *The Wishing Ring* had been a

Shubert production, one of two plays that marked the return to Broadway of playwright Owen Davis in 1910, after a year's hiatus.[6] Although the play was only afforded a single matinee performance before going on the road, it nevertheless received critical praise: the *New York Times* reviewer remarked that, although somewhat juvenile, it was a great improvement over Davis's previous, overly melodramatic, works, and that the audience clearly enjoyed it.[7]

The storyline in Tourneur's version of *The Wishing Ring* is simple. Giles (Chester Barnett) is expelled from college as punishment for his perennial misbehaviour. His disappointed and gouty father, the Earl of Bateson (Alec B. Francis), declares that he will have no more to do with his miscreant son until the latter is able to prove his worth by earning half a crown. Meanwhile, while filling in for his godfather's recently fired gardener, Giles falls in love with Sally, the parson's daughter (Vivian Martin). Giles and Sally court, although Sally initially believes Giles to be a poor gardener rather than the estranged son of the Earl. When she eventually learns the truth, she decides to reconcile father and son. Unbeknownst to Giles, she makes regular visits to the Earl, whom she soon succeeds in charming. However, she falls from a cliff while attempting to collect herbs to cure the Earl's gout, and while rushing to Sally's bedside, the Earl's horse goes lame. He searches for another horse and inadvertently borrows Giles's—for half a crown. When Giles and the Earl inevitably meet at her bedside, Sally points out that Giles has proved his worth and earned his half a crown, so should now be forgiven. Giles and the Earl embrace and an epilogue shows Sally, Giles, and many of the film's supporting players at Sally and Giles's wedding feast.

While film reviewers praised *The Wishing Ring*, they observed that the story was small in scale and did not really require feature-length treatment. Peter Milne argued that there is 'something engaging, something fascinating about this pretty little comedy-drama that results in it being unusually attractive, even though the story could have been told in far less space than five reels [sic] embrace'.[8] Hanford C. Judson found that the film was attractive not in spite of its unsubstantial story, judging that the slightness of the story enhanced the film's idyllic qualities, and arguing that the film's only true subject 'was human joy, which, like sunlight gathered in a cup to be appreciated for itself, is best enjoyed when the cup is as thin as possible'.[9]

Feature Films and Narratives

That the thinness of the film's story was of interest to film reviewers is neither surprising nor insignificant. Critical and professional discourse at the time focused on the density and articulation of stories as a central problem for the increasingly popular feature-length film. Given the dominance of single-reel and two-reel films in the period leading up to the feature film's emergence in the USA, the transition to feature-length films represented a radical departure. Single-reel films had functioned as part of an efficient, modular system of programming, and had to be produced both rapidly and uniformly: 'filmmakers came to know exactly what was required to turn out a story lasting approximately the same amount of time for each title'.[10] The feature-length film disrupted this system, prompting discussion as to what did and did not suit its multi-reel format.

Kristin Thompson, Tom Gunning and Barry Salt have all pointed out that, in recognizing that the feature film demanded more than the simple elongation of a single-reel or two-reel story, filmmakers turned to the theatre for models of story construction, and that in doing so they appropriated the playwright's ideal of dramatic unity.[11] As Thompson points out, this ideal was first articulated by Edgar Allan Poe with regard to the short story, then expanded to encompass unity of motivation and continuity of action, both of which became hallmarks of classical cinema.[12] However, unity was not the only goal, and as Thompson has observed, those who wrote scripts for early feature films 'achieved balance by splitting their story up into thirds or quarters, with their high points or major breaks between them', much like their successors.[13] In this way at least some early feature-length films could be said to be prototypical, demonstrating a considerable degree of continuity with later classical films.

Thompson's emphasis on these forms of continuity is useful for establishing the lineage of classical Hollywood cinema but it tends to obscure the problems posed initially by increased length and to downplay some of the non-classical solutions that were tried out in the early- and mid-teens. Although contemporary critics generally espoused the values and directives that Thompson identifies, their implementation was by no means always straightforward. And although the number of theatrical adaptations made in the early years of the feature film indicate a reliance on plays as models, critics like Louis Reeves Harrison warned against leaning too heavily on the theatre as he noted that exposition in films could be handled in ways that differ from those in plays.[14] Moreover, as Ben Brewster has demonstrated in his analysis of *Traffic in Souls* (1913), feature-length films did not always adhere to the protocols of balanced, large-scale design observed by Thompson: some of them were marked by idiosyncratic structural designs, conforming neither to the three-act or four-act model, nor to the reel-based constructions that marked a number of early multi-reel films.[15]

In all these ways and for all these reasons, early feature films did not simply progress towards classical cinema. Instead, they revealed the challenges inherent in what was still a novel form. Writing in 1913, critics such as W. Stephen Bush, Louis Reeves Harrison and Epes Winthrop Sargent decried what they perceived to be the weak and cumbersome structures of US feature films. Bush claimed that 'the multiplicity of reels was made to cover a multiplicity of sins',[16] while Harrison emphasized the need for writers who could devise photoplays with structural integrity: 'It is no longer denied that the visualization of a story of human life is bound to suffer from structural defects without two architects', he wrote. 'Few authors of merit have more than a general idea of how the photoplay should be shaped. . . . One result is the scarcity of good features.'[17] The most frequent and detested problem was 'padding', which referred broadly (and intuitively) to anything that opposed condensation and compression (values that critics had appreciated in single-reel films). Padding was considered a problem whenever there was not enough action to occupy the duration of a film or when too much time elapsed between climaxes. Critics and practitioners upheld the belief that dramatic high-points should be frequent in order to support the burden of extended film length,[18] and critics in particular identified padding as a problem wherever films contained an excess of incidents that did not propel the narrative forward. Narrative events that operated on a descriptive or paradigmatic level were considered inessential and least damaging when limited.[19] However, the challenges that made multiple-reel films prone to structural problems also permitted interesting variations in story construction, and this is one of the most interesting aspects of *The Wishing Ring*.

The Wishing Ring: Deviations from the Norms of Classical Narration

The Wishing Ring is marked by an elaborate narrative structure that not only deviates from the emerging norms of classical cinema, but also violates many contemporary practices. At a macro level, however, *The Wishing Ring*'s structure adheres to the classical and pre-classical models defined by Thompson, particularly insofar as it is divisible into four more or less equal parts. Although these parts do not always end at a high point or climax, they are unified in terms of narrative function and they each introduce or conclude a shift in action or character motivation. The first quarter of the film depicts Giles's delinquency up to the point at which he agrees to tend his godfather's garden. This segment establishes Giles's character and explains his strained relationship with his father. At the beginning of the second part Giles meets Sally, and a new line of action—their romance—is initiated. This segment develops the romance and ends when the Earl writes his ultimatum to Giles, and when Giles buys Sally a purportedly magical ring from a community of gypsies. The third segment begins halfway through the film and features the festivities at an outdoor party, at which Giles and Sally's romance continues. This segment advances the love story while also underlining Sally's belief in her ring's magical powers, which appear to have eventuated in the new dress and shoes that she wears to a party. At the end of this segment, Sally discovers a note, written by the Earl calling for the half crown he lent to Giles earlier on to be returned. This is a high point in the story, revealing Giles's true identity and providing Sally with a brand new goal—the reparation of Giles and his father's relationship. The film's penultimate segment builds to a climax when Sally accidentally falls off a cliff. But Sally is rescued and father and son are united by their love for her.

Despite its relatively classical segmentation, *The Wishing Ring* has a decidedly idiosyncratic feel. It does not build towards its climax, and for the most part its story is only sparsely punctuated with essential events and points of narrative tension. It was probably these qualities that prompted *Variety*'s declaration that 'there isn't a dramatic moment in the story'.[20] The film does, though, contain moments of conflict and narrative suspense. The Earl's reprimand to his son in the film's first quarter, the search for Sally, the parson's discovery of his daughter's limp body and, of course, the race to Sally's bedside are all moments of high drama. But while it is not unusual for the dramatic moments in a film to be concentrated in its final quarter, the preponderance of non-causally linked incidents leading up to the climax, the conscious reduction of anticipated conflict, and the extent to which this limits goal-motivation among its characters all work to attenuate the film's drama and exaggerate its capacity for elaborative narration.

Rather than depicting essential story elements, the first three quarters of the film are marked by an excess of material that does not propel the narrative forward, but rather serves a descriptive, elaborative function. Much of this is tangential to the story proper. For instance, at seven points in the film (not including the film's framing device, which will be discussed later) we see four unnamed young women sometimes observing Giles and Sally, sometimes interacting with townspeople and sometimes being observed by other peripheral characters. These women never engage directly with any of the principal characters, nor do they shape the progress of the story in any way. Other marginal storylines are briefly developed, but never become entwined with the central one. Thus in one shot we see a young woman depart home for the party at which Sally discovers the Earl's note to his son. This woman soberly says goodbye to her mother, then once the front door is shut trots off happily with her boyfriend (who has been onscreen all along but outside the mother's view). At the end of the party we see this couple coming back, nearly getting caught kissing goodbye as they do so. It is divergent moments such as these that tend to characterize the film. Other examples include two extended passages in which Giles is shown wandering more or less aimlessly through town, the first after he escapes from his tutor, and the second while Sally is with Giles's father. These passages have no clear causal motivation, nor do they lead to any subsequent actions. On the contrary, they serve a descriptive and unifying function: they permit Giles to wander through the town, and they invite the viewer to compare the circumstances of each of his wanderings.

If the excess of descriptive material delays the forward movement of the film's narrative, the leisurely pace of the film is further amplified by its relatively self-conscious effacement of conflict. In fact, the possibilities for the development and resolution of conflict in the film version of *The Wishing Ring* are significantly pared down in comparison to the play, which contains a parallel love story in which a girl with aspirations to marry into wealth falls in love with a gardener disguised as a rich man. The exclusion of this secondary inverted romance in the film not only makes room for the elaborative, descriptive passages discussed above, but also eliminates an additional source of dramatic interest and conflict. Moreover, the remaining central romance in *The Wishing Ring* is oddly unproblematic. Sally and Giles fall in love with each other almost immediately, and face no obstacles in their romance. The most obvious sources of potential conflict—mistaken identity and class discrepancy—are consciously eschewed in favour of a complication-free relationship. In the stage version, Sally is heartbroken by her discovery of Giles's true identity.[21] In Tourneur's version, Sally's discovery does not endanger her relationship with Giles: she is perturbed neither by Giles's true identity, nor by the fact that her assumptions about him prove to be incorrect.

The only instance of sustained dramatic tension in the story is produced by the strained relationship between Giles and his father. However, even this is minimized, and one of the remarkable features about the narrative is the extent to which it refuses to rely on goals to drive the story. In most classical (and most pre-classical) Hollywood films, goal-motivated characters push the narrative forward and generate suspense as to whether or not they will achieve their aims. But most of the characters in *The Wishing Ring* lack clearly articulated goals. Thus on his expulsion from college, Giles is depicted as aimless, and since his romance with Sally is uncomplicated and relatively static, whatever goals or desires it prompts are almost immediately satisfied. Thus, when Sally requires a suitable dress to wear to the lawn party, Giles buys one for her straight away.

Meanwhile, Giles's apathy about his relationship with his father results in a notable lack of motivation. Although he sulks after escaping his tutor, Giles is largely indifferent to his father's anger and disappointment, and makes no plans or efforts to make amends. This is emphasized by the passages of intermittent cross-cutting to and from the Earl in the second and third parts of the film. While eight separate shots of the Earl gazing forlornly into the distance or at Giles's photograph remind the audience of Giles's troubled relationship with his father, they also underscore the extent to which Giles remains unmoved. In a more classical film, the Earl's ultimatum to Giles to earn half a crown would immediately trigger the formation of a goal. But goal formation is delayed in *The Wishing Ring*: we do not see the Earl compose and send his letter to Giles until approximately halfway through the film. Moreover, the film not only delays the introduction of the letter, it also reduces its effect as a source of motivation for Giles. Shortly after the Earl writes his note, Giles receives a letter. We assume that this is the letter challenging Giles to earn the half crown, but an insert shot reveals that the letter Giles has received is not the letter from his father, but an announcement that his godfather is returning home. The film never shows Giles receiving the letter from his father and the audience is denied seeing Giles's reaction to the challenge posed to him. We learn that Giles has received the letter only because Sally eventually finds it. In the meantime, a single shot and intertitle are all that there is to mark how Giles has to earn the half crown in the film's fourth quarter and in the end, it is Sally, not Giles, who becomes *The Wishing Ring*'s principal goal-motivated character.

Avoiding the 'Padded' Pitfall

The qualities described above differ not only from the later classical cinema, but also from the recommended practices of the early feature period. The film's relaxed pace and its insistence on elaborative, descriptive passages put it at risk of seeming padded, and of violating Epes Winthrop Sargent's advice that: 'each scene should have a direct bearing on the story and contribute to the general effect a result equal to its footage. If this is not the case, the development is poor no matter how tricky and "cute" the planned action may be.'[22] *The Wishing Ring*, however, was praised precisely for its elaborative aspect which helped de-emphasize or stall the advancement of narrative. The reviewer for the *New York Dramatic Mirror* pointed to specific incidents of this kind, a cat drinking milk while its owner slept, and a dog howling in response to some bad singing, and for him these constituted high points.[23] Why, then, was the film not criticized for padding? Although it is undoubtedly digressive and marked by retardation, it is carefully constructed. The excess of divergent moments, the elaborative features of the film, consistently operate in the service of the film's impression of diegetic completeness and narrative unity. These traits are bolstered by Tourneur's aesthetic choices, and specifically by his patterned use of highly edited sequences and sequences comprised of long takes.

Jan-Christopher Horak has identified a tendency in Tourneur's later silent films to revert to archaic modes of representation that present 'fractured' diegetic worlds.[24] There are moments in *The Wishing Ring* in which the unity of the film's diegesis is indeed weakened. As is typical for the period, the main actors are identified and their characters introduced individually before the inception of the story. However, the actors and their introductions are not in any way integrated into the world of the story. Chester Barnett, for instance, steps out from behind a tree and mugs directly into the camera, and after registering his awareness of the camera, he ducks behind the tree again. But the most blatant source of diegetic weakening in *The Wishing Ring* is the framing of the story. *The Wishing Ring* opens with a shot of the four women who appear intermittently across the film. They gracefully part the curtains on a stage's proscenium while smoke from the footlights wafts upward (Figure 1), and as the film concludes these women close the curtains and curtsey towards the camera. This framing device not only alludes to *The Wishing Ring*'s status as a theatrical adaptation, but also marks the film as a performance presented before an audience. Tourneur minimizes the disruptive effect of this device by including the women in the film's diegesis. But their integration into the world of the story proper is arguably at odds with the integrity of the film's diegetic world, a world articulated in and through long takes and highly edited sequences alike.

A brief analysis of the opening sequence of *The Wishing Ring* will demonstrate how Tourneur's highly edited sequences work and how they enhance the film's sense of diegetic unity. The sequence depicts Giles's unscholarly behaviour and subsequent arrest. While this might have been depicted simply and concisely, Tourneur elaborates on the local impact of

THE WISHING RING (1914)

Figure 1

the event by means of its highly edited structure. The sequence consists of forty-four shots, up to and including the shot in which Giles is thrown into a jail, and it alternates between shots of Giles and his schoolmates' drunken carousing in an inn and the various townspeople and animals these young revellers disturb. More specifically, it shows five distinct spaces peripheral to the inn in alternation. These include: two separate windows through which a number of townspeople lean out to register their annoyance; Sally's bedroom, in which Sally herself is kept awake by noise; a field with a grazing donkey; and the town's streets, through which law enforcement officers make their way en route to the inn. The alternation between the interior of the inn and the two windows is structured around eye-line matches created when the townspeople look out at each other and down to the inn below. These eye-line matches serve a number of purposes. In the absence of an establishing shot linking the inn to the local residences, their most apparent purpose is to suggest the spatial relationships between them. But they also serve to set up a gag, which occurs when one of the townspeople exacts revenge on Giles by dumping a pitcher of water on him as he is dragged off to jail. One of their most obvious additional functions is to enhance the effect of diegetic completeness by suggesting a unified space that extends beyond the frame of any individual shot.

Tourneur's pointed use of eyeline matches shows how an essential narrative event—the loud partying of Giles and his cohorts—extends outward to a range of peripheral locations and characters. This event is not confined to the place in which it is set, but has sonic and social consequences beyond its immediate vicinity. Thus in addition to articulating a sense of diegetic unity, the elaboration of the effects of Giles's rowdiness establishes narrative and aesthetic resonances that are reiterated across the film. The appearance of Sally long before her introduction as a central character is a fairly typical instance of narrative 'planting'. (In a similar manner, Giles encounters Sally's pet dog before he meets Sally herself.) The film's opening sequence also sets up resonances through less formulaic means. One of its comic effects occurs when a donkey brays to express its displeasure at the noise emanating from the inn. Although the donkey's appearance seems gratuitous—a merely descriptive and humorous moment—it is mirrored later on when Sally's tone-deaf singing elicits a similar reaction from a dog. These parallels are comic elaborations on the quality of particular sounds. As individual incidents they are digressive, since they delay rather than further the narrative's causal chain. But their rhyming structures create compositional unity from what might otherwise have been purely local, one-off gags.

If Tourneur uses highly edited sequences to develop an elaborative rather than a streamlined or propulsive method of narration, he accomplishes the same thing with minimally edited scenes and lengthy shots. Although the cutting rate in *The Wishing Ring* is quite brisk (with an average shot length of just over seven seconds), Tourneur employs exceptionally long takes at a number of different points.[25] Two examples stand out: Giles's first encounter with Sally, and the Earl's visits with Sally. The average shot length for these sequences, which include intertitles, cutaways and shot reverse shot passages, and which greatly reduce the average shot length) are fourteen and twenty-one seconds, respectively. But both sequences contain shots that last well over a minute, and like the highly edited

Figure 2

sequences described above, these long-take sequences contribute to the aesthetic unity of the film even as they retard the progress of the story.

Although the two sequences in question contain relatively casual staging, their lengthy single-shot duration and their long-shot scale permit the elaboration of the actors' performances. For instance, while Giles spreads jam on a piece of bread for Sally, Sally lifts her napkin off the table, holds it up in front of her, turns it, then looks down at her dress (Figure 2). Her facial expression suggests that she is contemplating whether her dress requires the protection of the napkin. She decides that it does not and places the napkin on Giles's lap instead. Later on, in another long take in this sequence, Sally and Giles stand in the foreground facing the camera. Giles holds a bunch of grapes while he speaks. Without invitation, Sally reaches over and takes just a few grapes, then the whole bunch. After eating several more grapes, she tosses the bunch behind her onto the ground. Giles glances at the grapes as Sally takes them and looks behind her to see where they land, but their conversation is otherwise uninterrupted. The business in the scene is incidental rather than consequential. But through the elaboration of gestures, the performance embellishes the characters, conveying Sally's charming unpretentiousness and Giles's lack of concern about her uncouthness.

As in the sequence in which Sally meets Giles, the long takes that comprise Sally's meetings with the Earl allow the actors to convey their characters' growing friendship. In one of these takes, the inclusive framing of Sally and the Earl helps articulate their growing friendship—and their mutual delight in mocking one of the Earl's butlers. Here, Sally and the Earl in the foreground wait as the butler enters from the right. The Earl is about to ask the butler to bring in a chess set when Sally leans over to whisper to him. The Earl nods, half covers a delighted smile and agrees to allow Sally to request the chess set (Figure 3). After a few false starts—and additional encouragement from the Earl—Sally asks the butler for the chess set. She smiles and bites her fingernail with childish glee while the Earl tries to conceal his amusement, first by turning his back to the butler, secondly by turning round to face him with an expression of mock severity, and thirdly by turning away again in order to stifle a laugh. When the butler ignores Sally's request, the Earl turns round to face him and strikes his stick on the floor's wooden boards. The butler then exits background left as Sally marches behind him mocking his pomposity—and his ample girth. In addition to facilitating the elaboration of character traits, long-take sequences such as this help bolster narrative unity. The repetition of emphatically long takes establishes parallels between events: as the reconciliation between Giles and the Earl is effected through Sally's

Figure 3

influence on each character, the formal similarities between the sequences in which Sally charms each man highlight the functional similarities between them.

In 1916, Maurice Tourneur asserted that Shakespeare would have loved moving pictures, because his works showed 'his *flair* for embellishment'.[26] With the increased length of films in the early feature period, filmmakers were now afforded the time and space to embellish. The opportunity brought challenges, however, and many struggled to tell stories without resorting to padding. I believe it inaccurate to posit a linear development from short to classical films, or to characterize the cinema of the early- to mid-1910s in terms of a set of stable characteristics. Early feature-length films such as *The Wishing Ring* are evidence of the ways in which filmmakers were able to engage in elaboration and embellishment, neither falling prey to the hazards of padding nor adopting what would become the fundamental norms of classical cinema. The opportunities for alternative modes of representation were perhaps at no time more abundant than during a transitional period. Although our purview is often limited by the dominance of classical cinema, further study of early feature films will yield greater insight into the range of narrational strategies tested by filmmakers who were confronted with the challenge of telling stories over a long duration in compelling ways.

5

The Phantom Carriage (Körkarlen) (1921)

John Gibbs and Douglas Pye

The reputation of *The Phantom Carriage* is in some respects securely established. In film histories and surveys of Scandinavian cinema the film is cited frequently as a highlight of director Victor Sjöström's pre-Hollywood career and as one of the great films of Swedish silent cinema. Yet the film has attracted surprisingly little detailed discussion. Almost invariably, writers note its unusually elaborate temporal structure and its powerful and extended multiple-exposure special effects, but have very little to say about other aspects of the film.[1] Even in the field of silent cinema scholarship, which has transformed received histories of film in recent years, *The Phantom Carriage* tends to have a walk-on part. It may be that the film's two most striking stylistic features, as well as what can seem its overt didacticism, have deflected or discouraged closer scrutiny. Tom Gunning, for instance, partly establishes his case for *Mästerman* (1920) as 'Victor Sjöström's Unknown Masterpiece' by reference to *The Phantom Carriage*:

> In contemporary historiography, *Mästerman* has been eclipsed by . . . Sjöström's *Körkarlen* (*The Phantom Carriage*; French title *La Charrette Fantôme*, 1921). I don't intend to deny the beauty and quality of this famous film but, frankly, I think it is unfortunate that for many people, if they know one silent Swedish film, this is the one . . . *Körkarlen* wears its technique on its sleeve, overtly displays its unquestionable mastery of superimposition and complex narrative

structure. *Mästerman* tucks its mastery of editing and composition up its sleeve, so to speak, and refuses to make explicit its character's psychology as does the rather too-pat allegory offered by *Körkarlen*.[2]

Our view of *The Phantom Carriage* is rather different. We do not wish to promote its claims to recognition over those of other Sjöström films. But we do want to argue that the film's remarkable qualities are not limited to the widely noted multiple exposures and complex narrative structure—that in fact they include a 'mastery of editing and composition', a flexibility and fluidity in the construction of dramatic space that has been largely overlooked in discussions of Sjöström's, and the cinema's, stylistic evolution. We will also argue that Sjöström's dramatic achievements in *The Phantom Carriage* go well beyond 'too-pat allegory'.

The Novel and the Film

The Phantom Carriage was adapted from a short novel by the Nobel-Prize-winning Swedish writer Selma Lagerlöf, whose work formed the basis of several major films in what is often referred to as the 'Golden Age' of Swedish cinema. Of the eight features Sjöstrom himself directed between 1917 and 1921, four were based on Lagerlöf's work. In the afterword to his translation of *Körkarlen* (first translated into English as *Thy Soul Shall Bear Witness* but here as *The Phantom Carriage*, the most familiar English title of the film), Peter Graves describes Lagerlöf's 1912 book as 'both a novel of social realism, set in the slums and focusing on the evils of alcohol, family abuse and tuberculosis, and a ghost story, in which the focus is on the reforming and healing power of love'. He also makes clear that Dickens's *A Christmas Carol*, a story frequently evoked by viewers of *The Phantom Carriage*, was very much in Lagerlöf's mind as she wrote.[3] Like Dickens, Lagerlöf tells a story of the moral redemption of a character who is taken on a supernatural journey during the course of a single night (New Year's Eve in *The Phantom Carriage*).

The novel has two interconnected narrative centres: a young Salvationist, Sister Edit, dying of consumption in her mother's house; and David Holm, spending a drunken New Year's Eve in a churchyard with two companions. Edit repeatedly asks for David to be brought to her and for her colleagues go out to search for him. Talking among themselves, Edit's colleagues relate parts of the backstory of her meeting with David the previous New Year's Eve, her love for him, and her later attempts to reunite him with his wife and family. In the churchyard, David tells his companions the story of a friend, Georges, who was terrified of dying

THE PHANTOM CARRIAGE (KÖRKARLEN) (1921)

at the stroke of midnight on New Year's Eve and having to become the driver of death's cart (the phantom carriage), charged with collecting the souls of the dead. When the companions fight over David's refusal to go to Edit and he dies after suffering a consumptive fit, the carriage, driven by Georges, comes to collect his soul and Georges informs him that David must replace him as death's driver. Georges both relates the other parts of the backstory and takes David on a ghostly journey to show him what is happening to Edit and to his family in the present.

In the novel, then, we gain access to the past entirely through dialogue, one character talking to another. What is told in the novel is shown in the film: scenes of the past are bracketed in the film's present by a character looking back, their dialogue given to us in titles, but the scenes are dramatized so that we witness rather than merely hear about them. This gives the film its unusually elaborate temporal structure, with four main flashbacks, one of which contains a further, embedded dramatization—not strictly a flashback—of what one of the characters relates.[4]

Sjöstrom's adaptation is in many respects faithful to the novel, but he also made significant changes. One major subplot involving David's brother is omitted. The role of David's wife is considerably enhanced so that she becomes a substantial third character and the value of the marriage is given greater weight. Sjöström also rationalizes the ways in which the backstory is introduced so that in the film only David and Georges introduce flashbacks. Perhaps most significant in dramatic and filmic terms is that Sjöstrom both expands brief passages in the book into major sequences, including the mission hall scene, in which Edit first realizes that David is married, and invents new scenes to develop or replace those in Lagerlöf's original, including the film's most shocking episode, in which David deliberately sets out to infect his children with tuberculosis and then, after being locked in an inner room by his wife, hacks his way out with an axe.

We want to develop our analysis, however, from the detail of sequence construction and to move from there to some broader perspectives on the film. Specifically, we will look at a segment which is in several respects at the heart of the film: it shows the first meeting between the two central characters, David Holm (Victor Sjöström) and Sister Edit (Astrid Holm); it spans the film's exact midpoint; and at almost twelve and a half minutes, it is the longest uninterrupted passage to take place in a single setting.

The Meeting between David Holm and Sister Edit

This segment forms the third of the four extended flashbacks and the second in which Georges (Tore Svennberg), Death's coachman, requires David to recall crucial episodes in his life. The setting is a new Salvation Army hostel (Slumstation) on New Year's Eve, the first night on which it is ready to receive guests, and the action extends from the two Salvation Army Sisters, Edit and Maria (Lisa Lundholm), making final preparations for the hostel's opening and David's unexpected arrival just before midnight seeking a bed for the night to his departure the following morning. The flashback contains three sequences, divided by elisions of time marked by fades to black: (1) the two Sisters hanging a final framed text in the dormitory, David's arrival, his falling drunkenly asleep and Edit beginning to mend his tattered jacket; (2) later that night, Edit completing the sewing, praying for David, taking the jacket into the dormitory, covering David with a blanket and going to bed; and (3) David finding the jacket the next morning, being given breakfast by Maria and asking to see the person who did the mending; when Edit enters, David violently ripping out all of Edit's work; and Edit eliciting David's contemptuous agreement to return on the following New Year's Eve.

Most of the action takes place in the large living/dining room of the hostel, though in each sequence one or more characters move into and out of the adjoining dormitory for guests and the bedroom which Edit and Maria share. Sjöström gradually reveals that four doors open from the central room, respectively into the entrance lobby, the kitchen, the dormitory and the bedroom, and he makes significant use, as he does throughout the film, of doors and doorways, including here shots from one room into another. The only room the camera does not enter is the kitchen, seen briefly behind Maria as she carries David's breakfast to the table. The set was clearly designed to accommodate intricate stylistic intentions, and the dramatic and structural centrality of the hostel segment is paralleled by its remarkably rich and fluent articulation of the relationships between action, character and space. Our discussion will centre on the third sequence, from David discovering his mended jacket to his departure, which can be broken down as shown in Table 1.

By the beginning of this sequence, Sjöström has already introduced most of the spaces he will use. We have seen, for instance, both ends of the dormitory in which the sequence begins, the end farthest from the door in the first shot of the flashback, in which the two women are seen through the doorway hanging the framed text, and the opposite end in a number of set-ups when David is shown into the room and falls asleep, and again later when Edit returns his jacket. We have also seen enough of the main room to place the doors to dormitory, bedroom and entrance lobby in relation to each other.

THE PHANTOM CARRIAGE (KÖRKARLEN) (1921)

Table 1

Shot	Camera set-up	Action and visual field
1	A	David, framed knees up, sitting on bed, smoking, pulling on jacket. Head of second bed visible behind him right rear, table and chair behind him left rear. Looks down and discovers mending. Examines it in detail, begins to look up.
2	B	Main room. Part of table at right with lamp above. Part of window visible on wall left, doorway looking into what seems to be kitchen centre frame on rear wall. Maria walking through doorway towards camera, carrying tray. Places it on table and looks out of frame front left.
3	A	David looks up out of frame front and right (as though hearing Maria). Looks down, up and down at coat again, smiles, then coughs.
4	C	Looking into corner of main room with dormitory door partly visible left, harmonium along wall left, door to lobby at rear right, table in foreground with lamp upper right partly visible. Maria behind table, looking towards door at left, hands still on tray (i.e. 90 degrees to set-up B). Maria goes to door, camera adjusts left. She listens, with hand on knob.
5	D	Same axis as A, but slightly wider, with more of stove visible right of frame and part of head of David's bed. David looking out of frame towards door, laughing, looks down and coughs again.
6	E	Inside dormitory, looking at door (i.e. reverse of D). Door opens, Maria stands in doorway, looking out of frame down and left. Main room, including table, lamp and bedroom door at rear.
7	A	David looks up and out of frame front and right.
8	E	Maria opens door wider, smiles, seems to greet David.
9	D	David coughing, looking out of frame as before and returns greeting.
10	E	Maria, looking at David out of frame, gestures with her head towards main room.
11	A	David nods out of frame towards Maria, coughs, begins to rise.

Shot	Camera set-up	Action and visual field
12	F	Wide shot on same axis as D, looking towards door, table partly visible in foreground left, parts of two beds beyond, another right of door. Maria in doorway, facing David, seen from rear, standing up. Pulls on jacket, picks up hat, walks past Maria through door. Maria closes door.
13	G	Bedroom, facing window. Edit, seen almost full length wearing dressing gown, her hair down, making bed. She is looking out of frame front and left as though hearing noise from main room.
14	H	David sitting where Edit was sewing the night before. Maria leaning on table in left foreground towards David. David opens coat and gestures to mending.
Title		'Did you mend my coat?'
14 contd	H	Maria shakes her head. David speaks again.
Title		'Would you mind fetching the person who did this?'
14 contd	H	Maria nods and smiles, turns and leaves frame left.
15	I	In bedroom. Edit at mirror left; door right of frame opened by Maria, who speaks to Edit, smiling. Through doorway, view of main room, table with David seated behind and door to dormitory beyond him. Edit nods and turns back to mirror as Maria closes door.
16	J	Reverse field of I, looking from between David and dormitory door, David in foreground, looking away towards Maria closing door. She turns and smiles at David. Her smile fades as he doesn't respond but slowly puts down his cup, puts on hat, stands and leaves frame left.
17	K	Iris. Close to lobby door, centre frame, David approaching from left, large shadow behind him. Turns at door, buttoning coat and looks unsmiling out of frame front and right (towards Maria).
18	L	Reverse angle of K, Maria standing centre frame next to bedroom door (at left) and looking with concerned expression out of frame front and left (eyeline match).
19	K	David looking fixedly out of frame (at Maria).
20	L	Door opens and Edit comes out. Maria staring out of frame at David. Edit closes door. Turns front and left, looking at David and smiling, her shadow on door behind her.

THE PHANTOM CARRIAGE (KÖRKARLEN) (1921)

Shot	Camera set-up	Action and visual field
21	K	David staring out of frame and doing up coat.
22	M	Iris round Edit. Same axis as L but closer (waist up). She looks out of frame towards David.
23	N	Iris round David. Matching scale to M. Same axis as K. David staring stony-faced out of frame at Edit.
24	M	Edit smiles and speaks to David, rubbing hands together gently at waist height.
25	N	David stares but does not respond
26	M	Edit walks forward and out of frame left.
27	O	Framing to left of K. David and door to left of centre frame; Edit enters from right, stops in front of David and speaks to him, rubbing/twisting hands. Both cast large shadows. David sneers and hands move down to his coat.
28	P	Iris. David alone in front of door, closer framing than O. Violently rips out all the repaired sections of his coat, pushes hands in pockets and laughs, looking out of frame right (at Edit).
29	O	David laughing at Edit, who stands back, startled.
Title		'It's a shame you went to all that trouble, Miss, but I'm used to having it like this.'
29 contd		David looking down, smiling and gesturing at coat. Turns away from Edit and opens door. She catches his arm and pulls him back.
Title		'Before you leave, I'd like to ask you to visit me next New Year's Eve.'
29 contd		David turns to Edit. She speaks to him.
Title		'You see, I prayed that our first guest would have a good year. And I wanted to find out if my prayers were answered.'
29 contd		Edit speaking to David. He laughs and replies.
Title		'Oh, I'll be there. I'll come and show you God didn't give a fig for your twaddle.'
29 contd		David finishes speaking, laughs, turns and leaves, closing door behind him. Iris in on Edit looking after him. Iris closes to black.

Across the three sequences, Sjöström uses a large number of camera set-ups (39 in the 65 shots) to develop our understanding of the hostel's layout,[5] each defining a relatively small arc but each meticulously designed and juxtaposed to build a clear and coherent sense of the space. The dormitory and bedroom are filmed using reverse angles (in the third sequence, set ups A & E, G & I), a method Sjöström had used extensively in earlier films.[6] Here, however, direct reverse-field cuts only occur some way into the episode, and initial shots in each direction are separated in time and show only fragments of each room. The space in the main room is also built up in fragments, but the camera angles are much more varied.[7] At different points during the hostel episode, action is staged in ways that show each of the four walls of the central room, although we never see any of them in their entirety. It is a method which would have been both time-consuming—the large number of set-ups—and technically challenging—the creation of coherent space.[8]

It would have been perfectly possible for Sjöström to use wide shots showing significant areas of the room, but he chose a riskier strategy. Crucially, there are no establishing shots—we never see even half the room in a single view, and those shots which directly connect different rooms (shots from dormitory or bedroom across the width of the main room towards the other door) are deployed some way into the episode rather than at the outset (shots 25 and 27 of the first sequence). Across the three sequences, twenty-three set-ups are used for the main room, but there is no sense of a modified 'fourth wall' view of the action, with frontal staging and closer views cut in on the same axis, the method still in common use at this period, including, for instance, much of Sjöström's *The Monastery of Sendomir*, made just a year before *The Phantom Carriage*.[9] Here it is as though the camera can look, and characters can move, in any direction.

Sjöström's scene dissection means that our understanding of space is developed in a number of inter-related ways: through overlapping decor from shot to shot, match cuts, consistent screen direction and lighting, and eyeline matches—the whole repertoire of continuity editing. The third sequence opens (1) with a medium shot of David discovering his jacket has been mended, followed by a cut to Maria crossing the main room towards the camera from a doorway—to the kitchen—we have not previously seen (2). David looks up (3), registering the sound of Maria in the other room, and we are shown Maria from another angle (4), facing left of frame and putting the tray down on the table, the camera panning slightly to the left as she moves to listen at the door. Although we have not previously seen the kitchen door, it is characteristic of Sjöström's method

THE PHANTOM CARRIAGE (KÖRKARLEN) (1921)

Figure 1

that the second shot of Maria (4), matching action and screen direction with shot 2, enables us to place the kitchen within our evolving sense of the main room's layout. At the same time, David's eyeline in shot 3 both shows us that he is responding to the sound of Maria in the other room and matches her direction in shot 2—in effect, a reverse-field cut through a wall. There then follows a passage of precise angle/reverse angle editing with eyeline match (shots 6–11), and with parts of the main room visible behind Maria (E, F).

When David leaves the dormitory (shot 12), there is a cut to Edit making her bed (shot 13), and she in turn seems to respond to sound from the next room by looking out of frame front and left towards her door and David and Maria beyond. Shot 14 is almost at right angles to Edit's eyeline and to the view of David leaving the dormitory, and shows David sitting for breakfast, with Maria in the left foreground, leaning on the table towards him (Figure 1). Sjöström now juxtaposes two shots cut across 180 degrees along the axis between the doors to bedroom and dormitory, the first framing Edit at the mirror in the left foreground and a view to her right through the bedroom doorway across the main room to where David is sitting at the table, and the second with David in the

Figure 2

Figure 3

foreground, looking across the table to Maria closing the bedroom door (Figures 2 and 3). In the run of shots 14–17 (set-ups H, I, J and K), the space is viewed from four different 90 degree angles, triangulating, or quadrangulating, the positions of characters, revealing parts of all four walls and showing variously in the background a Christmas tree and a sofa (14), the door to the dormitory (15), the doorway to the bedroom shared by Edit and Maria (16), and the door to the lobby (17).

In its context, the most striking aspect of the hostel sequences is the confidence with which, using multiple set-ups, Sjöström creates a detailed and coherent three-dimensional environment for the characters, a commitment to the creation of naturalistic space that even extends to the mirror on the chest of drawers at which Edit is attending to her appearance seeming to reflect the wall behind the camera (shot 15)[10] (Figure 2). At the same time, there is a strong reciprocal relationship between this spatial naturalism and the film's performance style. Ben Brewster and Lea Jacobs identify Sjöström as a film-maker who in these years pursued 'the renunciation of expressive gesture' and 'systematically explored naturalist technique in this sense', and they associate 'this reduced style' with a high cutting rate.[11] Certainly, here the fluid articulation of space through editing, together with the proximity to the characters that Sjöström's methods makes possible, is paralleled in the naturalism of the acting. Across the film as a whole this is particularly marked in the subtlety and restraint of Astrid Holm as Edit and Hilda Borgström as Mrs Holm. But they are not alone. As David, Sjöström engages the broader, declarative register appropriate to a character determined to assert his bitterness and malevolence, but this is by no means unvaried. Here, on one of the few occasions when we see David alone and in repose (shots 1, 3, 5, 7 and 9), Sjöström's framing and the restraint of his performance create a moment of significant ambiguity. David's reactions to discovering the repairs to his coat—in shot 1 registering some degree of bewilderment and in shot 3 looking down at the coat after hearing Maria put the tray down in the next room, a half smile playing across his face before he breaks into a cough—could suggest either genuine pleasure at the act or amused contempt at the effort someone has taken on his behalf. As he interacts with Maria, in the dormitory and the central room, his manner seems benign and his conversation measured, polite in its phrasing, nothing he does contradicting the optimism with which Maria receives and conveys his request to meet the person who repaired the coat. In shot 15, we watch Maria joyously talk to Edit, and can see David sitting at the table, searching but impassive, observable by us but not by the others. Then, in the reverse (16), it seems that something in David's face—partially obscured to us—causes Maria's expression to change and the mood of the moment to darken. It is Maria's sudden uncertainty as she returns to him that suggests the imminent reversion to his public persona. The whole brief passage of action is beautifully modulated in the relationship between the understated acting and Sjöström's staging: the shift from the apparent mutuality of the angle/reverse angle exchange to the wider, more layered framing of the performances across the extremes of main room.

Cinematography, Lighting and Decor

The stylistic development in the films Sjöström directed, from the wonderfully expressive long takes in *Ingeborg Holm* (1913) to the mastery of découpage displayed here, owed a great deal to his collaboration with two cinematographers, the brothers Henrik and Julius Jaenzon.[12] Julius shot *The Phantom Carriage* and was responsible with his team for the remarkable multiple exposure special effects. But his cinematography, which includes, as Casper Tybjerg notes in the commentary for the Criterion release, the dramatic (and at this point still unusual) night-for-night shooting in the graveyard, is also the vital basis for the complex orchestration of large spaces such as the mission hall and the bar, and for the effects achieved in the hostel sequences, while Jaenzon's handling of light—notably the sophisticated use of practicals—is also central to the clarity with which space is developed here.[13] Even when a lamp is not visible, Jaenzon's lighting evokes its off-screen presence. For instance, the lamp in the dormitory which Edit has insisted, in the first hostel sequence, on leaving lit for the sleeping David is not visible until the twelfth shot of the third sequence, but the light it sheds helps us to orientate ourselves in the conversation between David and Maria in the doorway. The ornate lamp which illuminates the dining room also helps our apprehension of the different angles on the space, and is a unifying physical presence in every shot in our sequence which features that room, until David moves towards the exit (shot 17), in readiness for his confrontation with his benefactor. But it is also a bright, welcoming illumination, lighting the dark of a Scandinavian winter's breakfast.

Jaenzon's lighting, which provides plausible sources of illumination throughout, also adjusts to create heightened effects. In the later stages of the sequence, when the emphasis shifts from the hospitality of the Salvationists to its rejection by David, the direction of the dining room lamp, now off-screen, remains consistent, but the contrast of the light is greatly increased, casting strong shadows on the wall behind David, Maria and Edit as the tension of the situation increases with Maria beginning to doubt David's motives, or as Edit responds to David ripping the patches out of the coat. (The close-up of David savaging the coat is an exception here, and while it shows a prominent use of iris, as do a number of other shots at this end of the sequence, the lighting in this close-up is more diffuse.)

Other aspects of Sjöström's mise-en-scène take on a more discrete interpretive force. This section of the film is partly built on the extreme contrasts between David and Edit, evident throughout but sharply present at the end with David's hostility and contempt. But the hostel sequences also represent the chronological starting point for the most surprising dimension of Lagerlöf's tale, Edit's love for David. In the novel, Maria reveals to her Salvationist companion, just before she relates the events of that New Year's Eve, that Edit is in love with David. The film omits this revelation, dramatizing Edit's feelings for David through her actions, particularly in the later Mission Hall scene, but subtly preparing the ground by paralleling the characters in their first encounter here. Each responds from their bedroom to noise in the adjacent room, their eyelines just off camera, in David's case to the right and in Edit's to the left, the shots separated in time but matching in action and staged almost as reverse angles. They sit in the same chair at the table, that nearest the dormitory door, Edit to mend David's coat and David to take breakfast, the framing for each not identical but closely related, both characters viewed with the dormitory door to frame right and at the rear of the shots the adjacent walls with sofa and Christmas tree (Figure 4). These parallels, seemingly against the grain of the drama's moral contrasts, form part of the film's negotiation of Lagerlöf's tale, in which the impossibility of a relationship between David and Edit in this life is shadowed by suggestions of their spiritual kinship.

Sjöström's design and staging create other links between the pivotal hostel section and the rest of the film. The film is keenly interested

Figure 4

THE PHANTOM CARRIAGE (KÖRKARLEN) (1921)

in the materiality and social distinctions of its world, even as it tells a story of the supernatural. It is a film of textures and differing decors: from the middle-class conviction of the Slumstation to the horrendous shack in which Mrs Holm and the children live in the film's opening and closing sequences; from the mansion of the wealthy suicide in the film's first flashback and the well-dressed apartment in which Edit reunites David with his family to the deserted flat to which he returns from prison. The ornate lamp, prominent in the hostel, is a slightly less elaborate version of Edit's mother's lamp, noticeable in the room next to the one in which Edit lies dying as the film opens. Indeed, the hostel is decorated as a middle-class home, with Christmas tree, sofa, pictures and intricately printed wallpaper. It is as though Edit is trying to export the ideals, and perhaps values, of her mother's house. Even the dormitory is papered in a decorative nineteenth-century print—no rough rendered finish like the walls of the prison cell or the other hostel dormitory where David encounters Georges in an earlier flashback. Indeed, our first view of the Slumstation and the first shot of this segment of the film is of Edit and Maria positioning the sampler which is the finishing touch to the establishment, a shot which foregrounds the neat symmetry of the room, viewed through the doorway (Figure 5). David rages or crashes against the ambitions which Edit's designs imply: tearing at the repairs to the coat, slumping drunkenly across the harmonium on arrival at the hostel, arriving ominously late, a shadowy figure who becomes the first guest, a challenging response to the women's careful preparations and attempt to imbue respectability alongside redemption.

Perhaps the most insistent element in the film's design and staging is the use of doors and doorways. David's assault on the coat takes place in front of the door to the lobby, his movement towards the exit seemingly premeditated, preparation for a swift departure that will preclude any further interaction with the women. It is one of many moments featuring

Figure 5

doors and doorways in the hostel sequences—the opening or closing of a door and/or movement of characters through a doorway occur no fewer than twenty times, with eight in the third sequence alone. In addition, there are numerous shots through doorways, looking from one room to another, or in which the action is staged in front of a closed door. There are naturalistic dimensions to this plethora of doors and doorways: as part of the action, characters move or look from room to room in the hostel, while in filmic terms movements through doorways facilitate cuts on action, a set-up in one room smoothly replaced by one in the next. Cumulatively, these movements from one room to another are important in developing the sense of three-dimensional space we have been describing. But there was nothing inevitable about either the deployment of rooms and doors in the set or Sjöström's staging. The mutually informing decisions taken by the film-makers enable the seemingly naturalistic deployment of doorways to become the material basis for the wider resonance that the motif takes on.

To the best of our knowledge, only Darragh O'Donoghue, in his perceptive short piece on the film in *Senses of Cinema*, has commented on the film's use of doors. Making a wider point about the significance of thresholds and liminal spaces, he notes the 'many doors that physically, psychologically and spiritually block characters'.[14] As O'Donoghue indicates, one major dimension of the motif's significance involves the characters being 'blocked', physically separated and enclosed or even imprisoned. This gives further weight to the studio-bound nature of the film and its predominantly night-time setting.[15] The cumulative presence of the motif allows Edit's opening of doors for David in this section of the film—she leads Maria to the external door to answer David's ring and opens the dormitory door to gesture him towards his rest—to carry an unforced metaphorical significance: it is her Salvationist role to 'open doors' spiritually and in terms of life chances. Yet in the material world of the film, the affirmative connotations of 'opening doors' are overshadowed by darker implications of the motif. There is, for instance, a systematic patterning of the spaces in which Mrs Holm lives, two of which are similar both in appearance and in their orientation to hallway and stairs, and all three of which are marked by contested access through the door. The prison, too, with its heavy gate at which no one waits for David and the movements along a row of cell doors between David's cell and that in which his brother is incarcerated, shares an emphasis on doorways, corridors and difficulties with access—the film's most extreme vision of separation and isolated lives.

The prison sequence ends with David being released, seemingly determined to reform and re-establish his family life. On his return to the family home, however, he finds the door locked against him and his family gone. As he vows revenge, listening to the mocking laughter of his neighbours in the corridor, he leans against the closed door of the apartment. After Edit persuades Mrs Holm to take David back and brings them together in a bright new apartment, we see David return drunk and vengeful to the family. Finding the door locked, he kicks at it in fury until his wife lets him in. Set on a hideously destructive course, he roughly wakes his children, coughing in their faces with the intention of infecting them with his tuberculosis. When he moves into the adjacent room, his wife locks him in, in order to escape with the children, and David savagely hacks the door open with an axe.

Spiritual Dimensions

Even though, in the material world of the film, doors often 'block' and isolate, inhibiting human connectedness, they still feature in its spiritual dimension, though not as barriers. As spirits of the dead, Georges and David can pass through the material world without impediment. Yet, rather than taking advantage of the spectacular opportunities for them to pass through walls, windows and floors, Sjöström restricts them to the same entrances and exits as the living. In the first part of Georges' tale, the Coachman passes through the doors of a fine mansion to collect the soul of the suicide within, and thereafter Georges and David enter and leave only through doorways. There could well have been practical dimensions to these decisions in some cases, such as economizing on set design, using camera set-ups required for the living as the basis for the double exposure, but the effect as the film goes on is both to parallel and contrast the living with the dead. In the spirit world, material constraints do not exist; what constrains Georges and David is that they cannot make contact with the living, except those on the point of death. Obstruction operates on both material and spiritual planes.

Like doorways, David's disease and accompanying cough have both naturalistic and metaphorical significance. The mending of the coat, so brutally rejected, has a keen physical cost. In his commentary, Casper Tybjerg talks of tuberculosis in the novel as being 'a metaphor for the harm the characters do to one another', and it carries a similar charge in the film. That the characters cough is the symptom and means of transmission of the illness. But beyond this, and beyond its status as a manifestation of the dangers of human contact, the choice as to when David coughs is Sjöström's. In the third shot of our sequence, his smile (and chuckle?) in response to the discovery of the patches in his coat, and at the sound of (Maria's) movement next door, lead into a cough. The night before, he suffers an attack of coughing as he enters the dining room, surveys the space, falls into a chair and slumps across the harmonium. Elsewhere in the film, he coughs on rejecting Edit's request, conveyed by Gustafsson (Tor Weijden), to attend her deathbed; he coughs on being woken by Georges in the dosshouse; next in screen time, but the first time chronologically, we see him cough viciously as he hardens his heart with thoughts of vengeance, leaning against the door of the empty apartment, listening to the neighbours' laughter after discovering that his family have fled. He breaks into a cough at the mission hall, after laughing at Gustafsson's conversion, and at the point of being perceived by his (unseen) wife. His deliberate cough over the children, at least partly a way of distressing his wife, is another way of rejecting the home which Mrs Holm and Edit have restored for him, an impulse then taken up with the axe. David tends to cough at moments of psychological disjunction. With the partial exception of the cough in the company of Georges, all these moments of physical breakdown coincide with situations where the two aspects of David's life—family man and self-absorbed drunkard—come into painful relief, where David rejects the social, the spiritual and the respectable, or where this rejection is challenged by the attempts of others at making a human connection.

Such moments, often involving touch, are associated particularly with Edit and Mrs Holm. In the hostel sequence, after David has rejected the offer of connection made manifest in the repairs to the coat, Edit's dismay is expressed by the way she holds her hand to her side, as if feeling a physical injury from the assault on the garment. However, though dismayed, she tries again, reaching for his arm to prevent his departure, and pulling him back into the room to ask him to return in twelve months' time. In the next flashback after the hostel section, we see Edit offer David a handbill in the bar, which he crumples into a ball and throws back, hitting her in the face. In another doorway—that of the mission hall in the same flashback—Edit again reaches out to restrain David, this time at his determination to leave the town. Edit's gesture—echoing her attempted restraint in the hostel—and a second, moments later, unwittingly expresses an interest in David that is not purely spiritual. David registers, and Edit implicitly acknowledges, what she has revealed and when she discovers shortly afterwards that the person David is seeking up and down the land is his wife, guilt at her feelings for a married man inspires her plan to restore the Holm family, a reconciliation that proves disastrous.

The one occasion on which David does respond to these different

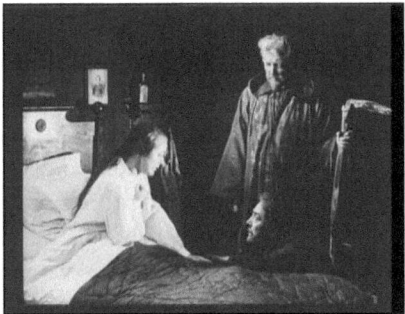

Figure 6

attempts to touch his soul, or his body, is in the scene which ends with Edit's death. She is able to see Georges and realizes what his presence portends, but David, increasingly distressed and remorseful at what he has heard and seen, is still invisible to her, on the floor at the foot of her bed. He manages to free his hands (Georges had earlier bound him hand and foot) and struggles to Edit's side, reaching to touch her hand, and she is suddenly able to sense his presence and to feel his touch, though she cannot see him (Figure 6). It is a moment that movingly dramatizes the dying Edit's uncanny ability to 'see' and to 'perceive' and to connect in ways not normally given to the living, but it is part of the film's telling mixture of the material and the supernatural that this touch is realized through David's translucent spiritual body rather than his earthly one. At the moment of Edit's death, there is a mutual connection through touch that is paradoxically both physical and yet intangible. It is an uncanny bond that signals that David has responded to her, acknowledges her desire for him as a man and promises that his redemption is possible, although this is predicated on the restoration of the Holm family, to the inevitable exclusion of Edit. Georges now frees Edit's spirit and she falls back onto her pillows.

Conclusion

This is, perhaps, a fitting image on which to conclude our discussion. We have wanted to demonstrate aspects of Sjöström's achievement in *The Phantom Carriage* that go beyond the widely recognized multiple exposure cinematography and complex narrative structure. The hostel sequences are the most complex examples in the film of what in its context is a remarkably sophisticated—but largely uncelebrated—construction of three-dimensional dramatic space, incorporating a strikingly confident handling of continuity. At the same time, we have pointed to a range of ways in which the film's drama and its social themes are inflected and enriched by the inventiveness of Sjöström's direction, both within individual scenes and across the film's informing motifs and patterns. Edit and David's ghostly meeting of hands can stand as a culminating example of the ways in which the technical and stylistic virtuosity of *The Phantom Carriage* is fully integrated with its dramatic situations and thematic concerns.

    A two-part audiovisual essay, made to complement this chapter, can be found at https://warwick.ac.uk/fac/arts/film/movie/contents/gibbs-pye._the_phantom_carriage.pdf

6

Dr Mabuse, der Spieler (*Dr Mabuse, the Gambler*) (1922)

Steve Neale

As if engaged in a game of cards, a hand in close-up fans a set of photographs of a man in various different disguises. A second hand adds more photographs from a pile on a table and we dissolve to a medium closeup of this self-same man in shirt sleeves. He shuffles the photographs then stacks them up on the desk in front of him, and from here we cut back to the stack as he selects one of photographs, then back to the desk as he holds out the photograph, looks up and summons an as-yet-unseen interlocutor.[1] The interlocutor is a servant called Spoerri (Robert Forest-Larringa) and the man who summons him is Dr Mabuse (Rudolph Klein-Rogge). The former has been taking cocaine and is admonished for doing so. The latter, his office full of costumes and disguises, is planning to steal a confidential commercial contract in order to make a killing on the stock exchange. Having done so, he will pose as a lowly member of the proletariat while employing a group of blind men to counterfeit banknotes, and will challenge other legal, moral and social norms as we witness acts of vengeance, kidnap, suicide and murder; demonstrations of physical and mental strength; displays of superstition, frustration and erotic entertainment; a headlong car ride through the streets of Berlin; and a full-scale battle between the forces of law and order and those of Mabuse and his henchmen. These ingredients will be examined in more detail during the course of this essay. However, in a film that begins with the serial repetition of images and disguises, it is important first of all to say something about the aesthetic traditions and industrial formats from which these ingredients emerged and on which they drew. These include sensational fictions, stories of adventure, and stories of crime and detection. They also include serials, series and tie-ins.

Serials, Series and Tie-Ins

Dr Mabuse, der Spieler was directed by Fritz Lang, scripted by Lang and Thea von Harbou, and produced by Erich Pommer in Germany in 1922. Pommer was head of Uco-Decla-Bioscop, the newly formed product of a merger between Decla and Deutsche Bioscop and the formation of Uco by Decla-Bioscop and the Ullstein publishing company. Its aim was to gain exclusive access to Ullstein's publications as a regular source of story material while providing tie-in publicity both for Ullstein's books and Uco-Decla-Bioscop's films. Along with *Phantom* and *Die Prinzessin Suwarin* (*Princess Suwarin*) (both 1922), *Dr Mabuse* was one such film.[2] According to David Kalat, the serialized edition of the novel, which was written by Norbert Jacques, was composed and published in instalments in the *Berliner Illustrierte Zeitung* prior to its publication as a full-length hardback in February 1922.[3] Serial publication had been a hallmark of popular stories for many years. In this case, however, seriality was apparent not just in the initial mode of publication of the novel, but also in the film's multi-episodic structure and two-part release.

Mabuse was 6,056 metres in length (approximately four to four and a half hours long, depending on projection speeds). It was shot at the Decla-Bioscope and Jofa studios, and premiered (and released more widely) in two distinct feature-length parts: *Dr Mabuse, der Spieler: Der grosse Spieler—Ein Bild der Zeit* (*Dr Mabuse, the Gambler: The Great Gambler—A Portrait of Our Time*), which was first shown at the Ufa-Palast am Zoo in Berlin on 27 April 1922, and *Dr Mabuse, der Spieler: Inferno—Ein Spiel von Menschen unserer Zeit* (*Dr Mabuse, the Gambler: Inferno—A Play About People of Our Time*), which was first shown at the Ufa-Palast on 26 May.[4] Both parts were divided into six numbered episodes or 'acts',[5] and both parts were accompanied by a programme brochure that served to explain and underline the differences between them. Hence the following rather fanciful extract from the brochure for part two:

> Where the first part of *Dr Mabuse the Gambler* attempted to depict the breathless, chaotic battle of our time, how the fates of individual people are thrown about in a crooked whirlwind, drawn helplessly into the vortex of a strong, evil will—the second part, *Inferno*, is concerned with showing the inescapable consequences of these

destinies—not the least of which is the fate of this powerful criminal himself, whose final ghostly gamble loses.[6]

With or without the help of programme brochures, it may seem strange to release a film of this kind in this way. However, as Rudmer Canjels has pointed out, two-part serials and multi-part feature films were by no means uncommon in Germany and other European countries in the late 1910s and early- to mid-1920s.[7] In the USA, the production, distribution and format of serials had become rigidly routinized. Emerging in the early 1910s, serials such as *The Perils of Pauline* (1914) and series such as *The Hazards of Helen* (1914–17) entailed the release of episodes featuring a central character engaged either in an ongoing or overarching narrative (in the case of serials) or in a set of similar but self-contained stories (in the case of series). These episodes were released on a regular basis and were usually tied into the publication of instalments in magazines and newspapers. The episodes themselves were initially shown as components in a varied programme of single, split or two-reel films. However, with the spread of self-contained, multi-reel, feature-length films in the mid- to late-1910s, and with the advent of an oligopoly of companies founded principally on their production, distribution and exhibition, episodes of serials were increasingly produced by minor companies and programmed as two-reel supports to longer features in secondary venues. The nature and dissemination of serials was different in Europe. In Holland, US serials were often programmed in longer multi-episode blocks;[8] episodes of *Fantômas* (1913–14), *Les Vampires* (1915–16) and other French series and serials were often of variable and sometimes feature length;[9] and one of the first German serials, *Die Herrin der Welt* (*The Mistress of the World*) (1919–20), consisted not of two-reel episodes but of eight six-reel, feature-length parts.

Die Herrin der Welt was produced and directed by Joe May. May had already produced and directed a number of series, a far more common format in Germany in the early- to mid-1910s. But *Die Herrin der Welt* was something new. It was also a huge domestic success, partly because of its impressive scale, partly because of its imperial trappings and partly because of the nature of Germany's distribution system, which was based on regionalized monopolies and afforded long exclusive runs of the kind necessary to recoup the costs of expensive productions such as this.[10] However, *Die Herrin der Welt* encountered difficulties in foreign markets and a serial of this magnitude was never attempted again. Lang, who was a devotee of Karl May and other writers of pulp fiction, and who had already submitted a number of scripts to Joe May while serving in the German army, co-scripted the final episode of *Die Herrin der Welt* and worked as an assistant director. He also co-scripted (and was initially slated to direct) *Das indische Grabmal* (*The Indian Tomb*) for May in 1921. Like *Mabuse*, and like *Die Spinnen* (*The Spiders*) (1919–20), which had been written and directed by Lang for Decla-Bioscop, *Das indische Grabmal* was one of an increasing number of two-part serial features produced and released in Germany in the late 1910s and early- to mid-1920s.[11] Among the latter was *Die Nibelungen* (*The Nibelungs*), which was directed by Lang, scripted by Lang and von Harbou, and released in 1924.

Like *J'Accuse* (1919), *La Roue* (1923) and a number of other multi-part French features, *Die Nibelungen* was a prestige production. In contrast, most serials and series, however long or numerous their parts, drew on the traditions of crime, sensation and international adventure evident in *Fantômas*, *Die Herrin der Welt* and *Die Spinnen*.[12] *Die Spinnen* interweaves all three. Although the novel *Mabuse* encompasses aspects of international adventure too, the film version focuses almost exclusively on crime and sensation, and is localized not just in Germany (nor specifically in Munich, in which the novel is largely set) but, as Lang himself recalled in an interview in 1968, in post-war Berlin:

> The period after World War I in Germany was a time of hysteria, cynicism, deep despair and unbridled excess. Newly acquired riches existed alongside abject poverty. In Berlin, the term *Raffke* was coined for the excessive accumulation of money and applied to the nouveau riche. Dr Mabuse is an archetype of this time.[13]

Aside from Mabuse himself, *Raffke* is represented in *Mabuse* by the owner of Schramm's (a high-class restaurant, casino and cabaret venue), whose rise from poverty to riches in the period between 1912 and 1922 is shown in a remarkably sardonic montage sequence. There is no direct equivalent to this sequence in the novel. Schramm's is a setting that von Wenk, the State Prosecutor,[14] visits on two occasions in the novel, and it is on and around these visits that he ponders and recalls conversations about this and other recent developments in Germany. As we shall see, other evocations of Germany's, and Berlin's, recent past can be found in the film, but they occur only intermittently, and serve largely to provide an aura of sensational up-to-dateness. This is particularly evident in the stock-exchange sequence, the printing of counterfeit money, scenes of gambling and erotic entertainment, scenes of crime and criminality, and the examples of contemporary painting and fashionable tribal art on

DR MABUSE, DER SPIELER (DR MABUSE, THE GAMBLER) (1922)

display in the mansion owned by Count and Countess Told (Alfred Abel and Gertrud Welcker).

Part One

Acts One and Two

Noel Burch suggests that the images that begin *Dr Mabuse* 'descend from techniques which date back prior to 1910: vignettes at the beginning or at the end of a film for the presentation of the actors and the characters they play'.[15] Mabuse's location in a room surrounded by make-up and costumes adds weight to this suggestion, and the fact that *Spieler* can mean 'actor' as well as 'gambler' is literalized here as well. Moreover, these images appear specifically to evoke the prologues to all but one of the episodes of *Fantômas*, each of which begin with a series of close-ups of Fantômas (René Navarre) in various disguises and each of which feature Fantômas-Navarre's intimidating head-on gaze to camera.[16] Gazes of this kind can be found towards the end of Act One of *Mabuse* (and in many of Lang's later films, which sometimes erase their aggressive characteristics and replace them with the signs of trauma). But here as elsewhere in Act One, Mabuse's gaze is either directed to the side of the camera or aimed at other characters.

The theft of the commercial contract that follows—a justly celebrated tour de force—draws on parts of episode one of *Fantômas* and episode four of *Les Vampires*.[17] It functions not only as a demonstration of Mabuse's power, but as an introduction to three key filmic devices: alternation, cross-cutting and parallel editing. As Tom Gunning observes, all three of these devices entail cutting back and forth between different spaces, characters and actions, each of which either converge or remain temporally or spatially distinct, and each of which imply either temporal simultaneity or temporal succession. In the case of this particular sequence, temporal succession and the coordination of events in time are crucial. They are marked not only by their precisely timed structure, but also by successive insert shots of watches that show the passing of a time on a minute-by-minute basis as the contract is stolen from a courier on a train and transferred to a car.[18] For Gunning, these events 'literally unwind like clockwork' and 'Mabuse appears as the evil genius of modernity, able to extend his power through space through his careful control of time'.[19] Insofar as this is the case, though, Mabuse is an avatar of the master criminal, the arch-villain, 'not simply a clever or prestigious criminal with a long array of crimes to his credit', but the ultimate incarnation of 'energy and hubris'.[20]

Having cut back and forth between Mabuse and his henchmen as the theft unfolds, we return once more to Spoerri and Mabuse. Mabuse is now in disguise and, although framed behind a desk in the foreground as before, he and Spoerri are now in a larger room, with books rather than racks of clothes on the walls. This is one of a number of examples of framing and staging that reiterates the frontal presentation of Mabuse and that constitutes one of the film's visual motifs. But it is also potentially confusing, and would probably not have occurred in a contemporary Hollywood film without making the change of interior location much more evident. Moreover, if Lang was a master of cross-cutting and parallel editing, he was not yet adept at constructing lengthy passages of scene dissection or adopting modes of staging that involve complex patterns of movement. Thus, when Pesch (Georg John), another of Mabuse's underlings, enters, approaches Mabuse at his desk and recites the current prices of a number of commodities on the stock exchange, he does little more than step forward from the doorway mid-ground right into a space behind the desk in the foreground.

Having listened to Pesch's recitation, Mabuse admonishes Pesch for his tardiness and leaves. A planned but apparently coincidental car accident enables the transfer of the stolen contract to Mabuse's limousine and, following Pesch's expressions of discontent to an unsympathetic Georg (Hans Adalbart Schettlow) and the aforementioned scene with the blind men, we move on to the sequence at the stock exchange. Aside from the conversation between Pesch and Georg, there are few equivalents to any of these scenes in the novel. There are distant echoes of theft, the accumulation of commodities and even a verbatim version of Pesch's recitation of their prices later on in the novel, when Mabuse and his henchmen are on their way to Mabuse's hideout on Lake Constance, but in the novel these and other money-making ventures are designed to enable Mabuse to establish the Kingdom of Citopomar in Southern Brazil and thus to realize a long-held dream. There are no traces of this in the film, in which, as is evident in the earlier scenes described above and in the ensuing stock-exchange sequence, Mabuse is much more preoccupied with the accumulation of money and power as such. The stock-exchange sequence itself is marked by the intercutting of shots of a relatively motionless Mabuse with those of the frenzied individuals, groups and crowds around him. At a point at which the evocation of the prologues to *Fantômas* is at its most overt, Mabuse's head-on gaze is on show here and serves to mark his triumph. His powers of hypnosis, though, are not unveiled until Act Two, which is introduced as 'He and his night'.

Underlining the range of his guises and mental powers, and the

DR MABUSE, DER SPIELER (DR MABUSE, THE GAMBLER) (1922)

film's theatrical tropes, Act Two begins with Mabuse delivering a talk on psychoanalysis from a stage at the Philharmonic. From here, we cut to the Folies Bergères nightclub, where the customers are entertained not by a lecture, but by a nude tableau prior to the appearance of Cara Carozza (Egeda Nissen), its heavily publicized star. As Carozza begins her performance, we cut to Mabuse, who is in a limousine applying the finishing touches to yet another disguise. He enters the club and makes his way to his box, where he finds a note from Carozza identifying Edgar Hull (Paul Richter) as his next potential victim. Uninterested in Carozza herself (whose love for Mabuse is clearly marked—and clearly unrequited), Mabuse looks up, gazes at the camera, then looks through his binoculars at Hull, who at this point joins in the applause as Carozza finishes her act. From here, we cut to an even closer shot of Mabuse and his penetrating gaze, then back to Hull, who clutches his head in response to its power, and who reacts in a similar way when he encounters Mabuse in the lobby and finds himself agreeing to accompany Mabuse to the Pontoon Club.

The scene at the Pontoon Club is the last scene in Act Two, but the first to feature card games and gambling in their literal sense. It is also the first scene in the novel, which begins with the card game involving Hull and an initially unidentified Mabuse as banker, and which results in the former's losses as a result of the latter's hypnotic powers. In the novel, this scene is followed by an abortive search for the banker, who identifies himself as Hugo Balling, to whom Hull has pledged to pay off his debts. Balling, however, cannot be found, and it as this point, towards the end of the first chapter, that Hull is reported as meeting Carozza. In the film, the search for Balling and the meeting with Carozza do not occur until Act Three. Thus, in contrast to the novel, the outcome of the card game serves as a further indication of Mabuse's powers rather than as an introduction to them, and the anticipated meeting between Carozza and Hull is delayed until Act Three.

Acts Three and Four

In addition to the search for Balling and the meeting between Carozza and Hull, Act Three (the equivalent of chapter two in the novel) sees the introduction of von Wenk (Bernard Goetzke), who visits Hull to inform him that he has been the victim of criminality and that a number of criminals—or a single criminal in numerous disguises—may be involved. Wenk asks Hull to get in touch with him should Balling make contact. Hull, however, is more interested in Carozza, who now enters Hull's apartment in order to establish their affair—and hence to further Mabuse's plans. As Hull and Carozza converse, we cut to a shot of Mabuse in his laboratory extracting venom from a snake, from where we cut back to Hull and Carozza and on to Schramm's, whose activities and settings are introduced one by one, beginning with the restaurant. It is here that the montage of its owner's changing fortunes is placed and it is here that we re-encounter von Wenk, who is sharing a meal with Karsten (Julius Falkenstein), a friend whom we first encounter in the scene at the Pontoon Club. It is here, too, that we first encounter Countess Told, who walks through the restaurant and draws von Wenk's eye while on her way to the casino. Like von Wenk, who visits the casino in order to keep tabs on Hull and Carozza and who hopes to catch a glimpse of the mysterious Hugo Balling, the world-weary Countess is content to observe rather than participate in the casino's activities. Then Balling (Mabuse) arrives and we witness another of his hypnotic performances as banker in a card game. When he later sends an IOU to Hull, von Wenk is convinced that Balling is the man he has been looking for. However, he delays his search in order to respond to an invitation from the Countess to visit the Told mansion.

Like most of the other scenes set in large-scale interiors (notably the stock exchange, the Folies Bergères, the lobby of the hotel in which Hull searches for Balling and the apartment in which Hull himself resides), the lighting, framing, editing and staging of the scene at the mansion tend to differ from their contemporary Hollywood equivalents. Although the attention paid to the scale of the room and to the nature of the artworks is part of the scene's initial purpose, the decor dwarfs its inhabitants and the lighting is even and flat. No use is made of back lighting (which was unpractised in Germany at this time) and (as was also typical in Germany at this time) at least one cut involves the production of an inconsistent eyeline.[21] Lang's later penchant for diagonal compositions and empty or unoccupied spaces is not yet in evidence.[22] In contrast, his practice of placing his actors in or near the foreground, often at a desk or a table, has been in evidence since the film's first scene, and as we cut forward to von Wenk at his office desk trying on a false moustache, this scene is specifically evoked as a point of comparison and contrast.

Von Wenk is preparing to visit the Palais Andalusia, a far less affluent club than those we have encountered so far. It is here that he is nearly hypnotized by Mabuse, and it is here that Mabuse's powers fail him for the very first time. Mabuse rushes off and von Wenk tracks him to the Hotel Excelsior. However, Mabuse escapes and von Wenk is captured by Georg, and, as Act Four comes to end, von Wenk is tied-up and tossed into the sea.

DR MABUSE, DER SPIELER (DR MABUSE, THE GAMBLER) (1922)

Acts Five and Six

Drawing on the opening sequence in episode three of *Fantômas*, Act Five begins with von Wenk being rescued by fisherman. From here, we cut to Mabuse, who is enraged that von Wenk has escaped, then on to von Wenk, who is now back in his office. We then cut to Hull and Carozza on their way to the Petit Casino later that evening, where they re-encounter Karsten and von Wenk. The Petit Casino is a brand new nightclub. Offering erotic entertainment as a prelude to the gambling, and equipped with every kind of up-to-date device, we are introduced to its lavish setting via a series of semi-circular camera movements. Along with the circular design of its gambling table (and along with the circular aperture in which its master of ceremonies is placed), these movements and designs serve to establish a motif that links, contrasts and compares the club and its activities with those of a seance at a respectable household elsewhere in the city. In a film as digressive as *Mabuse*, visual patterns often substitute for causal chains. Thus, when we cut to the household, we find Countess Told sat at a circular table in the foreground, turning from right to left as she listens to a man who is walking round the table in the same direction. The nature of their conversation is not made clear, but the patterns of their movement and their parallels with the circular motifs in the casino are. Moreover, when the man leaves (and just before Mabuse arrives to conduct the seance and to reacquaint himself with the Countess), the Countess is shown tracing the circular pattern on her dress with her finger as she waits for the seance to begin (Figure 1). Involved again in a systematic pattern of alternation, we cut back to the casino. The camera continues to circle as the master of ceremonies inaugurates the erotic entertainment, then reappears to announce that 'The game can begin'. A shot of the gambling table from above re-establishes the circle

Figure 1

Figure 2   Figure 3

motif, and this is further reinforced by an iris out as we cut to an overhead shot of the hands of those at the seance placed on top of a circular table (Figures 2 and 3). As we cut back and forth between the seance and the casino, the circle motif continues. It comes to an end when von Wenk leaves the casino in order to summon the police. Carozza, Hull and Karsten depart in a hurry, but as the police arrive in the streets, Hull and Karsten are killed by Georg and Carozza is captured. Along with Mabuse's gaze, violence, death and incarceration are the dominant motifs from this point on.

Act Six begins with another sequence of alternation, though this one entails more locations and narrative threads. Starting with a shot of Carozza in jail, we cut to a scene in which Mabuse declares his indifference to her fate then on to von Wenk, who tries but fails to enlist Carozza's help. Following a conversation scene between the Count and Countess in the Told mansion, we cut back to von Wenk in his office then on to the mansion as von Wenk tries to persuade the Countess to visit Carozza in order to get her to reveal Mabuse's plans. From here, we cut to Mabuse, who is now alone his office, then back to von Wenk and the Countess, who agrees to the visit, then back again to Mabuse, who climbs the stairs at the end of a corridor and enters an old and dilapidated bedroom. Clearly thinking of the Countess, Mabuse stares at the bed and orders Spoerri to refurbish the room. As he does so, we cut to the Countess herself, who at this point enters Carozza's cell and seeks to engage her in conversation. Carozza, however, is only interested in declaring her devotion to her master, and the Countess, unable to garner any real information (and impressed by Carozza's commitment), leaves. From here, as the patterns of misplaced, displaced and contested desire involving von Wenk and the Countess, Carozza and Mabuse, Carozza and Hull, and Mabuse and the Countess begin to accumulate, we move on to a soirée at the Told mansion.[23] Mabuse, who has been invited to the soirée and who is now actively pursuing the Countess, uses his hypnotic powers to force the Count to cheat at cards and his physical and organizational ones to kidnap the Countess. As Part One draws to a close, he drives the Countess to his house, places her on the newly refurbished bed, leans over her with his arms outstretched and, like many another melodramatic villain, utters simply 'Mine!' For all its narrative digressions, proliferating plot lines and multiple lines of action, Part One thus concludes with a single, emphatic situation.[24]

Throughout Part One, Mabuse's powers have been marked not only as multiple, but also as more or less omnipotent. Adopting various guises, he has made millions on the stock exchange, overseen the forging of banknotes, hypnotized Hull and the Count, delivered a lecture on psychoanalysis, conducted a seance, outwitted von Wenk on a number of occasions, resisted the charms of Carozza while seeking those of the Countess, and intimidated his henchmen into doing his bidding at each and every turn. The powers of Lang as director are also in evidence, as has been discussed both here and in some detail by Thomas Elsaesser and Tom Gunning. For Gunning, Lang is capable not only of alternation, cross-cutting and parallel editing, but also of arresting assertions of hypnosis, intoxication, desire and, in the second part in particular, the staging, filming and editing of at least two 'impossible' events—the Sandor Weltmann sequence and the final sequence in which Mabuse succumbs to madness—both of which involve the presentational melding of subjective and objective perceptions. For Elsaesser, Lang's film is 'made up of internal rhymes, representations, echoes, and counterpoints, drawn from a strictly limited repertoire elements' and 'typically generated from the two couples Cara/Hull, Countess Told/Count Told, flanked by two men: von Wenk and Mabuse, and their multiple disguises and aids', each of which are 'mirrors, doubles and split halves of each other'.[25] The end of Part One will leave its spectators not only with a well-defined situation, but also with a set of vivid characters, actions, motifs and narrative threads. Part Two will see Mabuse's powers finally thwarted, but not before they have been extended in yet more episodes of murder, mayhem, hypnosis and death.

Part Two

Prelude and Act Two

Following a summary of the key events in Part One, Part Two opens with a Prelude entitled 'Nights without Sleep', which begins with a shot of

Carozza in jail, then cuts to a number of characters, locations and scenes: Told in his mansion; von Wenk in his office reading a letter from the Countess informing him that she no longer wishes to pressurize Carozza; Mabuse carousing with his underlings; the Countess drugged and asleep in the bedroom; the Count leaving his mansion; von Wenk re-reading the letter from the Countess, spotting the Count in the rain and inviting him into his office; and Mabuse and his henchmen becoming more and more intoxicated. Further sequences follow as the Count tells von Wenk about the incident with the cards, as the Countess is awakened by the noise downstairs, as Mabuse and his henchmen continue to carouse and as Mabuse joins the Countess in the bedroom again. At this point, Spoerri enters and informs Mabuse that the Count is on the phone. Prompted by von Wenk, the Count has called to enlist Mabuse's psychological expertise in coming to terms with events at the soirée and, as the Prelude comes to an end, Mabuse agrees to see him.

Along with its structure of interwoven alternation, this sequence is marked not only by misplaced or displaced motives and actions, but also, to cite Elsaesser again, by a particularly overt logic of point and counterpoint, question and answer, anticipation and implication, and consequence and cause.[26] This logic governs most of Part One and nearly all the sequences that follow in Act Two, which begin with Carozza being taken out of her cell and moved to a women's prison, Mabuse advising the Count to isolate himself completely, and von Wenk's concern as to the whereabouts of Count and Countess Told. The Countess is trying to escape from the bedroom in which she has been locked, but Mabuse catches her and warns her that he will kill the Count should she try to escape again. From here, we cut to Mabuse visiting his workshop. Having ensured that the workshop's outer door and trap door are working, Mabuse departs and we cut forward to another scene between Mabuse and the Countess. The Countess tells Mabuse that her husband will be looking for her, but Mabuse is aware of the Count's true situation and remains unconcerned. From here, we cut to Mabuse's laboratory, where Pesch is mixing poison, Georg is fixing a timer on a bomb and Spoerri is preparing a package for the bomb's delivery.

At this point, we cut back to Mabuse, who tells the Countess that he himself has been advising her husband, then back to the laboratory, where Mabuse's henchmen are finishing their tasks. Noting yet another instance of entrapment and desire, we cut to von Wenk, who arrives at Carozza's cell and enters, then on to Georg, who changes places with a guard at the women's prison, then back to van Wenk and Carozza and onto the police station, where Pesch arrives with his bomb. As these narrative threads

DR MABUSE, DER SPIELER (DR MABUSE, THE GAMBLER) (1922)

become more and more tightly interwoven, and as Act Two moves to a crescendo, we cut back and forth between von Wenk and Carozza in the cell, Georg listening to their conversation outside in the prison corridor and Pesch in the police station. Von Wenk leaves, Pesch primes the bomb and Georg (ever the misogynist) advises Mabuse that Carozza 'may squeal'. Mabuse tells Georg to 'remove her' and we cut to the police station, to which von Wenk has now returned. Von Wenk is caught up in the explosion when Pesch sets off his bomb but remains unscathed and, as Pesch is captured, we cut back to the prison, where Georg forces Carozza to take the poison he has brought and where a resigned and helpless Carozza finally dies.

I have noted these events because they are rarely discussed in any detail: in a densely packed chapter of over thirty pages, Gunning omits any reference to them at all, and in an equally packed chapter of nearly fifty pages, Elsaesser only alludes to some of them in brief. For Gunning and Elsaesser, these events are not of major interest. It is worth drawing attention, however, to the ways in which these particular acts begin with stillness (Figures 4-7), build slowly, then gather pace and action, culminating in the explosion of Pesch's bomb and the death of Carozza,

Figure 4

Figure 5

Figure 6

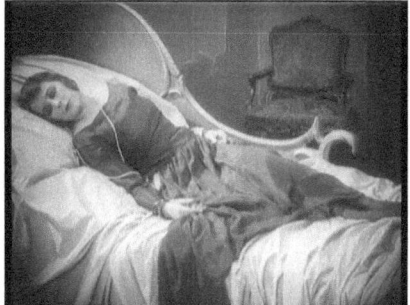
Figure 7

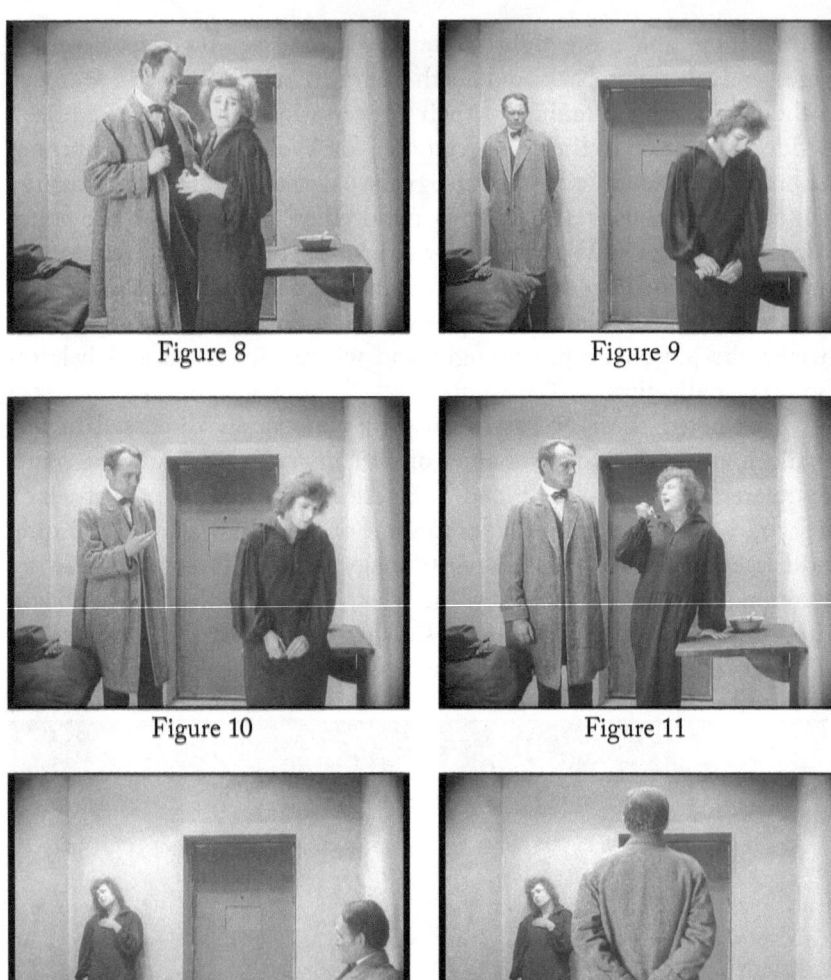

Figure 8

Figure 9

Figure 10

Figure 11

Figure 12

Figure 13

the former in major key, so to speak, the latter in minor. Even at the Ufa-Palast am zoo, hand-cranked projection would have resulted in differing tempos, but it is clear, at least to me, that the slowly mounting scale and significance of events was carefully planned, and this is evident in the acting too.

The registers of acting as a whole tend to vary, partly keyed by the nature of events and characterstic actions, partly keyed by the nature of the characters. Thus Rudolph Klein-Rogge's performance tends to be

DR MABUSE, DER SPIELER (DR MABUSE, THE GAMBLER) (1922)

Figure 14

Figure 15

Figure 16

Figure 17

Figure 18

Figure 19

marked not only by his trademark gaze and the power inherent in the stillness of his bulk, but also by his emphatic gestures and movements; Robert Forster-Larringa, and to a lesser Alfred Abel, by their fluttering, nervous hand gestures; Gertrud Welcker by her languid deportment; Bernard Goetzke by his largely self-contained responses to events around him; and Egeda Nissen by the perpetual frustration evident in her facial expressions and by the growing number of resigned poses she exhibits in reposnse to her incarceration and what she finally knows to be her death.

Here the gestural interplay between Nissen and Goetzke and Nissen and Schettlow is especially worthy of note—evidence that silent film acting can be subtle, emphatic and moving all at once (Figures 8–19).

Acts Three and Four

The events that follow Act Two mark a step-change as large-scale actions, large-scale plans, and large-scale displays of physical and mental power begin to take centre stage once more. At the beginning of Act Three, von Wenk enters Carozza's cell and finds her body. Pesch is brought in and threatened, but he refuses to name the person responsible for Carozza's death and von Wenk orders his men to take him back to the police station. From here, we cut to a bar in the Millernstrasse, where Mabuse in yet another disguise whips up the crowd by claiming that Johannes Gutter, one of its staunchest champions, has been arrested. The crowd spills out into the streets and, during the ensuing commotion, the van conveying Pesch back to the police station is stormed and Pesch is shot and killed by Georg. Once von Wenk is informed of Pesch's death, we cut to Mabuse, who is in his dressing room removing his disguise, then back to von Wenk, who is trying to determine the identity of the agent provocateur in the Millernstrasse.

Along with growing inflation, and alleged allusions to real-life gangsters in the film's denouement (of which more below), this is yet another point at which attempts to parallel events in the film with contemporary events in Germany are simply misconceived. Gunning points out that inflation began to rise in November 1921 and to rise more steeply at the point at which *Dr Mabuse* was released.[27] But hyperinflation was a phenomenon of the latter half of 1922 (and a number of years thereafter) and was thus not necessarily a mark of the film when shot. As for attempts to parallel Mabuse and events in the Millernstrase with the Spartacist uprising, Gunning is sceptical. Noting that Lang told Lotte Eisner that *Dr Mabuse* had originally opened with a 'breathless montage of scenes of the Spartacus uprising, the murder of Rathenau, the Kapp putsch and other violent moments of recent history',[28] he also notes that the 'assassination of Rathenau by members of the Freikorps . . . took place two months after the Berlin premiere of the first part of *Dr Mabuse, the Gambler*' and goes on to suggest that Lang was in fact 'mis-remembering' the opening of his later film *Spione (Spies)* (1928), not the first *Mabuse*.[29]

Back in the bedroom, Mabuse tells the Countess that he wants her to come with him. Following an interposed shot of the Count, who is clearly in drunken despair, the Countess refuses. 'You have now pronounced

DR MABUSE, DER SPIELER (DR MABUSE, THE GAMBLER) (1922)

your husband's death', says Mabuse, as we cut back to the Count, who wanders his mansion in a stupor, envisions a card game with multiple ghostly Mabuses, then collapses on the floor. Mabuse himself arrives the following day and tells the Count that his wife has left him. A little while later, as Act Three ends with another suicide and yet another death, the Count's servant informs von Wenk that the Count has slit his throat.

Act Four begins in the Told mansion, where the servant reveals to von Wenk that Mabuse had been advising the Count prior to his death. From here, we cut to Mabuse, his servants and the Countess, then back to the servant and von Wenk, who requests and is given Mabuse's address. Von Wenk visits Mabuse's house and is told that Mabuse is out, but on returning to his office, and behind the curve once more, von Wenk finds Mabuse waiting for him. Mabuse tells von Wenk that the Count must have acted 'under the influence of a superior and hostile will'. He also invites von Wenk to a forthcoming performance by Sandor Weltmann, who conducts experiments in mass hypnosis. Von Wenk accepts the invitation and, as we alternate again—and as Act Four comes to end—von Wenk issues orders to his men and Mabuse dons his Weltmann disguise.

Acts Five and Six

Act Five begins with Mabuse on stage as Weltmann. As in the seance sequence and other earlier scenes, his performance is addressed to a public eager for illusions and sensations. These include the aforementioned impossibilities, the real but illusory events that follow as he 'moves to the side, closes his eyes and concentrates. Through an overlap-dissolve, a desert landscape appears on the stage's back curtain. From the depths of the landscape, an Arabian caravan emerges, crossing over the stage and descending into the audience (horses, camels and all), parading down the central aisle, to the astonishment of the spectators'—those in the theatre and those in the cinema alike. Only then does he make the caravan vanish (by means of an edit by Lang), and only then is he greeted by 'wild applause'. It is at this point that Weltmann invites von Wenk to come on stage, where the latter is not just hypnotized (as so many others have been earlier on), but hypnotised into leaving the theatre and driving at breakneck speed towards an open quarry. Rescued by his men in the nick of time, von Wenk is now aware that his antagonist is Mabuse and, as Act Five comes to an end, he summons reinforcements as Mabuse's henchmen discover that Mabuse's house is surrounded by policemen.

Act Six, the film's last act, begins with the arrival of more and more policemen. Mabuse is now in his office destroying documents, and from here we cut back to the police, then back to Mabuse, then on to von Wenk, who phones Mabuse and asks him to surrender. Mabuse is defiant. He tells von Wenk that the Countess is 'here in my house'. Von Wenk decides to call in the army as we cut to the Countess, who is still entrapped in Mabuse's bedroom. The army arrive and join the police in besieging Mabuse's house.[29] Mabuse is wounded and a number of his underlings are killed, and as von Wenk and his men break into the house, Mabuse and Georg carry the Countess out of the bedroom and head for the laboratory. Georg tells Mabuse to 'let the woman go and save your own life'. Mabuse escapes into a tunnel, but Georg and Spoerri are arrested and the Countess is rescued by von Wenk, and from here we move on to the film's denouement.

Mabuse emerges from the tunnel and into his workshop. Once inside, (and for reasons that are never explained), he finds that the outer door and trap door are no longer working and that he is unable to get out.[30] As he becomes more and more frantic, and as we cut to the blind and bewildered forgers, we alternate between von Wenk and Spoerri and a shot of Georg in jail. Mabuse is now not only frantic, but also disturbed. Recalling the techniques of superimposition used to convey the Count's hallucinations of Mabuse, Mabuse himself begins to hallucinate his victims, first in 'ghostly' then in 'real' form, and from here we cut to Spoerri giving von Wenk the key to Mabuse's workshop, then on to Georg, who prepares to hang himself, then back to the workshop, where Mabuse plays cards with his victims amidst animated machinery on the workshop's walls. The card game recalls a number of earlier ones; it also literalizes the allusion to cards and card games in the film's first scene. As he descends into madness, flinging papers and counterfeit banknotes into the air as he kneels on the floor, Mabuse is now drained of his earlier powers, and as the hitherto unstoppable process of alternation comes to end, he is finally led away by von Wenk in two-shot.[31]

As is well known, this was not Mabuse's final appearance. If his resurrection in *Das Testament des Dr Mabuse* (*The Testament of Dr Mabuse*) (1933) and *Die 1000 Augen des Dr Mabuse* (*The 1000 Eyes of Dr Mabuse*) (1960) is testimony to Lang's enduring fascination with criminal power, his appearance in a subsequent cycle of Mabuse films in the 1960s and the early 1970s is testimony to the self-same commercial values that governed the writing of the novel in the first place and the production of the initial Mabuse film. All kinds of connotations have been attached to Mabuse and all kinds of meanings have been attributed to *Dr Mabuse, der Spieler*, most of them based on Ufa's programme brochure, on contemporary reviews and on Lang's own interviews (many of which were conducted some years later, and most of which are unreliable). Amidst them all, and despite the allusions to *Raffke*, it is important to remember that *Mabuse*'s origins lay for the most part not in socio-political events, but in sensational tales of fictional criminality built on improbable actions and situations on the one hand, and chains and clusters of motifs on the other.

7

Lazybones (1925)

Scott Higgins

Lazybones, which was produced and directed by Frank Borzage for Fox in 1925, is a curious film for the director, the star and a major Hollywood studio. Whereas goal-oriented protagonists in causal narratives were the studio era's common currency, *Lazybones* offers Western star Buck Jones as a hero defined by passive inaction, or, as the *Chicago Daily Tribune* critic put it, 'a big, husky, six-footer [who] goes gumptionless for eight reels'.[1] Billed by Fox as the 'picturized' version of Owen Davis's stage play about a 'lovable idling villager', *Lazybones* was Frank Borzage's debut effort for the studio after moving from MGM.[2] Well known for sentimental melodrama since his hit *Humoresque* five years previously, Borzage delivered an understated picture on the theme of suffering and acceptance. Often regarded as a minor work in a silent career that boasts *7th Heaven* (1927) and *Street Angel* (1928), *Lazybones* stands as a remarkable intervention in melodramatic form and the director's most thoroughgoing experiment in tempering sentiment with the emerging brand of Hollywood naturalism. Few films better reveal his skill at managing the viewer's relationship to story and translating subtle emotion to the realm of the visible.

Lazybones and Borzage's Authorial Imprint

Borzage's most celebrated works hinge on the obstruction of keenly desired unions. Hervé Dumont aptly describes Borzage's central theme as 'the apotheosis of the couple' played out in narratives in which 'redemption is achieved through embrace'.[3] His late-silent trio of Janet Gaynor and Charles Farrell romances all elaborate scenes that protract and delay the lovers' climactic clinch. In *7th Heaven* and *Lucky Star* (1929), Farrell's blind or crippled characters fight against all odds to reach Gaynor's before she, unaware of his struggle, falls into the arms of another. At the close of *Seventh Heaven*, for example, Borzage cross-cuts between Diane (Gaynor) coming to terms with Chico's reported death, inching ever closer to a comforting embrace from the opportunist Colonel Brissac (Ben Bard), and Chico (Farrell), sightless but implausibly alive, beating his way against Armistice day celebrants to reach her. In the romantic equivalent of a race-to-the-rescue, Chico bursts into the room in the nick of time, restoring Diane's faith at precisely 11.00 a.m., the hour they had set aside to profess their love while separated by war. Borzage's 1930s oeuvre also abounds with transcendent embraces between lovers (*Man's Castle* [1933], *History is Made at Night* [1937], *Three Comrades* [1938]) and, in one case, the too-late embrace of mother and child (*No Greater Glory* [1934]).

This authorial preoccupation began in *Humoresque*, which was scripted by Frances Marion and similar to *Lucky Star*. The film focuses on the musically gifted violinist Leon Kantor (Gaston Glass) who rises from poverty to fame only to sustain crippling injury to his arm at the front during World War I. Upon his return, Leon sinks into despair and rejects his family. Then, in the film's final moments, Leon miraculously recovers when he embraces his dejected wife Gina (Alma Rubens). This context highlights the experimental nature of *Lazybones*. Marion and Borzage present a virtual meditation on transcendent union, unifying the film's five parts around scenes that deny characters the mutual recognition of love. In a career founded on staging love's transcendence, *Lazybones* is a film of failed embraces.

Lazybones is organized around episodes from twenty-five years of Steve Tuttle's (Buck Jones) shiftless, small town life. Out fishing one day in 1900, Steve rescues Ruth Fanning (Zasu Pitts), who has thrown herself into the river and abandoned her secret infant beside it. Steve offers to keep the baby and her secret until Ruth musters the courage to tell her over-strict mother (Emily Fitzroy). When Mrs Fanning threatens, beats and forces her daughter to marry local businessman Elmer Ballister (William Bailey), Steve adopts the child and names her Kit. Steve's mother (Edythe Chapman) accepts the situation without question, but Steve's girlfriend, Ruth's sister Agnes (Jane Novak), leaves him. Ruth dies broken hearted without revealing her secret and Kit (Madge Bellamy) grows into a vivacious young woman. While Steve is fighting at the front in World War I, Kit falls in love with Dick Ritchie (Leslie Fenton), and together they build a thriving auto-repair business named Steve's Garage. Upon his return, Steve, struck with Kit's beauty, falls in love with her. He plans to propose, but when he overhears Dick asking Kit to marry him, Steve gives up his courtship. The film closes in 1925 as Steve, once again, goes fishing.

Adaptation and Adjusting Viewer Knowledge

Frances Marion's adaptation shifts Owen Davis's plot to address what *Variety*'s theatre critic perceived as the play's great failing: its ending. The play withholds Kit's parentage until the final act. By this point, Kit has cured Steve's laziness and, as *The Billboard* review put it, 'the child, grown to young womanhood, realizes that her love for her rescuer is changing from that of a child to that of a full-matured girl'.[4] Meanwhile, Ruth's odious widower commences to woo Kit, unaware that he had been married to her mother. For his part, Steve wrongly assumes that Kit is enamoured of neighbourhood boy Dick Ritchie, and so is oblivious to her feelings. Steve stands up to Ballister and quashes his predation, but then is accused of desiring Kit himself. When the now elderly Mrs Fanning reveals Kit's identity, she clears the path for her marriage to Steve. For *Variety*, this 'is the principal fault with the story' because

> it is as repulsive as if Ballister had gotten the girl—the thought that a man who had acted as her father, who had reared, trained and cared for her since babyhood, should enter into a state of marriage with one so young—for he is fully 25 years older.[5]

Davis's play generates tension around the question of Steve's paternity, which the climactic revelation resolves, unblocking romantic closure. This melodramatic contrivance came across to the critic as 'an effort to give in to the hokum which it is commonly supposed that New York theatre as an institution demands'.[6]

The film substantially 'opens out' the play, which takes place entirely on an exterior set of Steve Tuttle's house. Beyond adding scenes in the house and around town, Marion invented Steve's accidental heroism at the front in Northern France. Marion's major innovation, however, was to reveal immediately that Ruth is Kit's mother, changing what had been a welcome surprise into a steady source of pathos. The situation in which the viewer, Ruth and Steve, but neither Kit nor Agnes know of their sacrifice creates the melodramatic discrepancy of knowledge identified by Steve Neale in his seminal essay 'Melodrama and Tears'.[7] Neale explains how melodramas can place viewers in an emotionally charged position of powerless awareness by blocking or delaying the coincidence of character and spectator knowledge. Neale sums up the dynamic with the phrase 'if only', which he borrows from *Letter from an Unknown Woman* (1948):

> if only this character realized the other's worth, if only she or he were aware of the other's existence, if only they had met in different circumstances in a different time, in a different place, 'if only you could have recognized what was always yours'.[8]

Working from a psychoanalytic perspective, Neale theorizes that melodrama addresses an innate fantasy of union with the mother, which is literalized in films like *Stella Dallas* (1937) and *Imitation of Life* (Douglas Sirk, 1959), and certainly in Ruth and Kit's relationship in *Lazybones*. Whether or not unconscious desire is at play, it is clear that, by granting viewers knowledge of Ruth's maternity, Marion and Borzage activate a powerful melodramatic narrative structure that amplifies our desire for character union to the point of tears.

From the play, Marion and Borzage inherited an elliptical structure that presents slices of action from across several decades. Their adaptation multiplies Davis's three acts, set in spring 1904, summer 1920 and autumn 1924, into five parts, occurring in 1900, 1905, 1915, 1917, 1918, and finally 1925. This arrangement allows the film to complicate the action somewhat with the inclusion of World War I, while allowing the story to leap between emotional turning points and skate past exposition and motivation. Borzage and Marion need offer no explanation for Ruth's life-threatening decline in health at the start of the second part, or of Steve's uncharacteristically active decision to enlist in the army at the start of part three. Instead, we move swiftly from scenes of Ruth relinquishing her child, to defending Kit against neighbourhood bullies, and to her now-teenage daughter witnessing her mother's death. Likewise, Steve's teary-eyed departure for the front and his discovery of Kit's blossoming romance with Dick are tightly compressed. The plot thus maintains episodic intensity as it deploys situations from the melodramatic lexicon, including self-sacrifice for kindred, free union impeded by opposition of relatives and false suspicions drawn upon oneself to save a friend.[9] More specifically, the plot is an efficient vehicle for Borzage to explore and repeat the dynamics of 'if only'.

Rural Naturalism and Guarded Sentiment

For all its melodramatics, however, *Lazybones* sharply differs from the glorious hysterics of such sentimental box-office hits of the era as *Flesh and the Devil* (1926) and *The Big Parade* (1925), or even *7th Heaven* and *Street Angel*. In tone and approach, *Lazybones* evinces the kind of Hollywood naturalism that Lea Jacobs identifies as part and parcel of the decline of sentiment in the 1920s. In the years before Erich von Stroheim's *Greed* (1925) helped to align naturalism with serious, literary, prestige films, Jacobs finds the mode in a trend of sparely-plotted rural dramas that includes *The Old Swimmin' Hole* 1920) and *Miss Lulu Bett* (1922).[10] In addition to its rural setting and everyday characters, *Lazybones* shares *The Old Swimmin' Hole*'s anecdotal plotting and reticence with intertitles, and *Lulu Bett*'s anti-nostalgic 'oppressive domesticity'.[11] In a 1922 interview with Peter Milne, Borzage champions commonplace characters over 'the blood-and-thunder sort of interest'.[12] He describes the 'dramatic picture with average people' as a kind of film-making challenge:

> It's all very well to say that there's drama in the life of the man who delivers the milk and in the lives of those in the apartment next door. It's there all right. But find it! That's what I try to do and that's what I try to do in my pictures. That makes them a little bit different from the usual picture perhaps.[13]

As Jacobs points out, upon arriving at Fox, Borzage arranged for the film rights to plays about 'plain everyday people', which he had lauded to Milne, and which included *Lightnin'* (written by Winchell Smith and Frank Bacon, and brought to the screen by John Ford in 1925) and *The First Year* (written by Frank Craven and adapted by Borzage and Marion in 1926). *Lazybones*, which *Billboard*'s theatre critic had compared to *Lightnin'*, was part of this package of acquisitions, and is Borzage's fullest engagement with rural naturalism.

In bringing his version of Hollywood naturalism to such a highly melodramatic story, Borzage steers a careful course around sentiment. *Lazybones* exemplifies the director's attitude towards explicit and overwrought emotion, which he explained to critic Cecelia Ager in 1933: 'Sentiment's been abused; people are ashamed of it. It dare not show its face, it's got to sneak up on them from behind.'[14] In her brief but illuminating column in *Variety*, Ager reported that:

> Mr Borzage ... believes the judicious use of sentiment gives a picture its surest crack at hearty audience appeal ... But he lets the audience find that out. 'Don't point to it', he adjures, see that it's there but don't mention it. Leave its discovery to the audience. Make the audience sentimental instead of the player. Make the audience act.[15]

Borzage's defence of sentiment, and his concern that it be surreptitious, adds evidence to Jacobs' argument, when she charts an irrevocable shift in critical taste during the 1920s, 'a rejection of blatantly didactic or highly moralized narratives', when it became an insult to describe a film as "Pollyannish"'.[16] Instead, congruent with their literary counterparts, film critics began to value general features of naturalism occurring in a wide range of genres: 'one finds praise for simple over complex plots, for dedramatized scenes and situations, and for restrained modes of storytelling'.[17] *Lazybones* partakes in this aesthetic transformation, though without the irony and confrontational vulgarity of films like *Greed* (1924).

Lazybones joined a small trend of rural dramas produced by Fox, which included *Just Pals* (John Ford, 1920), *Lightnin'* and *Lucky Star*. *Just Pals*, itself Fox's answer to *The Old Swimmin' Hole*, is *Lazybones*'s closest relative. In *Just Pals*, Buck Jones stars as the town bum who rescues and adopts a young runaway boy and courts the local schoolteacher. The film is more broadly comic and eventful than *Lazybones* (Jones foils a robbery and wins the girl), but its focus on the pathos of paternal bonding (similar to Chaplin's *The Kid* released the following year) and conflict between narrow-minded small-town traditionalists and a good-hearted vagrant strongly anticipate Borzage's feature. Akin to *Lazybones*'s Steve Tuttle, Jones's character in *Just Pals* is an inveterate layabout who first appears lazing in a hayloft and complaining to two labourers: 'just watching you work makes me tired'. The films' chief similarity lies in the casting of Fox's Western star Buck Jones. The *Los Angeles Times*, which compared his performance to Charles Ray, hailed Jones's 'startling transition from the Western cowboy hero to the character of a lovable, Yankee small-town loafer—a type in utter contrast to a two-fisted, gun fighting, hard-riding puncher'.[18] Jones, to whom the paper attributes 'innate modesty and reticence of speech', brings restrained expressiveness to both roles, and Borzage draws on this star image to simultaneously underplay and magnify emotional situations. In combining rural naturalism, a cowboy star and melodramatic plotting, Borzage forges a place for 'if only' in an environment that was becoming increasingly wary of sentiment.

1900: Setting the Deadlock

Lazybones opens with a comic tone of folksy hyperbole that seems more in line with *The Old Swimmin' Hole* or *Just Pals* than the plot that follows. Steve Tuttle possesses a single character trait, reiterated visually and verbally: he is lazy. An emblematic cutaway to thick blackstrap molasses slowly engulfing a pancake illustrates the expository title 'Steve was as slow as molasses in winter, so they gave him the nick name of "Lazybones"'. Spiders have woven a thick web between his shoe and the fence he props his feet against, and his mother must shoo a fly from his nose when it threatens his slumber. Borzage underlines Steve's lethargy through repetition. Within moments, his mother remarks that his underwear blowing in a breeze on the clothesline 'never get that much exercise when Steve's in 'em' and assures Mrs Fanning that 'my boy ain't lazy—he's just tired from grown' too fast', but Agnes complains bluntly 'Oh, Steve, you're so Lazy!' Despite his passivity, however, Steve has a romantic goal, which is comically introduced as he nuzzles a goat, mumbling 'Agnes dear' in his sleep. At first, his desire serves as a vehicle for comedy when he incompetently attempts to woo Agnes with a ride in his car, which travels a few feet before breaking down.

Borzage uses the occasion not just to generate humour, but to hint at the game of emotional revelation that will overtake the film. After Mrs Fanning angrily berates Steve and Elmer Ballister arrives to drive her and Agnes home in his finely appointed carriage, Borzage ceases intertitles and lingers on character reactions. Framed in close-up over her shoulder, Steve nods slightly as Agnes consoles him. Meanwhile Elmer invites Mrs Fanning into his carriage and she turns to glare off-screen, motivating a reverse shot of Agnes gazing at Steve in the foreground. At her mother's command, Agnes climbs onto the back seat, where she continues to stare in Steve's direction. Borzage alternates close-ups of Agnes and Steve smiling ever so slightly, then drops back to a long shot that reintroduces Mrs Fanning, who glances in his direction and scoffs. Agnes's look remains fixed as the carriage pulls out of frame and we cut to a pictorial soft-focus deep shot of the road, the carriage raising a dust cloud while Agnes peers over the back seat and watches Steve.

This is a fleeting moment of unspoken understanding between the couple, a moment made poignant, however, by Elmer and Mrs Fanning's callousness. Borzage uses silent cinema's flexibility with regard to the spoken word to his advantage. Bereft of intertitles, the exchange between Agnes and Steve plays out through glances and subtle acknowledgements that suggest desire without grounding it in language. This dynamic, in which the viewers align with lovers who are pulled apart by unsympathetic forces, would become something of a Borzage trademark, and it quietly initiates the film's structuring pattern of interrupted or missed embraces. The moment also strikingly illustrates Ager's observation about sentiment in Borzage: 'He handles it carefully, gingerly . . . He checks it with underplaying, safeguards it with humor.'[19] Climbing out of his car, Steve discovers that he's been sitting on a chicken egg that he had placed there earlier. The scene closes with a gag, our hero bashfully wiping his pants, which deflates and deflects the emotional pressure.

The opening sequence is deceptively light; it doesn't prepare the viewer for the stark revelation of Ruth's unwanted child or her subsequent suicide attempt. Even so, Borzage loads the scene with visual motifs that will accrue emotion, including Steve's shoes, his posture of reclining with his feet propped up, the broken front gate, the hitching post that Agnes leans against and the shot of the carriage pulling away into the distance leaving Steve behind. The film's elliptical structure and drifting protagonist grant these motifs prominence and weight. They knit the episodes together and carry the load for underplayed or unexpressed pathos.

Ruth's situation is the melodramatic engine that drives *Lazybones*, and Borzage's exposition is direct and efficient. A brief scene of Ruth reading her mother's letter reveals the infant Kit lying on her bed. As Ruth tearfully embraces her daughter, the last time in the film she will do so, we cut to a comic vignette of Steve awakened from his slumber in the crook of a tree by a tug on his fishing line. He clumsily drops the fish and settles back into his nap when Ruth appears beside the river, carrying Kit in a basket. Borzage silently communicates Ruth's decision through point-of-view shots of the town before her and the river below. Unable to face her mother, she deposits Kit beside the river and leaps into the rushing current. In a suite of uncharacteristically successful actions, Steve dives from his tree, rescues Ruth from the raging river and offers to take care of the baby. Only Ruth and we are privy to Steve's burst of action, which opposes the shot of molasses that opened the film. The sequence is Frances Marion's invention, and it powerfully introduces the essential knowledge discrepancy. When she explains her plight to Steve, Borzage gives us a single subjective tableau of Ruth's shipping-office wedding to her ill-fated sailor. She begs Steve to believe what her mother will doubt, and the flashback, negligible in terms of exposition, serves as visual proof shared between the viewer and the characters. From here on, viewers are firmly on Steve's side, vividly aware both of his virtue and his reason for hiding it.

Ruth's maternal crisis creates a deadlock in which characters are prevented from pursuing their desires. Steve must forsake his love for Agnes to protect Ruth's secret, and Ruth, unable to stand up to her mother's abuse and threats to institutionalize Kit, forsakes her child. Rather than push the story towards a resolution of these tensions, Marion's screenplay exploits the situation for a series of 'if only' moments, the climactic embrace held in abeyance. Under Borzage's direction, these become set pieces of restrained sentiment. The first such moment is brief but kinetic.

Steve, feeding the infant Kit in his garden, catches sight of Ruth and Agnes riding in Elmer's carriage. He holds the child up and waves her hand towards the passing coach as Ruth and Agnes react silently, so as not to draw the attention of Mrs Fanning in the front seat. As in the flirtation that closes the first scene, Mrs Fanning once again provides the dampening presence of a disapproving authority figure. Now, however, secrecy between the sisters also prohibits emotional expression.

With characters necessarily underplaying, Borzage wrings pathos through imagery and editing. We first see Ruth in a master shot of the carriage's four occupants as she catches a glimpse of her child. Elmer, Mrs Fanning and Agnes are engaged in conversation, while Ruth gazes off-screen. Borzage delivers Ruth's point of view in one of the film's three dramatic tracking shots, a long shot composition of Steve lifting the baby as the camera sweeps past. The picket fence that whips by in the foreground, the camera's pan to reframe and keep Steve and the child centred as it begins to lose him and the soft-focus vignette that narrows this image's point of clarity mark the brief shot as ephemeral (Figure 1).[20] As soon as we, and Ruth, recognize the moment's import, it is already moving off frame. A cut back to the carriage in medium shot reveals that Agnes has also taken notice, and Ruth raises her hand to her chest as they both glance over the back of the coach. The shot activates divergent points of view, adding Agnes's secretive interest in Steve (once again behind her mother's back) to Ruth's maternal gaze. Ruth's subtle gesture of desire is matched in a medium close-up of Steve holding Kit; he furrows his brow and gently bounces the infant's hand to mimic a wave. Ruth reacts in close-up this time, shot from behind the carriage as she peeks over the seat's edge, smiles slightly and raises her hand to wave back. Editing has moved

Figure 1. Panning, tracking, and focus mark Ruth's view of her child as ephemeral.

us successively closer to our suffering characters as the distance between them expands. Borzage continues the pattern of alternation while shifting the range of knowledge. Steve lowers his hand and a medium two-shot of the back of the carriage reintroduces Agnes, who begins waving, while beyond her Mrs Fanning takes notice. Steve once again raises his hand, this time to acknowledge Agnes, but in reaction Borzage returns to Ruth's close-up, and her halting wave appears all the more furtive because of Mrs Fanning's growing awareness.

This exchange is narrationally complex: we register that Steve's acknowledgement of Agnes is, in part, a pretext for connecting the mother and child: he pretends to flirt while embracing Kit on Ruth's behalf. The playfulness of his gesture, making an infant wave, amplifies through contrast the moment's barely expressed emotional depth. Borzage interrupts this exchange of reactions with a shot of Elmer and Mrs Fanning, and the first intertitle of the sequence: 'There's Lazybones with that nameless brat!' Her devastatingly timed interjection marks the impossibility of union, lending an air of futility to the final alternations between Steve and Ruth. It is a scene of high sentiment, safeguarded by underplaying and bracketed by comedy. The sequence begins and ends with light touches. At the start, Steve milks the family cow directly into a baby bottle for Kit, who playfully rejects the offer. In the final shot, the impulsive infant grabs Steve's face and he breaks into gentle laughter. As Borzage commented to Cecelia Ager: 'A laugh takes the curse off [sentiment], holds it from spilling over.'[21]

1905: A Failed Maternal Embrace

The remainder of *Lazybones*'s '1900' section deepens the intractability of Ruth and Steve's situation. In an act of iconic cruelty, Mrs Fanning takes a whip to her daughter and threatens to send Kit to an orphanage if she reveals her parentage. Agnes breaks things off with Steve because he refuses to name Kit's mother. With the deadlock now seemingly insurmountable, the film jumps forward to a brief and emotionally dense second part, signalled by an art card depicting the riverbank and reading 'Summer 1905'. This six-minute sequence is our only glimpse of Kit as a young girl (played by Virginia Marshall), and Borzage generalizes the action with lush pictorialism. Three scenes linked by Kit's walk home stand in for the whole of her childhood, each a variation on 'if only'. First, Ruth intervenes in a skirmish and rescues Kit, who meets her mother's embrace with incomprehension. Next, Agnes and Mrs Fanning watch as another young girl tries to befriend Kit only for her mother to send the foundling away. Near to tears, Kit runs home to Steve and he comforts her, telling her that she's been rejected because 'I'm so lazy and good-for-nothin''.

Ruth's encounter with Kit is a variation on the melodramatic mainstay, noted by Neale with reference to *Stella Dallas* and *Imitation of Life*, in which hierarchies of knowledge intensify the failed union between mother and child. Ruth catches sight of Kit through her parlour window while her insufferably smug husband admires a newspaper story about his own promotion to bank president. She rushes out to disperse the bullies picking on Kit and kneels down, gazing upward into her daughter's eyes. The girl answers her mother's regard with a tragic lack of recognition: 'please don't look at me like that'. Meanwhile, Borzage cross-cuts to Elmer taking notice of his wife's absence, thus imposing a perceptible time limit on Ruth's interaction. The moment is fragile. When she finally forces a kiss and embrace on the girl, Elmer interrupts and sends Kit away. The incident concludes with a comic beat as Kit slingshots a rock at Elmer's backside.

In her screenplay, Marion has fashioned a situation that prevents characters from expressing themselves, and Borzage uses this to motivate underplaying while film style and narration take on emotional force. Cutting between slow and tightly confined actions in the Ballister parlour and Kit's energetic trot down a country road throws the stiff reserve of Ruth's marriage into relief. Her nervous glances between her husband and the children outside her window frame Ruth's intervention as an escape from domestic tyranny. The soft-style cinematography of Glen MacWilliams and George Schneiderman combines with brilliant edge lighting and a diffuse background to give the medium and close-up shots of Ruth and Kit an ethereal abstraction. These compositions, which place the desiring character lower in the screen gazing upward towards light and into the face of another, are a favourite arrangement of Borzage, most memorably on display in the Gaynor and Farrell films. (See Figure 2.) Here, the staging technique is especially poignant, the mother looking to the child for comfort. Zazu Pitts keeps her expressions to carefully modulated glances, and her gestures are small and aborted; her kiss is cut short by Elmer's arrival. Mundane flat lighting and crisp focus break the spell when Elmer chastises Kit and sends her away. No one is allowed to cry.

As Kit continues her trek, the film shifts focus from the mother's to the child's dilemma. Her rejection by her young friend's mother, viewed with sympathy by Agnes and with steely intolerance by Mrs Fanning, is an iterative event, presented once in the plot but imagined as a regular

LAZYBONES (1925)

Figure 2. Borzage's signature composition: Ruth gazes upward into the light.

occurrence in the story. Borzage interjects an anticipatory shot of Steve leaning against a half-painted fence drifting off to sleep, brush in hand and feet propped up on a wheelbarrow. The cut establishes an endpoint for Kit's journey, a destination towards which she begins rushing with growing urgency. The film's second dramatic tracking shot keeps Kit in medium shot as she first walks and then runs down the lane. She holds her hand to her mouth, on the edge of tears but not crying, picking up momentum and jostling about the frame. It is an expressive moment, carried by movement within and of the frame, and Marshall's delicate performance remains just short of an outburst. Before the girl's emotion fully crystallizes, Borzage cuts to a ravishing extreme long shot of Steve's front gate and the road stretching beyond it, Kit's slight edge-lit figure bounding up the sun-dappled path as storm clouds gather above. The composition is *Lazybones*'s pictorial highpoint, a breathtaking view that both brakes and resonates with the energy built by the tracking shot (Figure 3). In the following action, Kit plays against the building drama when she struggles with the still-broken front gate and repeats the comic refrain (already voiced by Elmer and Steve) 'Darn that gate!'

Borzage's subtle organization of emotion climaxes in the film's sole moment of mutual understanding between central characters. Kit enters the frame and sits down in the crook created by Steve's propped-up legs, making use of what had been a posture of indolence. The matter-of-fact gesture encapsulates their easy acceptance of one another. Finally, the director grants viewers emotional access to Kit crying in close-up. The simplicity of her question boosts its emotional depth: 'Why won't no one play with me Uncle Steve?' Borzage offers a lingering exchange of soft shot and reverse shot close-ups, then holds over Kit's shoulder for Steve's shifting reaction. First he deflects her by blaming his laziness

Figure 3. The film's pictorial highpoint both brakes and resonates with Kit's emotions.

and she comforts him with a hug. Then he cheers her up with some unintertitled remarks, and they embrace again. This time, his expression shifts enigmatically, a forced smile dropping away as she buries her head in his neck. After a few moments, Steve's eyes drift skyward and the image fades out. The characters' momentary union gently eases tensions built by Kit's rejection of her mother and the community's rejection of Kit. The sequence's kinetic and pictorial beauty lifts it from the flow of events while characters, Steve in particular, continue to underplay.

1915: A Mother's Death

The elliptical structure of *Lazybones* pays large emotional dividends in the decade-long leap that brings us to spring 1915, which finds Kit a teenager (Madge Bellamy) and Ruth on her deathbed. The ten-minute sequence presents the climactic failure of maternal union, the very fantasy that Neale suggests is at the root of melodrama's rehearsals of loss. The first three minutes of the segment pass with a single intertitle. Ruth condenses her situation with shocking economy: 'I'm dying—I want to hold Kit in my arms and hear her call me "mama".' With this, she locks her mother inside the room and then forces past her husband at the gate. She dies seated in Steve's living room, her arms around her uncomprehending daughter. Steve observes, keeping Ruth's secret to her end and unable to reveal his feelings. Her passing introduces a more extended exchange of dialogue titles, but the emphasis remains on unstated import. Steve attempts to explain the woman's death to Kit and to offer Ruth the belated closure she so desired. He explains death in terms of family, 'people get weary and tired—they're just called home', and asks Kit to offer a prayer. The young woman's teary supplication finishes in a title asking and granting mercy: 'and if she's done anything wrong forgive her—for God's sake, Amen'. Coming too late and without recognition, Kit's acceptance of her mother firmly places the viewer to wish 'if only'.

Borzage embroiders the sequence with contrasts and motifs that emphasize time as an insurmountable obstacle to union. Editing juxtaposes the dynamism of Kit in the sunny garden, collecting worms as a stiff wind buffets her edge-lit hair, to the stasis of Ruth's compositions, first in her own bedroom, then seated in Steve's parlour. Youth and vitality counterpoint age and lethargy. Elmer once again tries to stop Ruth at her gate, but this time she repels him. The swift tracking shot that covers Ruth's brief trek to Steve's house recalls Kit's walk home ten years, but also scant minutes, before: the mother's attempt to follow her child comes too late. Similarly, Steve's mother seats Ruth in the parlour, a composition that recalls the day fifteen years earlier when she placed the infant Kit's basket in that room. More broadly, Ruth's attempt to have contact with her daughter parallels the carriage scene and the scene at her gate. Steve is again the knowing mediator between the two, and the encounter leads to another awkward maternal embrace.

Differences in knowledge continue to shape the emotional and visual dynamics. Beckoned to the door, Steve pauses and glances first to Ruth in the house and then to Kit in the garden. The exchange of eyeline matches underlines a disjunction between character points of view. Steve alone connects mother and daughter through his look. Once Kit enters, Borzage delays the moment of embrace across eight shots as she crosses the room to her mother. The deceleration of action stands out against the bustle of Ruth's escape, escalating the tension. Steve, meanwhile, turns away, bites his thumbnail and fidgets with his shirt, unable to reveal emotions that the viewer must provide. A strong sidelight seemingly emanating from an unlit hearth behind the actresses provides dramatic facial modelling and makes palpable the unexpressed.

Ruth collapses in the act of embrace. She looks upward, off-screen and silently mouths the words 'my . . . my . . .' before burying her head in her daughter's lap (Figure 4). We see only her hand against Kit's back grasp and then release her dress. Kit drops her head and then, turning away from the camera and into semi-profile, hand to mouth, looks towards Steve. Borzage's great achievement lies in understatement, in withholding expression during an exceptionally well-defined melodramatic turning point. After her prayer, we linger on Kit's half-comprehending close-up, looking for approval from Steve. His glance in medium shot is briefer, and he looks down as we cut to a medium long shot of all three characters: the

Figure 4. When Ruth dies we see only her hand against Kit's back.

back of Steve's head and shoulders obscure Ruth's body as Kit, sympathetic but unsure, looks on. Again, the high point of emotion coincides with a discrete fade out.

1917: A Soldier's Departure

A climactic episode, Ruth's death exhausts the film's maternal situation, leaving Marion and Borzage to draw out romantic complications in *Lazybones*'s final third. Their plot briefly revisits Steve's failed courtship with Agnes, but devotes most time to his unrequited affection for Kit, which does not grow organically from Ruth's sacrifice. Melodramatic story structures often conglomerate episodes, in contrast to an elegant Aristotelian dramatic curve. However, in a departure from melodrama, and from the play, *Lazybones* uses the format not to offer increasingly spectacular reversals and revelations, but to deliver a series of anticlimaxes. The last part of the film takes a naturalist turn, culminating in a failed embrace and Steve's acceptance of his lot.

Borzage initiates a new form of blocked desire, that between Kit and Steve, with the scene of his departure for the front. The play made a point of Kit's romantic interest in her former father figure, but Marion and Borzage steer clear of direct expressions. The embrace does not trade on the dissonance of knowledge that earlier scenes involving Kit have, and the union doesn't fail so much as it is cut short. Instead, Borzage invests the moment with emotional potential that will linger after the war. A title alerts us that the year is 1917, but motifs reaffirm Steve's molasses-like pace of change. Kit is now at work painting the fence, which hasn't seen much progress since 1905, and Steve once again draws attention to the broken gate, another of Borzage's humorous deflections. Steve and

Kit's farewell recalls his parting with Agnes at the film's opening. Small gestures and looks stand in lieu of intertitles to hint at romantic yearning without settling the issue.

While mother and son say goodbye, Kit crosses through the gate to the hitching post where Agnes stood nearly twenty years earlier. Three shots of Kit glancing towards Steve over her shoulder orient us to her experience of the moment, and her quick turn away just as he might notice indirectly suggests furtive desire. Borzage then charges their parting kiss by marking the couple's awareness of others. Steve first tries to cheer Kit with a parental gesture, squeezing her nose and lifting her head, in a shared medium close-up. Then, from a close-up of Steve over Kit's shoulder, Borzage cuts twice to follow his glance, first towards his mother and then up the road to gathering soldiers. In a return to the medium close-up, Steve kisses Kit on the lips, their contact discreetly occluded by his hat brim, and they both glance off-screen towards his mother (Figure 5). Kit forces a smile, which transforms into a brave but serious look as she turns back to Steve. These visual reminders of the presence of others motivate the characters' underplaying (in front of mother) and amplify the moment's urgency (Steve must meet his comrades). Borzage interrupts their nearly tearful separation with a pictorial extreme long shot of Steve walking down the road away from home, then teases the viewer with two brief shots: Kit nervously plays with the hitching post, her lip trembling in close-up, and mother gazes stoically into the distance in medium shot. The scene closes with a return to the extreme long shot, Kit and Mother at the left, Steve in silhouette among a group of enlistees marching up the road in the distance. From the iconic and sentimental action of a soldier's departure, Borzage crafts a scene of tentative union

Figure 5. After they kiss, Steve and Kit glance off screen at his mother, which motivates their underplaying.

in the face of separation. The situation seems a rehearsal for Diane and Chico's hurried marriage as his detachment prepares for deployment in *Seventh Heaven*, but without the operatic elaborations. Cinematography and editing privilege Kit's point of view, yet she controls her expressions until just before Borzage cuts away, channelling emotional resonance into the landscape before the fade out.

1918: An Abandoned Proposal

The tone of this scene sets the wheels in motion for Steve's failed courtship of Kit upon his return. *Lazybones* spares fewer than four minutes on Steve's accidental heroism, in which he awakens behind an enemy advance and the German battalion mistakenly believes they are surrounded when he appears. More important to the film's emotional trajectory, Marion and Borzage introduce a new instance of knowledge disparity with a brief scene of Kit and Dick Ritchie running Steve's Garage and sharing a private embrace. Steve's homecoming begins with an expository title that returns to the comic distance of the opening: 'Steve was too darned lazy to write back home that he was alive—so one evening he just casually returned.' Before entering the house, Steve lingers at the hitching post and assumes the posture that he struck during his farewell to Kit. Placing his elbow on the post, he buries his eyes in his forearm, obscuring his expression, while the framing and gesture begin to signal the troubling import of Kit's new love. His reunion with Kit merely alludes to romantic tensions: Dick's expression drifts from a half-smile to one of concern as he watches Kit embrace Steve, and Kit's introduction of Dick features a telling stutter: 'He's been such a comfort to—to us.'

The art card that introduces the next section, however, brings the issue to the fore: 'This was the romantic season—Spring.' Steve's mother makes concrete what Borzage has been intimating. When she discovers her son playing his banjo, she exclaims, 'I ain't heard you singin' since you was courtin' Agnes!' Then her expression shifts from joy to concern as she watches Steve give Kit a goodnight kiss. When Steve gazes into his bedroom mirror and asks 'I'm still kind o' youngish lookin', ain't I ma?' cross-cutting underlines both his mother's realization and the pathetic impossibility of this union. Her gaze moves from her son towards Kit's off-screen bedroom, and Borzage cuts twice to the girl, clad in a glowing white gown, vigorously brushing out her hair. Contrasts in pace and light drive home the basic incompatibility between the two. Steve's mother becomes increasingly concerned and, finally, she meets his uncharacteristic declaration of enthusiasm for work and 'new store clothes' with an expression of resigned sympathy and the intertitle: 'Steve, you're in love with Kit.'

Steve's blocked desire for Kit varies the film's 'if only' structure in that Borzage and Marion do not align viewers with his wish. Where Ruth's blocked union with Kit, or even Steve's with Agnes, plays on a conflict between the viewer's knowledge and desire, this romance is never portrayed as a worthy endeavour. Steve's mother, having unfailingly defended her son previously, models our response to his infatuation as pathetic, but worthy of our empathy. Before the dance, Steve awkwardly informs his mother that he intends to propose, she gently frowns and Borzage cross-cuts to Kit and Dick already together at the front gate, the designated place for romance. We wish to spare our protagonist the inevitable rejection; if only he understood that Kit was happily in love. When Steve overhears Dick's marriage proposal at the dance and our hierarchy of knowledge flattens out, his quiet acceptance comes as a relief. Having taken off his stiff dress shoes to soak his feet in a nearby pond, Steve looks downward and wades off frame, leaving the movement and light of the dance floor in the distance behind him. Reverting to type, abandoning goals and passively meeting the world, proves to be *Lazybones*'s best course of action.

Within this drama of misplaced affection, Marion and Borzage devote one final 'if only' moment to Agnes. The scene recalls Ruth's encounter with five-year-old Kit, only now Agnes catches sight of the passing hay ride carrying revellers, Steve and Kit among them, to the dance. The cut from the boisterous hayride to the Fanning home's customary stasis presents a staggering tonal shift. In place of Elmer, Mrs Fanning scowls disapproval in the background as Agnes lingers at the window. The elderly woman, now suffering from dementia, blurts out the truth about Ruth's baby leaving Agnes in disbelief but unable to cry. Though it is the only thread that ties the film's last third to Ruth's initial sacrifice, the sequence is peculiarly out of place. Mrs Fanning's revelation has been shorn of the narrative utility it offered the play. Instead of clearing the way to union between Steve and Kit, Agnes's discovery merely torments her with too-late recognition of an unnecessary sacrifice. An episode of blunt pathos, Borzage invests little of the pictorial or narrational refinement that he brings to other turning points. True to form, though, Agnes reacts without intertitles and the scene ends quickly, before she can fully divulge her feelings.

Lazybones's actual climax fully displays Borzage's orchestration of reserved sentiment. The scene after the dance fades in on Steve's uncomfortable shoes as the camera tilts to reveal that they are tied to a 'Just Married' sign fastened to the back of Dick's car. The image dissolves

Figure 6. Borzage evokes previous failed embraces as Kit leaves home.

to a side view of the car parked before Steve's gate, Kit and Dick already seated inside. Borzage has spared us the wedding and Steve and Kit's farewell embrace. The director cues emotion not with action or dialogue, but through motifs, like the shoes, the gate and the car, which recalls Steve's aborted drive with Agnes at the film's start. After a brief exchange of medium shots in which Steve diverts his attention to the car as Kit and Dick smile blissfully, Borzage cuts to a soft-focus long shot of the car pulling away into the distance, leaving Steve, his mother, the hitching post and the front gate in the foreground plane. Kit turns to wave over the back seat, her hair a blazing highlight beyond the range of focus as Steve and his mother, backs to camera, return the gesture (Figure 6). The composition condenses other scenes of failed or interrupted embrace: the car's path away from the house recalls Agnes's departure in Elmer's carriage; Kit's wave from the back of the car echoes her mother's wave to her as an infant; and the camera position and pictorial effect recall the shot of five-year-old Kit arriving at the gate after encountering but not recognizing her mother.

Borzage extends the moment by alternating variously framed reactions of Steve and his point of view. A medium frontal shot of Steve against a velvet-soft background shows him tearing up, his jaw moving and a hand raised in a hesitant wave. He watches the car recede down the lane, kicking up a cloud of dust that catches the sunlight. The next reaction withholds direct emotional access by framing Steve's back, his hand slowing. When we return to his point of view the car is no longer visible, replaced by a thinning cloud of dust hanging at the end of the road. Finally, the camera moves in for a close-up of Steve in paper-thin soft focus. His eyes glisten as he breathes in and starts to sob. The road is now empty, a light haze marking the car's recent departure. In a return to medium shot, his mother's hand enters the frame and gently halts Steve's waving, he looks down, hat covering his face as he wipes a tear, and turns away. Borzage elegantly restrains and regulates emotion through cutting, interspersing brief glimpses of Steve with the play of light in the car's wake. Steve wipes a tear, forces a smile and jokes weakly in the scene's first title: 'Well anyway, I got rid of those darned shoes.' His mother hands him his fishing pole and a can of worms, Steve tenderly pats her face and makes his way up the road. Humour cuts the sentiment while clarifying our protagonist's brave suffering. Gesture, glance and movement all carry it forward.

1925: Gone Fishing

Restrained as it is, Borzage and Marion do not close the film on so poignant a note. A final art card introduces 'Summer 1925' and we fade in on Steve, feet up and asleep in the crook of his fishing tree. Awakened by a tug on his line, Steve reprises his heroic leap into the river, this time emerging with a miniscule fish that he tosses back. His life has returned to its drifting cycle of non-events, and comedy softens the film's measured pathos. It is an audacious way to close a melodrama, signaling the protagonist's acceptance of failure, the continuity of mundane life and the absence of character change. The epilogue encapsulates Borzage and Marion's experiment in embedding situational turning points in the idiom of rural naturalism, but it can obscure the film's emotional virtuosity.

Lazybones disappointed at the box office and few critics tolerated Borzage's experiment.[22] They variously seized on the film's apparent lack of incident and its melodramatic plotting for reproach. *Variety* panned the film, pointing out its implausibility, 'dullness, platitudes, and maybe unconscious humor', and concluded, 'you will have to think a lot of Buck Jones to forget this one'.[23] The *Chicago Daily Tribune* review, noted earlier, regarded Steve as 'too DURN no account' and the story 'a long drawn out soppily melodramatic affair with a hero in anything but a sympathetic role'.[24] Only the *Los Angeles Times* was fully supportive of the project, and of Borzage's understated pathos. In an unusually insightful review, the paper's critic observed that:

> The story ambles along in quiet fashion without any startling dramatic moments, and yet when analyzed it possess all the main elements of tense drama. However, this fact is seldom thrust into the foreground . . . It is one of those pictures which gives a quiet satisfying entertainment without apparently struggling to do anything in particular.[25]

Clearly the movie was, and still is, an outlier in terms of Hollywood storytelling, and this tends to mask the way it dexterously intervenes in both melodrama and in Borzage's particular brand of romance. In lieu of a classical protagonist overcoming obstacles, Borzage unifies his film around repeated emotional impasses, which gather resonance from pictorial and narrational patterning. Putting brakes on overt sentiment while maintaining episodic plotting encouraged Borzage to burrow deeply into poetic structures of motif, indirect expression and manipulation of viewer knowledge. The movie is a quiet exemplar of American silent cinema's visual intensity, and it testifies to the depth and diversity of Hollywood's melodramatic tradition.

8

Lady Windermere's Fan (1925)

Steve Neale

Billed in its opening title as 'A Warner Brothers Classic of the Screen', the 1925 version of *Lady Windermere's Fan* was produced and directed by Ernst Lubitsch, premiered at the Casa Lopez theatre in New York City on 1 December, then released in New York on 26 December and in Los Angeles on 30 January 1926. Adapted by Lubitsch and screenwriter Julien Josephson from Oscar Wilde's play, the film was one of a number of Lubitsch productions designed to establish Warners as a major studio capable of undertaking prestige productions.[1] As has been documented in detail by Charles Musser, it appears to have been influenced by an earlier adaptation scripted by Benedict James and directed by Fred Paul for the Ideal Film Company in Britain.[2] Initially released in Britain in 1916, this version was eventually released in the USA by the Triangle Distributing Corporation in 1919, though the nature and extent of its circulation is not yet fully documented.

Eschewing Wilde's epigrammatic dialogue (as James and Paul had done), Lubitsch sought here and elsewhere in his silent films to maximize the use of visual means to convey the nature of physical and social settings; the nature of the characters and their predicaments, relationships and motives; and the nature of their thoughts and feelings. To 'produce a perfect photoplay', he wrote in 1924, 'one must first of all realize that the art of the screen is wholly visual'.[3] This did not mean rejecting titles entirely. In the case of *Lady Windermere's Fan*, though, it did mean trying to 'stalk and bag the game hiding under his [Wilde's] words and translate that . . . into a moving picture'.[4] In doing so, he also sought, as Wilde had done, to address issues of power, wealth, gender and behavioural double standards in the rule-bound milieux of upper-class societies—issues he had already addressed in a number of earlier films (including those he had produced and directed in his native Germany) and that he also went on to address in a number of later ones.[5]

The Play

Wilde's play was premiered in London in 1892. It consists of four separate acts. The first and last are set in the morning room of Lord Windermere's house, the second in the drawing room and the third in Lord Darlington's rooms. In the first, we learn that it is Lady Windermere's birthday, that her husband has given her a fan, that a party is planned for the evening and that Lord Darlington, an early visitor, is in love with her. Having rebuffed Darlington's advances, Lady Windermere discovers cheques made out to a Mrs Erlynne in her husband's desk and assumes that he is having an affair with her, especially when he reveals that he has invited Mrs Erlynne to the party. Lady Windermere is angry, and Lord Windermere tries to reassure her: 'Mrs Erlynne was once honoured, loved, respected. She was well born, she had position—she lost everything . . . She wants to get back into society, and she wants your help.' But Lady Windermere is adamant and her husband is not sure what to do: 'I dare not tell her who this woman really is', he says. 'The shame would kill her.'

The second act is set at the party. Among the guests are Darlington (who restates his love for Lady Windermere) and Lord Augustus Lorton, who is pursuing an affair with Mrs Erlynne. Lady Windermere is angered by the presence of Mrs Erlynne and her rapid acceptance by a number of society's scions. She is also disillusioned by her husband and tempted by Darlington, so much so that she leaves a note telling the former that she is leaving him for the latter. Mrs Erlynne discovers the note, and is horrified. 'Why do I remember now the one moment of my life I most wish to forget?' she says. 'Does life repeat its tragedies? . . . The daughter must not be like the mother—that would be terrible. How can I save her? How can I save my child?'[6] Mrs Erlynne decides to save her child by taking the note and a cab to Darlington's rooms. Here, in the play's penultimate act, she confronts Lady Windermere, burns the note and persuades her to return to her husband. At this point, Lords Darlington, Lorton and Windermere and a number of other aristocratic men turn up for a nightcap. But just as Windermere leaves, one of the men spots a fan and assumes that its owner has arranged an assignation with Darlington. The fan belongs to Lady Windermere. A scandal is in the offing, and at this point Mrs Erlynne enters, draws everyone's attention and claims that she took Lady Windermere's fan by mistake (thus implicitly confessing to a liaison with Darlington), in this way affording her daughter the chance to escape.

The fourth and final act takes place the following morning. Lord Windermere now views Mrs Erlynne as 'a worthless, vicious woman', but Lady Windermere is much more sympathetic, as is apparent when Mrs Erlynne calls to return the fan and say goodbye. Mrs Erlynne asks for a photograph of Lady Windermere and her child, and Lady Windermere willingly agrees. However, the only photograph she can find belongs to her husband, so Mrs Erlynne asks for and is given Lady Windermere's fan instead. At this point, Lorton arrives. He is delighted. Mrs Erlynne has explained that she went to Darlington's rooms because she had been unable to find Lorton at his club. 'She is just the woman for me', he says. 'All the conditions she makes are that we live entirely out of England. A very good thing too. Demmed clubs, demmed climate, demmed cooks, demmed everything. Sick of it all!'

The Lubitsch Film and the Ideal Version

In constructing their screenplay, Lubitsch and Josephson added a number of scenes and reordered a number of others. The film opens prior to Lady Windermere's birthday. Lady Windermere (May McAvoy) is at her desk planning the seating arrangements for a meal. She is trying to decide where to seat Lord Darlington (Ronald Coleman) when he himself arrives. Professing his love for her, he follows her from seat to seat around the room as she gently but firmly rebuffs him. In the meantime, Lord Windermere (Burt Lydell) is at his office desk pondering a request for a meeting in a letter signed by Mrs Edith Erlynne.[7] As Lady Windermere and Darlington enter, Lord Windermere tries to hide the letter (the hiding of letters and notes are as important in the film as they are in the play). Lady Windermere does not notice, but Darlington does, and assuming that Windermere is involved in an affair, and aware that he is trying to retrieve the letter without his wife noticing, Darlington nudges the letter into Windermere's hand, thus facilitating Windermere's departure and ensuring that Darlington will be alone with Windermere's wife for a while at least.

Along with dalliance and inference, 'deceptions and misapprehensions' and 'partial understandings and false viewpoints'[8]—all of them marked by irony, all of them dependent on omniscient narration and all of them involving the precise staging, framing and editing of shots—pervade the opening scene and establish many of the film's dominant devices and preoccupations. But the second scene, while also marked by irony, is much more concerned with sincerity and truth. Mrs Erlynne (Irene Rich) is sitting at her desk gazing at a photograph of Lady Windermere in a society magazine. She carefully removes the photograph, then turns to ponder the unpaid bills that litter her desk. Lord Windermere enters, brandishes the letter she has sent him and demands to know who she is. 'I am the mother of your wife', she replies, and as the remainder of the scene unfolds she offers proof and vows not to reveal the truth in return for his help in paying her bills and in providing a financial settlement sufficient to afford her the chance to re-enter society. Windermere agrees, and in exchange she offers him the photograph. He takes it, turns to leave, then has second thoughts and offers it back to her. She gratefully accepts, then puts it in her desk drawer and locks it.

There is no equivalent to this scene in the play, or to the later sequence that charts the evolving relationship between Mrs Erlynne and Lorton (Edward Martindel) via the latter's visits to the former's apartment, the racetrack sequence that precedes it or a later visit by Windermere in which Mrs Erlynne requests and is eventually promised an invitation to Lady Windermere's birthday party. There are, though, partial equivalents to the some of the scenes in Mrs Erlynne's apartment in the Ideal version (which sets them in a hotel suite), and an additional form of equivalence in the latter's opening scene, which at one point shows Mrs Erlynne in bed reading a society magazine, seeing a photograph of her daughter and recalling her past. The caption to the photograph notes that Lord Windermere has won a substantial sum of money at the racetrack. There is no racetrack sequence in the Ideal version, though there is in the Lubitsch version (as noted above). There is, however, a partial equivalence to it in the dog-show scene that follows Windermere's (much more hostile) visit to Mrs Erlynne's apartment in the Ideal film.

The racetrack sequence will be discussed in more detail below. The site of the initial meeting between Mrs Erlynne and Lorton, it leads on both to the latter's visits to the former's apartment and to the establishment of a relationship that serves in turn to motivate Lorton's help when Mrs Erlynne finds herself at her daughter's birthday's party with a written request from Windermere not to attend rather than the invitation she had been expecting and that he had agreed to earlier on. Windermere has changed his mind because, prompted by Darlington, Lady Windermere not only suspects that her husband is engaged in an affair, but also believes she has proof when she breaks into his (firmly locked) desk drawer and discovers the cheques he has been paying to and on behalf of Mrs Erlynne. Like the other desk-drawer sequences, this sequence underlines the importance of concealments and secrets. Its peculiarity, however, lies not in its narrative significance but in the way the events it involves are handled. While her husband is out at Mrs Erlynne's apartment, we witness Lady Windermere attempting to open the drawer. Having no apparent access to a key, she tries but fails to prise it open with a letter opener. At this point, she is interrupted by a visit from Lady Berwick (Carrie Daumery). The two of them converse, and we cut to Windermere and Mrs Erlynne (who at this point requests the invitation to the party), then to Windermere arriving home as Lady Berwick leaves. Windermere enters and finds his wife disturbed and angry, then notices that the drawer is ajar, walks across the room, pulls the drawer open and sees the cheques. We can only presume that the drawer has been forced by Lady Windermere—but we never know for sure.[9] In a film so heavily marked by elision and inference, this may have been an experiment in both that does not quite succeed. Either way, it concludes with a sequence of recrimination, embarrassment and anger that is one of the most touchingly acted, staged and edited scenes in the film. Beginning with a medium shot of Lady Windermere and her husband sitting silently side by side, the scene eventually ends with a pair of medium long shot singles: the first of Windermere visibly shaken, embarrassed and upset as he turns to the left, props himself against the door frame and lowers his head; the second of his wife as she rushes into frame from the left, throws herself onto an armchair, then buries her head in its arm on the right and sobs (Figures 1 and 2).

This scene is followed by the party scene. Its purport and overall shape are similar to the corresponding act in the play. Mrs Erlynne succeeds in flattering Lady Berwick, winning over her acolytes and attracting the attention of a number of upper-class men. Although she does not make a scene, Lady Windermere is still upset with her husband, angered by Mrs Erlynne's presence and increasingly tempted by Darlington's declaration of

Figure 1

Figure 2

love—so much so that she eventually decides to write her husband a note, pick up her fan, put on her coat and leave. However, there are number of changes in detail and substance. At one point in this scene in the play Mrs Erlynne dances with Lord Windermere (in order, she claims, to make Lord Lorton jealous). Potentially courting disapproval from audiences, this does not happen in the film. And in the film, but not in the play, Mrs Erlynne intervenes to persuade Windermere that his wife is in bed with a headache when in fact she is on her way to visit Darlington, thus trying to protect her daughter while making Windermere's concern for his wife evidence of genuine care.

It should also be noted that the set in the play contains an illuminated terrace towards the back of the stage on the right from the point of view of the play's spectators. In the play, some of the characters walk out onto the terrace and back; and in the Ideal version, the camera is placed at various points outside on the terrace itself as we cut back and forth between Darlington and Lady Windermere, Mrs Erlynne and Lorton, other pairs and groups outside and other guests in the drawing room inside. In the Lubitsch version, however, the exterior is opened out to include a large and spacious garden, which becomes, along with a much more spacious terrace, a major site of character interaction and misunderstanding as Darlington tries to persuade Lady Windermere to go away with him and as Lady Windermere later assumes, when she sees Mrs Erlynne in conversation with a hidden interlocutor, that she is talking to Lord Windermere when in fact she is talking to Lorton. As we cut back and forth between momentarily hidden characters, fully or partially visible ones, what they can and cannot see, and what they do or do not know, the sequence as a whole becomes not just an exemplary exercise in visual narration, but one of the film's most celebrated highlights.[10]

Acts Three and Four

The party scene is famous, not just because of the garden sequence, but because of the extent to which, as David Bordwell has pointed out, Lubitsch plays with the norms of framing. Thus, on the one hand, a number of improbable symmetries involving pairs of similarly clothed, posed or coiffed female guests pepper the drawing room when Mrs Erlynne first arrives, while, on the other, an unusually asymmetrical shot of one of Lady Berwick's cronies is matched later on by an equally asymmetrical shot of Lady Windermere.[11] However, perhaps because they seem less flamboyant, the film's remaining scenes and sequences have rarely been discussed. Act Three in the play is set solely in Darlington's rooms. But after a brief series of shots showing Lady Windermere arriving at Darlington's front door, pressing the doorbell and being let in by an unseen servant, Lubitsch cuts back to Windermere's house to show that the party is over, that guests are leaving and that Windermere is on his way to look in on his wife when he is waylaid by a group of men in gleaming black top hats, strikingly framed from above on the staircase.[12]

Only then do we return to Darlington's apartment, this time to show Mrs Erlynne's arrival. Like Lady Windermere before her, Mrs Erlynne presses the doorbell and is admitted by an unseen servant. Then we cut to an extreme long shot of an interior door as she enters one of Darlington's capacious rooms (Figure 3) and on to an equally extreme long shot of Lady Windermere sitting on a sofa on the other side of the room. Lady Windermere stands (Figure 4), and we cut back to Mrs Erlynne, who begins to walk towards her daughter, then on to a closer two-shot framing them both. Lady Windermere speaks, and Mrs Erlynne reveals Lady Windermere's note. We cut to a close-up of Lady Windermere, who is angry and shocked. Then we cut to a close-up of Mrs Erlynne, who speaks in reply, crosses the room in long shot and throws the note on the fire, giving rise to a number of wounding comments from Lady Windermere. Trying to ignore these comments (and hold back her tears), Mrs Erlynne tries to persuade Lady Windermere to leave before it is too late (Figures 5 and 6). However, just as she seems to be having second thoughts, Lady Windermere, who is now framed with Mrs Erynne in two-shot, appears to hear sounds from outside (Figure 7). We cut to the source of the sounds as a high-angle long shot shows an automobile drawing up outside. Framed from closer in, the women turn their heads in unison. We cut to an exterior shot of a window as Mrs Erlynne enters and looks down towards the street below. The automobile has come to a halt; Darlington and Windermere get out and stand on the pavement. As we cut back and

Figure 3

Figure 4

Figure 5   Figure 6

forth between window and street, Lady Windermere gazes in growing horror as she joins Mrs Erlynne in a two-shot to observe more and more men (all of them wearing gleaming black top hats) alight from a series of automobiles and gather below.

The women hide in the library as the men enter Darlington's apartment and begin to gather in the room next door. Mrs Erlynne looks through a keyhole—and sees Lady Windermere's fan lying on a sofa. Lorton sits down on the sofa, sees the fan and draws it to the attention of his host and fellow guests with a knowing smirk. Mrs Erlynne and Lady Windermere are terrified; Darlington is puzzled; and Windermere is stunned. Realizing what is at stake, Mrs Erlynne walks in from the room next door, finds herself flanked by Darlington's guests, picks up the fan and tells Windermere that she took it by mistake. A series of medium close-ups interleave shots of Mrs Erlynne with shots of Lorton (who is angry and upset), Windermere (who looks away in embarrassment) and Darlington (who is bewildered), before cutting to a shot of Lady Windermere leaving in haste, then back to Mrs Erlynne surrounded by men. The men peel away and begin to leave. Mrs Erlynne offers Windermere the fan. He

Figure 7

shakes his head in refusal. Then he shakes Darlington's hand, crosses the room to leave with Lorton and closes the door. Assuming that her relationship with Lorton is now at an end, Mrs Erlynne is inititally fearful, then resigned. Standing in a two-shot beside her, Darlington converses with her briefly, then averts his gaze, and we cut to a wider two-shot as she turns away and leaves.

The film's last scene is much shorter than the corresponding act in the play. It begins with the Windermeres sitting together at breakfast. Lady Windermere crosses the room and sits on her husband's lap. Lord Windermere is facing foreground left; Lady Windermere's head is on his shoulder facing away from the camera. Lord Windermere speaks: 'You were right about Mrs Erlynne', he says. 'She is thoroughly bad . . .' , and as we cut back and forth between close-ups of Windermere's contented expression and reverse-angle close-ups of his wife's wide-eyed face (Figures 8 and 9), we register not only the differences between what they know about events the previous evening, but also, as Lady Windermere returns to her seat and Mrs Erlynne is paged, the differences between what they know, what Mrs Erlynne knows and what we know. In contrast to the play, there are no requests for a photograph. Mrs Erlynne and Lady Windermere simply greet each other warmly in medium two-shot. Windermere leaves the room, and Mrs Erlynne returns the fan to Lady Windermere and proffers a word of advice: 'Don't tell him. You will kill his love—and spoil the only decent thing I ever did.' She says goodbye and leaves and we cut to a shot of her standing outside, then to a shot of Lorton on his way to Windermere's house. Lorton catches sight of Mrs Erlynne and is not best pleased. But Mrs Erlynne decides that attack is better than defence: 'Your conduct last night was outrageous!' she says. 'I have decided not to marry you.' Then she turns away and walks out of shot. Lorton stops and thinks. Mrs Erlynne is an attractive and spirited

Figure 8

Figure 9

woman; this may well be his last chance. He follows her over to her taxi cab and speaks to her, then he joins her in the cab and they drive off together.

I have dwelt on the framing of shots in these and earlier scenes because Lubitsch uses them to indicate the nature of the relationships between different characters at any one point in time. Hence the fluctuating two-shots and singles as Lady Windermere and Mrs Erlynne argue back and forth in Darlington's rooms—and hence the ubiquitous use of point-of-view shots to chart the numerous glances, looks and inferences that pepper the film throughout. As Kristin Thompson has pointed out, shots and framings such as these were underpinned by the practices of uncluttered set design, three-point lighting and continuity editing prevalent in Hollywood (but not in Germany) in the early- to mid-1920s.[13] Moreover, while Lubitsch's penchant for metaphorical, ironic and oblique representation had already been established before he went to Hollywood, the example set by Chaplin's *A Woman of Paris* (1923) helped him to hone his style—and in doing so to contribute to the cycle of 'sophisticated' comedies, farces and dramas that emerged in its wake.[14] To contemporary reviewers, Lubitsch's films were full of distinctive 'touches', concise, allusive or elliptical means of conveying narrative information and the feelings and thoughts of characters: repeated shots of doors and objects; repeated framings, actions and gestures; and repeated glances, stares, looks and point-of-view structures. Touches of this sort are nowhere more evident than in the racetrack sequence in *Lady Windermere's Fan*.

The Racetrack Sequence

As Musser points out, this particular sequence—the last to be filmed—was shot at the Woodbine racetrack in Toronto over several days in late September and early October 1925.[15] As he also points out, and as noted above, it appears to have been inspired by the scene in the Ideal version that is set at a dog show.[16] During the course of this scene, Lorton and Mrs Erlynne visit the show, and at one point we witness a woman gazing through a lorgnette at Mrs Erlynne as the latter walks off and out of frame left (Figure 10). Along with its public setting and a context involving the display of competing animals (along with the aforementioned reference to the Derby in the opening scene in the Ideal version), it is this particular shot that seems to have inspired not just the racetrack sequence but also the tropes of looking and being looked at that so clearly lie at its heart. As we shall see, lorgnettes are by no means the only optical devices used in the racetrack sequence (spectacles, binoculars and a mirror are used as

LADY WINDERMERE'S FAN (1925)

Figure 10

well). Nor are they confined to members of the crowd—Mrs Erlynne uses a lorgnette too.

Preceded by a title informing us that 'Thanks to Windermere's cheques, Mrs Erlynne lived in extravagant style—not accepted by society but the subject of its gossip', the sequence starts with five expository shots of the racetrack setting. The sixth shot begins with a view of a board listing runners and riders. Then the camera pans down right to a high-angle view of Mrs Erlynne framed from behind and surrounded by men (and a single woman). Most of the men turn to look at her one by one, but she ignores them as she turns towards the camera and walks into the foreground, gazing out of frame. Having mounted two sets of steps in a pair of consecutive long shots, she stops and looks around. We cut to a group of spectators sitting together in the stands. Three of them are men, three of them women, the former sat in a row behind the latter. They raise their binoculars in turn (thus recalling and underlying the tropes of intrusive observation that began in shot six). Then we cut back to Mrs Erlynne, who is now matted to simulate the view through a pair of binoculars as she scans the stands through her lorgnette. We cut back to the group. One of the women is now wearing spectacles. Then cut to a closer matted shot of Mrs Erlynne, and on to a shot of two men looking through binoculars, then back again to Mrs Erlynne, who is still matted but who is now framed in long shot from below. A shot of the race officials follows and one of them raises his binoculars. The other officials follow suit, and we cut to a series of matted shots of Mrs Erlynne looking through her lorgnette as a man and a woman in the crowd behind her raise their binoculars. We cut to a series of matted views linked by dissolves as Mrs Erlynne turns around and gazes through her lorgnette, puts her lorgnette down and inspects her appearance in the mirror in her handbag, puts her bag away, then turns around in a low-angle long shot and looks through her lorgnette again. Only then do we cut to a group shot of the Windermeres and their party; only then does an intertitle introduce us to Lorton; and only then do we move on to another segment.

Throughout the previous phase, Mrs Erlynne has been the principal object of attention as she searches for a glimpse of her daughter, and it is at this point that the focus shifts to the Windermeres and their party as they too become the object of optical scrutiny, and as discrepancies in awareness and knowledge build multi-layered tiers of ignorance, knowledge and irony. Thus although Mrs Erlynne spots Lady Windermere, Lady Windermere is unaware of her presence throughout, and while other members of the party respond to Mrs Erlynne's presence in a number of different ways, Lubitsch's narration makes clear who can see who, who cannot see who, and how and why they respond as they do. This is made clear in David Bordwell's account of this part of the segment:

> We can infer and compare characters' reactions: Mrs Erlynne would like to speak to Lady Windermere, Lord Windermere is anxious about her presence, and Lord Darlington begins to suspect a liaison between his friend and the mysterious Mrs Erlynne. The Lord Augustus Lorton notices Mrs Erlynne and, inferring that she is flirting with him, gives her a sly smile. When Mrs Erlynne sits, three gossips in the Windermere party [The Duchess of Berwick, Lady Plymdale and Mrs Cowper-Cowper] start to spy on her through binoculars [and a lorgnette]. They tell Lady Windermere to have a look, but then we see, from her vantage point, that two other spectators block the view. The narration thus distinguishes precisely what can and what cannot be seen from the adjoining seats. Then the gossips use their binoculars [and the lorgnette] to scrutinize Mrs Erlynne's one stray grey hair and her expensive ring, When Lord Windermere urges the women not to slander Mrs Erlynne, all members of the party look studiously down at their racing cards, at the cost of ignoring the race itself.[17]

The racetrack sequence concludes with a coda, a stationary shot of Lorton in pursuit of Mrs Erlynne as they cross the frame from right to left outside the racetrack, followed by a combined collapsing-matte-and-tracking shot as he begins to catch her up. In both these shots, the walls of the racetrack are peppered with advertising posters. Although they are much more mixed, these advertisements recall those that pepper the dog show scene in the Ideal version (see Figures 11 and 12). Whether they constitute clues to the source of the racetrack sequence itself will probably never be known. Whatever the case may be, though, they are as striking

LADY WINDERMERE'S FAN (1925)

Figure 11   Figure 12

and inventive as the collapsing-matte-and-tracking shot and, indeed, the other devices that make the racetrack sequence so special and distinctive.

Coda

Following *Lady Windermere's Fan*, *So This is Paris* was the last Lubitsch film to be produced and directed under the auspices of Warners. Lubitsch left Warners for MGM, and Warners embarked on its sound shorts, part-talkies and all-talking feature-length films. Then Lubitsch produced and directed a series of operettas for Paramount, all of which used sound, song and music to augment the oblique style that he had already honed in the silent era, and from this point he tended to work either for MGM or Paramount. Lubitsch died in 1947, and in 1949, Otto Preminger directed a version of *Lady Windermere's Fan* entitled *The Fan*. This version opened in London in 1949 and is structured by flashbacks; its initial scene takes place in an auction, and when we first see an ageing but sprightly Mrs. Erlynne (Madeleine Carroll), she is looking at Lady Windermere's fan through a lorgnette.

9

The Strong Man (1926)

Joe Kember

In a perceptive 1927 *Picturegoer* article on the recent release in Britain of the Harry Langdon vehicles *Tramp, Tramp, Tramp* (1926) and *The Strong Man*, staff writer Lionel Collier adopted an apparently paradoxical opinion of the comedian which, in various guises, has dominated assessments of Langdon's performances ever since. Although Langdon was 'irresistible', 'an absolute scream' and always dominated the scenes in which he starred, the means by which he did so seemed founded less on the customarily active business of comic stardom than on a kind of deliberate self-negation:

> Langdon's nervous methods indicate a philosophy of self-effacement. So ingrained is this trait that you feel he would hate to be famous, and that he is conscious to-day that he has butted into notoriety without wiping his feet on the map.[1]

According to this reading, and unlike the star personas and performances of Charlie Chaplin, Buster Keaton or Harold Lloyd, with whom Langdon was regularly contrasted, Harry's shtick, if he could be said to possess one, depended fundamentally on a kind of poetics of absence in which comic performance somehow emerged from the failure to communicate or indeed to be meaningfully engaged with the world around him at all. As Langdon himself explained in an article that revealed more about his comic persona than any general comedic principles: 'Any individual is comic who automatically goes his own way without troubling himself about getting in touch with the rest of his fellow beings.'[2]

In one emblematic scene in *The Strong Man*, for example, Langdon sets about the comic business of suffering from a bad cold on a crowded bus, a slender premise that enables him to play out his disconnection from others across eight and a half minutes of elaborate, impotent pantomime. Typically, rather than fitting smoothly into the action of the movie, the scene is 'announced' very obviously by the preceding intertitle, in which Langdon's boss and travelling companion, the strongman Zandow the Great (Arthur Thalasso), who sits in the cab with the driver, explains that it had been a 'dirty trip' and that he had given his 'boy' a bath the preceding night. This narrative cue is answered immediately by the following establishing shot, which frames Langdon's performance of 'having a cold' as if within a proscenium arch, with his character, Paul Bergot, posed frontally at one end of the coach (Figure 1).

The following sequence is instantly established by this shot as a more or less self-sufficient episode, with plenty of likely internal tensions: Paul's ailment is apparent at first glance; the bus is tightly packed, with four passengers to each side of him, exaggerating the problematic social etiquette of this constrained space; and Zandow's introduction has already suggested that Langdon's presence within it will be akin to that of an irritating child amongst adults. Given this densely populated and narratively loaded *mise en scène*, it might seem likely that interactions between fellow travellers will occupy much of the scene, or at least that the eight other individuals in the coach will serve as an onscreen audience for Langdon. However, we see surprisingly little of them en masse, since the scene is largely composed of alternating medium close-ups and close-ups of Langdon, who dominates almost every shot. Moreover, on the few occasions when the other passengers do engage our attention collectively, they are most often notable for their attempts to ignore the imbecile in their midst: one reads a newspaper, another reads a book, others gaze in any direction other than at Paul. All conduct themselves in a manner that seeks to exclude him from the social space of the bus. Only when forced by

Figure 1

Paul's more violent ejaculations (his theatrical sneezes, his wide-mouthed coughs, his snorts and scratches) do we get a collective reaction shot of the passengers, who respond with outright displays of disgust and rejection. Later on, following a gag involving Limburger cheese, they seek to eject him, brutally, from the bus, moving as one to kick him off it. However, in Langdon's world, all such gestures are pointless: Paul rarely notices explicit social rejection, and when thrown from the bus he plummets down a hill only to land back in the coach in exactly the same position as before, gazing in prototypical bewilderment.

This sequence clearly exemplifies the 'Harry' persona. Personable and well intentioned, he is also unreservedly feckless, lacking the facility and initiative to recognize the problems that beset him or to take positive decisions that might improve his position. Yet the world shifts beneath him, most often in his favour, moving the narrative forward without any effective input from its leading protagonist. At the same time, the staging and framing of the action ensures that the audience's attention remains almost exclusively fixed on his gestures, and especially his face, as if it had something significant to express. As Joanna Rapf explains in one of the more recent echoes of Collier's reading, Langdon's films are characterized by 'long scenes in which absolutely nothing happens' except for the exhibition of 'virtuoso performance technique':

> His is a non-generative comic style that is all about what one might call 'performance'. Performance covets immediacy, delights in virtuosity, and captures the resonance of the moment and the timeless realm of dreams. In some ways it is the difference between 'art for humanity's sake' (Chaplin, perhaps) and 'art for art's sake'. In this, Langdon's eloquent pauses are akin to what we experience when listening to music, where we are not concerned with pushing through to the end, where we revel in the beauty and artistry of the moment, in a flow that does not have to take us anywhere in particular.[3]

To some extent this reading of Langdon's technique as a form of 'play' and 'flow', likened both to the appreciation of music and to the experience of dreaming, explains the pleasures to be gained from watching such a scene. Certainly, nothing narratively significant happens: Paul's cold is not referred to before or after the episode; the other characters in the bus play no further part in the film; indeed, the entire scene could have been cut from the film without any damage to its principal storyline. Its comedy therefore emerges from our moment-to-moment reactions to

Langdon's restricted arm movements and astonishingly mobile face. These create a fascinating and funny internal economy of their own (one might compare such scenes with non-narrative films of variety performances, which had been popular from the late 1890s and which also tended to present performance as a self-sufficient spectacle within static theatrical framings), and it is this that differentiates Langdon's performances from those that are more transparent and narrative-driven, this that motivates his character's social isolation—his failure to connect with others or to make an effective impact on his world. Whereas the other characters on the bus are engaged in the future-oriented business of travelling from New York to Cloverdale and in the attempt to make the journey as comfortable as possible, Paul seems locked into an eternal present, constantly prey to immediate and unfiltered physical sensations, nervous impulses and unknowable drives, all of which end up written fleetingly across his face.

More than an object of 'musical' appreciation, I would argue that Langdon's face on such occasions presents audiences with a prolonged opportunity to study his expressions, and that a great part of the pleasure of this scene is bound up with the challenge of deciphering Paul's capricious moods and dispositions. Indeed, the scene provides us with at least one model for this type of investigative activity: unlike the other passengers, the man sitting immediately to Paul's left as the scene begins stares fixedly at Paul's face as it undergoes its rapid transitions, an attitude repeated in a series of two-shots when Paul attempts to swallow unpalatable medicine, removes a mustard plaster from his chest and applies Limburger to his chest instead of the ointment he intends (Figure 2). Besides serving to characterize the growing distaste for these unsavoury goings-on, the prolonged period of staring-at-attention that marks it also serves to prompt the spectator's curiosity. Like Gertrude Astor's vamp, who appears in an earlier scene, and a long line of other Langdon antagonists, the stranger expresses excessive verbal and physical hostility to Paul. But unlike the

Figure 2

other antagonists in this scene, he also attempts to understand Paul, rather than simply excluding him. His unwavering gaze reflects unflatteringly on the invasiveness and persistence of our own attempts to read Paul's character from his face, triggering the sense of pathos that nearly always accompanies Langdon's comedy.

Of course, as Carl Plantinga, Murray Smith and others have shown, the ability to read facial expressions and to 'catch' emotions from them via processes of emotional contagion play a prominent role in all forms of character-driven cinema.[4] These are skills that we customarily acquire as socially functional individuals in the course of everyday life. Langdon, however, routinely exposes the fact that his characters have never figured this out and thus that they repeatedly fail to control and channel emotion. Hence, in spite of the expression of an astonishing array of facial registers during the bus episode, Paul fails to enter into the routine exchange of glances that might otherwise have characterized the scene. Moreover, prompted by extensive and apparently unmotivated close-ups of Paul's mobile features, as well as by the unfriendly attention of the hostile stranger, we as spectators undergo a uniquely intensive experience of face reading as we speculate on the significance of Paul's facial registers—a very different proposition from the transparent expressions and overt emotions associated with the performances of Chaplin or Lloyd.

The Trouble with Harry

As Collier and Rapf suggest, this episode is far from unusual among Langdon's films. The 'Harry' persona, fully formed by the time it featured in *The Strong Man*, was fundamental to their structure, and its characteristics are easy to identify: Harry is almost always present on the screen and humour emerges primarily from his mastery of bodily gesture while, at the same time, nothing, besides Harry's persistent bewilderment and failure to connect, seems to happen. His film-making career had begun with a series of shorts for Mack Sennett in 1924, much later than other major slapstick comedians. Later that year, Tamar Lane had noted that, in contrast to Lloyd and Keaton, Langdon did not depend upon 'outside props and gags' for his comic business; instead, 'the greater percentage of his humor *comes from within*'.[5] Unlike Keaton's trademark blend of practical intelligence and chronic absent-mindedness, which was carried principally in his relationship to narrative and to the immediate features of his *mise en scène*, in the case of Langdon, 'the comedian's own facial expressions and reactions to the scene' tended to dominate.[6] First National's advertising campaign for *The Strong Man* emphasized similar qualities: Langdon's 'facial contortions', his presence 'alone on screen for long periods' and the 'pathetic something' in his performance, 'which arouses sympathy'.[7]

Langdon's characteristic style was self-referential and centripetal, and his emphasis on performance was cited by several writers as evidence of his genius, leading to frequent comparisons with Chaplin.[8] For some critics, Langdon's comedy, like Chaplin's, was even understood to typify the most vital aspects of American character and ambition: 'Harry Langdon is infinitely more than a man; he is a symbol of America and the motion picture. A symbol of persistency and the victory of a dreamer.'[9] Meanwhile, surrealist artists and critics in Europe, including Salvador Dali and Luis Buñuel, believed that Langdon represented a new and exemplary vehicle for the dream-like immediacy and anti-logical stubbornness that they had earlier found in Chaplin.[10]

Alongside these positive responses were others that emphasized the unbalanced, disjointed or claustrophobic narratives that Langdon's performance style also seemed to create. This became increasingly apparent between 1926 and 1928, when seven Langdon features were hurriedly released, seeking to capitalize on the Harry craze. The first three to be released, *Tramp, Tramp, Tramp*, *The Strong Man* and *Long Pants*, were mostly positively received (though only *The Strong Man* made a notable profit). But the next three, *Three's a Crowd*, *The Chaser* and *Heart Trouble* (1928), received mixed reviews and made a loss. The seventh feature, *His First Flame*, was in fact the first to be filmed, though its release was delayed until 1927, at which point it contributed to Langdon's overexposure and helped cement his decline.

Led by Frank Capra's influential but notoriously unreliable reminiscences, this change in Langdon's fortunes has often been read as a cautionary tale for aspiring stars whose creative ambitions outstretched their creative talents. According to this account, Langdon fired Capra (and an extensive retinue of gag-men) from the set of *Three's a Crowd*, assumed control of production and direction, and thus occasioned a series of commercial and critical flops. Gertrude Astor later recalled that Langdon had depended entirely upon Capra's direction, claiming that between takes he 'would wander a block away and sit alone on a bench until Frank Capra needed him for a scene' and that he preferred to retreat 'into his private world of silence' rather than engage with those on set.[11] Capra expanded on this characterization in several publications from the late 1940s onwards, and James Agee's description borrowed strongly from these, furnishing a generation of critics with an easy analogy: Langdon was 'almost as childlike as the character he played'.[12] In Capra's 1971 autobiography, *The Name Above the Title*, Langdon is denigrated as little more than an adept performer of pantomime, with no understanding of the significance of effective storytelling and direction.

Since Joyce Rheuban's landmark 1983 reassessment of Langdon's work, Capra's account has usually been rejected as unfair and self-serving by film historians and biographers, who have accused him of deliberately conflating the 'simp' Harry persona with Langdon himself in order to exaggerate the impact of his departure on Langdon's fortunes.[13] This story neatly elides a range of other factors in Langdon's decline, not the least of which were contractual difficulties with First National and an overabundance of Langdon's features.[14] Nevertheless, there are indications that the basic conflict between Langdon's performances and the demands of effective storytelling had been a bone of critical contention throughout the comedian's silent film career. Reviews of Langdon's work had always been divided between those that found the films static, poorly plotted or plain half-baked and those that emphasized their episodic structure and the independent charms of Langdon's languid pantomime. The US trade journal *Motion Picture News* recognized that well-executed Langdon films, such as the three-reel *Saturday Afternoon* (1926), were 'well adapted to the eccentricities of this droll comedian'.[15] However, it also advised exhibitors that their audiences would find *Long Pants* to be 'a little lengthy and repetitious', and recommended that their promotional efforts should 'feature the gags' rather than the story and 'play up the pathos'.[16] Laurence Reid, a regular reviewer for *Motion Picture News*, lavished praise on *The Strong Man*'s bus scene, which he claimed 'makes the most of [Langdon's] expressive pantomime'.[17] His advice to exhibitors about the film was heavily qualified by his criticism of its episodic structure: the movie was ultimately little more than 'a series of strung-together gags' and these 'aren't tied together very strongly'—though fortunately 'no-one will pay attention to its flaws, so sure is its comedy'.[18] Only two years into Langdon's film career, this type of equivocation was already a familiar trend in critical responses to Langdon's features, and it would come to dominate criticism in the years that followed; indeed, the notion that Langdon movies were little more than opportunities to showcase his performances would dog him for the remainder of his career, ultimately coming close to destroying his reputation altogether.

Sympathetic commentators in the fan magazines were similarly conflicted, though they also tended to ape studio publicity in playing up Langdon's virtuosic performances and effective evocation of pathos. The *Motion Picture Magazine* found in Langdon a comedian 'who knows how to blend the pathos with the fun—if his wistful expressions and bashful gestures are any criterion',[19] later describing an audience at the Mark Strand Theatre as 'convulsed, ransacked, doubled-over with mirth at Harry Langdon in *The Strong Man*', even though the reviewer himself 'felt more like weeping over the mishaps of the futile little fellow'.[20] For Collier, writing at the height of Langdon's career, the comedy of self-effacement proved compelling for audiences because it conveyed 'the unassuming fortitude that the modest citizen assumes when his hat has been crushed beneath a brewer's dray', evoking in them a 'fellow-feeling of the average man' far removed from the athleticism of Lloyd or Keaton, or the performative precision of Chaplin.[21] *Three's a Crowd*, according to an extended review in *Hollywood Vagabond*, was 'built around Harry and it loses none of its value for that fact. There are certain scenes that are carried by Langdon alone that can be classified as the high spots of this picture.'[22] Even Langdon's final silent feature, *Heart Trouble*, the flop which finally ended his starring career, received some equivocal recommendation in the *Motion Picture Magazine*: 'if Harry's futile ways still make a joint attack on your heart and sense of humor, this will do as well as any'.[23] Nevertheless, the majority of reviews for Langdon's final features played up the problematic consequences of building a movie around Harry. *Photoplay* condemned *The Chaser* as 'just a series of gags with little or no story',[24] while *The Film Spectator* was more explicit, connecting this problem, as Capra later did, to Langdon's failure as a film-maker:

> The spectacle of Langdon insisting upon writing his own stories and directing them is a sad one. There was a time when he had the reputation for knowing something about acting. His lamentable failure as the master of his own destiny is creating the impression that he doesn't know much about anything.[25]

Such rhetoric certainly became more charged and spiteful following the Capra affair, but it did not represent a sea change in criticism about Langdon; rather, it perpetuated and extended the familiar and reasonable critique that Langdon's performances, while brilliant, were often played out to the detriment of his feature-length narratives. In this sense, we might regard Langdon's features as exemplary comedian comedies: more than any of his contemporaries, his success or failure turned on his ability to sustain his enigmatic, unsettlingly mobile, but bizarrely magnetic performance style across a full eighty minutes, even in spite of the narratives designed to contain them. The balance customarily achieved by other comedians between storytelling and delivering gags was therefore routinely overturned in Langdon's features. Instead, the nature of his self-referential gags left him purposefully isolated from the story world, leaving audiences with the primary pleasure of reading the intricate detail of his performance—always provided that they were willing and able to undertake this unusual and intimate task.

Reading Harry

Summarizing the argument thus far, one might usefully borrow terms from Roland Barthes to suggest that Langdon's performances tended to engage less than was customary with the proairetic code of narrative progression than with hermeneutic codes that presented audiences with a series of enigmas. This is a relatively unusual strategy for texts in any classical narrative tradition and it helps to explain the deeply felt exasperation with Langdon that emanates from so many of his critiques. Not only was this type of intensive character reading relatively demanding, requiring its spectators to scrutinize the details of performance in order to glean their significance, but it was frequently frustrating, since more often than not Langdon's swiftly changing expressions did not lead to any conclusive understanding of the character or of his world. This type of guessing game is inherent to most protracted Harry episodes, but it has also inspired numerous attempts to define the 'essential' Harry persona. In contrast to Rapf, these accounts recognize that Harry is never doing nothing and that his remarkable facial mobility betrays a restless agency at work. What requires explanation is his failure nevertheless to act upon the world around him.

Most pervasive among these explanations are those that have characterized Harry as a child or infant, repeating *Photoplay*'s 1926 assertion that he had 'gone younger' than the other film comedians.[26] In doing so, they have followed the cue of Langdon's Capra-directed movies, not least *Long Pants*, which presents Harry in a coming-of-age scenario, and *Tramp Tramp Tramp*, which concludes with a bizarre tableau of Harry playing his own baby. *Photoplay* added a further assessment, however, that tallied more closely with the 'simp' persona that Langdon had crafted during his years in vaudeville: 'In brief, he is the eternal moron.'[27] Among more recent variants of this kind of reading, Joyce Rheuban has argued that Harry is best explained as an individual suffering from cognitive or motor impairment of some kind, 'whose rational faculties are almost totally subordinated to sleep, dreams, hallucinations, alcohol and drug induced intoxication, and semi-conscious dazes induced by physical blows or by a woman's kiss';[28] Alan Bilton contends that Harry seems to suffer from a form of physical disorientation that has left him stranded between sleep and waking life, further arguing that this can be seen as psychological symptom of shell shock;[29] and Seth Soulstein endorses the surrealist admiration for Langdon's anti-rational, naive, man-child or sleepwalker persona.[30] Finally, in his analysis of Langdon's performance style, Noël Carroll notes a number of these and other features in turn: his 'inability to execute movements precisely . . . as if, to a certain extent, the character is not in complete control of his body'; his embodiment of 'the slowest thinker in film history'; and his 'revelation of the child in the man, that is, of the child's gestures in the man's body'.[31]

Each of these arguments has proven highly productive, having quite different consequences for our understanding of the humour and morality at work in these films. The Harry-as-infant reading, for example, tends to foreground the darker sexual undertones of several of the films, especially in Harry's encounters with various vamps. The shell-shock reading leads to an emphasis on wartime scenes in several of the films, notably *The Strong Man*, which opens with the 'dough-faced doughboy', Paul Bergot, lost in no man's land somewhere in Belgium.[32] However, close analysis of Langdon's performances tends to suggest that, for all their explanatory power, these potential metanarratives in fact mark branching, transient possibilities in the ongoing series of speculations that the viewer customarily engages in when viewing Harry's face. Thus, in returning to the bus scene in *The Strong Man*, what seems most striking is the range of dispositions Paul's predicament allows Langdon to express and the speed with which he moves from one to another. The opening two minutes are, as noted above, largely dedicated to Paul's discomfort, and we watch as he is repeatedly roused from a heavy-lidded, semi-conscious state (Figure 3) to work through each symptom in turn, first coughing, then sneezing, probing his swollen parotid glands, unblocking his ears and scratching at his itchy nose. His cold clearly provides enough motivation to justify his dreamlike disconnection from his surroundings. But the sneezes

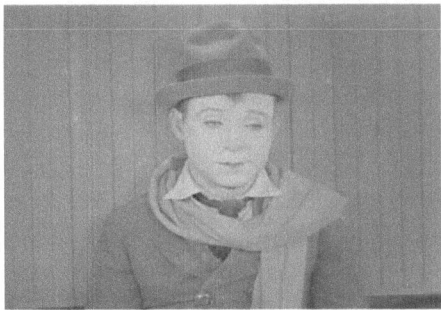

Figure 3

Figure 4   Figure 5

that punctuate the scene permit a subtle, ephemeral switch in this mode of performance, taking him by surprise as they might an infant, and momentarily awakening him to his surroundings (Figure 4). Later in the scene, Paul will react in a similar though exaggerated fashion to other basic physical stimuli, such as the ripping of the mustard plaster from his chest and especially the clearing of his sinuses, at which point his face becomes a picture of dreamy, physical delight (Figure 5). Indeed, it is in this spirit of open-eyed naivety that Paul interacts with the other passengers on the coach, responding with little more than a blank glance to the intensely hostile scrutiny to which his neighbour is subjecting him, and innocently asking the time of passengers who have already signalled their collective antipathy towards him. These occasional attempts at communication are perhaps the strongest markers of the pathos embedded in such scenes, for Harry's gestures are nothing if not open and supplicatory. Nevertheless, they prompt little fellow-feeling in his travelling companions and rarely occasion the shot reverse shot exchange of complementary glances we might expect.

During the following two minutes, this dynamic is intensified as Harry attempts to take medicine. First, his childish reluctance to swallow a pastille is followed by a further moment of wide-eyed physical surprise as he momentarily acts out the sensation of feeling it slipping down his throat. But the swallowing of a liquid medicine presents a far greater challenge, his fear of the spoon captured across a lengthy static shot that only ends when he sneezes the medicine all over the hostile stranger. Good boy that he is, Harry immediately attempts to clean up the mess with his handkerchief, and the ensuing fracas sees him run frantically through an array of facial expressions in a little over thirty seconds: from surprise at the sneeze (Figure 6) to relief that the medicine has disappeared (Figure 7), to consternation over its new location all over the stranger's suit (an upset mildly softened by occasional coughing and nose-wiping) (Figure 8), to glimmers of hurt and rejection as the stranger pushes him away and

THE STRONG MAN (1926)

Figure 6

Figure 7

Figure 8

Figure 9

Figure 10

commences a sustained verbal barrage (Figure 9). In one especially potent moment, Harry even turns to address the other passengers in what looks like the beginning of an appeal for clemency (Figure 10). But, as always, this is to no avail. As is often the case during Harry's episodes of stress or confusion, each of these attitudes seldom endures for more than a few seconds, though each will sometimes reappear several times, marking his inability to adopt any stable subject position that might permit him to communicate effectively with others.

The scene's structure, thus far, has been almost entirely dictated by Langdon's performance, with the intensifying facial action captured throughout by a series of long and static takes. This trend recommences in the following sequence, though here Rheuban's reading of Harry's cognitive and motor impairment seems more appropriate than variants on the man-child trope. Harry is always remarkably slow to rouse, and here his obliviousness to the hostile stranger's harangue (and to a couple of gags at his expense delivered by intertitle) provides a good example of his delayed reactions. Eventually provoked, he responds with a typically ineffectual punch, but even the immediate, adrenalin-driven stimulus of anger is somehow deferred: his face freezes into a mask-like caricature of fury, his gaze finally directed back at his enemy across two static shots that last for an endless fifteen seconds before the blow is delivered. Following the brief scuffle that ensues, the camera dwells for a further forty-five seconds as his anger subsides. The hostile stranger, who immediately settles back to grumpily reading his newspaper, provides a good point of comparison here: Harry does not seem to have an intermediate disposition such as 'grumpy' in his emotional vocabulary, so his face passes back and forth between his anger mask and his earlier, heavy-lidded despondency, his fist rising to renew the attack and falling again to match this tidal facial routine (Figures 11 and 12). Elaborating upon this odd disconnection between Harry's internal agency and his expressive actions, one might well speculate here upon the relationship between this performance and the compulsive, repetitive symptoms of some forms of shell shock.

The internal complexity of episodes such as this is borne almost exclusively by Langdon's performance, and especially by his face. These scenes are notable, therefore, for the extent to which they exploit native face-reading skills, calling upon spectators to decipher Harry's internal condition from his puzzlingly inconsistent exterior. Other scenes in *The Strong Man* deliver up a similar blend of ephemeral facial theatrics and mask-like grimaces. However, the effect in each case is subtly varied, providing room for different forms of speculation which, in turn, constitute the emotional movement we experience during the film. In

Figure 11   Figure 12

the opening scene, for example, even the experience of being shot at in no-man's land barely stirs Paul from the lethargic, unfocused gaze he maintains throughout; indeed, the entire scene dramatizes his failure to pay attention to the salient features of his surroundings. Only the arrival of a letter from his American sweetheart, Mary Brown (Priscilla Bonner), focuses his attention for a significant period, generating an emotional clarity absent from the remainder of the scene as his face passes from expressions of delight to dreamy anticipation. Similar expressions will recur in the later New York episode, when Paul misrecognizes Astor's vamp as Mary. Here, though, his facial register shifts abruptly from expressive delight to a mask of abject terror when he starts to suspect her of barely-guessed-at, dark sexual motives. Significantly, when Paul finally stumbles upon the real Mary and discovers that she is blind, this initiates his one sustained episode of emotionally lucid characterization, his face eloquently expressing attachment as he regales her with tales of his attempts to find her and finds that she reciprocates (Figure 13). His performance here shifts decisively into a Chaplinesque mode of repartee, akin to the Tramp's romance with the blind flower girl (Virginia Cherrill) in *City Lights* (1931), and replete with expressive leg swings, gleeful wide-eyed supplication and shared fun.

Thus, although Paul plays no intentional part in directing the journey from Belgium to New York to small-town America that will ultimately lead him to Mary—he is dragged there by Zandow—it is Langdon's face that reminds us of the emotional orientation of the narrative. Independent episodes such as those on the bus, in no-man's land or with Lily in New York, which are largely carried by our fascination with Langdon's multifaceted pantomime, therefore intensify the emotional resonance of his eventual unification with Mary. It is this long-desired goal that stimulates Paul's emergence into conventional facial transparency and Langdon's adoption of a recognizable variant of comic stardom.

Figure 13

Langdon's Scenes of Isolation

Langdon episodes such as those in *The Strong Man* can be instructively compared with what Plantinga calls the 'scene of empathy' in classical narrative film. Citing a range of scenes, including the celebrated ending of *City Lights*, Plantinga argues that these moments occasion a pause in the narrative during which 'the interior emotional experience of a favoured character becomes the locus of attention'.[33] Crucially, these scenes are designed to take full advantage of the face-reading skills most of us already possess, giving them a degree of independence from the narrative:

> Closeups of protagonists' emotional faces are often presented for much longer than is necessary for the mere communication of emotion, or for the cogitation necessary to comprehend the character's situation. In such cases their purpose must be to promote spectator empathy through facial feedback and emotional contagion.[34]

Langdon's scenes frequently provide audiences with longer than necessary opportunities to examine his face, but they rarely allow us to settle on an emotional theme that might evoke empathy in this way. Instead, Harry's face is notable for the variety of dispositions it expresses and for its persistent failure to express the individual-expressive mode of performance we have come to expect from classical cinema. In place of this, it most often substitutes a full vocabulary of what we might call 'weakly expressive' performance styles, often deploying one after another in an attempt to ape the normative performances of the characters that surround him. Thus, in place of Harry the adult, conscious, socially functional individual, we see a succession of poorly emoting faces: infant or baby face, dough face, sleepwalker face, mask face, grimace face, debility or illness face, and so on. Pathos emerges from the failure of each of these variants to live up to the affective promise of the fully empathetic face, which stars such as Chaplin routinely delivered, leaving Harry effectively isolated from the social environments of his films.

Langdon's peculiar form of versatility was premised to a large extent by the designedly vacant thematics of his face. Even straight publicity shots reveal it as a relatively featureless expanse, with the large eyes standing out and other features minimized, the mouth and eyebrows narrow horizontals, wrinkles or other signs of skin texture and coloration entirely absent (Figure 14). Missing the obvious markers of age which we might call 'character' or 'experience', the large eyes easily evoke the idea of the child; however, in motion, the face's minimal features are precisely

THE STRONG MAN (1926)

Figure 14

calculated to permit a much more inclusive range of weakly expressive modes of performance while resisting the more definitive, individual-expressive forms of characterization that might emerge from sensual or drawn lips, from a furrowed forehead or laughter lines, or from rosy or sallow cheeks. Most often during performance, the individual-expressive mode develops only fleetingly across these features, occurring when Harry attempts to make some form of contact with the characters that observe him from such an emotional distance. Scenes such as Paul's first romantic encounter with Mary Brown, which most closely resemble traditional scenes of empathy, provide a relatively unusual payoff in Langdon's work, and this goes some way towards explaining the regular complaints made about his fragmented narratives. Langdon's characters rarely proved capable of completely growing up, rousing themselves from their torpor or overcoming their cognitive deficiencies in order to demonstrate emotional and practical competence. In this sense, they remained eternally in stasis, incapable of generating the sustained emotional allegiance with audiences that might permit them to evolve and becoming apt objects, instead, for the emergence of curiosity, pathos or sheer exasperation.

The Chaser, for example, prompted perhaps the most hostile press of Langdon's feature career. The premise of this film differed slightly from that in earlier films, playing directly upon Harry's effeminacy rather than his childishness or semi-consciousness, with the comic business emerging from a divorce court judgment that Harry must switch roles with his shrewish wife (Gladys McConnell) in order to learn the meaning of responsibility in marriage. But the episodes comprising this film demonstrate repeatedly that he is incapable of such learning, and also that he cannot accomplish the bullish mastery that the movie imagines as an ideal form of manhood. Its lumpish critique of women's growing prominence in the professional workplace and the presumed effeminization of men is therefore incomplete. Instead, the film repeatedly stages variants of *The Strong Man's* bus scene, with Harry's incompetent performances of adult, male, conscious selfhood rigorously scrutinized by a series of onscreen antagonists. These antagonists are characterized much more extensively than in *The Strong Man*, with protracted shots emphasizing their confident, but malign self-possession in close-up and offering a powerful contrast to poor, isolated Harry. The pattern is established strikingly in *The Chaser's* opening sequence, in which first the wife, then her mother (Helen Hayward), then both together are depicted in medium close-up and close-up delivering a hideous tirade down the telephone. Following a full seventy seconds of this unbroken and rather disturbing display of animosity, the husband, Harry, is inevitably revealed at the other end of the line, deeply entrenched in his semi-conscious state and only occasionally roused by the volume or pitch of his assailants into ephemeral moments of expressiveness.

This type of scenario will be repeated, with variations, throughout the film: when Harry returns home to face the music; when he is depicted in court as an object of derision for wife, mother-in-law and judge (Charles Thurston); when he encounters the amorous intentions of a series of tradesmen (who are unaccountably confused by the pinafore he has been forced to wear by the terms of the judgment); and when admonished by his buddy (Bud Jamison) that he must get back into his pants and 'Be a man before your voice changes'. Once again, emotional disturbance and confusion inspire the film's most dynamic facial episodes, though in this case much of this action takes place during the inordinate amount of time Harry occupies the screen alone; in these scenes, long takes of his performances and a surprising number of direct gazes at the camera invite the audience to play the role of interrogator. During one fascinating sequence, roused from his torpor by a tradesman's kiss, Harry decides that suicide is his best option, but fails to shoot, poison and hang himself in turn. The scene, much criticized in the press for its poor taste and bleak, broad humour, provides an exquisite example of Langdon's face-play, allowing him to run through a full gamut of weakly expressive gestures in succession, varying from decisive bravado as he confronts himself in the mirror to abject terror when he considers the instruments of his demise. Indeed, at points such as that at which Harry convinces himself to swallow the castor oil he believes to be poison, the transitions between these and other dispositions are handled so quickly that they become overstrained and almost impossible to read. The interminable forty-five second scene

THE STRONG MAN (1926)

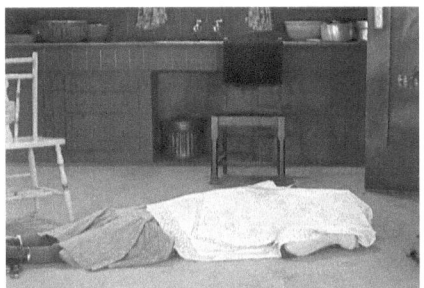

Figure 15

which follows, in which Harry lies still on the floor waiting for death, his face and body covered by a sheet, not only postpones the inevitable castor-oil/laxative gag, but also has a further structural role to play. For some minutes, Harry's face has been becoming progressively more mobile and less comprehensible, reaching a pitch of intensity we might regard as a type of facial 'white noise'; now, covered by the sheet, it disappears altogether, visibly absent on the screen for a protracted period—a perfect image of dissolution (Figure 15).

The Harry of *The Chaser* derives no reward for his efforts to act on the world around him; rather, the film's central episode depicts him at his most detached, his hyper-mobile face passing first into a cacophonous illegibility, then into absence. This creates a profound sense of isolation within the scene, even for Langdon, since his characteristic evocation of pathos has been deliberately stymied. *The Strong Man* is less radical than this because it always encourages spectators to share in the challenge of interpreting Langdon's inept facial routines and to develop sympathy for an individual who seems systemically unable to act effectively on the world around him. Equally, *The Strong Man* ultimately rewards spectators with the triumphant emergence of competent selfhood when Paul Bergot enters into a reciprocal and emotionally articulate relationship with Mary Brown. This is a form of social contract expanded in the film's closing shots, when Paul reappears as the town's unlikely (and again, strikingly Chaplinesque) new sherriff. Nonetheless, Langdon's extended scenes of isolation in this film retain their power to unsettle as well as amuse an audience. Confronted with a face that failed, most of the time, to emote in a familiar or conventional manner, spectators are also implicated in a series of difficult social interactions. Like the passengers on the bus, who are in an awkward social position we all recognize, we are required to work hard if we wish to decipher Langdon's ineffectual facial communications. The alternative is troubling for another reason: we may decide, instead, to avert our eyes.

10

Miss Mend (1926)

Vincent Bohlinger

A coffin bearing the body of a murdered man travels on a ship across the ocean on a voyage home to New York. In rough seas, the coffin overturns and the corpse begins to move. The man is alive, and he is terrified. He is discovered by his wife—technically, his second wife—and she fearfully reports back to her husband's assistant, who is both her lover and the would-be murderer. The once-dead man is quickly recaptured and seemingly murdered again, as his corpse is then displayed at a funeral stateside. But the body is snatched from its tomb, and we witness the man's resurrection yet again before he is killed for one final time. A female employee of the dead man, the eponymous Miss Mend, contests the man's will, claiming that he has fathered another son. Moments later she is struck over the head with an iron rod and her unconscious body is thrown into the Hudson River, where she is rescued by three male admirers. A young boy, the purported second heir to the man's fortune, is lured away by the prospect of seeing an elephant, but is then released after being given a poisoned apple. Miss Mend finds her way to the police station to retrieve the boy, but it is too late: he has already bitten the apple and drops dead upon her arrival.

    For those of us weaned on the likes of Sergei Eisenstein's *Battleship Potemkin* (1925), *Miss Mend*, a 1926 Soviet trilogy of feature-length films directed by Fedor Otsep and Boris Barnet, must seem curiously un-Soviet. The descriptive summary provided above covers less than half the story: additional events include a handful of other murders, a barroom brawl, a collision between a car and a locomotive, and an elaborate chase on foot, horseback and automobile. Still to come are mass murders involving chemical and biological weapons, along with scenes of impersonation, hypnosis, imprisonment and torture—not to mention a suicide and a poorly timed enema. Outlandish and zany in any context, a narrative such as this must seem especially unusual—far less Soviet and far more akin to what Ben Singer has described as the sensational 'blood-and-thunder' melodramas common to the USA in the 1910s.[1] Yet *Miss Mend* represents, or perhaps epitomizes, a film-making practice that existed alongside Soviet montage film-making in the 1920s.

Soviet films such as *Miss Mend* have long been overlooked in favour of the montage classics that are now taught in practically every introductory course on film history. In his canon-forming *The Film Till Now* (initially published in 1949 and revised in 1960), Paul Rotha describes Fedor Otsep, the principal director of *Miss Mend*, as 'not a director of any standing, his work being uneven and lacking in dramatic quality'.[2] Rotha groups Otsep with co-director Boris Barnet as 'second and third-rate directors', whom he characterizes as 'not of unusual consequence'.[3] Meanwhile, in his field-defining *Kino* (initially published in 1960 and revised in 1983), Jay Leyda makes only a single brief reference to *Miss Mend*, which he calls a 'good start', before grouping it with other films he labels as 'scattered jobs' and 'signs of . . . demise'.[4] While we may question the value judgement and reasoning of Rotha and Leyda, they are hardly alone. Film historians have collectively demonstrated a much more sustained interest in those Soviet films that we now consider overtly *Soviet*. Indeed, Leyda's lone comment on *Miss Mend* feels merely like an aside amidst the half-dozen pages devoted to *Potemkin*, *Mother* (1926) and *The End of Saint Petersburg* (1927).

In her book *Movies for the Masses*, Denise Youngblood has helped to refocus critical attention on the alternative film-making that coexisted alongside Soviet montage within the greater context of Soviet audiences' affection and preference for Western, and particularly American, movies and stars. She followed up this pioneering study on the influences of Soviet popular cinema with an exploration of the notion of 'Americanitis' (a term used by Lev Kuleshov) to demonstrate in greater detail the simultaneous affection and repulsion that Soviet film-makers and critics felt towards US cinema and culture.[5] In this context, Kuleshov's films, particularly *The Extraordinary Adventures of Mr West in the Land of the Bolsheviks* (1924), seem less like an outlier of Soviet montage and more like a bridge linking Soviet montage to popular films like *Miss Mend* and a wider array of Soviet films, styles and practices.

The Western influences on films like *Miss Mend* were well understood by Soviet film-makers, critics and audiences alike, and these influences were often approved of and even promoted by Soviet political and cultural elites. My intention in this essay is to consider the *Miss Mend* trilogy as a prime example of how the Soviets attempted to conjoin Western inspiration with Soviet circumstance—a process more complicated than simply adapting Western forms to Soviet content. The resulting films are an eclectic mishmash, and in this same spirit I aim to explore *Miss Mend* from a variety of angles in order to highlight the very eclecticism of these films. I begin with a discussion of the curious blend of Western influences on *Miss Mend*, both literary and cinematic, and then describe how these elements are simultaneously altered and amplified so that the films serve as both propaganda and parody. I conclude with a summary of *Miss Mend*'s mixed reception: an overwhelming commercial success, but generally a critical failure.

The Hybridity of *Miss Mend*

Miss Mend was an adaptation of the serialized novel *Mess-Mend: Yankees in Petrograd*. It was published in ten fortnightly instalments from late 1923 to 1924 in cheap paperback editions featuring photomontage-style colour covers designed by the constructivist artists Aleksandr Rodchenko and Varvara Stepanova.[6] Russian literature scholar Boris Dralyuk explains that the author of *Mess-Mend*, Marietta Shaginian, was one among many Soviet writers who sought to reproduce the aesthetic qualities of films—especially US and Western European films—in Soviet literature.[7] Samuel D. Cioran, the translator of the English-language version of *Mess-Mend*, points to the 'terse, episodic nature of cinematic art' as appealing to these authors: 'the action was rapid, the intrigue was quickly laid bare, character development was pared to the bone, and superfluous material was quickly skimmed away'.[8]

Shaginian's identity was unknown to the public during the course of the novel's initial release. The purported author was identified as an American named 'Jim Dollar', and the book's introduction offered a brief biography: 'Jim Dollar' was supposedly the name given to an abandoned orphan by his adoptive parents. He was said to have grown up in New York, before inheriting a fortune and then writing *Mess-Mend*, reputedly 'inspired by the October Revolution'.[9] This introduction positioned *Mess-Mend* as an extremely popular American import that, as 'our readers know', was 'sold out in the first eight days and is presently appearing in its twenty-second edition'.[10] Overtly declaring Shaginian's stylistic ambitions, the introduction asserted the book's affinities with film: 'one must be reminded that [Dollar's] traditions are linked to the cinema and not to literature. He never studied bookish technique. He studied only in the cinema.'[11]

The film takes numerous liberties in its adaptation. The original title, *Mess-Mend*, refers to a secret passcode used often in the novel wherein one person would whisper 'Mend-Mess' and another would answer 'Mess-Mend'. As Cioran explains, the covert alliance of heroes is 'mending the mess created in the world by capitalism and fascism'.[12] The title of the film, however, derives from the book's heroine Vivian Orton, 'a marvelous, flawless beauty . . . the most perfectly beautiful woman imaginable'.[13] In the film she is renamed Vivian Mend (played by Natalya Glan), hence the film's title, and she is a typist at a cork factory (whereas in the book, her mother was the typist). The main protagonist of the novel is Mike Thingsmaster, 'a curly blonde giant' who is helped by a seemingly innumerable crew of devoted sidekicks, as well as his extraordinarily gifted dog, Beauty.[14] The film, however, offers a trio of heroes, two of whom are named after the actors portraying them: Barnet (Boris Barnet, the film's co-director, who was married to Glan in 1926–27), a 'muckraker, who gets the news a half hour before it happens'; Fogel (Vladimir Fogel), 'melancholic by nature, snapshot-taker by trade'; and Tom Hopkins (Igor Ilyinsky), a 'love-sick clerk'. Among the remaining principals are the doomed factory-owner Gordon Stern (Mikhail Rozen-Sanin)—originally named Jeremy Morlender in the book—and his son Arthur (Ivan Koval-Samborsky), who happens to look exactly like the ill-fated Engineer Berg (named Vasilov in the book). Stern's deceitful second wife Elizabeth Stern (Natalya Rozenel) is Elizabeth Wesson in the book (though Wesson claims to be his wife only after his death). The central antagonist Chiche/Signor Gregorio Cice (Sergei Komarov) remains as nefarious as he is the book—though in the book his evil qualities are revealed more gradually. While there seems to be an abundance of players here, the film actually features far fewer major characters than the book.

Mess-Mend was an answer to the call for so-called 'Red Pinkertons' by Politburo member Nikolai Bukharin, who was at this point one of the highest ranking and most influential political figures in the Soviet Union. In a 1921 essay in the pages of *Pravda*, Bukharin suggested that works such as Pinkerton novels would appeal to young people and could be used for the purposes of indoctrination.[15] Boris Dralyuk reveals that this strategy arose from anxieties over the declining number of recruits to the Komsomol, the Soviet Young Communist League.[16] As Dralyuk points out, Bukharin 'stressed the importance of approaching young people on their own terms and paying special attention to their psychological demands'.[17] The goal, therefore, was to take the formulas that were already popular among Soviet youth and to use them to encourage young people to join the Komsomol. Russian literature scholar Julia Vaingurt summarizes this as 'an ingenious ploy: to adapt a popular genre to serve ideologically correct aims, to not only win an audience, but educate it politically'.[18]

Unsurprisingly, then, *Mess-Mend* adopts many of the characteristics of American detective fiction. These include what literary scholar George N. Dove calls 'the hermeneutics of detection' and 'hermeneutic specialization'.[19] Dove argues that the process of narration in a detective story, more than any other kind of story, gives a task to its readers: we are charged with trying to solve a mystery, so we must attempt to locate and decipher clues hidden in the text while trying to exclude false leads and premature suppositions. In *Mess-Mend*, Cice is a curiously opaque figure for most of the time. He is often described without being identified, so the reader must constantly surmise 'who is that' and/or 'who did it'. However, whenever questions like this arise in the film version they are usually answered fairly quickly. Early on in the film, for example, the character we come to know as Arthur Stern initially identifies himself as 'Engineer Johnson' when Vivian Mend jumps into his car in an attempt to elude the police after participating in the strike at the factory. When the police finally catch up and threaten to arrest him, he gives them a card and tells them to leave Vivian alone. We do not know what makes him so special at that moment, but the mystery is quickly over as he is soon revealed to be the factory owner's son. Thereafter, what follows in their scenes together involves unrestricted narration, a simple hierarchy of knowledge, in which we know that he is lying to an unsuspecting Vivian; only she is fooled. In the film, Chiche appears in genuine disguise only once, when he interrupts the brawl at the Valencia Bar and successfully steals Gordon Stern's letter. Immediately afterwards, however, he reveals his true identity when he removes his prosthetic nose in front of a mirror. Throughout the trilogy, he wears a range of accoutrements that distort how he looks (e.g. driving goggles, gas masks), but there is no mystery behind his appearance and we know who it is (Figure 1).

Despite the detective fiction influences of its source material, I would argue that the film is far more influenced by American serial queen melodramas, or more generally by what Michael Walker calls 'action melodramas', in which

> the basic story is concerned with the hero or heroes in conflict with the villains/the enemy/the bad guys/a hostile environment (with a resolution of triumph heavily emphasized in American culture, at

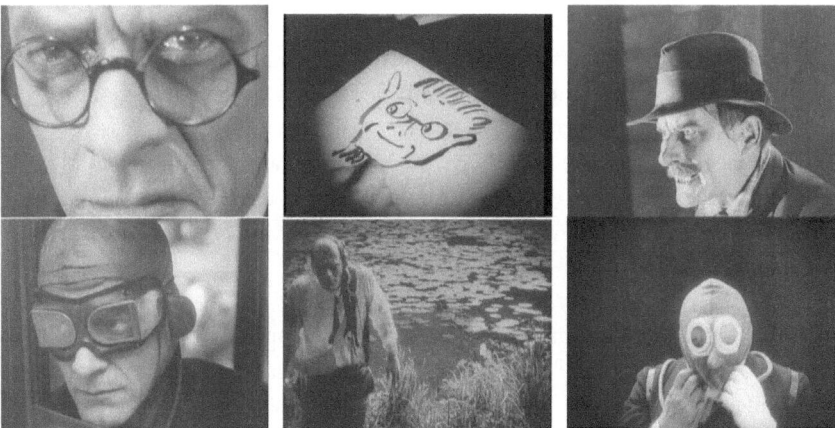

Figure 1. The many faces of the diabolical Chiche (Sergei Komarov).

least) and in which the 'love interest' is to a greater or lesser extent peripheral, with the strongest emotions, for both characters and audience/reader, reserved for the excitement and suspense of action and conflict.[20]

In their study of Russian melodrama, historians Louise McReynolds and Joan Neuberger focus on a long-standing Russian tradition that Walker calls 'melodramas of passion'.[21] McReynolds and Neuberger characterize Russian melodrama as 'Evgenii Bauer and Douglas Sirk . . . Vera Kholodnaia and Dorothy Malone',[22] wherein melodrama is conceived of as involving an elaborate *mise en scène* ('a world of *things*'), 'the return of the repressed' (an 'engagement with social issues') and 'cultural commentary' ('mediating political and social conflict').[23] However, they also evoke melodramas of action in 'the genre's association with the disreputable crowd', 'primal sensationalism', 'accusations of escapism', 'reliance on coincidence' and 'an aesthetic of excess: inflated emotion, stylized sets and acting, and wildly unbelievable plots'.[24]

Russian literature scholar Julie Cassiday informs us that in the 1920s some Soviet elites were calling for the appropriation of melodrama in a manner akin to Bukharin's call for the adoption of the Red Pinkerton. Cassiday explains that Commissar of Enlightenment Anatoly Lunacharsky and author Maksim Gorky found the 'persuasive moral message of melodrama highly attractive'.[25] (Lunacharsky, it should be noted, was married to Natalya Rozenel, the actress playing Elizabeth Stern.) Cassiday summarizes their reasoning as follows:

the ability of melodrama not only to attract a mass audience but also to elicit tears—that is, to produce a visible token of spectators' intense emotional engagement—provided proof positive of the genre's affective and persuasive impact. In addition, melodrama's cast of stock characters (the noble hero, the hidden villain, the innocent and vulnerable heroine, et cetera) caught in the struggle between good and evil provided an accurate aesthetic model for Russia's Marxist revolution.[26]

Yet the term 'melodrama' was not officially applied to films like *Miss Mend*. Like Pudovkin's *Mother*, it was officially classified as 'adaptation'— the standard generic designation for any film based on a literary source.[27] But both the novel and the trilogy were modelled on melodrama, its basic conventions summarized by Steve Neale as follows:

> (1) an unequivocal dramatic conflict between good and evil; (2) the eventual triumph of the former over the latter; (3) three principal character-types or functions: hero, heroine, and villain; (4) a demonstrative and often hyperbolic aesthetic by means of which characters were typed, dramatic conflict was established and developed, and motive, emotion and passion were laid bare; (5) an often highly episodic, formulaic and action-packed plot, normally initiated and often driven by the villain, dependent for its initiation, development and resolution on fate, chance and coincidence, and characterized throughout by 'an abundance of reversals and recognitions' [quoting Lea Jacobs]; and (6) the generation of what were called 'situations'.[28]

Thus, the heroes—and the heroine—in *Miss Mend* are unequivocally good and the villains resoundingly bad. The only character with any shade of grey is Arthur Stern, but he soon reveals his villainy after being misled about the murder of his father. Such circumstances have the potential to make him a more sympathetic character, but the film instead details his antipathy to the Bolsheviks and the lustful threats he poses to Vivian Mend.

Chiche is the mastermind who drives the plot forward with his elaborate schemes. The heroes' actions are almost always responses to what he does. At the same time, however, the development of the plot frequently depends on coincidence. For example, Barnet and Fogel happen to walk by the Valencia Bar at the very moment that Tom Hopkins is attacked inside that bar by hired gunmen sent to retrieve Gordon Stern's letter to the district attorney. Later on, Barnet, Fogel and Hopkins leave the same bar after making it known that they are looking for the men who tried to steal the letter, only to see one of these men leaving this very bar as well. They chase after him and find themselves unwittingly caught up in Chiche's plan to replace Gordon Stern's will. At times, coincidences such as this are openly acknowledged. As Vivian flees the police at the beginning of the film and jumps into Arthur Stern's car, she exclaims, 'How lucky that your car was just passing by'. When Fogel lands in Petrograd, he encounters a street urchin who informs Fogel that 'You're lucky to run into a man like me'. And, sure enough, Fogel is with the urchin selling newspapers on the street when he spies Elizabeth Stern.

The most notable situations—moments of stasis in the plot—are the cliffhanger endings at the end of each instalment. The first part ends with Vivian struck unconscious and thrown into the river. (In the book, Vivian is knifed and thrown overboard. She is in disguise, wearing a club leg and a large prosthetic humpback that absorbs the knife wound but makes it impossible for her to swim.) The second part ends with Fogel quarantined on a ship in Petrograd's harbour while his fellow passengers are dying of a mysterious illness unleashed by Chiche, while Barnet and Arthur Stern are on shore engaged in a deadly knife fight.

Miss Mend as Soviet Propaganda and Parody

Despite its Western influences, few viewers would ever likely confuse *Miss Mend* for anything other than Soviet even though the film lacks the montage-style flourishes that would become widespread in Soviet films of the late 1920s and early 1930s. (Ana Olenina and Maxim Pozdorovkin report an average shot length of 3.8 seconds for *Miss Mend*,[29] which falls within the average range of shot lengths for Soviet montage films noted by David Bordwell and Kristin Thompson, including 1.9 seconds for *Battleship Potemkin* and 4.3 seconds for *The Extraordinary Adventures of Mr West in the Land of the Bolsheviks*.[30]) In the absence of overt stylistic hallmarks that would brand the film as Soviet, the Soviet-ness of *Miss Mend* is largely conveyed by its content.

Olenina and Pozdorovkin point to a central tension between influence and repudiation in the film, 'the conflict between *Miss Mend*'s love of America and the need to criticize it'.[31] Because the book and the trilogy are largely set in the USA, the propaganda is typically negative, showcasing all the ways in which the West is corrupt, capricious and unjust. The film plays up Soviet paranoia, the fear that the West was actively and endlessly plotting to destroy the new Soviet Union. As Fogel declares, 'the whole city seems to be in the grip of some gigantic criminal conspiracy'. The Soviets are blamed for Gordon Stern's murder, which is said to have been a Bolshevik plot, and the priest at Stern's funeral proclaims 'May the wrath of God fall upon those enemies of culture and humanity—the Bolsheviks'. Stern's new will has been rewritten by Chiche to declare that 'my entire fortune . . . I bequeath to the fight against the Bolsheviks—enemies of God, mankind, and civilization'. Chiche proclaims to his conspiratorial organization, sponsored by stock companies and banks: 'We must use our gold to fight these workers. Our organization must be a bulwark against their revolutionary struggle.' The obsessive hatred of all things Soviet is thus depicted as maniacal, and is perhaps best summarized in Chiche's proposal to test their chemical and bacterial weapons on the Soviet Union in order to 'combine scientific research with the practical benefit of eliminating this harmful nation'.

Other sins of Western culture are highlighted in the film as well. The district attorney, for example, is unable to meet with our heroes because he is in need of rest and is taking his morning bath. A policeman is bought off by Chiche at the church—albeit at gunpoint—when our heroes attempt to report their discovery of the empty coffin. In the brawl at the Valencia Bar, the moustachioed henchman (Chiche in disguise) abruptly stops the fighting by forcing everyone to 'Stick 'em up'. He proceeds to shoot the only African-American in the bar, and when the police arrive, an officer announces, 'No big deal; he's black'. Bureaucratic impassivity and ineptitude are here combined with casual racism, a recurring theme in the Soviet Union's propaganda against the USA.

Pro-Soviet propaganda in the film comes largely via the spoken word, printed in intertitles. At a shareholders meeting, it is Miss Mend herself who interrupts with a diatribe, 'You condemn our mothers to poverty, our sisters to prostitution, our children to starvation—You're stinking rich! Your greed has no limit!' In the novel, a parallel diatribe is also given via the spoken word, here by Mike Thingsmaster:

> But, my dear Miss, we are engaged in this struggle not because we hate individual people, and we desire no personal reprisal. We are engaged in this struggle because the children of the poor are perishing in cellars where they are deprived of the sun and the air, because in times of war our lads are being sent to kill others who are just as unfortunate as they are themselves, or because they are driven into the mines and factories during times of peace. We are engaged in a struggle not in order to have revenge. We want to establish

justice on earth and a bright life for every person, from the first to the last. Do you understand me?[32]

Both the film and the novel involve parody. But insofar as this is the case, how do they denigrate what they seek to imitate? In an admittedly different context, film scholar Maureen Turim has described the line between satire and celebration as 'perniciously thin',[33] so how does one goes about parodying a genre that favours 'outrageous coincidence, implausibility, convoluted plotting, *deus ex machina* resolutions, and episodic strings of action that stuff too many events together to be able to be kept in line by a cause-and-effect chain of narrative progression'?[34] If nothing is off limits and everything is over the top, then how can action melodrama be satirized effectively?

The film contains a number of stylistic markers that seem satirical in their sheer excess. For example, at one point in the film there are ten irises utilized within the span of just a minute and a half. These constant iris-ins and iris-outs reinforce the choppy, episodic nature of the film's narrative by suggesting frequent jumps in time and space. Another strategy is the insertion of comedy. Many action melodramas, particularly serial queen melodramas, are played totally straight, with their heroines

Figure 2. Igor Ilyinsky's direct address in *Miss Mend*.

gamely enduring the wildest exploits with no acknowledgement of their sheer implausibility. In *Miss Mend*, Igor Ilyinsky (playing Tom Hopkins) frequently breaks the fourth wall and looks directly into the camera as if seeking commiseration with the audience (Figure 2). In the 1920s, Ilyinsky's screen roles were all comedic, and direct address was a consistent characteristic of Ilyinsky's performance style. Combined with his portly carriage, which provides a disruptive and comedic contrast to the intense action all around him, Ilyinsky's character helps to satirize the film's Western models because he is so noticeably out of place.

Miss Mend also seems to have found an ingenious way to poke fun at the narrative structure of its source films. In describing the scene of the kidnapping and murder of the notary public Mr Craft, Olenina and Pozdorovkin argue that 'long before the final stunt, the episode stops being about heroes and villains and turns into a spectacle more concerned with taking the idea of an American chase scene and pushing it to its absurd limit'.[35] Chiche seeks to kill Craft in order to swap Gordon Stern's will. He gives Craft's deputy notary the doctored will and then proceeds to drive Craft himself. The deputy notary gets into a different vehicle and follows Chiche. Outside the Valencia Bar, Barnet, Fogel and Tom encounter the henchman with whom they had previously scuffled. They chase after the henchman, first on foot, then on horseback, only to find themselves pursued by policemen and the irate owners of the horses. Craft objects to being taken by a different route and Chiche beats him unconscious. The henchman kills a railway crossing guard in order to let Chiche drive his car on the tracks, where it (with Craft inside) gets decimated by a train. Craft's deputy notary arrives to pronounce Craft dead and switch the briefcases before our heroes arrive. Chiche and his henchman escape into an abandoned factory and engage in a shoot-out with our heroes, and the sequence ends when a policeman gives the deputy notary the briefcase that he had planted on Craft in the first place.

What is extraordinary about this sequence is not just the extent to which it is pushed to absurd limits; it is also its use of what I would call 'closed-loop' or 'dead-end' narration. The deputy clerk is given a briefcase by Chiche to plant on Craft's body, but the very same briefcase is delivered back to him. He therefore needed only to kill Craft in order to make the switch, and in this way seven minutes of action are rendered entirely superfluous in terms of plot efficiency. Something similar happens with Gordon Stern's letter to the district attorney. Stern hides it in a funeral wreath and Tom Hopkins finds it on the shore when he inadvertently drops the wreath. One of Chiche's henchmen spies him with the letter and trips him into the water. The henchman rescues Tom, who is still clutching the letter, and proposes that they go for a drink. At the Valencia Bar, the henchman tries to retrieve the letter from Tom's pocket, but Tom catches him and puts it in his other pocket. However, the one-eyed man sitting on the other side of Tom tries to steal the letter, too. A raucous brawl breaks out and Barnet and Fogel come to Tom's rescue. It is not clear whether all the participants in the melee are henchmen, but everyone seems to want the letter that none of them has read. Chiche arrives in disguise, pulls out a gun and demands the letter. Then he throws it on the fire and watches it burn. Fifteen minutes of screen time have been given over to complications surrounding this letter, but nothing more is made of it as no one has learned anything from it. It, too, constitutes a dead end that serves no greater narrative purpose.

An advertisement in the *Izdatel'stva* newspaper proclaimed: 'The heroes of *Miss Mend*—in water they do not drown. Miss Mend—in fire she does not burn.'[36] While water certainly flows freely in the film as our heroes either voluntarily or involuntarily take the plunge on numerous occasions, there are no scenes involving our heroine, or, indeed, any of our heroes, being endangered by fire. It is as though the specific details of peril do not even matter so long as there is peril, and narrative logic and efficiency is dispensable.

The film's finale involves the union of parody with propaganda. There is extensive cross-cutting and increasingly rapid-fire editing leading up to the 7 o'clock deadline when Chiche's poison will be unleashed upon the Soviet Union. However, at the point at which Barnet, Fogel and Vivian finally catch up with Chiche, he has already been seized by Soviet officers. 'You are late, gentlemen', says the principal officer. 'We got him already'. This is a *deus ex machina* ending, despite the traditional chase and build-up of suspense. The parodic dead-end narration also signals Soviet glory. It is not Barnet, Fogel and Vivian who catch Chiche but the Soviet authorities; the Soviets are the ones who are able to finally outwit the evil Americans and come to the aid of our supposed American heroes.

The Reception of *Miss Mend*

The release of the three films comprising *Miss Mend*—*The Dead Man's Letter*, *The Lookalike's Crime* and *Death by Radio*—began on 26 October 1926.[37] Despite the fact that all three films had their own title, they were almost always referred to in the press and in advertisements as *Miss Mend*, each respective film identified separately as either the first, second or third part. In Moscow, *Miss Mend* replaced Vsevolod Pudovkin's *Mother* at the Ars ('Arts') Cinema, an 800-seat theatre affiliated with the Mezhrabpom-Rus' film studio located on the fashionable Tverskaia Street.[38] Although *Mother* is widely recognized to be one of the most popular Soviet montage films, it played for just two weeks in its initial run.[39] *Miss Mend*, by contrast, remained on screen for several months, usually at the Ars Cinema, with simultaneous screenings a couple of kilometers away at the 750-seat Kolizei ('Coliseum') at Chistye Prudy and occasional screenings at the Union Theater on Nikitskaia Street (500 seats) and the Koloss ('Colossus') on Bol'shaia Nikitskaia Street (1,800 seats).

The different 'episodes' of *Miss Mend* were screened at overlapping times. By the end of November 1926, for example, the Ars Theater was screening Part One once a day, at 6.00 p.m., and Part Two three times a day, at 7.30, 9.00 and 10.30 p.m.[40] Yet, in early December 1926, the same theatre had returned to two daily screenings of Part One, at 6.00 and 7.30 p.m., with Part Two at 9.00 and 10.30 p.m.[41] Two weeks later, the Ars was screening Part Two at 6.00 and 7.30 p.m., with Part Three showing at 9.00 and 10.30 p.m.[42] By mid-January 1927, a number of theatres were still showing the first part, and these included the Liuks ('Lux') Theater (340 seats), the Prozhektor ('Projector') (216 seats) and the 1-i Rabochii ('First Worker's') Theater (550 seats).[43] Months later, at the end of May 1927, the Koloss Theater was screening all three parts in a single screening.[44]

Denise Youngblood reports that *Miss Mend* was the highest grossing Soviet film in the domestic market throughout the silent era, so such extended and repeated screenings were probably unprecedented in the Soviet Union.[45] While a critic writing in the journal *The Life of Art* (*Zhizn' iskusstva*) considered *Miss Mend* a successful bringing together of commerce and ideology, many other critics were less kind.[46] The single highest profile review of the film—in the pages of *Pravda*—was at best ambivalent.[47] As noted by Boris Dralyuk, as well as Ana Olenina and Maxim Pozdorovkin, the reviewer—author, screenwriter and literary critic Boris Gusman—characterized the film as trying to be too many things at once: a straightforward detective story, a Red Pinkerton and a satire-parody.[48] As Dralyuk explains: '*Miss Mend* was a strange amalgam of ideology, adventure, formal innovation, and parody. Such amalgams could not help but lead to confusion.'[49]

The box-office success of *Miss Mend* was not repeated and would not be surpassed until the first feature-length talking film in 1931. Soviet cinema in the 1920s and early 1930s suffered from a culture of criticism in which just about every film was met with at least some hostile reviews; therefore, no sustained attempt was ever made to repeat proven box-office formulas. Government officials were unclear and sometimes contradictory in their demands, and film-makers and critics tended to pursue their own agendas. It was this culture that encouraged film-makers to experiment and expand the boundaries of Soviet cinema, and it was this culture that led to the production of *Miss Mend*. However, it was also this culture that prevented a similar kind of film from ever being made again.

11

Wings (1927)

Sara Ross

When audiences gathered to see *Wings* at the Criterion Theater in New York on 12 August 1927 at the start of its record-breaking fourteen-month run, they witnessed what was perhaps the most spectacular film screening of the late silent era.[1] Portions of this World War I epic were projected in Paramount's Magnascope process, which magnified the film's four major sequences of aerial and ground combat across the entire width of the stage. These and other sequences were marked not only by unprecedented aerial stunt work and cinematography, and dramatic additive-colour battle scenes and explosions, but by in-theatre sound effects as well. Even in its ground-based sequences, the film employed kinetic camerawork and UFA-style unfastened camera ('entfesselte camera') shots. *Variety*'s reviewer described the overall effect as space being 'eaten up so fast that there's no calculating the rate it's consumed at. . . . So much to see that it actually can't be minutely consumed at one viewing.'[2]

Wings, then, is a grand spectacle of aerial combat, a 'superspecial' that climaxes in an epic re-enactment of the battle of Saint Mihiel.[3] But it is also a film of powerful emotions, telling a story of friendship, rivalry, love and loss. The war gave rise to the moral uncertainty that to this day results from trying to reconcile the idea that war is evil but that warriors (or 'our boys', at least) are good. Through the successful integration of the most powerful tools that cinema has in its arsenal, melodramatic storytelling and immersive spectacle, *Wings* creates the fable of a boy who is transformed by war into a killer, but who nevertheless comes home and is finally cleansed of his guilt by maternal forgiveness and youthful love.

Wings' reach also extends beyond the story of its principal characters. In the battle scenes, the action often veers away from these characters in order to chronicle the final struggles of nameless flyers and infantrymen. These miniature subplots are vehicles for the spectacle of the violent ends of their lives, the 'rolls, dives, slips and loops', and the 'deftly tinted' 'spouts of flame' praised in *Variety*'s review. However, as the review goes on to note: 'Some of these shots of aviators dying with their planes going out of control are realistic enough to make a house "freeze". Who these boys are isn't known. They're not the main characters in the story, just individuals in a combat group pictured as both American and German, all fighting.'[4] As the review suggests, it is not the tragic story of two young men alone that creates *Wings'* impact, it is the compelling re-enactment of the death struggles of many young soldiers and airmen. Meticulously staged and drawing on every cinematographic innovation available at the time, *Wings* cultivates an overwhelming feeling of presence in the moment of battle. At the same time, it provides a perspective of visual mastery that would not have been possible for actual participants in the war, and successfully balances this feeling of perceptual presence with narrative absorption. This must have had tremendous emotional resonance for audiences in the late 1920s, many of whom must have wondered about the last moments of their own loved ones far away.

Wings presents a view of combat that unites the spatial, narrative and emotional clarity at which the studio era Hollywood feature excels with the innovative thrill of superhuman movement through space. The enduring popularity of aerial combat in popular culture, from *Wings* to *Star Wars* (1977) to *Avatar* (2009), is surely connected to its success in reducing the wider chaos of war to one-on-one engagements: despite their groundbreaking spectacle, the aerial battles in *Wings* are comprehensible in a way that an actual battle cannot be. At the same time, though, a poignant lack of control is reintroduced, not through faceless, senseless carnage, but through familiar melodramatic devices, notably coincidence and the gap in knowledge between two characters that is reconciled 'too late'.

In the following analysis, I will consider *Wings* in the context of post-World War I trauma, a fascination with aviation, and the wartime experiences of members of its production crew, among them William Wellman, the film's director. I will also examine the film's sentimentality and its adoption of melodramatic storytelling strategies as a means of grappling with the moral issues of soldiering and sexuality, and its coordination of aerial spectacle and narrative. This will help to illuminate the ways in which *Wings* condemns war but also makes combat legible by transforming incomprehensible horror into the pathos and thrills that audiences could more easily understand.

William Wellman and the 'Conquest of the Air'

There is a contradiction evident in *Wings*' juxtaposition of thrilling air battles and a pacifist message that was noted by critics at the time of its release. Edwin Schallert noted in his review that 'Although it glorifies air warfare, "Wings" carries a curiously effective message for peace'.[5] But this fissure in its ideology was evidently accepted by audiences, who were both fascinated by aviation and aware of the horrors of air warfare, and who made *Wings* a box-office smash.[6] Its focus on air combat set it apart from its hugely successful predecessor, *The Big Parade* (1925), whose tagline was 'The Epic of the American Doughboy'.[7] Interest in aviation was running high following Charles Lindbergh's celebrated nonstop flight from New York to Paris in May 1927. Marketing by Paramount and various exhibitors played up the connection to Lindberg and other famous aviators, such as the World War I ace Captain Eddie Rickenbacker,[8] and the film itself makes this connection in two opening titles that cite Lindberg's admiration for wartime aviators. In this way, as Schallert noted in *Motion Picture News*: 'Coming at this particular juncture, when the interest in the conquest of the air is at its height, "Wings" would seem to be an ideal sales product.'[9]

At the same time, the legacy of the Great War was fresh in the minds of the audience and crew of *Wings* alike. Although American casualties were low compared to Russian, German and French casualties, the trauma of around 50,000 US soldiers killed in battle, 230,000 wounded, thousands more missing in action or taken prisoner, and countless others psychologically wounded was felt well beyond those directly affected.[10] John Monk Saunders, the author of the novel from which *Wings* was adapted, the director William Wellman and most of the flyers in the stunt crew were flight combat veterans. Wellman had been a member of the French Foreign Legion's Lafayette Flying Corps from 1917 to 1918. He was trained in acrobatics and gunnery at Pau in southern France and flew numerous combat missions, an experience that clearly informed his work on *Wings*. Like the characters in the film, his wartime career included fistfights in camp, wild furloughs in Paris and separation from his closest pal during a mission. In his letters home during the war, Wellman not only describes incidents and sentiments that closely parallel those portrayed in *Wings*, but also writes with a tone that is echoed in certain moments in the film, juxtaposing sentimentality with a defensive emotional flatness.

As in the film, rivalries and friendships among the men, as well as Wellman's devotion to his 'little mother', figure prominently in his letters. He also dwells on details that would become important motifs in the film, such as the flyers' use of photos and other objects as good luck charms, and the beauty of flying at dawn.[11] In a letter that he wrote to his father on 16 September 1917, Wellman details an incident that is replicated in the scene in *Wings* in which Cadet White, played by the youthful and charismatic Gary Cooper, dies in a training camp accident:

> Just two days ago, a chap by the name of Billie Meeker, from Washington D.C.: One of the finest boys I have ever laid my eyes on, and with whom I had become a kind of 'pal in misery' was killed at Pau. A wonderful pilot, so pronounced by the Captain of the school, yet he got his and in a very simple way. Motor stopped and he went into a wing-slip not many feet from the ground. He bucked his machine just a wee-bit to (sic) much. This is just the luck of the game.[12]

Wellman's tone in the letter, both elegiac and matter of fact, is echoed in dialogue titles in *Wings*. When Cadet White leaves the tent that he shares with Jack (Charles Rogers) and David (Richard Arlen) just before his deadly training accident, he makes the fatalistic comment that 'Luck or no luck, when your time comes you're going to get it'. After his accident, a close-up dwells on the half-eaten bar of chocolate that he shared with the others before he left and never came back to finish.

This incident is representative of the dangers that lurked even before young men reached the theatre of war. According to one account, only 25 per cent of flyers whose lives were lost in the war died in combat, while 75 per cent were lost in accidents, most of which occurred in flight school.[13] The trauma of the deaths and injuries caused by the war was compounded by the apparent senselessness not only of the loss of life as 'cannon fodder' on the battleground, but also seemingly random accidents such as the one that took the life of Billie Meeker.

The juxtaposition of fascination with the exploits of flyers and awareness of their deadly consequences was the context in which Wellman and his crew set out to create a facsimile of what they had experienced during the war. According to Wellman's own accounts, the climatic recreation of the Battle of Saint Mihiel was almost uncannily accurate, from the placement and depth of the trenches to the advancement of the troops and the choreographed planes strafing them. Wellman coordinated a remarkable array of variables, laying out a spectacular display of simulated carnage. He positioned himself on a raised platform at the apex of a triangle of seventeen camera crews, plus an additional twenty-eight electrically controlled eyemos that would record 'rehearsed bits of battle business' during the re-enactment. Rehearsals lasted ten days, and involved 3500 army personnel and about sixty-five pilots. Wellman oversaw all of the action and personally set off barrages just ahead of the advancing performers. 'I had . . . an organlike board with push buttons that controlled and positioned the creeping barrage that preceded the advancing wave of doughboys. This I had practiced until I could do it in my sleep.' However, Wellman states that he became momentarily distracted by a visiting executive about two-thirds of the way into the scene. 'I pushed the wrong button, and a couple of bodies flew through the air. They weren't dummies.'[14]

The authenticity of the re-enactment also had unintended effects on some of Wellman's performers. He describes a pilot going crazy during shooting of the scene and 'knocking the helmets off the advancing waves of doughboys'.

> The bastard was going nuts, he was slowing us down, screwing up the whole carefully planned advance . . . I suddenly realized that in all my planning I had forgotten one terribly important factor, the human element. This pilot had flown at the front. He had been decorated. He had flown missions just like this one. For five minutes, it was not 1926 to him; it was 1918.[15]

Wellman was deeply affected. He describes going on a drunken bender when the scene was successfully completed and later collapsing in tears. The control of the scene provided by Wellman's position of visual ascendency clearly had its limits, and managing the chaos of even a simulated and carefully rehearsed war proved difficult. Once the perspectives of the many cameras were spliced into a whole, however, Wellman provided the audience with a spectacular illusion of mastery over the battle that eluded him both as a participant and as a director.

'Girl Interest' Meets the 'Serious Business of War'

Amidst *Wings*' awesome display of cutting-edge spectacle, its sentimental story might be regarded as an afterthought. A number of trade reviews certainly treated it as such. *The Film Daily* said: 'The air sequences which carry the big wallops are without parallel. They are as thrilling as they are amazing. Any audience will get a tremendous kick out of them. It is unfortunate that the dramatic story was not stronger.'[16] In *Motion Picture News*, Laurence Reed praised the realism of the film's 'war spectacle', but found the story 'weakly-built' and thought that the characters should have been 'more genuine'.[17] *Variety*'s review devotes seven paragraphs to superlatives describing the thrills provided by the 'air stuff', the special effects and the theatrical presentation, not to mention 'trench warfare and tank action, too'. The plot is not mentioned until paragraph eight: 'The story? An average tale. And yet it was human enough Friday night to make 90 per cent of the women in the house cry.'[18] *Variety* thus not only dismisses the story as 'average', but hints that whatever success it does achieve is tainted with feminine sentimentality. *The Film Spectator* went still further in this regard. Despite calling *Wings* 'a magnificent picture', its reviewer complained that 'only the fact that "Wings" is powerful enough to carry the load kept it from being ruined by its story', and that its 'girl interest' distracts audience attention from 'the serious business of war'. 'The flutter of a skirt has no place among whirring propellers', it asserts. 'The picture deals graphically and dramatically with the affairs of war, and the presence of a girl behind the line for no other reason than to conform to the movie convention that there must be a girl in a picture detracts from its strength.'[19]

This disdain for the necessity of a romantic plot for 'girl interest', as well as the reviewers' generally held opinion that the story should be more serious or 'genuine', is consistent with Lea Jacobs's analysis of shifting critical attitudes of the period in her book *The Decline of Sentiment*. Jacobs has described *Wings* as among the more sentimental of the 1920s cycle of World War I films at a time when 'the male adventure story moved in a decisively anti-sentimental direction'.[20] She discusses the association between sentimentality and female spectators, as well as lower-class and small-town audiences. In short, a preference for sentiment was characterized as typical of less sophisticated moviegoers. The influence of pointedly unsentimental works such as the World War I play *What Price Glory* was evident in films like *The Big Parade* and the 1926 film adaptation of *What Price Glory*. However, as Jacobs points out, even these films were of necessity more sentimental than the controversial play and did not stray too far from 'the glamour typically associated with Hollywood protagonists and stars'.[21] She notes that the film version of *What Price Glory* 'retreats to a much more conventional love story than was present in the play' and that other films that eschewed romance plots for grittier all-male stories were regarded in the trade press as box-office gambles.[22] From a box-office perspective, then, the sentimentality of *Wings*' story might simply have served as a way to ensure a broad audience.

Beyond this, however, the very 'averageness' of the story may have helped to temper the film's overwhelming spectacle of war.

The combination of sentiment and thrills in *Wings* is typical of its melodramatic mode of storytelling, as is its incorporation of some up-to-date 'realist' strategies. Melodrama, like the overt sentimentality that often characterizes it, was increasingly denigrated by critics as best suited for unsophisticated audiences. But it was both a tried-and-tested and a flexible means for dealing with perplexing moral problems, such as the story of two young men who become killers but who are nevertheless also victims and heroes. Peter Brooks argues that melodrama serves as a means of providing moral legibility in modern societies,[23] and Linda Williams that melodrama allows popular culture to reveal moral good 'in a world where virtue has become hard to read'. She speaks of a common thread running through popular American novels, plays and films in which realism, sentiment, spectacle and action posess the capacity to effect 'moral legibility'. 'American movies . . . have been popular', she writes, 'because of their ability to seem to resolve basic moral contradictions at a mythic level.'[24]

In spite of its failure to impress contemporary critics, its comfortingly familiar story is the foundation on which *Wings*' 'curiously effective message for peace' is built, and is therefore worth considering in some detail. In typical melodramatic fashion, *Wings* begins in a place of innocence, offering a view of 'virtue taking pleasure in itself'.[25] In a small US town in 1917, young Jack Powell (Charles 'Buddy' Rogers) dreams of flying, but must content himself with tinkering with his automobile, with the somewhat unwelcome help of the girl next door, the smitten Mary Preston (Clara Bow). Jack and Mary name the car 'Shooting Star', and Mary paints a shooting star motif on its side. Jack believes that he is in love with city girl Sylvia Lewis (Jobyna Ralston), but Sylvia is in love with his rival, a wealthy teenage boy named David Armstrong (Richard Arlen).

Meanwhile, the corruption of the larger outside world, in its most brutal form of mechanized warfare, threatens the fragile innocence of this haven when both Jack and David sign up for flight training. Sylvia prepares a locket with her picture in it for David. But Jack thinks that the locket is for him and Sylvia does not have the heart to correct his mistake. When Mary gives Jack her own picture, he carelessly shoves it in his pocket, as the boys' weeping parents send Jack and David off to war.

To succeed in the tasks that face them, Jack and David must be willing to give their lives, but perhaps the deeper sacrifice is that they must also become killers. The process begins gradually, as the two boys go to training camp together. Jack's dislike for David leads them to a fistfight. But David's game reaction to being knocked down wins Jack's respect and friendship, while Mary signs up for the Women's Motor Transport Corps. Jack and David move on to flight school, where Cadet White (a young Gary Cooper) dies in a training accident.

Their training complete, the boys arrive at their airdrome. Jack adds Mary's shooting star logo to his plane and the boys go on their first dawn patrol, when they get involved in a dogfight with the famous Count Von Kellermann (Frank Clarke) and his 'Flying Circus'. This first major flying sequence does not appear until the third reel (approximately forty minutes into the film). The sequence is introduced by an intertitle that might be said to express the audience's, as well as the protagonists', anticipation of the long-awaited flight: 'His first dawn patrol! Here was his dream come true—here was the trumpet call to breathless hazards in the skies! Here—at last!' The sequence begins with a lyrical presentation of Jack and David's squadron taking off to 'the high sea of heaven'. However, despite its heroic preamble, neither main character emerges truly triumphant. Kellermann chivalrously lets David go when he sees that his machine gun is jammed, and Jack is forced to make a crash-landing.

Our heroes have come of age as flyers, and in the next battle they are allowed their share of the heroics. Here the narrative stakes are raised by the introduction of a menacing German 'dragon', the giant Gotha bomber that threatens the French town of Mervale, which houses a garrison of US soldiers. In a melodramatic coincidence, Mary is caught up in the bombing while delivering medical supplies to the town as Jack and David engage in a dogfight with the Gotha and its escorts. Like the narrative stakes, the stylistic stakes are escalated as flourishes of all kinds underline the action, cutting to and from the pilots in the air and Mary on the ground. But the climax of this scene is not only the defeat of the Gotha, but the moment when a soldier standing next to Mary recognizes the shooting star on Jack's plane and tells Mary about him. In a neat display of narrative efficiency, Mary thus discovers the identity of the hero who has just saved her, learns that Jack has become a famous flying ace and is given hope that her crush on him might be reciprocated when she sees the shooting-star mascot on Jack's plane (Figure 1). The flyers are awarded medals, the film's first part comes to an upbeat end and an intermission begins.

The second part of *Wings* begins with Jack and David on leave in Paris. Once again, they coincidentally cross paths with Mary, who discovers that the two men are unaware that they have been recalled to the front,

Figure 1

under penalty of court-martial. Mary catches up with them drinking champagne at the Folies Bergère. But Jack is drunk and doesn't recognize her, and shedding her uniform, she borrows a showgirl's dress and seduces Jack away from a young French party girl. Mary takes him to a hotel room to sober up. But when a pair of military policemen catch them there together, she covers for Jack and is sent home in disgrace.

As Jack and David prepare for the big push, David senses that he will not survive, and asks Jack to return his belongings to his family. Jack gets out the locket from Sylvia to show it to David and the picture falls out, revealing to David (but not to Jack) that Sylvia has signed its back with love to him. To hide this from Jack, David tears up the picture. But Jack misunderstands David's motivation and is furious. During the scuffle that ensues David forgets his lucky teddy bear, and as they take off on their mission, Jack refuses to take part in their customary pre-battle exchange of 'all set!'—both sure signs of David's impending doom.

Meanwhile, allied troops move en masse to join the battle. The patterns of stylistic escalation and the linking of flying action to character development continue in the third major flying sequence. While protecting Jack, David exposes himself to enemy attack. Jack reaches his objective and shoots a pair of Zeppelins from the sky but realizes that David is no longer with him. The young men's falling out in their rivalry for Sylvia is paralleled in this physical separation, and Jack is now concerned, looking for his friend in vain before heading back to base. David, meanwhile, has been shot in the shoulder and is forced to crash land behind enemy lines. Another sequence thus ends with a crash-landing, this time by David rather than Jack. David escapes and makes his way through enemy territory.

In the morning, Count Kellerman braves a flight into Allied territory in order to drop a note at the American airfield. The note states erroneously that David has been killed while resisting capture. Jack is heartbroken

Figure 2

and vows to 'square things up for Dave'. He flies behind enemy lines alone and makes several devastating attacks on German troops, convoys and a machine-gun nest. Meanwhile, David finds a German airfield and pulls off the daring theft of a German plane, then circles back to shoot down a would-be pursuer. David reacts in triumph and soars away, …but the camera lingers not on David and his plane, but on the limp body and empty eyes of the slain German flyer.

The allied forces eventually gain a victory. But we cut not to a shot of allied triumph, but to an emblematic overhead shot of a dead soldier lying on an iron cross outlined in stones on the ground, with an inserted close-up of his face (Figure 2). Underscoring the tragedy of loss on both sides, this quasi-diegetic sequence generates a pause in the narrative and a departure from the Manichean divisions of sympathy evident in earlier wartime films such as *Hearts of the World* and *The Heart of Humanity* (both 1918) or *Yankee Doodle in Berlin* (1919): it is war itself, rather than any specific character, that is depicted as the source of the characters' suffering.

The ambivalent treatment of David's triumphant but bloody escape in the German plane prefaces the deeper tragedy of his own slaughter at the hands of his blood-crazed friend in the film's final flight sequence, which represents the emotional climax of Jack and David's friendship. Turning for home, Jack spots a German plane heading for the American lines and, in a case of mistaken identity, relentlessly pursues its pilot and shoots him down. Jack follows the plane to the ground in order to claim its iron cross as a trophy and discovers David. Realizing what he has done, Jack kisses his mortally wounded friend, who dies as the propeller on his plane outside slows to a stop. The melodramatic standbys of fatal misrecognition and death-bed reconciliation are here overlaid onto the brutal and the senseless reality of death by 'friendly fire'. While no less tragic, it is thereby rendered more familiar for audiences used to exploring emotionally or ideologically fraught subject matter via melodramatic modes of storytelling.

Back at base, Jack discovers that Sylvia loved David all along. Returning home, he receives a hero's welcome, and David's mother forgives him for what he has done. He is then reunited with Mary, to whom he confesses his misspent night in Paris, unaware that she is the girl he was with that night. As they cuddle in his car, they see a shooting star, and, restored to the refuge of his small-town life, Jack kisses 'the girl he loves'. Here as elsewhere in the film, Clara Bow's character is a marvellous example of the ways in which, as Williams points out, melodrama can reinvent itself in order to adapt to modern mores. Bow's star persona was firmly tied to the ultra-modern flapper in the mid-to-late 1920s, and her character in the film is hardly demure, given her love for speeding cars, her active role as an ambulance driver and her success at out-seducing a Parisienne party girl. She nevertheless performs a nostalgic function in the film as the feminine personification of home and innocence. Though some critics took exception to the inclusion of Mary's subplot, Edwin Schallert conceded in *Motion Picture News* that 'Miss Bow will be greatly liked in this role which is both pepful and 'sympathetic'.[26] Mary's plucky 'flapper next door' enthusiasm remains constant, even as she herself ventures into the theatre of war. Her virtue is underscored through the melodramatic misrecognition of her as sexually transgressive during the scene at the Folies Bergère and the hotel scene that follows. Her anguish over the thought that Jack might be considered AWOL reassures us that her seduction is only motivated by concern for him. The fact she assumes the costume of the follies girl as a temporary masquerade further distances her from the implications of her provocative appearance while fulfilling viewer expectations and desires, a strategy that is typical in Bow's roles.

However, the final scene between them also introduces some ambiguity with regard to what happened between them in the hotel room. Though we have clearly seen that 'nothing happened', their dialogue here may lead us to question this in retrospect. Jack says in an intertitle that 'There was a girl—and I forgot myself—I don't know who she was—I never want to know'. He continues, saying '—and then', before hanging his head in shame. With tears in her eyes, Mary tells him to 'Remember—I saw the war, too, Jack! And I can't blame—anyone—for anything! What happens from now on is all that matters, isn't it, dear?' Although the dominant reading of this conversation may be that he has merely drunkenly misremembered what actually happened, there is at least a suggestion that they pair may have consummated their relationship in Paris. This exchange reminds us that more than one kind of innocence was lost for both the men and women who went overseas. But like the acts of violence that young men commit in battle, this particular transgression, real or imagined, is treated as an aberrance that was part of the experience of war, and can thus be bracketed off from life back home.

Bow's relatively small role in the film was thus a key moment for the resolution of another moral contradiction with which audiences were preoccupied, namely, the extent to which the young modern women could be both sexual and innocent. Bow's successful portrayal of a modern version of the girl next door in *Wings* bolstered her career, a career that depended on reconciling the superficial sexuality of the modern girl with the assertion of her fundamental purity.[27] The fact that Mary's seductiveness is a masquerade that she uses to protect the boy she loves, combined with the melodramatic device of a misrecognition of her virtuous behaviour, helped insulate Bow against moral suspicion. In this way the flexibility of melodramatic storytelling facilitates the reconciliation of Bow's modern flapper persona with the otherwise old-fashioned role of girl-next-door that she is called on to play in the film.

Theatres of Battle: Exhibition, Spectacle and Immersion

As we have seen, *Wings* matches rising narrative stakes and escalating spectacle over the course of the film. Closer analysis of the deployment of specific types of aerial spectacle further demonstrates how the powerful evocation of spatial mastery that they yielded was orchestrated to coordinate with and contribute to narrative absorption. In spite of the critics' dismissal of *Wings*' story, it is doubtful whether the film's lengthy sequences of air combat would produce the thrills that they did without such coordination.

Wings was a 'superspecial' and a road-show picture, and as such, it received special theatrical presentation when first released. Some of the aerial battles featured additive colour for the sky and clouds, as well as the flames of stricken planes. Additional enhancements to the presentation context increased the immediacy of the aerial battles. The musical accompaniment was halted occasionally during the dog fights, leaving only the sound of backstage effects to simulate the sound of engines 'in two tones to denote the American and enemy planes'. The distinct tones of the planes served an expository function that enhanced the narrative clarity of the dogfights, but the shift to aural verisimilitude also produced a direct sensory appeal to the viewer that reinforced the aural impression of being present for the battle. 'The result', *Variety* declared, 'will get under anybody's skin.'[28]

When the film was shown in Magnascope, as at the Criterion in New York and several other theatres, the experience must have been particularly overwhelming. Magnascope was a process in which some of the film's images were projected onto an expanded screen using a special wide-angle lens. It was one of a number of large-screen and large-gauge projects that Zukor and Famous Players-Lasky experimented with in the mid- to late 1920s, which, as Sheldon Hall and Steve Neale have discussed, served to show off both the technology that was the subject of the films and the technology that was used to present it.[29] As John Belton explains, Magnascope could produce an effect of gradual enlargement of the image through 'the projectionist's movement of the black maskings framing the projected image'. When applied to a shot of the USS *Constitution* sailing directly towards the camera in *Old Ironsides* (1926), the process produced 'an illusion of the image's movement into the space of the theater auditorium', somewhat like a protrusion effect in a modern 3-D film.[30]

Variety's description of a screening at the Criterion suggests that the use of Magnascope for *Wings* relied less on incidental effects than on a sustained alternation between smaller and larger screens. *Variety* stated:

> Midway in the first part the switch is made to Paramount's Magnascope, which spreads the screen and projection across the entire stage. This is retained until the finish of the first half. The same thing occurs in the second part, so that much more than half the footage is magnified.[31]

Rather than the temporary illusion of objects moving into the auditorium, then, the use of Magnascope seems here to have been designed to produce the more extensive immersive effects of later wide screen processes.

The idea of being 'immersed' in a film can indicate several distinct phenomena. Perceptual immersion, often associated with wide-screen processes, is based on 'the technological promise of erasing the frame'. As Allison Griffiths suggests, technologies in this tradition 'immerse spectators in the represented space and give them a heightened sensation of moving out of the immediate and into the hyper-real'.[32] 'On the other hand', as Scott Higgins has pointed out, 'immersion also implies that viewers are wrapped up in a film's story', consistent with theorist and film-maker Pia Tikka's definition of immersion as the 'embodiment of emotional situatedness and not about the perfect image projection'.[33] What makes *Wings* exceptional is its ability to invoke these two potentially conflicting modes of immersion at full throttle. As *Variety* noted, it was spectacle that could get under your skin.

WINGS (1927)

Fundamental to the film's balance of narrative absorption and perceptual presence is the careful orchestration of its spectacular aerial cinematography. The two most frequent shots in the flight scenes in *Wings* are front-on views of the pilots, produced by automatic cameras attached to the front of the planes, and aerial long shots of multiple planes. Both display their status as genuine aerial shots, enhancing the verisimilitude and underscoring the film's high production values. For example, the front-on shots often reveal impressive aerial compositions of other planes ranged in depth behind the pilot, while the long shots soar along with the flyers at varying heights above, below and on a level with them. The long shots establish the space for shots of the dogfights and other aerial attacks, while the close-ups provide the emotional punch of the flyers' reactions. The coordination of spectacle and story is impressive, as the staging of the automatic camera close-ups reveal the same planes in pursuit of the flyers as are visible in the long shots.

The close-ups also serve to set up the much less common point of view and over-the-shoulder (or what might more accurately be called behind-the-pilot) shots, looking forward as the pilots fly. As I have pointed out elsewhere, the restraint with which these forward-rushing point-of-view and behind-the-pilot shots are used is particularly interesting.[34] Shots such as the over-the-shoulder-shot of David passing through the smoke trail of a Fokker that he has just shot down are among the most bravura images in the film (Figure 3). What is more, allowing viewers to share the visual perspective of the flyers is probably the most perceptually immersive effect that aerial spectacle has to offer. While shots such as these could provide spectators with a powerful illusion of unmediated flight, they are used instead to underscore key moments in battle from a subjective perspective, providing an embodiment of emotional rather than a purely perceptual situatedness.

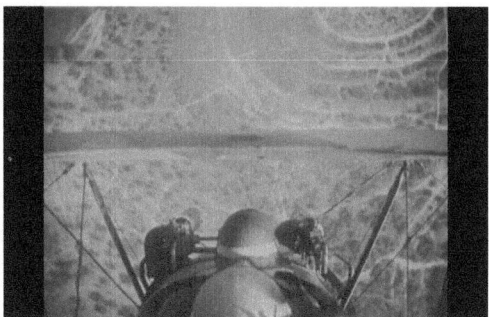

Figure 3

The first sequence of aerial combat, the dogfight with the Flying Circus, introduces the film's spectacular aerial photography primarily through long objective shots of the fight, including plummeting planes spouting animated engine fires. These shots are intercut with frontal shots of the pilots' reactions and inserts to show details of damage to the planes, and this particular sequence also includes a point-of-view shot of the ground rushing by during take-off.

The second sequence features more subjective camerawork. Its early part includes several aerial point-of-view and behind-the-pilot shots of the town and of the crowds taking cover, from the perspective of the Gotha crew. There are more behind-the-pilot shots of the American flyers in this sequence, as well as a swooping point-of-view from Jack's perspective of the underbelly of the Gotha.

These kinds of shots are used more liberally as the film progresses, raising the stakes of spectacle in close coordination with the dramatic progression of the story. They appear most frequently in the emotionally fraught climactic battle sequence, where they are tied to Jack's overwrought state of mind as he hunts down his enemies. This battle contains the most dramatic use of aerial footage to align spectators with the visual perspective of a pilot. The sequence includes not only aerial work, but also the epic ground battle, visibly staged beneath the air war. The flying action in the sequence can be divided into three distinct parts. The first of these is an elegiac take-off sequence that echoes and amplifies the dawn patrol sequence, this time portraying squadrons of planes taking off to join the 'big push'.

The second centres on Jack's crazed quest for revenge for what he believes to have been David's death. Here, spectators repeatedly have access to the kind of behind-the-pilot and point-of-view shots that have been used so parsimoniously in the film so far. This creates an uneasy and occasionally vertiginous subjective alignment with Jack as he engages in his most bloodthirsty and arguably least heroic actions: strafing essentially defenceless German troops, and gunning down a retreating German general in his squad car. When Jack swoops in to strafe a German machine-gun nest that has been decimating the advancing American line, an undercranked point-of-view shot (apparently filmed from a crane rather than an airplane) plunges down towards the dying gunners, then begins to swoop back upwards, before abruptly cutting.

Intercut with this action is the scene in which David steals a German plane. As with the shots from Jack's perspective, David's point of view underscores the bloodthirsty attitude to which the boys have been driven. After circling over the German airfield to shoot down a would-be pursuer,

David looks back over his shoulder to check his success. A point-of-view shot shows the downed plane and the ground rapidly receding as David pulls back up into the sky, then a cut to his reaction reveals his crazed laughter. A cut back to an objective, ground-based shot of the downed plane lingers on the other Germans pulling the limp body of their comrade out, dissolving, for emphasis, to a closer framing of his bloodied body and empty eyes as they carry him away. Like Jack, David is remorseless, while the viewer is made privy to a longer view of the consequences of his action. There is a guilty quality to the spectacle here, tinged as it is with the suggestion that their aerial viewpoint allows the flyers to soar away from the consequences of the hail of bullets that they rain down.[35] The spectacle is not only emotionalized, but is done so in a complex way that situates viewers alongside both the heroes and their fallen enemies.

In the final section of this sequence, forward-facing shots disappear once more, shifting the emphasis from the thrill (and guilt) of the hunt to the emotions of the two main characters as the story begins to reach its tragic conclusion. As Jack chases David, who is flying a stolen German plane, Wellman eschews shots that put the viewer 'in the hunt' via the visual perspective of the attacking pilot. Instead, the more objective style of shooting used in the earliest flight sequence once again predominates, with a particular emphasis on medium shots of David as he shouts and waves, trying to get Jack to recognize him, and corresponding shots of Jack's angry face as he hunts down 'another heinie'. The dissonance between the heroes' blood lust and its tragic consequences takes centre stage as both hunter and hunted are principal characters, and hence points of identification for spectators. Wellman's stylistic retreat in the scene from point of view and behind-the-pilot shooting emphasizes the contrasting emotions of the two friends rather than the vicarious 'thrill of the chase'. The climax of the character arc thus trumps visual spectacle, while the anti-war sentiments in this tragic sequence are powerful enough without point of view shots of Jack shooting David. At the height of the film's unrestrained melodramatic coincidence, the use of this type of shot is thus not only restrained, but orchestrated to coordinate with character development and to modulate emotional impact.

The emotional impact of *Wings* is achieved through an integration of spectacle and melodramatic narrative, providing a powerful illusion of visual presence in battle while maintaining the audience's emotional connection to the story. *Wings* does a masterful job of orchestrating its violent, balletic spectacle of air combat such that if spectacle is not always subordinate to linear narrative, it is certainly complementary to it. While spectacle often exceeds the immediate context of the plot, it is also thoroughly interwoven with the plot structure, character development and what might best be described as emotional scoring. In this way coordination of spectacle and sentiment in *Wings* is also central to its ability to pull off a complex ideological mix, in which the actions of the flying aces are both mythologized and problematized.

12

Palais de Danse (1928)

Martin Shingler

Introduction

At London's Palais de Danse, shop girls and playboys, society matrons and gigolos meet, drink and dance. Here the different social classes mingle, which is the main issue at the heart of *Palais de Danse*, and here we encounter Number Sixteen (Mabel Poulton), a young, impoverished woman from London's East End who joins the dance hall as a professional dancing partner. After meeting eligible bachelor Tony King (Robin Irvine), who performs the role of Prince Charming to her Cinderella in a charity tableau, she forgets her place and falls in love with him. As the only son of Sir William King (Jerrold Robertshaw), an eminent High Court judge, Tony is out of Number Sixteen's league. After their first meeting, however, he begins to court her at her workplace until his mother, Lady King (Hilda Moore), intervenes and forbids their bourgeoning romance, and further complications ensue when it transpires that Lady King has been having an extramarital affair with a man who calls himself Count Alban but who is in fact the head professional dancer at the Palais, otherwise known as Number One (John Longden). Once exposed for what he is, Number One exploits the situation by blackmailing Lady King. With the help of Number Sixteen, however, she manages to avoid being blackmailed—though not before her son has discovered his mother's association with the 'lounge lizard'. Resolution comes when Tony pushes Number One through the glass roof of the Palais, from where he falls to his death onto the dance floor. Finally reconciled, Number Sixteen marries her Prince Charming at the end of the film, proceeding down the aisle with Lady King's blessing.

Palais de Danse is, in essence, a modern-day version of the classic fairytale Cinderella. It is also a modern melodrama, consisting of pathos and action, tears and thrills, villains and victims, unrecognized virtue and moral conflict, all set in the racy urban context of London in the twenties. Modern music and dance crazes, modern fashion and hairstyles, modern types and attitudes are major features of this movie, which mixes fantasy and reality, dreams and nightmares, romance and crime. It also possesses many curious features, one of which is the naming of its principal characters according to their social status. While Lady King has a name that proclaims her elevated position (aristocratic *and* regal), the film's star and her leading man are unnamed (and are only identified by numbers). While situating these characters in the lower strata of society, these numbers still position them within a hierarchy, with Number One at the top. Poulton's character, by contrast, has the highest number of any dance partner at the Palais since, as the new recruit, she is the least experienced member of the team—and hence the lowest of the low. While labelling the characters according to social status may make the film seem rather antiquated, the characters themselves are modern types involved in modern relationships that challenge traditional social mores.

Palais de Danse is not well known, but its merits and points of interest have been discussed by Christine Gledhill in her groundbreaking book, *Reframing British Cinema, 1918–28*. Gledhill explores the peculiarities of the films of the 1920s by situating them within a broader cultural and aesthetic context, and which discusses *Palais de Danse* as an example of the penchant of British film-makers for whimsical tales that playfully recycle and update existing stories.[1] My intention here is to focus on the acting, and in particular to analyse the performances of the principal players Mabel Poulton, John Longden and Hilda Moore. In the interests of brevity and detail, analysis is restricted to just one scene: namely, the moment when Lady King realizes that she has been deceived by the Palais's premier taxi dancer. Before proceeding with this, however, some contextual information is provided below.

Maurice Elvey, *Palais de Danse* and his Principal Cast

> Maurice Elvey, the most prolific producer of popular British box office success, has done it again with 'Palais de Danse'—all the dramatic 'punch', romantic 'pep' and effective atmosphere which characterized 'Hindle Wakes', combined with the appeal of Mabel Poulton, make Elvey's latest Gaumont British film a certain winner at the box office.[2]

PALAIS DE DANSE (1928)

Produced by Gaumont British in 1928, *Palais de Danse* was directed by Maurice Elvey, one of Britain's leading silent film-makers.[3] Elvey had established himself as a notable cine-biographer during the First World War with such films as *Florence Nightingale* (1915), *Nelson* (1918) and *The Life Story of David Lloyd George* (1918). After the war, as the chief director for Stoll Picture Productions, he directed several prestigious literary adaptations, then worked in Hollywood for a year, before resuming his career in Britain by setting up his own production company to make *The Woman Tempted*.[4] In 1927, he joined the newly formed Gaumont British Picture Corporation to direct Lillian Hall-Davis in *Roses of Picardy* (1927), and then established a more durable and successful working relationship with the American actress Estelle Brody, who headed the cast of *Hindle Wakes* (1927), *The Glad Eye* (1927), *The Flight Commander* (1927) and *Mademoiselle Parley Voo* (1928). He also forged a productive association with actor-screenwriter John Longden. After taking a small role in *The Flight Commander* (1927), Longden wrote and starred in Elvey's film *Quinneys* (1927), and co-wrote and performed in *Mademoiselle Parley Voo*. In addition to performing the male lead in *Palais de Danse*, Longden developed the screenplay for the film, cleverly incorporating elements from *Hindle Wakes*.[5] Having starred in this earlier Elvey hit, Estelle Brody would have been an obvious choice for the leading female role of Number Sixteen. However, Mabel Poulton proved to be a more inspired choice.

At the end of February 1928, Mabel Poulton became a sensation in Britain with the release of the first film version of Margaret Kennedy's best-selling novel *The Constant Nymph*. With the help of director Adrian Brunel, Poulton performed as bohemian wild-child Tessa Sanger with such conviction and intensity that film critics and moviegoers were both impressed and astonished. Hitherto, Poulton had earned some good notices and favourable publicity, but none of her previous pictures had made her a major star. Her first film, *Nothing Else Matters* (1920), had catapulted Betty Balfour to stardom, but had done little for Poulton. Even after garnering good notices for her performance as Little Nell in the 1921 film version of *The Old Curiosity Shop*, and achieving a degree of international recognition for her role in Germaine Dulac's French film *Ame d'Artiste (Heart of an Actress)* (1924), Poulton had still not become a star. However, *The Constant Nymph* changed all that, as Poulton took 'a front-rank place among international stars' as 'Britain's Mary Pickford'.[6]

Maurice Elvey was the first to capitalize on Poulton's new-found stardom by offering her the female lead in his next production. However, as Christine Gledhill has observed, Elvey was not an advocate of the star system, favouring character actors over stars.[7] Consequently, Poulton found herself overshadowed by other members of the cast, many of whom were not only fine character actors, but also Elvey regulars. Reviews of *Palais de Danse* confirm this. On 2 August 1928, *Kinematograph Weekly* announced that, 'Mabel Poulton is very badly served' by *Palais de Danse*, adding that 'She does her best, but does not appear to best advantage'.[8] Meanwhile, on the first day of August, *The Bioscope* reported that, as far as acting was concerned, 'Chief honours are carried off by John Longden, who gives a clever and finished performance of the blackmailing dance professional'.[9] Of Mabel Poulton, the reviewer remarked that she 'is charming as the rather over-sentimental heroine', but made no further comment about her performance. Longden certainly makes a strong impression as *Palais de Danse*'s villain. The actor had plenty of scope for an eye-catching performance playing a working-class man with ideas above his station, masquerading as a European nobleman to deceive and ensnare the well-bred middle-aged ladies who frequent the dancehall in search of excitement and romance. Hilda Moore also created a compelling screen role as Lady Helen King, a rather intimidating society woman with a keen sense of her own superiority and little time for her social inferiors.[10] After it is discovered that she has committed adultery with Number One, she becomes increasingly sympathetic as a character and acquires greater depth as a more transgressive figure (i.e. as a woman seeking romance beyond her marriage). Ordinarily, such a woman would be punished, in accordance with the conventional laws of melodrama's moral order. Although she suffers the horror and indignity of being blackmailed, she is eventually exonerated and restored as the matriarch of the King family, her fate forming part of the film's 'happy ending'. Her story even becomes as significant as that of the romance of the young cross-class couple. As the main focus of the narrative during the second half of the film, she effectively becomes the central protagonist.

Naturalism, Expressionism and Melodrama in the Exposure and Blackmail Scene

The exposure and blackmail scene is preceded by the scene in which Number Sixteen is summoned to the manager's office at the Palais for an interview with Lady King. Here, the contrast between the two women goes beyond age and class. Poulton shifts from delight to confusion and sorrow with a mixture of ingratiating smiles, tears and trembling hands, while Moore remains implacable, making only minor movements and appearing to speak harshly, until Poulton leaves. In the next scene, Poulton stands alone in the adjacent room, her head bowed in an image of

PALAIS DE DANSE (1928)

dejection. Her eyes stare vacantly until she flicks her head back, projecting her chin forward and upward to assert her pride and determination. Mumbling something to herself, she raises her head further by extending her neck and turning as she looks towards the closed door leading to the room occupied by Lady King. Turning again, more bodily this time, she faces the door, holding her shoulders back, poised to propel herself forward. After hesitating, she advances, opening the door slightly, before hesitating again. Here she remains, rooted to the spot, captivated by the spectacle of Lady King being cajoled, accosted and blackmailed by Number One. Standing at the doorway for several minutes, Poulton's eyes convey embarrassment, disapproval, alarm, pity, shame, excitement and confusion (see Figure 1). Tilts and turns of her head emphasize her embarrassment and disapproval, while her breathing augments the sense of alarm and excitement. Eventually, towards the end of the scene, she bursts into action, fleeing from the room to avoid being discovered by Number One. As the camera pans quickly to the right, Poulton dashes across the screen, wrenches the door open and pulls it closed behind her to make her getaway.

Naturalness, hesitancy and spontaneity are the hallmarks of Poulton's performance here. She reacts quickly and in small ways to convey her character's changing thoughts and feelings. Her hands make a series of significant, though always slight, movements. They frequently reach out towards things only to hesitate, fail to connect and be swiftly withdrawn, as though she lacks the courage of her convictions, feeling self-conscious and out of place. Such gestures seem drawn from life rather than theatre. Instead of using stock poses, Poulton executes quotidian gestures and attitudes, so deft and fluid, so small and fleeting, that they are hardly observable. They are in no way striking or attention seeking. In contrast, Longden uses more obvious gestures to establish his character's social type, as well as his attitudes and intentions. With a series of elaborated

Figure 1

poses and expressions, he conveys concealment, shame, defeat, calculation and villainy. He begins the scene naturalistically, entering nonchalantly whistling a tune while reading a paper. From this point on, however, he becomes more emphatic and mannered. Spying Lady King out of the corner of his eye, he looks up, his lips freezing in shock. Stepping back (i.e. being literally taken aback), he attempts to cover his No. 1 badge, but, after looking down in shame, he drops his hand to reveal his number, grimacing slightly. He then registers defeat by dropping both hands to his sides, tilting his head forward and down. From this position, Longden establishes his character's villainy with more expressionist methods. At first, he gazes up at Lady King from under wolverine eyebrows, his mouth crooked beneath his moustache, while his tongue moves slowly and lasciviously from side to side between his lips, accentuating his canine qualities. His villainy is confirmed when he smiles, appearing to relish the woman's dismay. Despite being well dressed and groomed, his behaviour here proclaims that he is not a gentleman.

Number One's villainy is established more forcefully in the next shot sequence when, laughing, he attempts to take hold of the distraught woman. After she has wrenched herself free, Longden's hands remain suspended in the air, his fingers bent and claw-like, reaching out towards her (see Figure 2). Tensing, frozen and distorted, he could easily be in a German expressionist film, adopting a manner reminiscent of Conrad Veidt in *The Hands of Orlac* (1924).[11] This prolonged and exaggerated pose creates a vision of horror, producing terror on Lady King's face until Longden finally withdraws his hands and begins to stroke his fingertips with his thumb, repeating a gesture that he uses whenever his character is in contemplative mode. However, both tension and expressionism return when, after the dialogue intertitle ('What's the difference, Helen? It's *me* you love, not Count Alban'), Number One makes a second attempt to grab hold of Lady King. Rebuffed again, Longden's face appears distorted

Figure 2

PALAIS DE DANSE (1928)

Figure 3

by strong chiaroscuro lighting. A menacing smile and arched eyebrows accompany his whispered statement, 'Hating me, dear lady, contradicts a previous tribute in writing . . . on a photograph'. Longden's face sneers cruelly, wolf-like again (see Figure 3), as he pushes his tongue against his lower lip, bulging the left side of his mouth, heralding the next intertitle, 'As I am discarded, perhaps you'll buy back the photograph by TO-NIGHT—otherwise . . .' However, the actor instigates the blackmail plot by adopting a more casual manner as he picks up, examines and folds a sheet of paper while whistling, feigning nonchalance. Number One's demand for £500 is made as he temporarily leaves the room to deposit the paper on the manager's desk next door, returning to wish a devastated Lady King (whom he impertinently addresses as 'Helen') a 'Good Afternoon'.

Through emphatic gesturing, Longden not only establishes his character's type as a working-class man with middle-class pretensions, but also his individuality. What stands out here is his tendency to look up from under his eyebrows, his strange tongue movements and the repetitive rubbing of his fingertips. Such rhetorical gestures have their roots on the stage, where for decades actors used them to telegraph character traits and attitudes to audiences some distance away. Longden uses a scaled-down version to work more effectively in close-shots (e.g. the tongue in the cheek and the tongue moving between the lips). He also intersperses them with more quotidian or naturalistic actions, such as whistling and laughing. Even so, they remain attention-grabbing, being designed to attract and hold the audience's gaze.

Hilda Moore uses even more emphatic gestures in this scene to convey the strength of her character's emotions. She begins the scene by indicating that Lady King's harsh treatment of Number Sixteen was just an act designed to break the girl's attachment to her son. Consequently, once alone she relinquishes her formidable facade. As Moore shrugs her shoulders, the stern expression on her face dissolves. Having executed an emphatic sigh, she picks up her bag as she prepares to depart, only to hesitate, appearing to respond to a sound outside the room. Moments later, when Number One enters whistling, Moore registers a rapid sequence of emotions: surprise, welcome, shock, disgust, horror and sorrow. Having initially granted him a welcoming smile, she starts to breathe deeply, her shoulders rising and falling, registering shock as she realizes that he is a taxi dancer. Her eyebrows rise to convey horror and then her head tilts back slightly as she recoils, exposing her nostrils and displaying her disgust until her eyelids drop, as though she is about to faint, her eyes fluttering before closing. Seized by Number One, she immediately reacts by pushing him away. Retreating, she takes her left shoulder (which he had touched) in her right hand and holds this posture as Longden stands with his claw-like hands extended towards her.

Moore's performance now becomes more noticeably melodramatic, particularly when, with her face dissolving into tears, she raises her arm and buries her head against it, resting her forehead against her forearm. Although she briefly looks up to speak, heralding the scene's first intertitle, 'You've broken my heart', her head is mostly held low in shame. Bent and trembling, Lady King allows herself to be momentarily enfolded by her lover, although Moore keeps a clenched fist firmly between them. As she pulls away, her breathing calming a little, her hand moves hesitantly from her lips towards Longden, coming to rest against his chest (suggesting both acquiescence and indecision) before slowly but firmly pushing him further away. At this point, her attempt to master her emotions fails and she is overcome by them. Trembling, she returns her clenched fist to her mouth before executing another melodramatic gesture, putting her hands together (as though in prayer) and shaking them beseechingly (see Figure 4). Opening her hands, she holds her palms towards Number One (as though to declare, 'stay away from me!') before pushing him away again. Moore's hands return to her face, to cover her mouth (as if to say, 'I have nothing more to say to you'). After Number One has laughed at her and reminded her of the incriminating photograph she once gave him, Moore raises her head and holds a clenched fist to her mouth. Here, the actress assumes another melodramatic posture, swallowing repeatedly and tensing her forehead, holding this pose for several seconds. Moore stands transfixed once Number One has left the room after casually demanding £500 for the photograph, her clenched hand on her chest (i.e. her heart). Facing public scandal and social ostracism should her affair with the gigolo be disclosed, the once high and mighty Lady King now looks every inch a victim.

PALAIS DE DANSE (1928)

Figure 4

When Lady King finds herself in the hands of a predatory and mercenary male in this scene, Hilda Moore transforms her into a melodramatic victim by adopting a series of established gestures and poses: the fist held to her mouth as a sign of horror; the head thrown down upon the forearm as a gesture of sorrow mixed with shame and defeat; and the clasped hands as a plea for mercy. However, Moore constricts these through tension in her body so that they seem less exaggerated within the confines of medium and medium close-up shots. A concentration on hand movements, shoulders and neck, facial expression and breathing effects a reduction in scale of these well-known physical signs. Nevertheless, they remain noteworthy, even spectacular, and, as such, attract and hold the gaze of the audience.

Acting in Muted Melodrama

Christine Gledhill has noted that, as melodrama evolved during the late nineteenth and early twentieth centuries, a series of reductions occurred in the scale of its gestures, influenced in part by developments in photography and popular Victorian painting.[12] This produced an increasing movement away from grand rhetorical posturing to something more apparently 'naturalistic' (i.e. incidental and spontaneous), including minor facial inflections to evoke a sense of a character's internal dilemmas. After 1918, such gestures and inflections were adopted by many British actors in order to help film producers and movie-theatre owners attract wealthier and more 'sophisticated' middle-class and upper-class audiences.[13] Even so, as Gledhill observes, different registers of gesture persisted in British films of the 1920s.[14] Consequently, a single scene might include acting in three distinct registers: colloquial (or everyday); rhetorical (emphatically communicative, i.e. to heighten a significant moment or emotion); and epic (for grandeur, loftiness or the sublime).[15]

Analysis of the exposure and blackmail scene in *Palais de Danse* reveals that both colloquial and rhetorical registers are employed by the actors here. While the film's leading lady uses gestures that seem almost entirely drawn from everyday life, the character actors use mainly rhetorical gestures and postures, interspersed with some colloquial actions and expressions. While Longden constrains his rhetorical style of acting with the muscular tension and prolonged posturing associated with expressionism, Moore uses a more traditional style of melodramatic performance in order to portray her character's confusion, horror and distress. Nevertheless, even here an effort to restrict the scale of her gestures can be detected. By concentrating on smaller gestures that are drawn *into* the body rather than directed outward, Moore creates a sense of internalized feelings, evoking passion through restraint; in other words, through what is repressed rather than expressed.[16] As an upper-class English woman, Lady King appears to be bound by the social constraints of decorum, so that she remains intent on recovering her composure despite experiencing a high level of emotional turmoil. Moore conveys this through a series of gestures that suggest concealment and containment (e.g. bending over, placing her head against her arm, holding her fist to her mouth), and through maintaining a significant degree of muscular tension in her body and face. All of these suggest Lady King's internal struggle to retain her dignity and contain her emotions. While adding depth to Moore's characterization through the suggestion of a psychological struggle, they also attract the audience's attention, further inviting sympathy and understanding. There is, however, a tension here between 'toning down' melodramatic performance (in the interests of achieving an upper-class characterization, as well as a naturalistic and modern performance) and 'acting up' in order to draw attention to a character's strong feelings, on the one hand, and the actor's performance, on the other. This tension was, as analysis reveals, something that Mabel Poulton, John Longden and Hilda Moore negotiated and resolved in their own unique ways.

Conclusion

Despite top billing, Mabel Poulton did not receive star treatment from Maurice Elvey in *Palais de Danse*. In Hollywood, it is likely that after her successful pairing with Ivor Novello in *The Constant Nymph* she would have been given a star vehicle tailored to her acting style and screen persona, affording her maximum screen time with a greater proportion of close-up shots than any member of the cast. Furthermore, the supporting cast would have been chosen specifically to enhance her image and attributes without distracting attention away from her. In *Palais de Danse*, however, some members of the supporting cast were given greater prominence than their leading lady. Analysis of the exposure and blackmail scene reveals that the actors John Longden and Hilda Moore took precedence over Poulton. It also reveals that melodramatic acting was employed here by the two principal character actors to render their performances more visible. What is also clear is that Longden and Moore's acting methods were not only markedly different from Poulton's, but also subtly different from one another, with Longden's being more expressionist and Moore's being more traditionally melodramatic. Here, the expression of strong emotions (particularly horror, sorrow and shame) kept melodramatic gestures and attitudes in play, however restrained. Moreover, analysis suggests that in the work of Maurice Elvey, one of the most successful and prolific directors of British silent cinema, there remained a commitment to established tropes of melodramatic acting right through to the final phase of silent cinema.

Despite the use of stars (in this case, the nascent star Mabel Poulton) and the adoption of newer and more naturalistic performance styles, *Palais de Danse* indicates that stardom and acting in popular British cinema of the late 1920s stood in marked contrast to Hollywood. It would also seem to be the case that when Hollywood acting and stardom became the international standard during the era of the talkies, such films as *Palais de Danse* were rendered strange, to the point of becoming antiquated curios in danger of being edited out of the archives and history books. As it finds its way back into circulation, a film such as this not only has much to tell us about the distinctive modes of storytelling and acting in British cinema of the 1920s, but it also rewards repeated viewings and close scrutiny. As such, it deserves to be recognized as a significant technical and aesthetic achievement, not just in the context of British film-making, but in terms of world cinema more generally.

Postscript

After *Palais de Danse*, Mabel Poulton headlined in a number of minor productions by Nettlefold Studios.[17] Her last significant silent film was *The Return of the Rat* (1929) for Gainsborough Pictures, which paired her once again with Ivor Novello, her *Constant Nymph* co-star. Although the studio gave her the leading role in the romantic comedy *Taxi for Two* (1929), which was her first talking picture, she was subsequently reduced to playing a small part in John Galsworthy's *Escape* (1930). As Gledhill has observed, Poulton's 'ineradicable Cockney accent' prevented her from making a smooth transition to sound cinema, restricting her to character parts, for which her acting technique was ill-suited.[18] When Basil Dean directed the first sound version of *The Constant Nymph* for Gaumont British in 1933, recruiting newcomer Victoria Hopper to play Tessa, Poulton's film career appeared to be over, though she reappeared in small roles in Michael Powell's *Crown v. Stevens* and Louis Renoir's *Terror on Tiptoe* (both 1936 and both quota quickies), and she also appeared in *Bed and Breakfast* (1938) and *Strange to Relate* (1943) prior to retirement.

John Longden fared much better. After *Palais de Danse*, he carved out a long career as a character actor in British cinema. Although major stardom and a Hollywood contract eluded him, he did play the leading role (as Inspector John Bradley) in the Edgar Wallace crime thriller *The Flying Squad* (1929) and in the Warner Bros. UK-based production of *Murder on the Second Floor* (1932). Having made his sound debut as Detective Frank Webber in Alfred Hitchcock's *Blackmail* (1929), thereby securing a place in film history, he went on to appear in three more Hitchcock talkies: *Juno and the Paycock* (1929), *The Skin Game* (1931) and *Young and Innocent* (1937). His later films included *The Silver Fleet* (1943), *The Ghosts of Berkeley Square* (1947), *Pool of London* (1951) and *The Ship That Died of Shame* (1955). After spending most of the late 1950s and early 1960s working in television, Longden finally retired from film acting thirty-six years after his role as Number One in *Palais de Danse*, making his last appearance in the science-fiction fantasy film *Frozen Alive* (1964).

Hilda Moore's film career after *Palais de Danse* could not have been more different. Following her performance as Lady King, she was hired by one of Hollywood's biggest studios, Paramount Pictures, to support two of America's finest actors, Jeanne Eagels and Fredric March, in a screen version of Louis Verneuil's play *Jealousy* (1929). However, shortly after embarking on a new chapter in her acting career by becoming a Hollywood character actor, she contracted a blood disease from her five-year-old son and died in New York City on 18 May 1929 at the age of forty-three. *Jealousy* was released four months after her death.

13

Piccadilly (1929)

Jon Burrows

Following its restoration by the British Film Institute's National Film and Television Archive in 2004, 35 mm prints of Ewald Andre Dupont's 1929 British film *Piccadilly* have been screened on several continents, and separate DVD editions have been produced in five different countries. It is assuredly no longer 'among the finest silent pictures that nobody knows', as Sukhdev Sandhu put it when the restored version received its premiere.[1] *Piccadilly* is now probably the most famous British silent feature film not directed by Alfred Hitchcock.

This is a far cry from the situation in the late 1970s, when Herbert Luft, author of the first significant overview of Dupont's career, was unable to view the film and had to ask Paul Rotha for his recollections about it. Rotha told him that *'Piccadilly* was a mess'.[2] Writing about it in *The Film Till Now* shortly after its original release, Rotha had complained that *Piccadilly* 'was slow where it should have been fast and fast where it should have been slow'.[3] Similar criticisms have occasionally been voiced since 2004,[4] but the film has predominantly been received very warmly by modern audiences. This positive reappraisal is clearly in some measure due to the fact that *Piccadilly*'s restoration coincided with a major flowering of interest in one of its stars, the Chinese-American actress Anna May Wong, whose birth centenary was celebrated in 2005. Since 2003, there have been two biographies of Wong, two book-length critical studies and one play about her, and these have been accompanied by major retrospective film seasons at MOMA and UCLA, an exhibition at the National Portrait Gallery and two widely shown documentaries.[5]

The twenty-first-century canonization of *Piccadilly* has also been predicated upon the creative vision of its German director. Sandhu set the tone for the reappraisal of the film as a 'masterpiece' with his suggestion that Dupont

> brings to the filming of late 1920s England the curiosity and freshness of gaze that foreigners tend to do . . . The documentary textures and the director's anthropological impulses combine to reveal a side of [London] that we would never have expected.[6]

The idea that *Piccadilly* has something interesting and valid to say about England in the 1920s represents a complete reversal of the attitudes adopted towards this film upon its release in 1929. *Piccadilly* received fairly positive reviews within the mainstream British press, with critics praising its technical virtuosity and the quality of the lead performances. However, it was insistently asserted that, for all the skill and proficiency on display, the film delivered an entirely fanciful and inauthentic representation of contemporary London. One reviewer declared 'a personal regret that the film is a trifle foreign for its title'.[7] Another complained that Dupont had provided 'a continental rather than a typical London effect'.[8] There were many variations on this theme, including 'It must be admitted that the Piccadilly of the screen bears a somewhat foreign appearance'.[9] Dupont's nationality was obviously a crucial consideration in these verdicts: 'Herr Dupont has not troubled to accurately reproduce these phases of London life, nor is he sound in familiar detail', claimed *The Cinema*'s critic.[10]

It was at the time conventional to measure a national cinema in terms of the nationality of the film production personnel. Although *Piccadilly* was made entirely at Elstree, Rotha thought it appropriate to characterize it as 'not strictly the product of British studios'.[11] The prominent involvement of non-British nationals rendered the very concept of the British film industry absurd, according to Hugh Castle's review of *Piccadilly* in the avant-garde film journal *Close Up*:

> This is the perfect British film. That means to say it was made by a German, with a German cameraman; its leading lady is an American of Polish extraction and its second lady is an American of Chinese extraction; the leading man is English and the second man is Chinese; the art direction is by a foreigner and the story is by Arnold Bennett, who must have had the toothache or an Income Tax paper at the time. For the remainder, it is authentically rumoured that the great aunt of one of the men who trimmed the lights came from Aberdeen.[12]

PICCADILLY (1929)

It has now become a critical orthodoxy to suggest that various émigré directors (e.g. Alberto Cavalcanti, Joseph Losey, Roman Polanski) occupy a particularly privileged status in the pantheon of important British film-makers, their capacity for telling insight being sharpened by their automatic nonconformist status. Discussing British cinema of the 1940s and 1950s, Peter Wollen has argued that

> the best films about any country are frequently made by foreigners, film-makers who tend to look askance and from an unusual angle . . . Outsiders—and I might include 'internal outsiders' in this category—often see things about a country which insiders miss or discount or repress.[13]

So what exactly might it be that E.A. Dupont's 'outsider' perspective reveals? I think it is important to consider this question in a systematic way—something the nascent scholarship on *Piccadilly* has not yet attempted—to ensure that the 'émigré outsider' thesis is not being simply deferred to as a default critical reflex. I will attempt to provide an answer by situating this production in the context of concerted efforts within the British film industry of the late 1920s to collaborate with European partners and thereby achieve greater international circulation, and also by considering the film in pertinent generic contexts. Sandhu praises *Piccadilly* for presenting images of inter-war London that we would not ordinarily expect to see. He is referring here to the fact that parts of the film are set in the East End dockside district of Limehouse, the location of London's original 'Chinatown'. But it would actually be more accurate to suggest that cinemagoers of the 1920s must have found it difficult to avoid encountering screen incarnations of this famous Chinese quarter. Between 1919 and 1929, there were eighteen feature films, three long-running serials and three miscellaneous serial episodes made in Britain and America which featured prominent Limehouse settings.[14] *Piccadilly* was produced very much at the tail end of this pronounced vogue for exploring the world of London's immigrant Chinese community in the cinema. In order to assess the level of special insight, if any, which Dupont's émigré status afforded him, it is particularly important to understand if or how *Piccadilly* nuances, or conforms to, what was, by the end of the 1920s, a very well established visual discourse.

'Film Europa' and the International Touch

Some of the reasons why E.A. Dupont came to be employed at the

Elstree studio complex owned by British International Pictures (BIP) are well documented. *Piccadilly* was an Anglo-German co-production, financed jointly by BIP and a partnership put together by Dupont between the Berlin studio Gloria-Film GmbH and the Munich-based Emelka company (a.k.a. Münchner Lichtspielkunst AG). The ubiquity of international co-productions in the latter half of the 1920s has been the subject of extensive investigation.[15] Such initiatives have been studied in the context of coordinated contemporary calls for Europe's film industries to form a federalized body, or 'Film Europa', as the Germans called it, as a means of confronting competition from Hollywood from a position of comparable economic strength. Co-production agreements facilitated exchanges of ideas and creative personnel, which would theoretically enable European films to perform more effectively in a variety of different national markets. Shared investment also permitted increased production budgets, which were necessary to bridge what Gerben Bakker defines as a perceived 'quality gap' between post-war American and European films, exacerbated by the former's higher 'endogenous sunk costs',[16] and to thus enhance the possibility of successful distribution in the US market as well as across Europe.

Dupont would have seemed a plausible figure to spearhead a new assault on the North American market for one obvious reason: whilst a number of German films in the 1920s had been widely admired by American critics, only a handful had been substantial commercial hits in the USA, and the most successful of these was Dupont's 1925 film *Variété*.[17] Set, as its title suggests, in the world of metropolitan vaudeville theatre, *Variété* deals with a trapeze trio act which becomes a tragic love triangle: its middle-aged leader (Emile Jannings) is cuckolded when his mistress (Lya De Putti) gets seduced by their younger associate (Warwick Ward), and he wreaks murderous revenge. One measure of the impact this film made in America lies in the fact that certain key features were reworked by Paramount in their 1928 production *The Sins of the Fathers*. This lost film, about a middle-aged bootlegger (also played by Emil Jannings) whose young mistress absconds with another man, even adopted the same title as the American translation of the Felix Hollaender novel which *Variété* had been adapted from.[18]

Prior to *Piccadilly*, Dupont directed another Anglo-German co-production at Elstree, *Moulin Rouge* (1928). This first attempt by BIP to develop a successful 'Film Europa' amalgam also replicated various elements of *Variété*. It was similarly a tale of the entertainment industry demi-monde—the principal female character, Parysia (Olga Tschechowa), is a celebrated dancer at the Moulin Rouge theatre in Paris—and once again the narrative is powered by a knotty love triangle: André (Jean Bradin), the fiancé of Parysia's daughter (Eve Gray), becomes consumed by desire for the mother, and nearly causes a double tragedy when he plans a suicide attempt following Parysia's rejection of his advances. Most unusually for a British film of this period, *Moulin Rouge* is suffused with images of forbidden sexual longing. In one scene, André reaches an ecstatic reverie as he lies in bed staring at a theatre programme portrait of Parysia, and the way in which the programme slips off his bed as he drifts off to sleep slyly implies that it stimulated him to masturbate. Parysia subsequently shivers with barely suppressed desire as André first declares his infatuation and tries to grasp her hips whilst kneeling before her. And in what is perhaps the most provocative sequence in the film, Parysia dances in a musical number in which she is playfully ravished by a cast of leering minstrels in blackface. Parysia's stylized gestures of mock horror and fear imply a perfunctory resistance and even a measure of enjoyment, and Dupont underlines the stakes of this interracial transgression by showing a group of six black spectators watching the display with ambiguously impassive expressions.

As Andrew Higson has shown, *Moulin Rouge* encountered an exceptionally hostile reception from British film reviewers. Its 'persistent continental sex element' was roundly condemned.[19] As this reference to mainland European mores suggests, the film was perceived to be straightforwardly incompatible with any concept of British cinema. Its Parisian setting and pan-European cast (headed by a Russian-born star of German cinema and a French leading man) saw it condemned as an 'international hotchpotch'.[20] The *Daily Express* critic conceded that it may 'please Continental audiences who like this kind of erotic nonsense', whilst declaring it to be 'the most un-British film ever made in Britain'.[21]

The choice of primary setting and scriptwriter for Dupont's second British film were made in the immediate aftermath of *Moulin Rouge*'s disastrous premiere.[22] It thus seems reasonable to speculate that the decisions to hire Arnold Bennett, one of Britain's most celebrated modern novelists, to write a film with a London backdrop clearly telegraphed in its very title were probably made in order to try and achieve a more overt and successful connection with British tastes. Nonetheless, historians of this brief era of federalization in European film production have argued that whilst the need to respect distinctive national cultural traditions was 'invariably invoked by those promoting the wares of Film Europe, the success of its films surely depended on their ability to embrace hybridity in a meaningful way'. A process of 'extensive cultural and industrial internationalisation' has come to be seen as fundamental to the coherence and prospective success of co-production projects in the 1920s, necessitating a broadening of the concept of national cinema; after all, wide international distribution would require not simply addressing a broad range of European tastes, but also 'colluding with and borrowing from Hollywood'.[23]

Tim Bergfelder has made a strong case for the significance of the fact that one of *Piccadilly*'s most striking borrowings from Hollywood, Anna May Wong, appeared in numerous European co-productions in the late 1920s and early 1930s. Bergfelder argues that Wong's hybrid ethnicity, both American *and* Chinese, provided the ideal star image for 'Film Europe's narratives, which sold decentered identities to different national audiences'.[24] He also offers the highly suggestive observation that numerous co-productions of this era 'focus on the margins, boundaries and junction points of Europe... These spaces are inhabited by outsiders, people of indeterminate national identities.'[25] The kinds of recurrent 'Film Europe' narrative locations that Bergfelder has in mind here are train stations, ports and remote islands. He includes in this list the metropolitan nightclub setting of *Piccadilly*, but it is crucial to note that the Limehouse 'Chinatown' district potentially offered an even more suitable liminal space for teasing apart stable constructions of national identity.

Fashionable Limehouse

Following a less sophisticated commercial logic, a Limehouse setting in the 1920s offered other obvious advantages for an expensive co-production whose profitability was conditional upon achieving wide circulation in the continental European and North American markets. In the aftermath of the phenomenal success of D.W. Griffith's *Broken Blossoms* (adapted from a story in Thomas Burke's 1916 book *Limehouse Nights*) at the start of the decade, Limehouse had become arguably the most familiar district in England outside Westminster as far as Hollywood cinema was concerned in this period. From 1929 to 1938, Paramount had a permanent 'Limehouse Street' set kept *in situ* at its main studio facility on North Gower Street.[26] *Piccadilly* can be seen as a film which actually followed an established formula on the part of its production company for trying to secure US distribution. The outfit rebranded as British International Pictures in 1927 had been founded in 1925 as British National Pictures, and it is important to note that British National's first in-house production packaged a very similar combination of strategic casting, scriptwriting and location choices. The comparably titled *London* (1926), directed by Herbert Wilcox, featured an American star in its leading role (Dorothy

Gish) and was also partly set in Limehouse. (Dorothy Gish was, of course, the sister of Lilian Gish, the star of *Broken Blossoms*, and the script of *London* was written directly for the screen by Thomas Burke, the celebrated British author whose short stories of Limehouse life had inspired D.W. Griffith's iconic film.)

Maria Tatar has shown that the slums of East London also occupied a privileged position in German popular culture during the Weimar era, as a result of the widespread fascination amongst artists, novelists and film-makers with the Whitechapel murders committed by Jack the Ripper.[27] Dupont himself had previously been responsible for the German film *Whitechapel* (1920), and it is telling that another Anglo-German co-production made in 1929, *The Alley Cat* (*Nachtgestalten*), directed by Hans Steinhoff, was itself largely set in Limehouse.

Arnold Bennett's diaries present a clear chronology of when the script for *Piccadilly* was written, but they give no indication as to whether it was Bennett, Dupont or BIP's executive management who first suggested that the film should have a Limehouse element. It is possible that one or more of these parties may have derived some inspiration for their story of the murder of a young Chinese woman by her infatuated compatriot from a tragic real-life crime committed in June 1928 that had fascinated the British press: a newly married affluent young Chinese couple had been honeymooning in the Lake District when the husband, Chung Yi Miao, strangled his wife to death for no apparent reason.[28] What we can say for sure is that the district of Limehouse had intrigued Bennett for a number of years. As Anne Witchard has explained, it became fashionable in the 1920s for 'West End revellers, after a couple of champagne cocktails, to go slumming "down Chinatown way"'.[29] In common with various writers and artists of the time, Bennett had embarked upon a 'fact-finding' excursion to Limehouse on the evening of 28 April 1925, in the distinguished company of Lord Beaverbrook, the proprietor of the *Daily Express* and *Evening Standard*, and Baron Ashfield, the chairman of the company which ran the London Underground. He recorded in his journal that:

> We went to the Limehouse Police Station first. It took us exactly fifteen minutes to drive there from Ciro's. Great change in a short time. We saw some 'curios' (as the Chief Inspector called them) first. Explanation of 'Fantan' and 'Pluck Pigeons'. The first seems a purely childish game in which the bank plays 2 to 1 winnings on a 4 to 1 chance. Then out with the Inspector to Pennyfields. No gambling after 8 o'clock, he said, usually not later than 7. We entered two Chinese restaurants (11 p.m.) where lots of people were

drinking tea. Humble people. All very clean and tidy indeed, and all the people looked decent . . . We went into a Chinese Music Club, where four men were playing Mah Jong and one strumming a sort of Chinese guitar with very large string-pegs. Their singing nights were Wednesday and Saturday. A suggestion that they should sing was not well received. They were very polite but didn't want us . . . Then we went into a pub (closed) and found one or two old topers (friends of proprietor's) drinking stout after hours. We were taken upstairs and there saw a wonderful collection of Chinese carving of all sorts—chiefly picked up from sailors. Lastly, return to police station. No prisoners . . . On the whole a rather flat night. Still we saw the facts. We saw no vice whatever. Inspector gave the Chinese an exceedingly good character.[30]

Certain fruits of this 'research' evidently found their way into *Piccadilly*. When the club proprietor Valentine Wilmot (Jameson Thomas) undertakes his first trip to Limehouse, he is similarly greeted by the sights of tea drinking and 'Fantan' playing. The pub which Bennett visited is undoubtedly the Railway Tavern, near West India Dock, whose landlord, Charlie Brown, was famous for his collection of oriental antiques. During the making of *Piccadilly*, Anna May Wong apparently went to the Railway Tavern as part of her preparation for playing the role of Shosho,[31] and these experiences are echoed in the film: the office above the restaurant where Valentine goes to purchase Shosho's dress is similarly festooned with Chinese carved statuettes.[32]

Perhaps one can also detect the initial source of inspiration for *Piccadilly*'s defining narrative collision and collusion between the West End and the East End in Bennett's comment that his journey from Ciro's—a fashionable West End dancing club and restaurant, just like the Piccadilly nightclub represented in the film—to Limehouse was surprisingly brief and created a consciousness of 'Great change in a short time'. In the analysis which follows, I will argue that the film is centrally preoccupied with momentous changes occurring in quick succession, and that this can be plausibly understood as an attempt to address the Film Europe challenge of presenting meaningful and resonant forms of cultural hybridity.

Plot and Camera Revolutions

The basic narrative structure of *Piccadilly* is effectively geared around an uncertainty principle, as protagonists regularly shift places with each other. Paul Matthew St Pierre has suggested that *Piccadilly* conforms to the same scenario template used in *Variété* and all of Dupont's subsequent British films: the love triangle.[33] It would be more accurate to suggest, however, that whilst the film does deal in triangles, it delights in producing multiple formulations and repeatedly substituting the constituent points. In its opening scenes, *Piccadilly* directly emulates *Variété*. The middle-aged entertainment impresario's relationship with his principal female dancer Mabel Greenfield (Gilda Gray) is challenged by the amorous advances of her younger dancing partner Victor Smiles (Cyril Ritchard). Cyril Ritchard has a very similar gaunt physical build to Warwick Ward, the British actor who played the equivalent character of Artinelli in *Variété*, and Victor actually attempts to inveigle himself into Mable's affections using exactly the same seduction technique as Artinelli: he boasts that he has been offered a prestigious professional engagement in America and offers to take Mabel with him and make her a star on Broadway. But rather than setting the wheels of a *Variété* remake in motion, the formula is just as swiftly deconstructed: Victor is promptly ejected from the narrative, and relationships are realigned as the narrative turns like a carousel. Shosho replaces Victor as the star attraction of the Piccadilly and then replaces Mabel as the object of Valentine's affections; this new triangle is mirrored by another as Valentine in turn displaces the Chinese boy Jim (King Ho-Chang) as Shosho's sweetheart.

Dupont, a former newspaper journalist, slyly comments upon the significance of these plot 'revolutions' with a series of ironic newspaper inserts. The front-page story that conveys news of Shosho's tragic death plays second fiddle to a feature headline pronouncing that a 'London Bride Changes Her Bridegroom'. At the end of *Piccadilly*, a man reading the sensational newspaper report on the inquest abruptly transforms the mood of the film by turning over to the sports pages and happy news of a win on the horses. As he drops a cigarette behind him, he is immediately replaced as its owner by another man, who picks it up. The latter is one of a stream of 'sandwich men' advertising a new show at the Scala Theatre, whose title, 'Life Goes On', drives home the message that nothing stays still and no values hold immutable significance, whilst further subverting the tragic tone of the climax. The aphorism that today's seismic news stories will become tomorrow's fish and chip paper is effectively encapsulated in accelerated form by another prominent advertisement displayed in this scene: 'The World's Greatest Sin. See Tit-Bits.'

The fluid nature of attitudes and alliances in *Piccadilly* is reinforced by a highly distinctive approach to the representation of space, and an understanding of certain key stylistic techniques that Dupont employs brings his vision of everyday British life as thoroughly hybridized and cosmopolitan into clearer relief. The film begins by insisting upon a rigid hierarchy of spatial systems which reinforce important ideological distinctions: above/below, west/east. When Valentine investigates the disruption caused to Mabel's dance performance by complaints about food served on dirty plates, various tiers of employees deny responsibility by insisting that 'the restaurant is the restaurant and the kitchen is the kitchen', or 'the kitchen is the kitchen and the scullery is the scullery'. But these confident assertions of clear geographical boundaries are swiftly undermined. The very first dialogue titles in *Piccadilly* suggest that fast-changing entertainment trends make it impossible to offer a secure definition of what kind of environment the Piccadilly actually is. 'Is it a Club?', says one patron to her companion in the powder room; 'Do Clubs have electric signs?' 'Of course it isn't a Club', the companion unhelpfully elucidates. 'They *call* it a Club and so everybody wants to come to it'. (This brief exchange pre-emptively invalidates the confident West End 'insider' knowledge of one commentator, who complained that Dupont 'might have been filming Timbuctoo for all the relation his picture bore to its title'.[34])

The wider impact of the distractions caused by the Chinese dishwasher Shosho as she dances deep in the bowels of the establishment serves to demonstrate that the barriers between these realms are highly porous, as her actions ripple out to the dance floor and she is soon moved 'upstairs' to perform there. Before long, Valentine himself is being transported from the West End to the East End. On one of his visits to Limehouse he is introduced to the district's equivalent hot spot for dancing and drinking, and is told 'this is *our* Piccadilly'; distorted shots of the local revellers reflected by mirrored surfaces underline the suggestion that the two realms are not so distinct.

It is pertinent to discuss the qualities of some of *Piccadilly*'s stranger forms of camera choreography in relation to this issue. The striking use of camera movement in *Variété* to convey the dramatic transportation through space of the trapeze artists had been universally applauded, but the strikingly different effects produced by the moving camera in *Piccadilly* were generally perceived as awkward and misconceived. Meaningful looks or conversations between characters standing apart from one another are repeatedly conveyed via ostentatious back-and-forth camera pans or tilts rather than conventional analytical editing. Paul Rotha thought the balance between editing and camera movement in the film was fundamentally wrong:

Both the merits and demerits of panning were apparent in Werner Brandes's camerawork, at Dupont's direction, in *Piccadilly*. Several highly dramatic moments in this film lost their effect on the audience because the camera dawdled in its panning, in the very place where direct, quick cutting should have been used. It may be added that the technical accomplishment of the camerawork in this film was of a high standard and it was regrettable that it should have been misused.[35]

Hugh Castle found the camerawork straightforwardly laughable:

> If Dupont wants to show two people in different rooms, he pans from the attic, down the stairs, across the front room, through a brick wall or two, into the room, wanders around it and finally brings his camera to rest on his second character.[36]

This is obviously a caricature of the technique employed, but it does establish the most salient point about Dupont's preference for panning rather than cutting between characters: it links disparate spaces and people together rather than compartmentalizing them. I think it is feasible to suggest that Dupont and Werner Brandes experimented with such unconventional uses of panning as part of a considered strategy to elide the perception of barriers between different spaces, and perhaps reinforce the impression that, contrary to the view of the critics who denounced *Moulin Rouge* as irredeemably 'foreign', a sense of national boundaries cannot be easily stabilized or maintained.

It is certainly the case that this peculiar and sustained use of 'suture' panning to avoid the need for cuts represented a new stylistic departure for Dupont. Thomas Brandlmeier has suggested of *Variété* that there is 'one consistent stylistic feature in it: the fragmentation of space'.[37] *Moulin Rouge* has attracted the attention of a leading historian of editing techniques as a result of the 'exceptional number of different set-ups and framings' that Dupont frequently uses when simply dealing with two characters communicating in the same room. The fragmentation of space in his first British production is further intensified by persistent and deliberate violations of the 180° rule: Dupont regularly cuts across the line when showing two people in conversation so that their eyelines do not match.[38] Characters thus effectively become isolated in erratic shot compositions.

Deliberate cross-line editing does feature on a few occasions in *Piccadilly*, but its use appears to be thematically coordinated so that it can be subsequently undermined by sinuous pans. When Valentine conducts a job interview with Shosho, the incongruity of her presence—wearing tatty 'laddered' stockings—in his luxuriously furnished office and their significant formal and physical distance from each other is initially emphasized by cross-line cutting. However, at the moment when she explains that her previous experience of dancing in Limehouse resulted in 'trouble, men, knives', there is an elaborate pan across the room to Valentine, cementing their association and implicating him in the violent 'trouble' that their relationship will subsequently provoke.

The Ordinariness of Dupont's Limehouse

Ultimately, the key trope of cultural mutability and hybridity in *Piccadilly* is the Chinese community of Limehouse. The parameters for the conventional visual representation of Limehouse had been established in *Broken Blossoms*, where it figures as a space of endemic danger and exotic debauchery. The opium den frequented by the leading male protagonist is described by one intertitle as a 'scarlet house of sin', and young white women in the throes of an opium trance are shown making themselves easy sexual prey for lascivious Chinese men. It was presumably as a result of expectations raised by this kind of imagery that Arnold Bennett found himself disappointed by the 'rather flat night' he spent in the real Limehouse in 1925, when 'no vice whatever' was to be found. Indeed, the 'facts' of Limehouse were decidedly mundane: 'lots of people were drinking tea. Humble people. All very clean and tidy indeed.' Curiously, in the shooting script for *Piccadilly* written by Bennett, it is largely the myth of Limehouse which is embraced, rather than the 'facts' he had previously ascertained at first hand. The Limehouse denizens he envisaged for the film are far from clean and tidy: the restaurant Valentine visits to acquire a costume for Shosho is described as a 'wierd [*sic*] building which could hardly be considered a human habitation ... At a number of small tables sit unmistakeable Chinese in dirty, European clothes.' This first scene set in Chinatown is preceded in the script by a description of a planned montage:

FADE INTO:

258. A short panoramic view of Buckingham Palace.

QUICKLY FADE INTO:

259. A short panoramic view of the Houses of Parliament and Tower Bridge.

PICCADILLY (1929)

QUICKLY FADE INTO:

260. A short panoramic view of Trafalgar Square with the Nelson Column and the huge business houses in the background.

QUICKLY FADE INTO:

261. A short panoramic view of a characteristic street scene in Whitechapel and again

QUICKLY FADE INTO:

262. A typical [?] of 'Limehouse' the Chinese quarter in London. (These short pictures taken by the camera are intended to express the many-sidedness of the metropolis London, and above all show the contrasts between the east and the west end of London.)[39]

This had become an established and somewhat clichéd strategy for introducing Limehouse on screen. Much the same kind of montage features in a 1925 British film set in Limehouse called *A Girl in London*. A prologue sequence introduces 'London, flower of cities all', with a selection of actuality views of various London landmarks, including 'Splendid' Tower Bridge and 'Imposing' St Paul's cathedral, to emphasize maximum contrast with the last image of the sorry, 'Sordid' underbelly of London: a street scene in an east end slum.

It is surely significant that Dupont chose not to follow Bennett's suggestions for a binary juxtaposition between east and west: the final cut shows Valentine arriving in Limehouse with a minimum of fuss. Furthermore, there is no great suggestion of exoticism or filth in the scene that confronts him at the restaurant, and the dominant images are of immigrant assimilation. Perhaps Bennett told Dupont of his disappointment that the Chinese he saw in Limehouse were all peacefully drinking tea, because there are prominent notices for 'Lyons Tea' in the front window (Figure 1). On the wall to the right of the window is an amalgamation of an English newspaper headline and Chinese logograms. The Chinese men inside the restaurant are smartly if mundanely dressed in western clothes; we later see others sporting flat caps and macs. The process of cultural adaptation is seen to be reciprocal in some respects: a white woman plays 'Fan Tan' in the restaurant (Figure 2). This provokes a wry smile from Valentine, and the fact that the woman is mature and well built confounds the stereotype of delicate Limehouse waifs vulnerable to oriental sexual predators as popularized by *Broken Blossoms*.

Images of cross-cultural influence abound in this film. The Piccadilly's

Figure 1   Figure 2

scullery supervisor Bessie (Hannah Jones) swaps her overalls for a pigtail and silk gown when she becomes Shosho's maid. The character of Jim—a significant name—is particularly striking in this respect. He is first encountered eating regular English café food with a knife and fork. Bennett's shooting script presents Jim as a sinister 'half-caste': 'it is not quite certain if he is pure-bred Asiatic. He rather gives the impression of being mixed-race. His black slit-eyes seem to have discovered, followed up and retained more than one secret.' The script emphasizes Jim's irredeemable foreignness by having him speak in pidgin English (e.g. 'She wanted Mr Wilmot to give up white woman'). But there is no discernible suggestion in the film as shot that Jim is of mixed race, and the intertitles show him to be so thoroughly anglicized as to speak in a broad cockney dialect (e.g. 'It'll bring no luck to 'im as finds it').

It must be acknowledged that there is one cultural boundary in *Piccadilly* that is seen to permit no safe and acceptable breach: a tipsy white woman dances with a black man in the Limehouse pub and is roundly abused by her peers. 'Are yer blind, or wot?' the landlord seethes. The scene appears in Bennett's script, but Dupont adds an extra detail by showing the woman before she enters surveying the scene through a glass panel by peering through the two 'o's of the inscribed 'Saloon Bar' lettering (Figure 3). The comic effect this has of superimposing round 'spectacles' on her face could be taken as confirmation of the landlord's suggestion that she cannot see clearly. However, we might also consider the fact that Dupont has a marked fondness in his earlier films for playfully using instruments of optical magnification to signify a desiring gaze; I am thinking here of the vignetted shots in *Varieté* which mimic the point-of-view of an audience member with opera glasses, or the shot in *Moulin Rouge* of Andre's father, who is unexpectedly charmed by Parysia, examining her handkerchief through his monocle. There is no reverse shot in the scene from *Piccadilly*, but perhaps we are nonetheless being encouraged to see

PICCADILLY (1929)

Figure 3

this as a sly undermining of the vitriolic rebuke the woman receives, suggesting that her vision has been enhanced by a magnifying device, and that her senses and desires are calibrated to their maximum aperture.

My view that *Piccadilly* works hard to demythologize Limehouse's sinister reputation, and that it offers a highly iconoclastic portrait of the district by the established screen standards of the day, was not shared by contemporary reviewers. The critic for *The Times* looked for evidence of Arnold Bennett's signature authorial style, but found that the treatment of Limehouse was wearily familiar and straightforwardly 'conform[ed] with the mannerisms of the films as much as with Mr Bennett's novels'. He concluded that there was nothing in the film's 'romantic' Limehouse that remotely suggested the kind of observational realism that Bennett was famed for: 'it is curious and perhaps significant that the world which commonly provides Mr Bennett with so much material for description should be, on the films, the world of the films'.[40] A very recent scholarly appraisal of the film has concurred that *Piccadilly* replicates a very conventional visual discourse, showing the same kind of 'dangerously degenerate 'Othered' culture that lurks in the East End of London' as could be seen in a number of films produced earlier in the decade.[41]

I have argued in another context that, when dealing with films about Limehouse, critics in the 1920s adopted a standard interpretive strategy that vociferously repudiated any mimetic dimension, as if to deny that such a place as Limehouse even existed within the heart of the British empire.[42] This is obviously a quite distinct ideological response compared with the recent tendency amongst human geographers to also emphasize the fictive, constructed nature of representations of Limehouse as a means of deconstructing the denigration the region historically attracted as a perceived source of cultural 'infection'.[43] However, it would be unfortunate if this necessary critical vigilance served to prevent an adequate recognition of the mischievous fun which E.A. Dupont clearly had when playing with the stock tropes of Limehouse. Perhaps it was as a means of responding to the accusation that he was constitutionally incapable of understanding the true nature of Englishness that he highlighted its inevitable adulteration.

14

The Kiss (1929)

Patrick Keating

In the final scene of Jacques Feyder's *The Kiss* (1929), Irene (Greta Garbo) is sharing a kiss with André (Conrad Nagel) when they are interrupted by three cleaning women preparing to wash the courtroom where the story has been resolved. The women are delighted and amused by the sight of the two lovers kissing, though the intertitle ('Excuse me, but we have to clean the court') communicates their need to get down to work. The women function as stand-ins for the film's own viewers, who have just watched and perhaps enjoyed the glamorous spectacle that is *The Kiss*, but who are preparing to leave its frivolous tale behind. Just as the final scene presents us with a romantic kiss and then undercuts the romance by ending on an image of three women who are decidedly not movie stars, so too does the film as a whole offer a satisfying series of Hollywood pleasures that it proceeds to question. On its surface, *The Kiss* may be glamorous and even a little silly, but in this essay I argue that Feyder's film is unusually self-conscious about its own veneer, using polished visuals and a plot-twisting story to offer a reflexive commentary on the deceptiveness of Hollywood style and narration.

The film is remembered first of all for being last: Garbo's last silent film, and the last silent film from her studio MGM. Released late in 1929, with a synchronized score and some diegetic sound effects but no audible dialogue, it was the first Hollywood movie by the Belgian-born Feyder, who had made his name in France with large-scale productions like *L'Atlantide* (1921) and *Carmen* (1926), along with the smaller-scale impressionist character study *Crainquebille* (1923). The partnership with Garbo was successful enough that he was assigned to direct the German-language version of *Anna Christie* (1930), her first talking film, with a more famous English-language version directed by long-time Garbo collaborator Clarence Brown. Still, Feyder struggled in Hollywood, directing two mediocre Ramon Navarro vehicles (*Daybreak* and *Son of India*, both 1931) before returning to France with his wife Françoise Rosay in 1933. There, often working with the creative team of Rosay, the Belgian screenwriter Charles Spaak and the assistant director Marcel Carné, Feyder directed several successful films that are classified sometimes as precursors of the Poetic Realism movement associated more closely with Carné.[1]

The Kiss has not received much attention from scholars, though one notable exception is Lucy Fischer's superb analysis in her book *Designing Women*. Here she examines the way that the New Woman had come to be associated with art deco, or style moderne, the sleek lines of the latest design fashion becoming a visual shorthand for daring femininity, as in Figure 1, where the slim form of Garbo's dress echoes the thin vertical posts of the doorway and the stylized sculpture behind her.[2]

Indeed, the film's *mise en scène* is consistently up to date, from the numerous tight-fitting hats worn by Garbo's Irene throughout the film to the dozens of sculptures and other *objets* that decorate her well-appointed home. Feyder's camerawork is similarly modern, employing superimpositions, fast camera movements and unusual angles to communicate story information visually, demonstrating a familiarity with the cutting-edge style of his friend F.W. Murnau, a fellow European émigré.[3] On the narrative level, Fischer finds *The Kiss* to be one of the most radical presentations of Garbo's New Woman character, both because the ending does not punish the bold protagonist for her transgressions against social norms and because the story is told in a striking way, with a lying flashback that anticipates Alfred Hitchcock's *Stage Fright* (1950).[4] This essay will extend Fischer's project by examining another aspect of the

Figure 1

film's modernity, its reflexivity, an aspect that emerges in part through its experiments with unreliable narration.

The story of *The Kiss* is a tale of scandal surrounding Irene's relationship with three men: André, the man she loves; Guarry (Anders Randolf), her wealthy, easily ired husband; and Pierre (Lew Ayres), a puppyish young man infatuated with her. After Irene breaks off her relationship with the conscientious André, she begins to spend time with Pierre, arousing the suspicions of Guarry. One night, after Guarry has left to visit a business partner (Lassalle, Pierre's father), Irene meets with Pierre at her home and agrees to grant him a goodbye kiss before he leaves for school. After the initial kiss, Pierre grabs Irene forcefully to steal another. At this moment, Guarry appears and, through the window, sees Pierre gripping the struggling Irene. In a jealous rage, he attacks the now helpless Pierre, in spite of Irene's cries for him to stop. The ensuing struggle takes place largely offscreen, but it ends with a gunshot heard behind a closed door. A bleeding Pierre goes home to his father, who plans to protect his son from scandal. During the ensuing police investigation, Irene lies about the fateful night, excluding Pierre entirely and implying that her husband's death was a suicide. The police quickly spot the inconsistencies in her story and charge her with murder. André, who happens to be a skilful lawyer, defends her, securing an acquittal when he shows that Guarry, secretly facing bankruptcy, had a reason for suicide. After the trial, Irene finds the courage to tell André the truth: she shot Guarry to prevent him from killing Pierre. Though Irene expects her confession to destroy André's love for her, he reaffirms his devotion, leading to the final kiss amid the cleaning women.

This is a complicated story for a film that lasts little more than an hour. What is most striking about *The Kiss*, however, is not the story but the narration—that is, how the events of the story are organized in order to manipulate the spectator's response through the play of concealment and revelation.[5] The most overtly manipulative scenes are the murder scene, which uses a closed door to block our visual access to the crucial event, and the interrogation scene, which illustrates Irene's lies to the detective with false images of events that did not happen. A closer look at these two sequences will show that the film is working to draw a reflexive analogy between the dishonesty of Irene and the dishonesty of the film's own narration—and, by extension, the dishonesty of commercial Hollywood films in general.

In the murder scene, we see Guarry beating Pierre over a desk that previously was shown to contain a gun in a locked drawer. Irene stands behind Guarry, trying to pull him off the defenceless boy. The camera

Figure 2

views this scene from outside the office, through a momentarily open doorway, as in Figure 2.

But the door soon closes, and the camera dollies back to frame a shot of the door flanked by two art deco sculptures, the elegant balance of the composition counterpointing the violence we know to be occurring beyond. Just as the dolly is completing its manoeuvre, the frantic score slows to a pause, and we hear a gunshot on the soundtrack. The result is a curious mixture of concealment, obviousness, discretion and deception. The scene conceals information from us—we do not know what happens on the other side of the door. Of course, narratives conceal information all the time, but this is an unusually obvious act of concealment. The film heightens our awareness of its own manipulations of story information by stressing the concealment with the camera's gesture of pulling away from the action and the music's silence allowing the gunshot to be heard. The initial effect is to provoke sharp curiosity: we know someone has been shot, but we do not know who, or by whom. The secondary effect is to give the appearance of discretion, allowing us to infer what has happened while tastefully protecting us from the view of a gruesome act. For the next half hour, we are encouraged to follow the incorrect inference that Pierre committed the crime. Not only was he near the drawer with the gun when the door was closed, but his subsequent behaviour, appearing in his father's study bleeding from his temple and quickly collapsing, seems to confirm his guilt. Yet Irene's final confession reveals, among other things, that our initial assumptions about this act of concealment were wrong. The closing of the door, it turns out, was not a tasteful way of concealing an easily inferred but gruesome event, but a deceptive way of concealing a surprising story event that had been withheld systematically for half the film's running time. The film's narration—its organization of story events—had seemed tastefully discreet, only to be revealed as definitely unreliable.

THE KISS (1929)

The morning after the murder, the police interrogate Irene, who lies about the events to cover up the fact of Pierre's visit, apparently to help the presumably guilty Pierre. Here, Feyder makes a remarkably bold choice, illustrating Irene's story with visually illustrative flashbacks that are clearly incorrect. When the detectives ask her at what time she sat down to read, we see the hands of a clock swinging around until Irene settles on the time she wants to report. Then we see Irene leaving an outside door open and keeping the lights on, both represented by images that contradict what we have seen earlier. Next, Irene claims that the windows in the bedroom were closed, and we see a shot of the windows closing themselves automatically, as if by magic. The effect of this sequence is to position Irene as the film's internal narrator for a few moments, not just because she is telling a story, but also because she temporarily has control over the film's images, altering them to suit her present needs. She is an unreliable narrator to the questioning detectives, though at this moment the film's own mode of storytelling appears reliable by comparison, precisely because the visual contradictions expose Irene as someone whose account is not to be trusted. In the end, this assumption of the film's own reliability will be overturned. When Irene finally tells the truth, and we see the events as they happened, we realize that the film has baited us into assuming that she was trying to protect Pierre all along.

Because the film ends up exposing its own manipulations, the deceptiveness of Irene's act of narration is analogized to the deceptiveness of the film itself. Just as she has concealed information to mislead the detectives, the film has concealed information to mislead its audience. The analogy is reinforced visually through the motif of the door. In the murder scene, the act of concealment centres on the image of a door closing—indeed, appearing to close itself, since no character is nearby to push it shut. In the interrogation, Irene's own acts of concealment are visualized with an image of Irene closing a door and later with an image of windows closing themselves under her command.

We might contrast Irene's act of unreliable narration with a previous scene, in which a private detective had offered his report to the suspicious Guarry. The film dissolves from a close-up of the detective's face to a flashback of his investigation. When Irene emerges from her car, the detective spies on her via a reflection in a shop window. He then follows her into a 'canine exposition', and Feyder's remarkably mobile camera tracks along a series of adorable dogs, the editing clearly marking these travelling shots as representations of the detective's point of view, not of Irene's. Soon he spots Irene meeting Pierre, whose childishness is signalled efficiently through his association with animals. The detective's report is reliable, in the sense that it is factually correct, and yet unreliable in the sense that his judgement is suspect.[6] He incorrectly assesses the relationship between Irene and Pierre as an affair, when it is clear to the audience that it is just a harmless flirtation. In this way, the film stresses the gap between seeing and knowing. The detective's narration is not to be trusted, not because he is lying, but because he does not understand what he sees. The later sequence of Irene's interrogation will drive a further wedge between seeing and knowing, to the point at which we cannot trust the cinematic images we see with our own eyes.

In the interrogation scene, there is special significance in the fact that the theme of deception is visualized through the image of a static or slow-moving object appearing to come to life through movement, as seen in the image of the clock hands whirling around and the inanimate windows shutting themselves. Here, the film seems to be alluding to the cinematic image itself: a static picture that springs into movement. This observation might seem like an unbearable stretch were it not for the fact that Feyder's film consistently deploys the 'image' as a motif. In the opening scene, Irene meets André in the Lyons museum of fine arts, and a gag shows a docent leading a group of American tourists through the museum at a breakneck pace, contrasting their hectic movement with the more contemplative pace one might expect in such a distinguished hall. Yet Irene and André are no better than the American tourists, as they ignore the art to focus on their own concerns.

In the trial scene, courtroom artists are shown sketching Irene's image for the newspapers, and one of the drawings looks remarkably similar to a subsequent low-angle shot of Irene standing accused. Others look like sketches by a fashion designer, with Garbo's stylized profile in a distinctively pointed hat and chic back-draped dress. We know that the newspaper images are not really high art, but simply tools to sell more papers, and the visual similarity between the cartoon and the cinematic image itself undercuts the authority of the latter.

Similarly, the film features an extended motif concerning a publicity photograph that also works to cast doubt on the value of the film's own images. After Irene breaks up with André, an intertitle informs us of 'Weeks of loneliness—of social routine—of striving to forget'. The words prime us to expect an image of Irene suffering, as only Garbo can suffer, but the film instead dissolves to a tight close-up of Irene looking seductively into the camera. With William Daniels's impeccably smooth lighting, Irene looks glamorous, even in such a tight framing, and the illusion-shattering gaze towards the camera makes the image reminiscent of a publicity photograph. The camera dollies back, and we are surprised

Figure 3

to learn that Irene was looking into a mirror the whole time, applying make-up and preparing to go out with her less-than-glamorous husband. Later, the idea of a publicity shot comes back in the most literal way. Just prior to the murder scene, Irene offers Pierre a gift, allowing him to select one of several photographs she has of herself (see Figure 3).

Astonishingly, the photos are quite recognizable as pre-existing publicity shots of the film's star. For instance, the image in Figure 3 is clearly a portrait taken by the great MGM photographer Ruth Harriet Louise for the publicity campaign for *The Mysterious Lady* (1928).[7] The film extends this inside joke about the publicity shots after the trial begins. The trial is front-page news, and the papers, with alternating headlines in French and English, are filled with pictures of Irene—the same publicity shots we have seen her offer Pierre. The film wryly comments on how quickly a scandal can become old news, showing a grocer use one of these newspaper publicity photos to wrap up a fresh bunch of celery. Another newspaper shows the publicity photo from Figure 3 appearing under the headline, 'Did Mrs Guarry Kill Her Husband?' We might think of the publicity photo as a tool for commerce, separate from the film image, a tool for storytelling. *The Kiss* suggests that such distinctions are nonsense, at least in the context of a Garbo film at MGM. Just as pre-existing publicity photos of Garbo have become narrativized in this film, *The Kiss*'s own narrativized close-ups of Irene function as moving publicity shots for the studio's commodified stars. Irene finds herself caught in the publicity machine of the scandal-mongering newspapers, a form of storytelling that relies on games of concealment and revelation not at all dissimilar to the film's own mode of narration.

This interpretation of the film as a reflexive commentary on the status of the image within Hollywood narrative gains greater weight when we situate the film within the context of director Feyder's career. To be sure, we might also point to the influence of Hans Kraly, the film's screenwriter, who had plenty of practice using the motif of the closed door while writing scripts for Ernst Lubitsch, a master of suggesting all sorts of naughty behaviour going on in rooms unseen.[8] Yet Feyder had been exploring this territory in his French films for some time. For instance, in *Crainquebille*, the protagonist experiences various fantasies during the trial scene, including one in which a sculpture of justice comes to life, looking directly at him. In *Faces of Children* (*Visages d'enfants*, 1925), the boy's nostalgia for his lost mother is so strong that he imagines seeing a moving image when he looks at a painting of the departed. Feyder marks both moments as fantasies by showing a normally static object appear, shockingly, in motion. The moving objects of *The Kiss* can be seen as variations on this authorial motif.

More generally, Feyder's other silent films often deal with the theme of epistemological uncertainty that is at the core of *The Kiss*'s narrative strategy. In addition to the fantasy sequences in *Crainquebille* and *Faces of Children*—fantasy sequences that the characters respond to as if they are really happening—we might cite other examples in *Gribiche* (1926) and *Carmen*. In *Gribiche*, a young boy is adopted by a rich woman after he does her the favour of returning a dropped purse. The woman tells the story in flashback several times, each time exaggerating the poverty of the boy and the generosity of her response, and each time the film visualizes the lie with images we know to be incorrect. In *Carmen*, one sequence represents a future that José imagines, but that Carmen, consulting her tarot cards, knows will not take place. These characters seek to narrativize time: the past, in one case; the future, in the other. The moving image that illustrates their imagined stories is not to be trusted. Perhaps the flashback-within-a-flashback structure of *L'Atlantide* could be added to the list, a narrative structure that hints at the idea of epistemological uncertainly, within the context of a film whose desert setting evokes the idea of a mirage.

Following this line of thinking, it is tempting to classify the French impressionist Feyder as a modernist, making reflexive films that problematize the status of the cinematic image, expressing distrust for the narratives that image is consigned to tell. From this point of view, *The Kiss* becomes a radical film, subverting Hollywood narration from within. This reading, while plausible, may push Feyder's apparent modernism a little too far. In his authoritative discussion of French films in the 1920s, Richard Abel classifies Feyder's works as commercial, realist films, rather than as examples of the 'narrative avant-garde'.[9] Another look at the above examples confirms this proposal. Although Feyder's films often explore characteristically modernist themes of uncertainty, illusion and deception, they often contrast those negative values with the positive value of truth—in particular, a truth provided by a character's act of confession. The religious subtext of the confession theme is made explicit in *Faces of Children*. The protagonist's lie endangers his own stepsister, who is caught in an avalanche but is saved when she hides in a church. After the boy confesses his mistake, the members of the town are able to locate the girl because the cross of the church steeple peeks through the enveloping banks of snow. Similarly, *L'Atlantide* is structured around an act of confession, while *Crainquebille* reverses the motif, telling the story of an honest man who refuses to confess to a crime he did not commit. In *The Kiss*, Irene conceals the truth, a concealment aided and abetted by the film itself, hiding the murder behind a closed door. But Irene and the film ultimately come around to confessing the truth, the film's false flashback replaced by the real one.

During the course of pre-production, the film's ending changed several times. In the film's credits, the writing is credited to Kraly, and the original story is attributed to one George M. Saville. In the MGM files at the Margaret Herrick Library, the earliest complete treatment is signed by Feyder himself, suggesting that 'Saville' was nothing more than a pseudonym for the Belgian director. In this early version, Irene and André (here named Henry) begin their affair after the trial. Irene eventually confesses the truth to him, but his love is unbroken. In the end, Irene kills herself in order to free the devoted André to return to his dying wife.[10] In the first complete draft, Kraly reworks Irene's suicide scene significantly, not least by removing entirely the storyline about André's wife. Disgusted by Irene's confession, André (here called by his last name, Dubail) leaves her. Walking down the stairs, he begins to regret his decision when he hears the gunshot. Irene and André reconcile in the ambulance, but she dies before reaching the hospital. In this way, the script suggests that Irene deserves forgiveness, while punishing her all the same.[11] The next draft, written a month later, offers perhaps the most dramatic of the alternative endings. André initially is appalled by Irene's confession, accusing her of being in love with the young Pierre the whole time. After he leaves, Irene writes a full confession and gives it to a page to mail to the authorities. Regretting his decision, André comes back. The script reads:

> Irene points mutely to the street below. Dubail's eyes follow Irene's gesture, and both look upon the street below. Quick dissolve into: Ext. Street Opposite Hotel. Moving Shot. The camera moves rapidly from the vantagepoint of the two, at the window, downward, to the mailbox attached to the house-wall, opposite the hotel, until

the mailbox is in a Close Up. The page's hand is just dropping the letter into the mailbox.[12]

This scene adopts the just-missed timing of the tear-jerker. Seeing Irene's courage sweeps away all of André's doubts about his love for her. The result is an ending that carefully balances joy with tragedy: André's love for Irene is greatest just at the moment when she is most likely to be punished for the crime. The film as released destroys this balance, preserving the moment when André reaffirms his love for Irene while eliminating the suggestion that she may suffer for the crime. However, this ending might be the most radical, especially in its social implications. Lucy Fischer astutely points to an earlier French impressionist film, Germaine Dulac's *The Smiling Madame Beudet* (1923), as a relevant comparison. In the earlier film, the protagonist dreams of killing her boorish husband, but ends up trapped in her loveless marriage. Similarly, in a Hollywood film, the daring modern woman may challenge social norms for the bulk of the story only if she is punished in the end. In *The Kiss*, Irene longs to separate from her husband, a longing we are encouraged to endorse. One of the three cleaning ladies goes even farther, saying that 'Half us women would shoot our husbands—if we only had the nerve'. By the end, Irene has managed to challenge conventions, kill her husband (albeit only in defence of Pierre) and reunite with her lover, all without the sentence of jail or death that Hollywood normally would require for such a transgressive figure.[13]

Describing Feyder's time at MGM, his wife Françoise Rosay once suggested that he made an effort to satisfy MGM's needs, noting that he hoped his Garbo script would fulfil 'all the conditions required by the American public . . . love, sensuality, redemption, and "nobility"'.[14] Yet Feyder ended up embittered by his experience, criticizing the Hollywood system of story development in a 1931 interview with his friend Marcel Carné, then ridiculing the system a decade later in his autobiography with Rosay. In the former piece, he states:

> The directors of [American] film actually find themselves in a very paradoxical situation: the mentality of the inhabitants of the big cities has noticeably evolved, whereas that of the rural people remains a little rough. The entire problem is there: to make a film that does not unleash the laughter of the New York worker and makes torrents of tears flow from the farmers of San Bernardino.[15]

Here, in an admittedly self-serving argument, Feyder adopts the position of the sophisticated European who failed to connect with the more naive segments of the American audience.

My analysis of *The Kiss* suggests that Feyder's cynicism towards Hollywood emerged early on, well before he found himself directing MGM nonsense like *Son of India*. Indeed, a critique of Hollywood is built into Feyder's first Hollywood film. From a commercial perspective, *The Kiss* has it all: romance, fashion, celebrity, murder, a mystery, a trial and an abundance of glamour. Yet the film's reflexivity encourages us to criticize these elements even as we enjoy them to the fullest. The film's approach to storytelling is revealed as manipulative, even duplicitous. The film's deployment of a glamorous visual style is exposed as an accomplice in the narration's acts of deception. Though Irene Guarry finds love and freedom, on a deeper level Hollywood narrative is being put on trial in this film. And Feyder's verdict comes back guilty.

15

Love and Duty
(Lian'ai yu yiwu) (1931)

Anne Kerlan

Considered lost for more than half a century, a print of *Love and Duty* was eventually discovered in Uruguay, among the belongings of a former high-ranking officer in the Chinese Nationalist Army. Produced by the United Photoplay Service (UPS), which was otherwise known as the Lianhua Film Company (Lianhua yingye gongsi), *Love and Duty* was an important landmark in the history of the company and of Chinese cinema in general. Appearing at the same time as the first Chinese talkies, *Love and Duty* was a silent feature that UPS hoped would engage with and challenge aspects of Western culture. Sound technology and the vicissitudes of Chinese history would bring new challenges to Chinese cinema and relegate the silent version of *Love and Duty* to the past. Other versions followed, but the first is uniquely significant.

When *Love and Duty* was proposed, UPS existed mainly as a project and a name, as is clear from a manifesto published on the opening page of the issue of *Yingxi zazhi* (*The Film Magazine*) on 1 August 1930. The announcement somewhat ironically called for the Chinese film industry to exploit the opportunities provided by the advent of talking pictures:

> For the past twelve years the film industry has succeeded in playing an important role in the industrial world . . . But at the same time those who work in the industry have witnessed the extent to which imported foreign films have contributed the cultural and economic penetration of our country while national production has gone into

decline ... Now the United States, our principal provider of feature films, has stopped producing silent films, and the talkies it exports to China will face difficulties on account of issues of language. Those in our profession have to find a way of saving our cinemas from the crisis caused by the lack of films ... Now is the time to launch a 'movement for the renaissance of the national film industry'. We urge the national movie world to adopt this idea in order to grow and to benefit our people. Well-known film companies from Hong Kong, Guangzhou, Nanjing, Shanghai, Beijing, Tianjin, Liaoning and Harbin are in the process of amalgamation and will soon give birth to UPS ...[1]

Major players in the Chinese film industry—important businessmen, statesmen and artists—participated in founding the company. In the context of a semi-colonized China, where foreign powers were increasingly perceived as economic and cultural invaders, some of the principal personalities in the Chinese film industry, together with their colleagues among the Chinese bourgeoisie, declared their intention to battle for a stronger China. Their aim was to save an industry in crisis and to become a partner in the rebuilding of a nation led by Chiang Kai-shek and the Guomindang. In order to do so, they adopted the economic model of a vertically integrated Hollywood major. The UPS emulated Hollywood as the benchmark of artistic and technical quality and as a means of attracting educated urban Chinese audiences, even as it advertised itself as a national enterprise ready to lead the way in producing high-class Chinese films for Chinese people. In that regard, Hollywood was both a model and a counter-model.[2]

UPS had not been registered as a company when production on *Love and Duty* began. Indeed, as late as autumn 1930, those involved in the formation of UPS, including Li Minwei (Lai Man-wai), head of the China Sun Motion Picture Company (Minxin yingpian gongsi) and the main instigator, Luo Mingyou, head of the North China Film Company (Huabei dianying gongsi; an important network of film theatres in northern China), were still in discussion. They were soon joined by the Great China and Lily Film Company (Dazhonghua baihe yingpian), and it was these three companies that formed the basis of UPS. UPS was registered at the Ministry of Industry in Nanjing on 25 October 1930 (and in Hong Kong shortly thereafter) and its Shanghai branch was opened on 25 March 1931, by which time production on *Love and Duty* was more or less complete.[3] It was premiered a few weeks later, on 5 April 1931, in two important theatres in Shanghai and at two further venues in Beijing and Nanjing.

During the course of 1930 and 1931, the advent of sound films had become a topic of heated debate. Different companies adopted different strategies.[4] The Star Film Company (Mingxing yingpian gongsi) and the Unique Film Company (Tianyi yingpian gongsi) invested heavily in sound technology and produced their first sound films in 1931. The first Chinese talkie, *Songstress Red Peony* (*Genü hong mudan*), a sound-on-disc film made with Pathé technology, was released in Shanghai on 15 March 1931. Less than three months later, two minor Chinese companies produced the first Chinese optical sound film, which was made with Japanese technology, and in October 1931 Unique released *Pleasures of the Dance Hall* (*Ge chang chunse*) using Movietone technology.[5]

Why, then, did UPS produce *Love and Duty* as a silent film? The answer can be found in a series of articles written by the company's producers and published in *Yingxi zazhi* (*The Film Magazine*) between June 1930 and October 1931. While arguing that China was not yet ready for sound, the producers also pondered the ways in which it could be adapted to Chinese ends. China did not yet have the means to produce numerous costly sound films, and there were difficult issues of language to address. The nationalist government was keen to push towards a common language, but most people only spoke local dialects. What language should actors speak? How could audiences in a cosmopolitan city like Shanghai be helped to understand what was said on screen?[6] Another factor was the absence of a tradition of spoken Chinese theatre, and hence a lack of ready-made Chinese scripts and stories. There was a danger that Chinese-speaking films would be based on foreign stories and that Hollywood talkies would displace silent Chinese films before the Chinese film industry had a chance to come to terms with these and other fundamental issues.[7] UPS producers also thought that:

> while talkies arrived in the United States at a point at which silent film had reach its apex, silent Chinese films were as yet far from being perfect. By adopting the new technology straightaway, China risked destroying its yet unrealized potential.[8]

The strategy at UPS was to delay the production of talkies in order to gain economic strength and to devise alternatives to US productions. In the interim, the producers proposed the production of two types of films: silent films screened with live or pre-recorded music, and music and dance films based on the art of Chinese opera.[9] UPS met its target. Its second feature film, *Wild Flowers* (*Ye cao xian hua*), released in December 1930, was also China's first sound film, with five songs recorded on disc.

Then, in March 1931, UPS acquired a troupe of singers and dancers, who made their first appearance in *Two Stars of the Milky Way* (*Yin han shuang xing*), a sound-on-disc production mixing Western and Chinese music.[10] Four months after the release of the first UPS sound film, and only a few months before the release of *Two Stars of the Milky Way*, *Love and Duty* was released and promoted as a landmark example of the art of silent film—an example so successful that UPS would continue making silent films for the next four years.

From Novel to Film

The production of *Love and Duty* was initially advertised in the August issue of *The Film Magazine* in 1930, in which a set of photographs and stills was accompanied by an announcement that the film was

> based on an English novel by Miss Luo Chen, a female writer from Northern China, and is being made with her full cooperation. It deals with the situation of women of our country as they encounter love, duty, ideology and oppression . . .[11]

Luo Chen was one of a number of noms de plume adopted by S. Horose, the Polish spouse of a Chinese man.[12] As she explains in the preface to the French edition of the novel, she and her husband met as students in France. There they 'learnt what Justice was. With this word in our hearts and in our spirits we visited a number of countries where, unfortunately, injustice reigns and misunderstandings flourish.'[13] S. Horose and her husband went to live in China in or around 1911, and from that point on she considered China to be her second home.[14] She used it as a setting for a number of her novels, many of which, including *Love and Duty*, were initially written in English or French, then subsequently translated into Chinese.[15]

Love and Duty was written in 1921. The Commercial Press in Shanghai initially published the Chinese version in instalments in 1923, then as a book in 1924. (An English language version was published two years later.[16]) The status of women in China was a major topic of debate in the early 1920s, and the novel attracted the attention of the elite of Northern China. At this point, Luo Mingyou and Li Minwei planned to produce a film version. But it was not until they approached Zhu Shilin, head of the translation department at the North China Film Company, that they found a suitable screenwriter.[17] With Zhu Shilin on board, Luo Chen was hired as a consultant, Li Minwei was put in charge of production and Bu Wancang was chosen to direct.

The French edition of the novel, which was published in 1932 (and which appears to have been written at the same time as the script), tells the story of Yang Neifan and Li Tsoju, who initially meet on the way to school and fall in love.[18] Their relationship is cemented when Neifan is bitten by a dog and Tsoju comes to her rescue. The two young people dare not even speak to one another, and Neifan's father decides that it is time for her to marry Hwang Tajen, the man he has chosen as her husband. Tsoju and Neifan are parted. Hwang Tajen is an educated man, but he and Neifan are not in love. Tajen spends more and more time away from home, playing poker and having affairs with women, and Neifan's only joy lies in taking care of their two young children. However, while playing in a park, Neifan's little boy falls into a river—and is rescued by none other than Tsoju. Neifan and Tsoju meet again. They are still in love with one another, and as their feelings intensify, Tsoju asks Neifan to abandon her home and children and to come and live with him: a choice between love and duty. She chooses love. But her heart is broken as she and Tsoju are regarded as a scandalous couple, especially when she gives birth to their daughter, Pingel. Tsoju is unable to find a decent job. His father disowns him, and dies without bestowing his forgiveness. Devastated by a death that renders him impious, Tsoju falls ill and dies as well.

Poverty-stricken, friendless and ostracized by her family, Neifan is left alone with her baby girl. She brings her child up as best she can, giving her a modern education while working as a seamstress. Tajen meanwhile has reformed. Now a model father and enlightened spirit, he publishes a newspaper called *China's Future*, in which he defends such modern ideas as gender equality. Neifan is an eager reader, and she learns that her now grown-up children are due to perform at a local charity show. She also discovers Tajen's address and tries to catch sight of her children. One day, Tajen visits Neifan's shop to buy artificial flowers for his daughter's wedding. He recognizes Neifan and learns of her unhappy life, while Neifan realizes that her fate is to embroider flowers for her abandoned daughter as a common seamstress. When her fiancé's family rejects Neifan's daughter on account of her scandalous mother, Neifan decides that it is time for her to die. She writes a letter to Tajen asking him to take care of Pingel, and then swallows a fatal overdose of sleeping pills. Pingel becomes united with her siblings and eventually marries the man she loves.

As Zhu Shilin puts it, Luo Chen 'says things that most people do not dare to say . . . because she loves China as a second homeland but also because she understands its weaknesses. She sees things we cannot see about our country.'[19] He goes on to argue that the questions raised by the novel are complex, turning as they do around the 'battle between desire and reason':

> how do we judge a person who follows their desire, a person who knows that they are not doing the right thing but who does it anyway? Should we scorn them or pity them? The issue is that of individual free choice, and this is, in China, is a very new question.[20]

Engaging on the one hand with what Kristine Harris calls 'the competing concerns of intellectuals' involvement in China's New Culture Movement' and on the other with the contradictions between 'romantic dilemmas and Confucian obligations' evident in contemporary popular fiction, *Love and Duty* is a novel in which all the main characters have their own weaknesses and strengths, in which the traditions of marriage are questioned, in which women lack freedom and choice, and in which a character like Tsoju believes he can behave like a hero in an American or European novel.[21] As such, the issues at stake are multi-dimensional, and this is as true of the 1931 film as it is of the 1920s novel.

The Film and the Novel

The 1931 version of *Love and Duty* is similar in outline to the novel, but there are a number of changes, some of which are major. The sequence in which Neifan and Tsoju (Yang Nei-fan and Li Tsu Yi in the film) register as husband and wife is omitted, as is the sequence in which Tsoju finds a job as a clerk in a Western department store, which describes at length the relationship between the Westerners in the shop and their Chinese 'boys'. There is no mention of the relationship between Tsoju and his father, and in the film Tsu Yi dies of ill health. The film also omits the meeting between the older Neifan and Tajen. In its stead is an extremely touching scene showing an ageing Nei-fan measuring costumes for her grown-up children, who are unaware of her identity. Given that Ruan Lingyu, the film's principal actress, plays Nei-fan's daughter as well as her mother, this particular scene is all the more touching—and all the more important.

The film adds other telling details, too, such as the extent to which Nei-fan is tempted to commit suicide when Tsu Yi (played by Jin Yan) dies. It is only the thought of her baby girl that stops her. (Suicide was seen as a conventional option for a 'lost woman' in China, so it is perhaps unsurprising that Zhu Shilin added it to the script.) Similar motives underscore the scene with her grown-up children, which focuses more on Nei-fan as a mother than a spouse. For Chinese audiences, Nei-fan's tragedy resides in the loss of her children, who will never recognize her. As Zhu Shilin puts it, she loses her daughters not once but twice, the first time when she leaves them for her lover, the second when she has no choice but to hide her identity if they are to find any kind of happiness and any kind of 'face'.[22] Notably, while the novel ends with the marriage of Neifan's daughter, the film ends with Ta Jen (played by Lay Ying) nodding in approval as Nei-fan's children pay their respects to their mother, whose photograph hangs on Ta Jen's wall. This, as Harris points out, is one of a number of points at which photographs and visual effects are significant.[23] The film also raises the question of womanhood and marriage in a way that is slightly but significantly different from the novel. If both film and novel insist on the fact that Neifan/Nei-fen and Tajen/Ta Jen do not love each other, the novel describes a common and parallel drift away, while the film is more one-sided, showing Ta Jen in night clubs with his mistress while Nei-fan stays at home with her children. For Zhu Shilin, in addition to the issue of arranged marriage, there is that of the husband's responsibility in the family's happiness: 'when a husband becomes cold to his wife, bringing therefore unhappiness into his family, is it the husband or the wife who is responsible for that unhappiness?'[24]

A Chinese Film with a Taste for Hollywood

Like many late 1920s and early 1930s Chinese films, *Love and Duty* mixes Chinese and Western ingredients. The Hollywood model is particularly evident in the costumes and settings, as well as in the acting. Thus, while Luo Chen sets the beginning of her story in a district of Beijing which is 'not yet touched by Western civilization',[25] the film is set in Kiangwan, a westernized residential area with wide streets, pavements and elegant two-storey villas with fences and private gardens.[26] (Aside from foreign settlements, there were few such places in China in 1930.) The villas of the families of Tsu Yi and Nei-fan are decorated in art deco style, and the villa occupied by Ta Jen's family at the end of the film is a luxurious dwelling with its own private tennis court. The film is set in a kind of 'cinema land' that would appeal to the Chinese bourgeoisie.

Other details are consistent with a world that is less a reproduction of China and more a utopian depiction governed by Hollywood norms and westernized ingredients. While in the novel Neifan is bitten by a dog, in the film she is a hit by a car. Both afford Tsoju/Tsu Yi the chance to approach and help her. But the choice of a car—a modern, Western machine—is clearly of a piece with these ingredients. Later, when Neifan/

Nei-fan goes to the theatre to catch a glimpse of her children on stage, the novel makes it clear that she stands in order to see them, while in the film she borrows a pair of Western binoculars. In the film, Western culture is marked not as foreign, but as a milieu in which some of the wealthy characters live. Those aspects of the Western world that are shown—the car, the telephone, the binoculars—exemplify technological progress and help people to connect. The novel is different, questioning as it does the influence of 'modern books' and Hollywood films on Tsoju, and drawing attention to the racism of his Western employers. Its author's ambivalence in this regard is perhaps best expressed at the point at which Neifan kills herself by taking a Western drug, a drug that is 'foreign . . . a modern drug . . . sweet and terrible'.[27] None of this ambivalence is in the film. There are no Westerners (prejudiced or otherwise). And Nei-fan's death is very different: she returns to Tsu Yi's tomb, says that she is coming to join him, then walks away and disappears from view as she disappears from life. The episode in which Tsu Yi dreams that he is a hero saving his beloved in a Hollywood adventure sequence is a tribute to Douglas Fairbanks and Mary Pickford, not a critique. In a context in which US productions were particularly popular, this scene may have pleased audiences. However, it was also a means by which UPS was able to demonstrate that it possessed the technical and artistic wherewithal to produce entertaining films, but chose not to do so. For UPS, enlightenment was more important than entertainment.

As the film was directed by Bu Wancang, Hollywood's style influences the framing and editing of *Love and Duty*. Bu Wancang and his colleagues were working in a Western medium, and *Love and Duty* uses a vocabulary derived in large part from silent Hollywood films. They cite, draw on and transpose shots and scenes from a number of American films. Thus, when Tsu Yi follows Nei-fan down the middle of the street on their way to school, a lengthy reverse tracking shot evokes a similar shot in Buster Keaton's *Seven Chances* (1925), while Cecil B. DeMille's influence is evident in some of the scenes of married life. These scenes are dramatic rather than comic: Nei-fan and Ta Jen are engaged in separate activities in their living room in a manner reminiscent of some of the scenes and sequences in *Don't Change Your Husband!* (1919) and *Why Change Your Wife?* (1920).[28] Bu Wangcang emphasizes the lack of rapport between Ta Jen and Nei-fan, and in another dramatic scene he cuts back and forth between Nei-fan and her lover and Ta Jen enjoying himself with his mistress. The editing is similar to the point in *Why Change Your Wife?* at which Robert Gordon is trapped at Sally's place while his lonely spouse waits for him in bed.

Sounds and Silence

Love and Duty is a silent film, but it also highlights the power and presence of sounds. There are a number of points at which characters react to sounds, and these are often marked by changes in facial expression. Thus, at the point at which Nei-fan is about to be hit by a car, she is shown kneeling in the street with her back turned towards Tsu Yi. The car horn is shown in close-up, followed by Tsu Yi's reaction. But Nei-fan is in a still soundless world and appears to hear nothing. Later, Tsu Yi, who is waiting for a call from Nei-fan, reacts to the ringing of the telephone. An editing structure similar to that used in the car-horn sequence is used here as we cut to a close-up of the sound source then on to a shot of Tsu Yi's reaction, then to a shot of Nei-fan and back to Tsu Yi, who is listening and smiling, then back to Nei-fan, who begins to weep in silence. But the most striking depiction of sound in this silent film occurs at its climax, when a desperate Nei-fan (who is ready to commit suicide) hears the cry of her baby girl (who is shown in close-up) and decides not to jump into the river. Instead, she will live and bring up her daughter as a free and educated woman.

Love and Duty can be seen as the story of a voiceless woman. But this is more than a metaphor, for the extent to which Nei-fan is unable to speak is evident in her facial expressions, and this is particularly marked from the point at which her father tells her that he has decided to marry her to Ta Jen. The effect of her father's words is evident in the way she squeezes her hands and bites her lips. This is a woman who literally cannot speak, and Ruan Lingyu will replay this body language on numerous occasions, each time conveying the impression that Nei-fan would like to speak but cannot. But Nei-fan is not only a voiceless person; she is also brutalized by the words of the men around her. Following her father's imposition of a marriage that she does not want, she is forced by Tsu Yi to abandon her husband and her children. She tries to argue with Tsu Yi, but is physically intimated by his words. Close-ups show her speechless and tearful. Only later will she speak to him on the phone—at a point at which she makes a choice that she will regret for the rest of her life.

There are many other scenes that repeat this motif, particularly in the film's first half. After Tsu Yi's death, a desperate Nei-fan examines her options. Should she return to her father? Should she return to Ta Jen? In both cases the film depicts her fears, in both cases she is framed as a small and fragile figure bending in front of taller man who seeks to dominate her by using violent words and gestures, and in both cases it is as though she is unable to articulate words, as though she has not yet learned how to speak. Describing the violence imposed by those who speak on those who cannot, the film makes evident the paroxysm of being voiceless in a world of sounds.

Reception and Fate

As is the case with most early Chinese films, it is difficult to get an accurate idea of the commercial success (or failure) of *Love and Duty*. No box-office figures are available, and we are left with incomplete sources in magazine and newspapers. As already noted, the film was premiered in Shanghai (at the 1000-seat Beijing Theatre and the 900-seat Guanghua Theatre, both of which were located in the International Settlement). It returned to the Guanghua a month later and was subsequently advertised in *Shun Pao*, a Shanghai newspaper, as a production that 'shook the world', as a film that 'exported to America and Europe', and as a film that 'broke records at the box-office in forty theatres' in mainland China (a figure cited in *Yingxi zazhi* too).[29] The international circulation and reception of *Love and Duty* is even more difficult to trace. According to *Yingxi zazhi*, it was acquired for exhibition in France, South America and Canada,[30] though I have been unable to discover whether or not it was shown in any of these markets. (An article by S. Horose in the French film magazine *Pour Vous* announces that the film will soon be shown in Paris, though there are no further or subsequent details.)[31] There is evidence that the film was shown in the South Pacific, though, according to Luo Mingyou, and despite the presence of a relatively large Chinese population in the region, it was not a great success.[32] However, it was one of fifteen films selected by the Ministry of Education for the Chicago International Trade Fair (the Century of Progress International Exposition) in the autumn of 1933, and as such was adjudged to showcase the qualities of Chinese films and to possess international appeal.[33]

Leafing through the April, May and June editions of *Shun Pao* in 1931, it is clear that *Love and Duty* was released at a point at which competition between sound and silent films was particularly fierce: *Songstress Red Peony* was still on screen in April and May, the Youlian Company released *The Singing Beauty* (*Yu Meiren*), a sound-on-disc film, and *The Love Parade* (1929), a Hollywood musical talkie, was shown repeatedly. In the end, though, an anecdote about *Love and Duty* tells us something about its importance in Chinese cinema. A sound remake of *Love and Duty*, complete with songs performed by Bai Hong, was made in 1938, entitled *Qing tian xue lei* (*Days of Love, Blood and Tears*) in Chinese. Produced by Zhang Shankun at the Xinhua Company, it was directed by Bu Wancang.

Jin Yan again played the leading male role, while Yuan Meiyun played the part of Nai-fan (Ruan Lingyu, who went on to star in *The Goddess* (1934) and *The New Woman* (1935), committed suicide in 1935). It was in the 1938 version that a young man named Gu Yelu made his debut. Gu Yelu became a major star, and for him a part in *Love and Duty* was fate, for, as he recalls in his memoirs, the first Chinese film he ever saw as an apprentice in Shanghai was the 1931 version of *Love and Duty*. 'I came out of the theatre', he wrote, 'with the names of Bu Wancang, Ruan Lingyu and Jin Yan engraved forever on my mind and in my heart.'[34] The film attracted Gu's attention to the power of films and changed his destiny; it also raised the standards of Chinese film.[35] Although it was a silent production, it led the way to a new era of Chinese cinema.

16

I Was Born, But . . .
(Umarete wa mita keredo) (1932)

Alex Clayton

A pivotal sequence in *I Was Born But . . .* speaks of the capacity of film to bring us to see the world afresh. Two boys, Keiji (Sugawara Hideo) and Ryoichi (Tokkan Kozo), aged around seven and nine, attend a home movie screening hosted by their father's boss (Takeshi Sakamoto). This amateur film includes a reel of footage shot on company premises. On the screen, a dozen or so employees, including the boys' father, Yoshii (Tatsuo Saito), a clerk in the firm, are performing an aerobics routine on the company rooftop. Keiji and Ryoichi identify their father in the line-up of exercising bodies and exchange proud smiles as he is singled out by the boss's camera for a closer view. Perhaps distracted by a sudden awarenesss of being favoured, the clerk falls out of synch with his colleagues and makes a flustered effort to catch up. Back in the screening room, the boss and a fellow executive laugh fondly, turning to Yoshii, who looks a little bashful, beside them. The screen now shows a small gathering of company bigwigs, plus Yoshii at the boss's shoulder, frame left. Suddenly, the normally retiring clerk leaps to centre frame, adopts an outlandish squatting posture, points his hands out like wings and pulls a silly face—to the visible hilarity of his associates, who have evidently spurred him on. In the darkness of the auditorium, the faces of Keiji and Ryoichi drop. The boys watch numbly as a montage of their father's antics unfolds onscreen: a shot of him sticking his tongue out, another of a daft solo dance, and yet more grinning, gurning and goofing. The accumulated effect supplies the picture of a pleasing fool, constantly at pains to gratify his superiors. The boys glance over to a laughing projectionist and the reel of footage being excruciatingly unspooled. The boss pitches back and forth in laughter at the clerk's clowning, and tells Yoshii he would make a good comic actor. The boys glare at the screen and then at their father in the flesh. From their perspective, we are shown his seated figure as, in a characteristic gesture, he dips his head and rubs the back of his skull. Perhaps Yoshii senses his sons' eyes upon him, conscious of the incongruity between this on-screen frolicking figure and the preferred image of a patriarch he could count on the boys to respect. But all they see in the gesture is a confirmation of their father's wretched meekness, an inability even to claim the horseplay as his own. They leave the room, mortified.

A number of plain facts of the medium—that a camera strips an image away from its subject; that actions are extracted from context; that a succession of views forges continuity; that projection is automatic, relentless—are shown to be capable of producing a drastic shift in perception. They can even bring the basis of a social order founded on the eminence of the father into question. The transformative effect of this film within a film is an emblem of the medium's power and the ambition of Ozu's work: to bring us to see the familiar freshly, sharply, in a new light. *I Was Born, But...* seeks nothing less than to renew an apprehension of certain fundamentals of social life: power and status, discipline and deference, capital and labour, role-play and ritual. The film traces the experience of the two boys and their father as they adjust to a new life in the suburbs. From fragments of gossip, we learn that Yoshii has moved the family to live closer to his boss and thus ingratiate himself into the manager's social life in the vague hope of advancement. We see Yoshii as an authority figure at home—glaring at his sons to sit straight—but a sycophant at work. Meanwhile, we follow Keiji and Ryoichi as they encounter local boys, play truant from school and eventually become leaders of the neighbourhood gang. The episode at the home movie screening leads to the boys to dispute their father's rule and protest against the unfairness of a world ordered around money. They commit to go on hunger strike, but soon relent and apparently come to terms with their father's need to act deferentially towards his boss.

I Was Born, But... was released in 1932. In the global context, this is late for a silent film, but silent cinema endured in Japan long after most other countries had converted wholesale to sound. Even by the late 1930s, around one-third of Japanese films still had no synchronized soundtrack, and silent films were still commercially exhibited alongside sound films into the early 1940s.[1] This persistence is largely explained by the phenomenon of *benshi*, performers who would occupy a spot next to the screen and guide the audience through the film, supplementing narration, sometimes even supplying voices for characters and generally offering a kind of live moment-by-moment 'reading'.[2] These displays of virtuosity (and the power of those who provided them) remained a major draw through the 1920s and into the 1930s. If the swift conversion to sound in Britain and the USA was propelled by the notion that sound was a key addition, Japan's resistance had surely to do with the prospect of loss. It is easy to imagine how the automated sound film, devoid of the flourish and vitality of this theatrical supplement, may have seemed inert by contrast.

The long period during which silent and sound films were exhibited in parallel must have made film-makers specializing in silent films acutely conscious of the particularity of their medium, and keen to vindicate its survival. This could explain the curious subtitle of *I Was Born, But . . .: A Picture-Book for Grown-Ups*. It seems to declare the potential of silent film to renew and edify our vision. An infant's picture book is apt to identify basic forms, to give shape to the perceptual muddle of the child's world; a grown-up's picture book would serve to restore an appreciation of those elemental things of which perception may have dulled. The ambition of *I Was Born, But . . ..* is, in the words of Coleridge, 'to combine the child's sense of wonder and novelty with the appearances which every day . . . has rendered familiar'.[3] The underlying structures and patterns of a busy world are made more visible when a measure of its noise is held back.

Consider, for example, the early scene where Yoshii pays a social call to the home of his boss. As the characters interact on the terrace, the total absence of chatter we would otherwise hear gives special prominence to posture and makes a little comedy of manners. Nearly a minute of screen time, punctuated only by a single title card, is given to a veritable orgy of bowing, calling attention to the physical awkwardness with which Yoshii stresses his respect and allegiance to the executive. The initial cut to the scene is striking in that we join Yoshii at the deepest point of an excessively formal bow to the manager's wife. The manager then appears in frame, and Yoshii bows deeply again. The servile body language is pronounced not just by the lack of audible dialogue, but also by the camera position, which offers a profile view stressing the curve of Yoshii's back against the criss-cross of lattice windows. Indeed, the film repeatedly sets the bowing body against perpendicular lines which accent the gesture of bending forward and virtually measure its shape and gradient. Here the coordinates let us notice that the clerk bows a few degrees more deeply for the manager even than for the manager's wife, and the greater duration of the second bow gives us time to register the graphic similarity between

Figure 1

the arc of Yoshii's spine and the curved arm of the (equally docile and accommodating) bentwood chair, frame right (Figure 1).

Besides an emphasis on posture, the absence of synchronous dialogue allows the camera to observe whole groups in full-body shots as they interact, with less pressure than in talkies to clarify speakers through close-up. *I Was Born, But...* exhibits an almost anthropological interest in the arrangement of figures in groups. The scene of Yoshii's visit to his boss's house, for instance, briefly digresses to show the local gang of rascals gathered at the large fence at the property's perimeter, calling the manager's boy to come join them. As they convene to discuss martial strategy, we see the rascals clustered around their burly leader and tapering off to either side in strict height order (Figure 2). The neatness of their arrangement has a cartoon quality about it, a pyramid announcing the gang's hierarchy with comic blatancy. It speaks of an absurdly simple rule: the bigger the boy, the more power he wields. The next shot returns us to the scene on the terrace, where Iwasaki takes a seat in the bentwood chair while various fawning acquaintances gather round. The framing and grouping of figures ironically echoes the previous shot and thus invites direct comparison in terms of the configuration of bodies (Figure

Figure 2

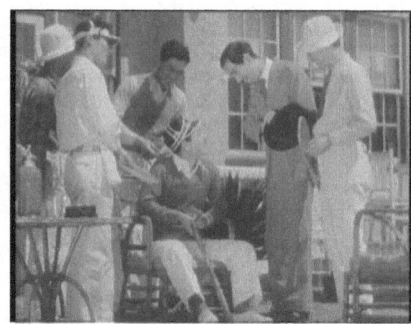

Figure 3

I WAS BORN, BUT . . . (UMARETE WA MITA KEREDO) (1932)

3). Here, the leader is once again central to the unit, but this time assumes the lowermost position, being the only person seated, legs firmly planted. His relaxed posture announces possession of the space and his identity as someone entirely comfortable in his station, with no need to assert his authority. The other figures arrange themselves respectfully in a semi-circle around him, courteously attending to what he has to say. The gathering may appear more casual, but it is no less formally structured than the neighbourhood gang. Indeed, the adult social order feels inordinately more fixed, less open to challenge: satellites securing the nucleus, rejecting the precariousness of the pyramid.

In these ways *I Was Born, But* . . . shows how different formations, rituals and rules hold sway in different social realms, placing emphasis on the thresholds between those realms. The picket fence running along the front of Yoshii's family house, for instance, gains particular prominence as the line where schoolboys repeatedly assemble to taunt Keiji and Ryoichi, marking the boundary between a protected space of parental rule and the 'wild west' of scrubland occupied by the neighbourhood posse. 'Home' feels like a series of adjoining boxes and parallel lives. Children and adults carry on separate routines within mutual view, but with little comprehension of one another's experience. An early view of the house interior shows the boys in the foreground, absorbed in their breakfast, whilst Yoshii, slightly out of focus, gets dressed for work in the background (Figure 4). The space is dominated by perpendicular lines (often accentuated by 'straight-on' camera angles), uneasily accommodating the boys' squat shapes and making it never feel quite like *their* space. Their world is defined by round things: baseball caps, bread rolls, bicycle wheels, balls. By contrast, the adult world is governed by straight lines, as exemplified by the early shot of Yoshii exercising in the yard (Figure 5). Posts, poles and wires form a busy network, accentuated by a long lens, which compresses layers of space to make a flat geometrical field. The line of Yoshii's arms as they

Figure 4   Figure 5

stretch out from his body is underscored by the passage of a train rushing by on tracks that evidently parallel the far boundary. The visual match between the shape of Yoshii's torso and the freshly laundered white shirt humorously evokes a regimented, ritualistic suburban world of exercise routines, wash cycles, cigarette breaks and commuter trains. Boxed in between fence stakes and rail tracks, Yoshii gazes into the distance, the line of his vision leading offscreen with other lines as if converging towards an unseen centre, making this view seem a peripheral segment of a vastly larger picture.

Another threshold space, the entrance to the school grounds, is marked by a small bridge and wooden pillars. This is the spot where Keiji and Ryoichi pause several times to decide whether to check in or play truant. We are twice offered their point of view through the gateway to an unenticing playground, which appears first as a space ordered rigidly by a schoolmaster (the children standing in lines for assembly), and then, even less invitingly, as a scramble of jostling bodies not yet checked by the school bell. Indeed, school is characterized not so much as a site of learning as a disciplinary institution, where the fidgeting bodies of reluctant schoolboys are shaped into the orderly citizens required for the worlds of work and war. The ragtag assortment of boys are lined up for military-style inspection and marched away in double-time. A tracking shot glides left-to-right against their movement, and the direction and pace of the camera motion is maintained across a cut to an office, where once-primed bodies, now tubby and wedged behind desks, yawn and stretch. The office is a bare grid of workstations chiefly defined by their proximity to a door marked 'Private'. The higher-level clerks flaunt their relative privilege by perching on the edge of desks in the area directly outside. When Yoshii is invited into the manager's office (to the visible envy of his colleagues), he pauses in its threshold space first, as if ceremoniously, to do up the buttons on his jacket. Arms by his sides, savouring the big moment, he pitches an exceptionally formal bow into the cavernous room.

As we saw earlier, the posture of Yoshii bowing is key to the film's presentation of his character and to its development of the theme of social deference. It also contributes to a pattern used to dramatize the shift in Keiji and Ryoichi's apprehension of their father. The way they habitually see him as towering and upright—a model of rectitude—is captured by the repeated alignment of his lean figure with telegraph poles. This is established right from the first scene as Yoshii confronts the problem of how to rescue their removals truck from a patch of mud. Directing from the front, the father's authority is accented by the compositional inclusion of a wooden post, parallelling and reinforcing his standing frame as he calls

I WAS BORN, BUT . . . (UMARETE WA MITA KEREDO) (1932)

Figure 6

the children to climb down from the vehicle and push. Having overseen the truck's release, we are then offered a shot from the boys' point of view of Yoshii instructing the hired driver (Figure 6). He is flanked by a series of telegraph poles, and the lines formed by the side of the truck and the receding row of poles lead the eye naturally to Yoshii's standing figure as the point where these lines converge. The effect of single-point perspective captures the way the boys envision their world, with their father as its unifying feature.

The vertical axis again emphasizes Yoshii's status as father several scenes later, when the boys seek his figure as refuge from a scuffle with the local bully. The lateral tracking shot of father and sons walking home is composed such that the horizon line bisects the frame into halves, a cluttered lower half of ground and an upper half of sky into which only Yoshii's lofty frame extends. The boys appear as if huddled below his towering body, linking their perception of their father's height to his provision of shelter. The tracking shot finally comes to rest as the family group recedes behind a foreground telegraph pole, associated firmly now with the father's steady guardianship. Where the sons see only an upright and eminent figure, we are shown another side of Yoshii, of work and weariness, servility and self-compromise.

The film establishes a pattern of point of view whereby we glimpse infirmity while the boys see only strength. In the opening scene, for instance, we are placed (as the boys, loafing at the rear of the truck, are not) to see Yoshii bent-double with exertion, straining to turn the crankshaft, his bowed figure paralleling the arc of the front tyre, striving and failing to keep his three-piece suit free from grease (an impractical outfit for travel, worn, we soon gather, for the 'impromptu' en-route social visit to his boss). In the aftermath of his morning aerobics, we alone witness Yoshii reeling unsteadily from his exercise, a shoulder complaint hidden from the kids. Later, during the commute to work, as Yoshii waits for the rail-crossing barrier to lift, briefcase in hand, and the boys use the occasion for an unscheduled toilet break, only we are placed to notice his sorry resignation to routine and his envy of childhood spontaneity. All the boys see, for now, is an upstanding figure of discipline. But their perception gradually begins to shift. When berated by their father for their truancy, they kneel before him in an amplified show of contrition. As he speaks grandly of 'important men' and the boys gaze down at their father's feet, they are startled to notice his socks bunched limply round his ankles. Two close-ups confirm the incongruous detail, reverse shots registering their peculiar surprise: the shock of the ordinary.

This is just the first and most fleeting of a series of episodes which progressively introduces doubts in the boys' minds as to their father's peerlessness, culminating in the episode at the boss's home movie screening. The next occurs after Keiji and Ryoichi have assumed power in the neighbourhood gang. Ryoichi spots Yoshii emerging from what appears to be a chauffeured car and proudly announces the arrival of his dad. The group gathers round to watch as now, from their shared perspective, we see Yoshii offer a couple of bows to the figure in the back seat. The vehicle drives on. 'That's my father's car', reveals the boss's son, Taro (Seiichi Kato). Apparently threatened by this as a challenge to their status, Ryoichi and Keiji invoke a long-standing gang ritual whereby the subordinate must lie flat on his back. Taro duly shows allegiance. But their rule is undermined when Yoshii approaches, shooting them angry looks. How dare they treat his employer's son like this? Keiji and Ryoichi stand there sullen, exchange glances and shove their hands in their pockets as their father preciously attends to their rival, helping Taro up from the ground, even squatting beside him to brush dust from his clothes. As a final touch, in what seems to them a grotesque inversion of the natural order, he bends to offer the child a fulsome bow (Figure 7). The placement of the father's bowed body, frame left, countered only by a wiry telegraph pole frame right (a distant echo of that proud ideal), makes an unbalanced composition to match the perception of things awry. The gesture and composition, with Taro centre frame, makes a centrepiece of the rich kid in the very spot where seconds earlier he was isolated to show subservience. The arrangement also registers a shift by breaking from the film's regular staging of action along a single axis line. Here two planes of staging—the cluster of rascals behind, Yoshii and Taro in front—are overlaid, registering the discord between incongruous systems of value.

This film's version of the coming-of-age narrative is to trace the boys' gradual move away from childish social arrangements based principally on physical stature towards more adult forms of status determination,

I WAS BORN, BUT . . . (UMARETE WA MITA KEREDO) (1932)

Figure 7

where money and resource play an increasingly large role. Key to this development is the figure of the teenage vendor, placed at the threshold between child and adult realms, who sells sake and beer from door to door. His first appearance shows him comically deferential to patrons. He turns up at the doorway of Yoshii's family house to see if he can hawk some wares, but, finding only the youngest son, glowers and haughtily tells him to fetch an adult. A reverse shot shows Ryoichi pulling an impudent face, knowing the sake-boy cannot cross the threshold to beat him up for fear of losing potential custom. The irritated sake-boy raises his fist in threat, but then suddenly his whole demeanour changes: his face widens into a toothy ingratiating smile, he tips the brim of his hat and crumples forward into a bob. The anticipated reverse shot, its reveal comically delayed to attend to this grovelling shift in body language, now confirms our suspicion: Ryoichi's mother has appeared beside her son. Sometime later, Ryoichi hatches a plan to exploit this advantage, effectively employing the sake-boy as hired 'muscle'. Knowing it to be his father's payday, Ryoichi supplies the tip that his mother will likely buy beer. In exchange for this precious information, the sake-seller knocks the neighbourhood bully around the head a few times, granting Ryoichi and his brother a route to power as the new gang leaders. However, the sake-boy's allegiance is strictly provisional; he refuses to beat up Taro, whose affluent household routinely buys more beer.

This episode seems to complicate the previously simple rule as to how the pecking order of the gang should be established. If standing within the gang is somehow linked to the buying power of fathers, perhaps the order can be negotiated. One boy appeals to the fact that his dad has dozens of suits. Another declares his father to have the most impressive car. Both claims to higher status are swiftly quashed, apparently on the basis that these are emblems of labour rather than disposable wealth—the first boy's father is a tailor; the second boy's father is an undertaker, his car a hearse. We see here, in light comic vein, how the economic hierarchy of the adult world filters into the realm of the child. A further step in this process, and more suggestive of how money and brawn intersect, is the boys' adoption of sparrow's eggs as a makeshift currency. One sparrow's egg is the price of admittance to the manager's home movie screening, payable to the boss's son, who loses no opportunity to capitalize on his father's wealth. Crucially, the value of the eggs is underwritten by the belief that on devouring, they bestow superhuman strength, so that he who holds the most eggs is also, by default, the strongest.

The allusion is to wondering whether the more or less latent capacity to exact violence is ultimately what secures status even in the more 'civilized' adult world. This again comes to mind when, after the screening, Yoshii resorts to beating his son in the absence of a good reason as to why Keiji should respect him. If moral distinction is cast in doubt, what is it, after all, that gives a father mandate? Yoshii initially appeals to his role as breadwinner, reminding Keiji that toadying ultimately puts food on the table. But if the provision of resource were the sole reason for esteeming one's parents, then filial deference would be hollow and mercenary indeed. Similarly, physical dominance and the threat of force may obtain status in the neighbourhood gang, but is a poor backing for family authority, perhaps only signalling its defeat.

Throughout the quarrel, Ryoichi hides behind Keiji but follows his lead, obediently copying his elder brother's gestures of dissent. This reminds us that some forms of deference are more habitual than pragmatic in nature, less about the promise of resource or the threat of violence and more to do with sheer force of habit. Yielding to seniority easily becomes customary, for better or worse. This offers a better explanation of Yoshii's relentlessly obsequious behaviour towards his boss, in the absence of any sign of actual potential for material gain. It is simply easier to go along with a culture of 'apple polishing', especially when one finds oneself rewarded with token favour, than it is to be fully one's own person. The suspicion that there is, after all, a failure of will on Yoshii's part—hence that the children's supposed achievement of maturity, their accession to 'the way the world works', is actually rather sad and sorry—accounts for the complexity of the film's ending, for our residual feelings of grief and injustice despite the ostensible reconciliations. In this light, Keiji's pledge to go on hunger strike, however impulsive, should be seen not as a tantrum preceding grown-up acceptance, but as a real step towards maturity, the resolve to self-determination which is the true break with childhood.

17

Street Without End
(Kagiri naki hodo) (1934)

Lisa Dombrowski

Although frequently described by both native and international critics as one of Japan's greatest directors—behind only Ozu Yasujiro, Mizoguchi Kenji and Kurosawa Akira, and the first Japanese director to have a film distributed theatrically in the USA (*Wife! Be Like a Rose!* (1935)—Naruse Mikio is nevertheless little known to audiences outside Japan.[1] The bulk of Western scholarship on his work focuses on the contemporary-life woman's pictures he directed in the 1950s and 1960s, primarily for the studio Toho. Yet Naruse's initial professional peak occurred in the early 1930s, when he worked at Shochiku's Kamata studio. In films such as *Apart From You* (1933) and *Every Night Dreams* (1933), Naruse paired overtly dynamic camera movement and editing with urban realism and a modern approach to female-centred narratives. His final film for Shochiku and his last silent picture, *Street Without End* (1934), is a snapshot of a director in transition, one delivering key elements of his studio's house style while experimenting with film form in a more subtle manner. *Street Without End* explores the contradictory status of young working women in urban Japan, free from parental influence and economic want, yet still restricted by gender, class and circumstances. Narrative parallels and patterned stylistic punctuation direct viewers to compare and contrast characters and chart their emotional journeys, highlighting the range of choices and identities available to modern women as well as the ongoing influence of tradition. While *Street Without End*'s urban modernism, comedic subplot and formal experimentation link it to Naruse's previous films, its relative stylistic restraint, open-endedness and ambiguity point towards his distinct contributions to the Japanese woman's film in later decades.

In Japan, the woman's film (*josei-eiga*) is a subset of the *gendai-geki*, or contemporary life film, and developed in the 1920s and 1930s to exploit changing economic and social roles for women. By the 1920s, increased female education and economic expansion brought more women into the Japanese workforce, particularly in offices and the retail and service sectors.[2] With economic prosperity among the urban middle class, the female consumer market developed, giving rise to magazines that provided new images of Japanese womanhood, such as the *moga* (modern girl), the self-improving housewife, the office worker and the café waitress.[3] Pointing to Shochiku's exploitation of the female market under the leadership of studio chief Kido Shiro, Mitsuyo Wada-Marciano argues the 1920s witnessed the advent of the woman's film in Japan. Kido noted not only that women went to the cinema with other women, thus multiplying the size of audiences, but also, 'the fact that the old moralistic ideas that have a repressive stranglehold on women present opportunities for us to create various theatrical stories for our films'.[4] Wada-Marciano suggests Shochiku targeted women viewers through female-centred stories, employing more actresses than any other studio (rather than using *oyama*—female impersonators) and shooting on location in Tokyo in order to highlight details of everyday life. This production strategy was part and parcel of Shochiku's aim to differentiate its product through an emphasis on realist *shomin-geki*, films about ordinary middle-class and lower-class people.[5]

The woman's films that Naruse directed at Shochiku reflect not only the studio's modern approach to visual style, incorporating Western continuity editing norms alongside avant-garde stylistic practices, but also its tendency to adapt stories from women's publications, nineteenth-century domestic novels and *shinpa* romantic dramas. Japan's most popular form of theatrical drama from the late 1890s to the mid-1920s, *shinpa* typically features handsome, gentle male protagonists whose weakness makes them undependable. Along with the oppressions of social convention, class status and family loyalty, these weaknesses cause much suffering for women and often give rise to noble self-sacrifice, ending in various combinations of betrayal, desertion and/or death.[6] In her book *The Cinema of Naruse Mikio*, Catherine Russell argues that, while *shinpa* formed the 'narrative core' of Shochiku's output, Kido Shiro's vision of the woman's film replaced *shinpa*'s conventional morality with more modern attitudes.[7] Tradition is not entirely abandoned, however. Instead, it forms one half of a dichotomy with modernity, often fluidly represented through the construction of female identity.[8]

Though Naruse had already shown himself adept at directing woman's films and providing critical and commercial success for Shochiku, he approached *Street Without End* with little enthusiasm. He had long been frustrated with the studio, drawing a lowly salaryman's pay while advancing significantly more slowly than Ozu, Gosho Heinosuke, Shimazu Yasujiro, Shimizu Hiroshi and other peers.[9] Naruse never enjoyed the full support of studio head Kido Shiro; Kido confided late in life to film scholar and historian Audie Bock that he disliked Naruse's 'monotone pace, the absence of dramatic highs and lows' in his work.[10] The two men clashed in temperament, too. Kido aimed for Shochiku to produce upbeat films with 'life goes on' endings: 'There are two ways to view humanity . . . cheerful and gloomy. But the latter will not do: we at Shochiku prefer to look at life in a warm and hopeful way.'[11] Yet Naruse was anything but warm and hopeful. Nicknamed 'Yaruse Nakio' (Mr Cheerless) when working at Toho, he held a consistently bleak worldview: 'From the youngest age, I have thought that the world we live in betrays us; this thought still remains with me.'[12] At Shochiku, Naruse searched for material that would allow him to tell the stories he wanted to tell while also providing the elements Kido favoured. Bock suggests Naruse agreed to direct *Street Without End* only because he was promised his next film would be more to his liking; the source material, a newspaper serial about the courtship and marriage of a young woman who works at a tea salon, failed to attract the interest of any other director.[13] *Street Without End* illustrates the ways in which Naruse balanced production imperatives with his own aesthetic sensibilities, combining modernity and humour with his interest in 'the fighting spirit of the independent woman'.[14]

Street Without End explores the lives and loves of two young women who are employed in a café in the Ginza district of modern-day Tokyo. The attractive Sugiko receives both an offer of marriage from her boyfriend, Machio, and a chance to become a film actress, but a car accident throws her into the path of a wealthy man from a respected family, Hiroshi, who falls in love with her. Misunderstandings cause Machio to break their engagement, but Hiroshi proposes to Sugiko and the two wed despite his family's opposition. The mean-spiritedness of Hiroshi's mother and sister drives him to drink and womanizing, prompting Sugiko to leave him and move in with her younger brother, Koichi, who is working towards becoming a taxi driver. After Hiroshi is badly injured in a drunk-driving accident with another woman, his mother begs Sugiko to return; instead, Sugiko berates Hiroshi's mother and sister for their coldness and abandons

Hiroshi. Meanwhile, Sugiko's more adventurous friend, Kesako, pursues the acting job offered to Sugiko, but cannot shake the affections of a sweet but fumbling street artist, Shinkichi. Kesako finds Shinkichi a job at her film studio as a painter, where his pursuit of her sets tongues wagging and keeps her from landing jobs. At the end of the film, Kesako has abandoned acting and married Shinkichi, while Koichi has earned his driver's licence and started to work as a taxi driver. Sugiko, on the other hand, is back where she started, working at the café. She spots Machio on a passing bus one day, but can only wonder what might have been.

One of the most distinctive elements in *Street Without End* that differentiates it from Naruse's later work and marks it as a Shochiku product is the manner in which it highlights signifiers of modernity. Shochiku was the only major studio operating in Tokyo from 1923 to 1934, and its frequent location shooting provided 'the dominant imagery of metropolitan life for a nation that was still in fact largely rural and unevenly modernized'.[15] *Street Without End* sandwiches its plotline in between a prologue and an epilogue that focus exclusively on streetscapes filmed on location in Ginza, Tokyo's bustling shopping district, imbuing the story with a sense of urban realism and vitality. Shots of streetcars and automobiles, buildings and pedestrians, signs, shoppers and people meeting on the street orient the viewer even before the plot begins. The rapidity of the editing, the quick variation in shot content and the camera movement all work together to introduce a world characterized by speed and variety. The rapid juxtaposition of the shots highlights the choices and opportunities available to urban dwellers: on a city street you can see and be seen, engage in a chance meeting or make a fateful choice. This is a theme that continues throughout the whole film, as does the location shooting. In the most extensive English-language analysis of the film to date, Catherine Russell argues that the 'fascination and significance of *Street Without End* lies in its transformation of urban space into a kind of abstract system where people's paths continually cross, or in [the] last scene, fail to cross'.[16] The city thus offers not only the spectacle of modernity, but also a formal tool to open up the narrative, allowing chance and coincidence to play a motivated structural role.

Modernity is also evoked in citations of Hollywood films and a *moga* character. In the opening montage sequence, a shot of a cinema marquee features the iconic face of American film comedian Harold Lloyd, complete with straw hat and round glasses. Sugiko later attends the cinema on a date with Hiroshi, and we see them watching the final sequence in Ernst Lubitsch's *The Smiling Lieutenant* (1931)—especially apt thematically, as it depicts the foreplay between Maurice Chevalier

Figure 1

and Miriam Hopkins following the latter's surprise transformation from an unfashionable woman into a jazzy flapper. The image of the modern Western woman is also embodied in *Street Without End* through an unnamed *moga* who functions as a rival for Sugiko (Figure 1). With her permed hair, westernized androgynous clothing and jazz dancing, the *moga* visualizes the cosmopolitan sensibility, wealth and sexual confidence lacking in Sugiko. Yet the audience is cued to view the *moga* in less than flattering terms: she is proud, rude to Sugiko, rejected by Hiroshi as a 'tomboy' and favoured only by Hiroshi's mother and sister, the two least likeable characters in the film. *Street Without End* thus illustrates a narrative pattern frequently found in Japanese woman's films that contrasts the *moga* with a more traditional female character;[17] the extreme nature of the *moga* allows Sugiko's independent working woman to appear more respectable by comparison.

Location shooting and self-conscious references to Western culture are specific to this period of Naruse's career; so, too, is a comic aspect. Naruse's first assignments at Shochiku were *nansensu* slapstick comedies, a staple of the studio. According to Audie Bock, Naruse realized with *Now Don't Get Excited* (1931) that if he sprinkled humorous gags and other bits of comedy throughout the film he could do what he wanted with the rest of it.[18] Thus *Street Without End* pairs its primary *shinpa*-influenced plotline with the secondary comedic plot of Kesako, lightening its tone and providing a best buddy and comic foil to Sugiko. But as with Sugiko, Kesako's primary choices involve love and work. While Shinkichi is consistently loyal and kind towards Kesako, his lowly profession (sidewalk artist) and bumbling manner (he continually trips, drops things and appears confused) undercut his appeal to her even as they endear him to the audience. The courtship of the two is structured as a lighthearted chase. In the opening scenes Shinkichi pursues Kesako with a series of generous gestures—he offers to walk her home, to eat with her, to make her coffee, to find her a new apartment—but each time he fumbles the gesture and Kesako expresses annoyance. Later scenes, however, cue the viewer to recognize that Shinkichi and Kesako may be better suited for each other than she acknowledges: both characters brush their teeth comically, both bite their handkerchiefs in concern and Kesako's humorous physical instability when opening Shinkichi's apartment door mirrors his earlier stumbles. The most inspired comedic sequence involves Shinkichi cluelessly wandering around a film set at the studio where both he and Kesako are employed—he ends up dreamily applying a coat of paint to a director's chair right before it is sat on—but his continued pursuit of Kesako becomes an obstacle to her success. After Kesako admits to Sugiko acting may not be right for her, her plotline disappears until after the completion of Sugiko's own character arc. In the last three minutes of the film, Shinkichi's pattern of pursuit is fully turned on its head: Kesako is now the one bringing Shinkichi his lunch, and their dialogue reveals they are happily married.

As with the *moga*, Kesako's character serves a dual purpose: she provides a specific appeal (comedy) while also offering an alternative image of the modern Japanese woman. Where Sugiko initially appears more reserved and hesitant, Kesako's dialogue and actions suggest she is more animated and impulsive. Kesako reprimands, 'Don't be so wishy-washy!' when Sugiko questions whether she should marry Machio; she argues becoming an actress is 'much better than being a "devoted wife"'; and after Hiroshi calls on Sugiko, Kesako encourages her, 'You should seize happiness while you can!' When Kesako consistently rebuffs Shinkichi and instead pursues an acting career, her decisions suggest she is more interested in advancing her lot as an independent woman than in fulfilling the traditional role of a loyal wife and wise mother. Yet by the end of the film, Kesako abandons her own career and embraces the role of a dedicated wife, seemingly content to stay with the less-than-upwardly-mobile Shinkichi. Kesako's character arc suggests love *is* enough. As long as a couple are well suited and their loyalty is intact, they can be happy in marriage even if not financially well off—just the sort of upbeat tone favoured by Kido for Shochiku's *shomin-geki*.

Although *Street Without End* weaves together the two plotlines of Sugiko and Kesako, more than three-quarters of its running time is devoted to the former, a far from comedic tale. Parallels structure the central plot of Sugiko's romance and marriage, encouraging viewers to compare and contrast different moments and choices in Sugiko's life as well as those of the other women. As with Naruse's earlier *Every Night Dreams*, the narrative transforms the conventional *shinpa* plotline: a

STREET WITHOUT END (KAGIRI NAKI HODO) (1934)

flawed, weak-willed young man is initially romanticized by a woman but later overtly criticized; the woman does not sacrifice herself throughout but faces her burdens with strength. The act structure divides the plot into three distinct phases: Sugiko's life before meeting Hiroshi, her primary suitor; Sugiko's life with Hiroshi; and Sugiko's life after leaving Hiroshi. The difference in the two defining turning points—the coincidental car accident that throws Sugiko in Hiroshi's path versus her determined decision to leave him—marks her development from a hesitant beauty who believes in the power of love into a decisive, independent woman who questions her earlier faith. Three sequences, one from each act, illustrate the range of stylistic strategies Naruse utilizes to punctuate the pauses, glances and figure movement of Sugiko, thereby shaping the viewer's perception of her subjectivity and the choices she makes.

A mere eight minutes into the film, Sugiko receives her first marriage proposal from her steady boyfriend, Machio, as the two meet at night on the street; the scene is a vivid example of Naruse embellishing the 'piecemeal découpage' approach to scene construction common at Shochiku. In 'Visual Style in Japanese Cinema, 1925–1945', David Bordwell describes piecemeal découpage as one of three period stylistic trends in Japan that combined Western classical norms with 'an experimental impulse mediated by a self-conscious sense of "Japaneseness"'.[19] Piecemeal découpage constructs each scene with a great number of shots, frequently with distinct camera set-ups, which provide close views of detailed elements; wider framings and depth staging may also be incorporated into the scene.[20] The thirty-two-shot scene of Sugiko's first proposal has six title cards and an average shot length of 3.3 seconds, less than the film's average of 3.8 seconds; only four camera positions are repeated. The scene is an elegant ballet of glance, movement and delay, as Naruse intercuts title cards and shots of street lamps (as well as one train) to punctuate and prolong the emotional beats of the proposal.

Naruse rigorously patterns the editing in the scene, creating seven segments marking the different turns in the conversation and the characters' reactions to each other. With A designating a street lamp or train, B indicating Machio and/or Sugiko, and C designating a title card, the editing pattern for the scene is as follows: ABABCA/BBCA/BBBBCA/BBCA/BBBCA/BBBCA/BA. The initial exchange between Machio and Sugiko sets up the reason for their meeting: Machio is contemplating marriage, and hopes that it will be to Sugiko. Each dialogue title is paired with a complementary lantern shot, as neutral moments or moments of emotional deflation are followed by distant shots of lights, while moments of optimism are punctuated by closer shots of lights more dominant in the frame.[21] After the lamp shots mark and prolong the emotional beat, glances and movements in the consequent shots of Machio and Sugiko visualize their resulting thoughts and emotions. The precise shot patterning, contrast within the frame and figure movement emphasize for the viewer each tentative step taken by the couple towards their engagement and the obstacles they must overcome.

The first and second segments establish the narrative context of the scene and its rigorous stylistic patterning. The first segment begins with a distant shot of a double lantern, then cuts to a medium long shot of Machio and Sugiko walking into the frame and positioning themselves near a wall, the shadows partially abstracting the space around them. A different angle of the distant double lantern follows; the shadows and street lights create graphic contrast in their respective shots. In a medium close-up over the shoulder of Sugiko, Machio then turns to face her, priming the viewer for his announcement, and begins the line of dialogue continued on the title card: 'My family wants to marry me off back home while my Dad's still alive.' The title card is followed by a third distinct shot of a far-off street lamp, the small, bright spot in the frame perhaps suggesting the hope of the couple overwhelmed by the darkness. The inclusion of the lamp shot prolongs the delay until viewers see Sugiko's response, allowing time to consider the implications of Machio's announcement and imagine how Sugiko might respond. We see the response in the following sequence: in a medium close-up over Machio's shoulder, Sugiko looks to the centre of the frame, down, then to the left, and moves to exit left. The glances and movement away from Machio sustain the glum emotional beat, embodying Sugiko's disappointment and the likely separation from her boyfriend. But the sequence takes a turn when Machio, after watching Sugiko walk away from him, follows and turns to face her. Machio continues the conversation, suggesting all may not be lost after all. The title card confirms this as Machio asks her to marry him. The segment concludes with a double street lamp bright and large in the frame, a beacon of hope that underlines Machio's desire and primes the viewer for Sugiko's relieved response.

The subsequent segments progress in a similar manner as the unusual editing pattern prompts viewers to pay close attention to the rhythm and details in each shot. As Sugiko and Machio consider their options and possible marriage, gesture and movement punctuate each stage in their thought processes, providing indirect access to character subjectivity. Tight framings and over-the-shoulder shots accentuate the dropping and raising of eyes, turns to and away from each other, and steps closer and further away, the editing and movement rhythmically creating a dance

STREET WITHOUT END (KAGIRI NAKI HODO) (1934)

between doubt and hope. After Machio announces he will refuse his parents' directive if Sugiko agrees to marry him instead, Sugiko looks up to meet his gaze, her hope ignited. Prior to admitting the two would not have much money, Machio looks down nervously, walks away from Sugiko, then turns to deliver the bad news; Sugiko walks into the foreground, turns and closes the distance between them before revealing, 'I don't care about that' (Figures 2–5). The characters' glances and movements thus visualize not only their immediate subjectivity, but also their potential fates—they may come together in marriage or they may break apart. The graphic contrast of the street lamps works redundantly with figure movement and dialogue to emphasize the characters' emotions and extend each narrative beat—bright lamps dominate following hopeful sentiments, the night sky engulfs the light in moments of doubt.

Yet a different visual element—the graphic contrast in the abstracted background—provides a troubling counterpoint to the scene's primary stylistic pattern. Following the title card announcing Machio's family's desire for him to marry back home, vertical blocks of light and shadow

Figure 2   Figure 3

Figure 4   Figure 5

visually divide Machio from Sugiko in more than half the two-shots that frame them together (as in Figure 2). Even at the end of the scene, as Machio asks Sugiko to marry him and she smiles in agreement, light and dark planes in the background split them in the frame, subtly suggesting a separation right when they agree to become one. The narrative and stylistic divergence raises a nagging question in the viewer's mind: are these two really united? Sugiko's admission to Kesako in the following scene—'I accepted, but I'm not sure I was right'—clarifies her doubt. Her ambivalence cues the viewer to wonder: is she worried about Machio's lack of wealth? is she worried about his family's desire that he marry another? or does she doubt her own feelings for him? The answer remains unclear, but one thing is certain: Sugiko is hesitating. The self-consciousness of this scene draws viewers' attention not only to the emotional beats, but also to the formal accents themselves. Yet rather than distancing the viewer, Naruse's visual style encourages close attention to subjective cues, especially those regarding choice. It is through the depiction of Sugiko's choices—as well as the role of chance—that the film highlights the contradictory status of the modern Japanese woman.

The film's second proposal scene prompts comparisons with the first through its parallel narrative action and its contrasting visual presentation. Six title cards punctuate the scene's emotional beats; all but one contain Hiroshi's dialogue, thus positioning Sugiko again as largely reactive. Both proposal scenes feature few repeated camera positions—only two of the second scene's twenty-five shots are duplicated angles. Both also rely on glances and movements in order to convey character emotion. Yet the *mise en scène* and editing in the second proposal scene vary dramatically from those of the first. Whereas Machio's proposal takes place during a furtive meeting at night on an urban sidewalk, Hiroshi's occurs during the day after a drive into the countryside; he and Sugiko converse at a scenic overlook underneath the majestic peak of Mount Fuji. The shadowy, abstracted background of the first sequence is replaced by the light-filled visual splendor of the second. Nothing divides Hiroshi and Sugiko within the frame. Moreover, instead of the piecemeal découpage that marks the first proposal, analytical editing structures the second scene, maintaining spatial and temporal continuity throughout. The initial medium long shot establishes the space and cuts into tighter shot reverse shot framings, then matches on action to wider framings re-establish the space as the characters move to punctuate a turn in the conversation. At 5.16 seconds, the scene's average shot length is nearly a second and a half longer than the overall average in the film, producing a more deliberate sense of pace. Completely lacking in self-consciousness, the visual presentation of the second proposal immerses the viewer in the sentiment of the unfolding emotion, punctuating Sugiko's hope and faith in Hiroshi and providing no obstacle to the viewer sharing her belief.

The central segment in this scene shows how Naruse uses differences in style to encourage viewers to compare and contrast the two proposal scenes. After Hiroshi and Sugiko disembark from the car in a long shot, Hiroshi lays his handkerchief down on the grass for her and the two sit side by side with Mount Fuji rising behind them. A match on action takes us to a 180 degree reverse angle, a medium shot of the couple smiling at each other. Sugiko glances offscreen right, motivating the title card as Hiroshi begins the conversation: 'Have you ever thought of us getting married?' The question is a leading one: in a prior scene, Hiroshi referred to Sugiko as his wife when the rival *moga* denigrated Sugiko's everyday kimono and lack of family status. In that scene, Sugiko told Hiroshi she did not mind being described as his wife—he did so, after all, in an attempt to defend her honour—so one might expect she has had a few thoughts on the subject since then. Three medium close-up shot reverse shots follow the title card with Hiroshi's question, as Naruse continues to break down the scene analytically in order to highlight its important gestures and expressions. First, in a shot over Hiroshi's shoulder, Sugiko glances at him with a half-smile on her face (Figure 6); then, in a reverse angle over Sugiko's shoulder, he looks at her with an eager grin. In a repeat of the shot over Hiroshi's shoulder, Sugiko turns her head away and down, raises her eyes up, stands and exits the frame to the right. As in the first proposal scene, Naruse relies on nonverbal cues to communicate each subtle shift in character emotion, from surprise, to anticipation, to possible doubt. Yet here the conventional nature of Naruse's stylistic choices masks their use, invisibly directing attention solely to character subjectivity without providing any contradictory cues.

Figure 6

The tone now having shifted with Sugiko's response, Naruse cuts on action to a re-establishing long shot, marking the beginning of a new emotional tangent. Sugiko walks into the midground left third of the frame with lips pursed and glances left, prompting Hiroshi to stand and walk behind her to the centre right of the frame. The two face straight ahead, allowing the viewer to see Hiroshi's keen expression while Sugiko's face betrays little. The ambiguity in Sugiko's reaction motivates the subsequent title card of Hiroshi's dialogue: 'Are you angry I brought it up?' Again Naruse cuts analytically straight into the established space, providing a medium two-shot of Sugiko on the left of the frame and Hiroshi on the right. Sugiko looks pensively ahead, while Hiroshi remains eager behind her; she looks down and shakes her head 'no' with a wry smile, cueing the title card, her only line of dialogue in the scene: 'I just don't know what your mother would say.' Here, as in the earlier proposal, Sugiko faces the obstacle of a family that desires a different spouse for their son; moreover, in this particular instance, class provides an additional—and possibly even greater—impediment. Naruse continues to cut analytically in to a pair of medium close-ups, carefully focusing the viewer's attention on each character's reaction: how they respond individually to Hiroshi's family's disapproval will determine the future of their relationship. Sugiko turns to the front of the frame and smiles up to Hiroshi over her left shoulder; Hiroshi steps to the right and looks down at her with intent. His line on the title card reads: 'As long as we're both sure of our feelings, that doesn't matter.' Hiroshi's response—his defence of his attraction to Sugiko in the face of family and class expectations—is the culmination of a narrative pattern developed from the moment of their meeting. Hiroshi's kindness to Sugiko in the hospital after the car accident, his persistent attentiveness to her, his defence of her during their date at the cinema, even his arguments in her favour to his mother at home, have all repeated and varied the same theme: Hiroshi will protect their love, and love will conquer all.

Rooted in romantic convention and sentiment, this idea is underlined in the composition that follows: in a pictorial medium two-shot, Hiroshi and Sugiko stand facing each other under Mount Fuji, Sugiko looking down in concern and Hiroshi encouragingly placing his hand on her shoulder (Figure 7). Both the mountain, an iconic symbol of Japan, and Sugiko's kimono (more visible here than in the earlier proposal) visually link the scene with Japanese tradition; their stance reinforces customary gender roles as well, with Hiroshi adopting a protective role and Sugiko maintaining her modesty and reserve. The title card iterates Hiroshi's plea to Sugiko: 'Please trust me!' In order to underline the earnestness of

STREET WITHOUT END (KAGIRI NAKI HODO) (1934)

Figure 7

Hiroshi's entreaty, Naruse cuts back to him in medium close-up, looking down at Sugiko. Naruse reserves the tightest framing of the entire scene for her response, thereby emphasizing the significance of her action: she looks up at Hiroshi and smiles her assent. Here, Sugiko makes her first fateful decision of the film, and it is a decision rooted in old-fashioned sentiment and faith. Unlike the first proposal scene, no stylistic element provides a counterpoint to the words and actions of the couple; instead, the stylistic unity and consistent narrative patterning cue the viewer to trust as the couple does, believing Hiroshi and Sugiko's love will overcome all obstacles.

As with the first proposal, however, a scene following the second proposal raises questions about the couple's future. In the first instance, Sugiko doubted whether she should have agreed to marry Machio; in the second, Sugiko's brother Koichi raises similar doubts: 'Wow, sis, you're more conventional than I thought.' Koichi explicitly asks Sugiko whether she will be happy as 'a bourgeois housewife', but Sugiko maintains the faith in Hiroshi she expressed during the proposal. Koichi encourages her, 'You should examine your feelings more closely', emphasizing not only how marriage will redefine her social status, but also the challenges of class difference and family opposition: 'How do you think his family will treat a working girl like you?' Sugiko responds by glancing up sharply and standing in reproof, followed by a title card: 'That makes no difference.' Koichi's query is not only logical but also motivated by his selfless concern for her—he even dismisses as unpalatable her suggestion that her marriage could help her support him. However, despite her brother's doubts, Sugiko's belief in the power of love remains steadfast. A title card spells it out: 'As long as we love each other . . .', then cuts to a medium close-up of Sugiko looking dreamily to the side with a smile, as if to suggest love can conquer all. Though some might view Sugiko's faith as naive (clearly her brother does), her motives are pure, and her uncharacteristic certainty in the face of opposition encourages the viewer to wish for her success. Yet, in true *shinpa* form, subsequent scenes soon prove Hiroshi's trustworthiness to be an illusion and Sugiko's confidence unfounded. A title card makes the villain explicit: 'Even today, feudalistic notions of "family" crush the pure love of young people in Japan.' Despite Sugiko's best attempts at fulfilling the role of a 'devoted wife', the abuse meted out by Hiroshi's mother and sister (and Hiroshi's own weakness) cause her to suffer, an innocent victim worthy of the viewer's sympathy and pity.

At this point *Street Without End* takes a modern turn, initiating a plot pattern in which the apologetic self-abasement that Sugiko initially exhibits in her marriage gives way to growing self-awareness and assertiveness. First, Sugiko meets Kesako in the café in which they both used to work and expresses a change of heart regarding Hiroshi: 'I didn't really think things through. I thought our love would be enough to make me happy. But I was wrong.' Subsequently, the decisiveness Sugiko displayed when marrying Hiroshi is replicated in ever more bold and socially transgressive ways: after Hiroshi turns to drink and becomes quarrelsome, Sugiko moves out of his house and back in with her brother (a daring move for a married Japanese woman of the era); when Hiroshi lies injured in the hospital after drunkenly crashing his car, Sugiko forcefully lays the blame at the feet of his mother and sister, accusing them of never loving her or Hiroshi but only the family name (a gutsy condemnation for a woman of a lower class); and Sugiko finally abandons the fatally injured Hiroshi in the hospital, ignoring his appeals of love and his family's desire to maintain a facade of happiness (a definitive rejection of female self-sacrifice). The patterning of Sugiko's actions emphasizes the increasing confidence with which she imposes her own will, rejecting as she does so the necessity of self-sacrifice and the traditional gender stereotype of the 'devoted wife'.

Naruse explicitly punctuates two of Sugiko's transgressive decisions with a rapid track into a tighter framing of her. Whereas his other surviving Shochiku films, particularly *Not Blood Relations* (1932), *Apart From You* and *Every Night Dreams*, frequently employ rapid tracks to express emotion, in *Street Without End* Naruse reserves the technique for when Sugiko decides to leave Hiroshi and when she resolves to go to the hospital and rebuke his family. The latter example is particularly emphatic, as a title card interrupts a track in to Sugiko: 'I have something to say to his mother and sister.' The track then resumes until framing an extreme close-up of her looking straight into the camera, the tight composition and direct address emphasizing her determination. The rarity of the tracks heightens their significance, marking these moments of firm resolve and independent thinking as key to Sugiko's character development. Their relative self-consciousness and rapid succession—they mark the end of two consecutive scenes—prime the viewer for the final confrontation between Sugiko and Hiroshi's family.

Naruse uses piecemeal découpage in the film's climax, as he does in all of Sugiko's confrontations with Hiroshi's mother and sister, rhythmically organizing glances, pauses and movements to punctuate emotional beats. In contrast to earlier scenes involving these three characters, however, here Sugiko abandons her reticence and becomes the aggressor. The 5 minute 24 second scene contains 104 shots and twenty title cards; more than half of the cards convey Sugiko's dialogue, a sharp increase from the previous scenes with Hiroshi and his family and a clear indication of her growing assertiveness. As with the piecemeal découpage of the first proposal scene, the average shot length is a low 3.12 seconds and fewer than one-fifth of the camera set-ups are repeated, creating opportunities for editing to rhythmically accent action. The scene unfolds in three sequences in the hospital where Hiroshi lies seriously injured: the first depicts Hiroshi's apology to Sugiko for making her suffer, to which she replies, 'You're a good man, but you're weak'; the second reveals Sugiko's rebuke of Hiroshi's mother and sister; and the third illustrates Sugiko's deliberations in the corridor afterwards when she hears Hiroshi has died. While the framing, staging and editing in the first two sequences emphasize Sugiko's consistent determination and strength, the third suggests that her resistance to the appeals of love and convention might be wavering.

In the first and second sequences of the hospital climax Naruse stages characters across the frame in multiple planes and uses 360 degree editing to maximize the emotional impact of small alterations in spatial relationships. The middle section of the second sequence provides a vivid example of Naruse's larger strategy. After Sugiko charges Hiroshi's mother and sister with causing his accident and decries his mother for never showing her any love, Hiroshi's sister counters, 'You're just jealous and bitter!' Sugiko admits, 'Perhaps', but her physical movement indicates she is not daunted. In a low height medium shot, Sugiko turns right in the left third of the frame to face Hiroshi's mother and sister, and then steps forward. Both of the movements, the turn and the step, bring Sugiko closer to Hiroshi's mother and sister, emphasizing her determination and prolonging her advance. The subsequent shots continue the visual pattern of pursuit, as Sugiko consistently moves to address Hiroshi's mother directly. A title card reveals Sugiko's next accusation: 'But you don't really love me or Hiroshi.' A medium shot staged in three distinct planes allows

Figure 8

viewers to see the response of all three characters simultaneously. Sugiko stands in the background left corner, with Hiroshi's family's manservant in the far background right corner; both are out of focus. Hiroshi's sister is in the midground centre, with Hiroshi's mother slightly closer (Figure 8). Hiroshi's mother retreats from Sugiko, faces the camera and steps into the foreground centre, then glances down. The triangular staging, with Hiroshi's mother at the apex obstructing her daughter, places the most conventionally respectable character in the foreground centre of the frame at the moment of her greatest shame. The downward tilt of her head emphasizes her recognition of her failure to be a loving mother. In the background, Sugiko begins to move right, prompting a match on action to a medium close-up as she crosses left to right, pauses, and turns towards the front. As with the previous pre-title shot, a series of discrete actions punctuate and extend Sugiko's relentless attack; the composition and rhythmic editing emphasize each of her moves.

The subsequent title card completes Sugiko's list of Hiroshi's mother's crimes: 'All you love is the Yamanouchi name.' A quick medium shot cuts more than 180 degrees behind Sugiko to reveal Hiroshi's mother centre in the frame and looking down to the right. Although Hiroshi's mother appears contrite, Sugiko steps towards her to continue her verbal assault. A match on action cuts to a multiplanar reverse angle, with Hiroshi's mother in the foreground right, looking down and out of focus; Sugiko centred and frontal, drawing the viewer's attention; Hiroshi's sister slightly behind them on the left third and facing left; and the manservant in the background, out of focus between Sugiko and Hiroshi's mother (Figure 9). Sugiko again steps forward to confront Hiroshi's mother, her movement and increasing size in the frame marking her as the primary compositional element and emphasizing her desire to fight another round. Hiroshi's sister glances at Sugiko, motivating the next title card. Sugiko questions Hiroshi's mother's maternal fitness, much as Hiroshi's mother once

STREET WITHOUT END (KAGIRI NAKI HODO) (1934)

Figure 9

questioned Sugiko's ability to be a proper wife: 'Can you really call yourself his mother?' A 45 degree cut holds Sugiko in the centre midground of the frame, with Hiroshi's mother out of focus in the foreground left, still looking down to the left, and Hiroshi's sister out of focus in the background right, glancing down and to Sugiko. The staging and eyelines diagonally link Hiroshi's sister to Sugiko and Sugiko to Hiroshi's mother, his sister's dropped head and silence suggesting she may finally be cowed. But Sugiko still does not let up her attack, taking yet another step towards Hiroshi's mother and asking again, 'Can you?' The final shot in the sequence is a tighter framing of the earlier multiplanar reverse angle, with Sugiko centred, in focus, and flanked by Hiroshi's sister on the left rear plane and Hiroshi's mother in the right foreground. Sugiko finally drops her head in concession, turns and exits the frame at the right, concluding her confrontation with Hiroshi's mother. The individual steps forward Sugiko takes in each shot (six in total) rhythmically accent her defiance of the conventional respect afforded to in-laws. The staging, figure movement and editing in this segment punctuate and prolong Sugiko's rebuke of Hiroshi's mother, emphatically illustrating the shift from her passive faith in sentiment to active independence from tradition.

In the final sequence of the scene, Naruse again uses accentual editing but for a very different purpose, highlighting Sugiko's hesitation rather than her determination. After Sugiko has sharply broken gender and social norms by abandoning her ailing husband and dressing down his imperious mother and sister, she retreats to the hospital corridor outside Hiroshi's room and, in a sign of emotional exhaustion, closes her eyes and leans against the wall. The Yamanouchi family's manservant reveals Hiroshi has taken a turn for the worse and begs Sugiko to return to him, but she takes only a step in his direction and pauses before Hiroshi's sister arrives with the fateful news: Hiroshi is dead. A procession of the servant, sister, nurses and others enters Hiroshi's room, leaving Sugiko alone in the corridor. Up until this point in the sequence, Naruse has kept the camera on one side of the 180 degree line, maintaining spatial clarity through consistent screen direction. The final four shots in the sequence break this pattern, repeatedly crossing the 180 degree line in tight framings. The editing thus confuses screen direction and raises questions as to whether Sugiko is returning to Hiroshi or running away. First Sugiko steps into the frame from right to left in medium close-up, glancing straight and to the right, and pauses (the camera is to her left, see Figure 10); then she steps into the frame from left to right in a profile close-up, looking right, and pauses (the camera is to her right, see Figure 11); then she steps into the frame from right to left in a profile close-up, looking left, pauses and swallows (the camera is to her left). The final shot cuts out to a medium shot as Sugiko stands in the midground, looking left, steps forward and glances right, then runs towards the foreground right (the camera remains on her left). David Bordwell describes the effect:

> The [first] three shots maintain narrational uncertainty: is she returning to the deathbed in a final gesture of love?; is she moving away in a definitive act of rejection?; is she hesitating? At the same time, the momentary disorientation provided by the empty frames and the sudden, accentual close-ups provide decorative geometricization.[22]

By the fourth shot, Sugiko's expressions and figure movement appear to suggest her hesitation is over and she has made a decision, yet the viewer seemingly never learns where she runs to.

Figure 10

Figure 11

STREET WITHOUT END (KAGIRI NAKI HODO) (1934)

Intriguingly, Naruse provides viewers with the means of unravelling the truth through the *mise en scène*, yet rather than stage and edit the scene for maximum clarity, he chooses instead to amplify expressivity and create ambiguity. The hospital corridor in which the scene takes place, though quite short and plain, is clearly laid out through wider framings and distinctive set design. When Sugiko is facing the end of the hall next to Hiroshi's room, she is facing windows open to the cityscape. A wall of frosted windows is to her left and a painted wall with doors is to her right. The far end of the corridor behind her contains a single frosted window. Together with rigorous adherence to the 180 degree rule and consistent screen direction, the visual differences between the ends and sides of the corridor help to clarify whether characters are moving towards or away from Hiroshi's room during the bulk of the scene. Once the accentual editing of the final four shots begins, the 180 degree rule and consistent screen direction are no longer maintained, but the background *mise en scène* still provides clues as to Sugiko's direction each time she takes a step. Although the conflicting screen direction makes it appear as if Sugiko is stepping away, then towards, then away again from Hiroshi's room, the set design reveals she is in fact consistently moving towards him, keeping the row of frosted windows to her left, the single frosted window behind her and the wall with doors to her right. Naruse could have shot Sugiko's step–pause/step–pause/step–pause/step–pause–run towards Hiroshi without crossing the 180 degree line, simply patterning the close-ups in an accented manner in order to develop rhythm and emphasize her hesitation with each step. Yet the choice to confuse screen direction does not merely underline Sugiko's indecision; it also suggests she may be walking away completely, raising the possibility in viewers' minds that the marriage has so embittered her she no longer feels even basic human sympathy for the man she once professed to love. The ambiguity—Sugiko may feel for Hiroshi after all or she may be so bitter she no longer cares—allows for opposing or even contradictory responses from viewers regarding Sugiko's bold act of liberation. Some might cheer her attempts to free herself from the oppressive yoke of her in-laws, others might fault her for appearing so hard-hearted, and still others might root for her but criticize her for going too far.

Sugiko's plotline concludes on an equally ambivalent note. Our last glimpse of her is on the sidewalk outside the café where she once again works. As she watches her newly licensed brother drive away in his taxi, a bus passes and she sees her old flame Machio inside it, looking downcast. Sugiko glances down, as if considering all that has come before (Figure 12). Then her image fades out. This open-ended conclusion prompts the

Figure 12

viewer to consider: what went wrong for Sugiko? Was she misguided in believing in the power of love? Is being a devoted wife not a job worth aspiring to? Or did she simply make the wrong choice? Although the second half of the film largely associates marriage with humiliation and servitude, Sugiko's rueful glimpse of Machio provides a 'what if' moment—what if she had been able to marry Machio after all? Perhaps marrying a different man would have brought her happiness—or perhaps he would somehow disappoint as well. Coincidence ended Sugiko's relationship with Machio and chance brought her Hiroshi, but Sugiko herself made the decision both to marry Hiroshi and to leave him. She gained the strength to earn her freedom, but she now pays a price in her solitude. The composition of the last shot of Sugiko presents her as an icon of the urban Japanese working woman, framed by Ginza's landmark K. Hattori clock tower and the street lamps that figured so prominently in the first proposal scene. In her westernized café waitress uniform, Sugiko could be any young working-class woman, trapped between the promises of modernity and the remnants of tradition.

'There are things that love alone can not change', Sugiko tells Hiroshi after he pleads on his deathbed for her to stay with him. Although *Street Without End* foregrounds the appeals of modernity, humour and romance, its central concern—highlighted through narrative patterning and expressive stylistic punctuation—is the maturation of a woman who loses love yet finds inner strength. As such, the film is both conventional and innovative, working within Kido Shiro's production imperatives to target a female audience with an overtly modern version of a *shinpa*-style narrative. The paralleling of the *moga*, Kesako and Sugiko offers a range of depictions of the modern Japanese woman and, together with the role of chance and the ambiguity inherent in the fate of Sugiko, allows for contradictory understandings of the choices available to them. Nevertheless, the expressive application of Naruse's visual style emphasizes the triumph of Sugiko's rebellion, even if only for a fleeting moment. *Street Without End* thus foreshadows what will distinguish Naruse within the Japanese woman's film, as he creatively punctuates the glances, movements and pauses of a stubbornly determined woman mired in bleak circumstances.

Notes

Introduction

1 Ben Brewster, 'Multiple-Reel/Feature Films: USA' in Richard Abel (ed.), *Encyclopedia of Early Cinema* (New York: Routledge, 2005), pp. 456–57; Sheldon Hall and Steve Neale, *Epics, Spectacles and Blockbusters: A Hollywood History* (Detroit: Wayne State University Press, 1910), pp. 9–18.

2 Hall and Neale, *Epics, Spectacles and Blockbusters*, pp. 21–48. For details on the advent, spread and characteristics of multi-reel films in France and Italy, see Richard Abel, *The Ciné Goes to Town: French Cinema 1896–1914* (Berkeley, Los Angeles and London: University of California Press, 1994 edition), pp. 298–428; Ivo Blom, 'Italy' in Abel (ed.), *Encyclopedia of Early Cinema*, pp. 335–39; and Giorgo Bertellini (ed.), *Italian Silent Cinema: A Reader* (New Barnet: John Libbey Publishing, 2013), pp. 79–122, 161–70, 263–74, 285–89. For an overview of history of multi-reel films in Europe as a whole, see Mark B. Sandberg, 'Multiple-Reel/Feature films: Europe' in Abel (ed.), *Encyclopedia of Early Cinema*, pp. 452–56.

3 For Britain, see John Hawkridge, 'British Cinema from Hepworth to Hitchcock' in Geoffrey Nowell-Smith (ed.), *The Oxford History of World Cinema* (Oxford: Oxford University Press, 1996), pp. 133–35; Nicolas Hiley 'Great Britain' in Abel (ed.), *Encyclopedia of Early Cinema*, pp. 284–86; and Rachael Low, *The History of the British Film*, vol. 3: *1914–18* (London: George Allen & Unwin, 1950). For Denmark, see Casper Tybjerg, 'Denmark' in Abel (ed.), *Encyclopedia of Early Cinema*, pp. 172–76 and Thomas C. Christensen, 'Nordisk Films Kompagni and the First World War' in John Fullerton and Jan Olsson, *Nordic Explorations: Film Before 1930* (Sydney: John Libbey & Company, 1999), pp. 12–18. See also a number the essays in Lisbeth Richter Larsen and Dan Nissen, *100 Years of Nordisk Film* (Copenhagen: Danish Film Institute, 2006). For Germany, see Thomas Elsaesser, 'Germany: Production', Elsaesser and Michael Wedel, 'Distribution', and Corinna Müller, 'Audiences' and 'Exhibition' in Abel (ed.) *Encyclopedia of Early Cinema*, pp. 270–77. See also Thomas Elseasser with Michael Wedel (eds), *A Second Life:*

German Cinema's First Decades (Amsterdam: Amsterdam University Press, 1996) and Paolo Cherchi Usai and Lorenzo Codelli (eds), *Before Caligari: German Cinema, 1895–1920* (Pordenone: Biblioteca dell'Edizioni dell'Immagine, 1990). For Russia, see Denise Youngblood, 'Russia' in Abel (ed.), *Encyclopedia of Early Cinema*, pp. 58–59, and *The Magic Mirror: Moviemaking in Russia, 1908–1918* (Madison: University of Wisconsin Press, 1999). See also Yuri Tsivian with Paolo Cherchi Usai, Lorenzo Cordelli, Carlo Montato, and David Robinson (eds), *Silent Witnesses: Russian Films, 1908–1919* (London: BFI, 1994), and Yuri Tsivian, *Early Cinema in Russia and its Cultural Reception* (London: Routledge, 1994). For Sweden, see John Fullerton, 'Sweden' in Abel (ed.), *Encyclopedia of Early Film*, pp. 615–18. See also Jan Olsson, 'Exchange and Exhibition Practices: Notes on the Swedish Market in the Transitional Era' and Astrid Söderbergh Widding, 'Towards Classical Narration? Georg af Klercker in Context' in Fullerton and Olsson, *Nordic Explorations*, pp. 139–51 and 187–203, respectively. Attention should be drawn as well to two unpublished doctoral theses: 'The Development of a System of Representation in Swedish Film, 1912–1920' by John Fullerton (University of East Anglia, 1994) and 'An Art of Silence and Light: The Development of the Danish Film Drama to 1920 by Casper Tybjerg (University of Copenhagen, 1996). These are available from the University of East Anglia and the UMI Dissertation Information Service, respectively. Meanwhile for Australia, China and Japan, see Ina Bertrand, 'Australia', Zhen Zhang, 'China', and Suresh Chabria 'Japan' in Abel (ed.), *Encyclopedia of Early Film*, pp. 50, 113, 319 and 345, respectively. See also Erik Barnouw and S. Krishnaswarmy, *Indian Film* (New York and London: Columbia University Press, 1963), pp. 12–20, and Suresh Chabria, 'Before Our Eyes: A Short History of India's Silent Cinema' in Chabria (ed.) *Light in Asia: Indian Silent Cinema, 1912–1934* (New Delhi: Le Giornate de Cinema Multo and the National Archive of India, 1994), pp. 11–15. It should be noted that the terms 'feature' and 'feature film' are North American and British. I have been unable to determine the precise equivalents (if any) in non-English-speaking countries.

4 Ben Brewster and Lea Jacobs, *Theatre to Cinema: Stage Pictorialism and the Early Feature Film* (Oxford: Oxford University Press, 1997). As an example, and as Brewster points out in a personal communication, in the 1912 edition of his book on theatrical directing, *Regie*, while recognizing the revolution Otto Brahm had brought about in the German theatre, Hagemann complains that at the Deutsches Theater, one had to watch carefully not to miss an actor's gesture or a movement of his eyes; by the 1918 edition, he asserts that, under Brahm, 'there was no theatre in the true sense—he had no use for anything primitive and elementary'. See Carl Hagemann, *Regie:*

Die Kunst der szenischen Darstellung (3rd edn, Berlin: Schuster & Loeffler, 1912), pp. 63–64, and *Regie: Die Kunst der szenischen Darstellung* (5th edn, Berlin: Schuster & Loeffler, 1918), p. 60.

5 Michel Marie, 'Place de *Germinal* dans l'histoire du cinéma', *1895*, numéro hors série: 'L'année treize en France' (October 1993), p. 230.

6 For an article that draws attention to a number of non-standard (or non-classical) Hollywood films and their styles in the late 1910s and the 1920s (including those directed by Tourneur after *The Wishing Ring*), see Kristin Thompson, 'The Limits of Experimentation in Hollywood' in Jan-Christopher Horak (ed.), *Lovers of Cinema: The First American Film Avant-Garde, 1919–1945* (Madison and London: University of Wisconsin Press, 1995), pp. 67–93.

7 Uli Jung and Martin Loiperdinger, 'World War I' in Abel (ed.), *Encyclopedia of Early Cinema*, p. 702.

8 Brewster and Jacobs, *Theatre to Cinema*, pp. 111–43. For the Danish films in particular, see also David Bordwell, 'Nordisk and the Tableau Aesthetic' in Larsen and Nilssen (eds), *100 Years of Nordisk Film*, pp. 81–96, and 'Nordisk and The Tableau Style', http.//www.davidbordwell.net/essays/nordisk.php.

9 For a detailed discussion of the role played by French director Paul Garbagni in tutoring Sjöström in the pictorial style and hence in adopting it in *Ingeborg Holm*, see Jan Olsson, 'Nils Krok's Social Pathos and Paul Garbagni's Style', *Film History*, 22.1 (2010), 73–94.

10 Kristin Thompson and David Bordwell, *Film History: An Introduction* (New York: McGraw-Hill, 2003 edn), p. 67.

11 Thompson and Bordwell, *Film History*, p. 59. See also the more detailed account provided in Paolo Cherchi Usai, 'Italy: Spectacle and Melodrama' in Nowell-Smith (ed.), *The Oxford History of World Cinema*, pp. 127–30.

12 For a comprehensive account of French films, the French film industry, and French film criticism and theory in the 1920s, see Richard Abel, *French Cinema: The First Wave, 1915–1929* (Princeton, NJ: Princeton University Press, 1984) and *French Film Criticism and Theory*, vol. 1: *1907–1939* (Princeton, NJ: Princeton University Press, 1988). See also Thompson and Bordwell, *Film History*, pp. 85–100.

13 Thompson and Bordwell, *Film History*, p. 101. For more details, see Thomas Elsaesser, 'Germany: The Weimar Years' in Nowell-Smith (ed.), *The Oxford Companion to Film History*, pp. 141–42, and Klaus Kreimeier, *The Ufa Story: A History of Germany's Greatest Film Company* (Berkeley, Los Angeles and London: University of California Press, 1996), pp. 29–47.

14 For a sceptical view of Expressionism in German films and the extent to which the examples usually cited contain genuine Expressionist traits, see Barry Salt, 'From Caligari to Who?' and 'From German Stage to German

Screen' in Salt, *Moving into Pictures: More on Film History, Style, and Analysis* (London: Starword, 2006), pp. 55–62 and 179–89, respectively.
15 Lea Jacobs, *The Decline of Sentiment: American Film in the 1920s* (Berkeley, Los Angeles and London: University of California Press, 2008), p. ix.
16 Ibid., pp. 91–101.
17 Amidst the numerous accounts of Soviet Cinema and its practitioners in the late 1910s and 1920s, standard overviews and reprinted documents include David Bordwell, *Narration in the Fiction Film* (London: Methuen, 1985), pp. 234–73; Ian Christie and John Gillett (eds), *Futurism/Formalism/FEKS: 'Eccentrism' and Soviet Cinema, 1918–36* (London: BFI, 1978); Vance Kepley, Jr, 'Federal Cinema: The Soviet Film Industry, 1924–32', *Film History*, 8.3 (1996), 344–56; Richard Taylor and Ian Christie, *The Film Factory: Russian and Soviet Cinema in Documents, 1896–1939* (Cambridge, MA: Harvard University Press, 1988); Taylor and Christie (eds) *Inside the Film Factory: New Approaches to Russian and Silent Cinema* (New York: Routledge, 1991); Thompson and Bordwell, *Film History*, pp. 119–42; and Denise J. Youngbloood, *Soviet Cinema in the Silent Era, 1918–35* (Austin: University of Texas Press, 1991) and *Movies for the Masses: Popular Cinema and Soviet Society in the 1920s* (Cambridge: Cambridge University Press, 1992). A recent account that focuses on the role of camera operators can be found in Philip Cavendish, *The Men with the Movie Camera: The Poetics of Visual Style in Soviet Avant-Garde Cinema of the 1920s* (New York and Oxford: Berghahn Books, 2013).
18 For more on Boris Barnet, who remains a relatively unexplored figure, see Mark Le Fanu, 'Revolutionary Road: Boris Barnet's *The House on Trubnaya Street*' at http://www.bfi.org.uk/news-opinion/sight-sound-magazine/features/greatest-films-all-time/revolutionary-road-boris-barnet-s> and Giuliano Vivaldi, 'Boris Barnet: The Lyric Voice in Soviet Cinema' at http://brightlightsfilm.com/boris-barnet-the-lyric-voice-in-soviet-cinema/.
19 Hall and Neale, *Epics, Spectacles and Blockbusters*, pp. 58–61.
20 Christine Gledhill, *Reframing British Cinema, 1918–1928: Between Restraint and Passion* (London: BFI, 2003).
21 In addition to Andrew Higson and Richard Maltby (eds), *'Film Europe' and 'Film America': Cinema, Commerce and Cultural Exchange 1920–1939* (Exeter: University of Exeter Press, 1999 and the other sources cited by Burrows, see Kristin Thompson, 'National or International Films? The European Film Debate during the 1920s', *Film History*, 8.3 (1996), pp. 281–96, and Thompson and Bordwell, *Film History*, pp. 167–73.
22 Donald Crafton, *The Talkies: American Cinema's Transition to Sound, 1926–1931* (New York: Scribner's: 1997), p. 207.
23 For a detailed account of the production, spread and changing characteris-

tics of feature-length sound films in Hollywood between 1928 and 1931, see Crafton, *The Talkies*, pp. 267–380.
24 Thompson and Bordwell, *Film History*, p. 209.
25 According to Thompson and Bordwell, *Film History*, p. 257, the Chinese market was dominated by imports: 'In 1929, only 10 percent of the 500 films released were made in China.'
26 David Bordwell, *Ozu and the Poetics of Cinema* (London: BFI, 1988), pp. 18–30, 'A Cinema of Flourishes: Japanese Decorative Classicism of the Prewar Era' in Arthur Molletti, Jr and David Desser (eds), *Reframing Japanese Cinema: Authorship, Genre, History* (Bloomington and Indianapolis: Indiana University Press, 1992), pp. 328–46, and 'Visual Style in Japanese Cinema, 1925–1945', *Film History*, 7.1 (1995), pp. 5–31. See also Thompson and Bordwell, *Film History*, pp. 186–87. As Bordwell points out, most pre-World War Two films have, along with a number of films made in World War Two era, either been lost or destroyed. As reported in a note to 'Visual Style in Japanese Cinema, 1925–1945' (p. 29 note 2), the survival rate for the pre-war films is estimated to be 'about 4 per cent'. The breadth of styles, and the extent to which idiosyncratic variants seem to have been cultivated by individual directors (including Ozu and Naruse), may have been the product of a rivalry between Shochiku and Nikkatsu and of rivalries within them. Unlike the Hollywood majors, these companies exhibited their own films in their own cinemas on an exclusive basis, and this may have encouraged forms of product differentiation. In addition, and given the status of many directors as salarymen who worked for the same companies for years on end, they probably had the freedom to experiment and hone their own styles.
27 Thompson and Bordwell, *Film History*, p. 186.
28 Ibid., pp. 208–09. Much has been written on the *benshi*. The most detailed account in English can be found in Jeffrey A. Dym, *Benshi Japanese Silent Film Narrators and their Forgotten Narrative Art of Setsumei: A History of Japanese Silent Film Narration* (New York, Ontario and Lampeter: Edwin Mellen Press, 2003).
29 Bordwell, 'Visual Style in Japanese Cinema, 1925–1945', p. 18.

Chapter 1

1 *Les Misérables*, released late in 1912, was longer in total, but was issued in four forty-five-minute parts, each of which made up only part of a theatrical programme, rather than the whole subject.
2 'Place de *Germinal* dans l'histoire du cinéma français,' *1895*, numéro hors série: 'L'année treize en France' (October 1993), p. 230.
3 Roberta Pearson, *Eloquent Gestures: The Transformation of Performance Style*

in the Griffith Biograph Films (Berkeley: University of California Press, 1992), especially Chapter 2, pp. 18–37.
4 When this article was originally written, Capellani's *L'Assommoir* was thought to be a lost film, but it has since come to light and can be viewed in the DVD box set *Le Coffret Albert Capellani* issued by Pathé Frères in 2006. It is, strictly speaking, not an adaptation of Zola's novel, but one of the play by William Busnach and Octave Gastineau first performed in 1879.
5 Ben Brewster and Lea Jacobs, *Theatre to Cinema: Stage Pictorialism and the Early Feature Film* (Oxford: Oxford University Press, 1997), p. 89.
6 *Eloquent Gestures*, pp. 113–18.
7 *Theatre to Cinema*, pp. 133–36.
8 The print of *Germinal* that I studied was that held by the Cinémathèque royale de Belgique, in a version restored for the Cinémathèque française by Renée Lichtig in 1968. An identical copy is available on DVD in the *Coffret Albert Capellani* box set referred to above.
9 For those not familiar with the film, and maybe unaware of the differences between the film and the novel, a plot summary follows: Étienne Lantier, a mechanic, loses his job in Lille one winter. He tramps the roads in search of work, and finally, through a chance encounter with Bonnemort, an old miner kept on as a surface worker, is taken on as a haulage man in the team led by Bonnemort's son-in-law Toussaint Maheu at one of the coal mines in Montsou in the *département du Nord*. He also finds lodgings in the Maheus' house. Another member of the team is Maheu's daughter Catherine, a haulage woman. Lantier and Catherine are attracted to one another, but Catherine has another suitor, the coal cutter Chaval, and Catherine marries Chaval because Lantier fails to put forward his own suit. Chaval mistreats Catherine, in part through suspicion and jealousy of Lantier, resulting in fights between the two men. The company enforces changes in the way teams are paid that effectively lower their earnings. The miners, inspired by the vague knowledge of socialist ideas gained by Lantier during his earlier working experience, protest the changes, and receiving no response from the management, they strike. Chaval, mostly out of spite for Lantier and jealousy of his ascendancy with the miners, becomes a management spy. As the strike drags on, Chaval leads a group of miners to return to work—a group he forces Catherine to join. Learning of this treachery, the strikers cut the cables to the cages while the blacklegs are down the mine, forcing them to climb the emergency ladders to get out and to run a gauntlet of the strikers when they emerge. Humiliated, Chaval denounces Lantier to the police, forcing Lantier to go into hiding in a disused pit. Troops are called to quell the disorders and, during an attack by the miners on the mine director's house, soldiers open fire on the strikers, killing a number of them, including

Maheu. The strikers decide to return to work, led by Chaval. Reluctantly, Lantier joins them. The anarchist machinist Souvarine sabotages the waterproof cladding of the pit shaft, and the mine is flooded while the miners are below. Many are drowned, but Lantier, Catherine and Chaval find themselves trapped by water in an old working. Led by the mine engineer Négrel and Maheu's son Zacharie, a rescue attempt is made via the old pit. Zacharie dies in a firedamp explosion during this attempt. Down in the mine, Lantier kills Chaval in a fight over food and Catherine dies of starvation in Lantier's arms, but Lantier is still alive when the rescuers break through. Once he has recovered from his ordeal, Lantier decides to leave to pursue a political career. He says goodbye to Maheu's wife, who has herself become a haulage woman in the mine, and sets out for Paris.

10 The baby is called Estelle in the novel. Like many of the characters in the film, she is not named in the intertitles. I will use the names in the novel without comment from now on.
11 Krauss had acted for Antoine at the Théâtre Libre in 1892 and had been a regular SCAGL leading man since 1908. He was the Quasimodo of *Notre Dame de Paris* and played Jean Valjean in *Les Misérables*.
12 Louise Sylvie appeared in a small number of films, mostly made by SCAGL, in the early 1910s, but acted mainly on stage, often, in the 1900s and 1910s, for the Théâtre Antoine and the Théâtre de l'Odéon under Antoine's direction. In the mid-1930s, she had a renewed film career as a character actress, culminating in her starring role in René Allio's *La Vieille femme indigne/The Shameless Old Lady* in 1965.
13 It should be noted that Jacquinet was a mime before he started to act in films.
14 Contrast the mess of the fight between Glenister and McNamara in the 1914 Selig film *The Spoilers*, which the film-makers clearly had no idea what to do with, despite the fact that it is the key moment of the film, and was known to be the key moment from its significance in the 1907 stage adaptation of Beach's novel—this despite the fact that William Farnum was accustomed to playing he-man parts on the stage and must have known how to do a stage fight. Perhaps the techniques of stage fighting had not been adapted to an edited scene such as was required in *The Spoilers*, which has the standard découpage of an American film of its date.

Chapter 2

1 Here is a summary of the film: one of Assunta's former admirers, Raffaele, sends a letter to her fiancé, Michele, falsely accusing her of consorting with another man. Assunta calms Michele's jealousy by agreeing to leave her

father's house and to run a laundry next to Michele's butcher shop. Later, Raffaele shows up at a birthday celebration for Assunta and the two flirt, prompting Michele to stalk off in a jealous rage. On the street, returning from the party in the company of friends, Assunta is assaulted by Michele, who slashes her face. Assunta is taken inside, where she calls for a mirror and tries to hide her face. After Michele is arrested, however, she lies in court in an attempt to have him acquitted. Outside the courtroom, Michele's mother-in-law berates her for ruining her son's life. Michele is sentenced to two years in prison in Avellino. Assunta bargains with the notary Funelli, agreeing to sleep with him if he will see to it that Michele serves his time close to home in Naples. Feeling guilty about the affair with Funelli, Assunta stops visiting Michele in prison and replying to his letters. After a year and a half, on Christmas Eve, Assunta appeals to Funelli to come to her house for dinner, and he agrees half-heartedly, having obviously lost interest in her. She confides to one of her friends that she is pregnant and hopes that Funelli will marry her and take her away before Michele is released from prison. Assunta's dinner preparations are interrupted by the arrival of Michele, who has been released six months early. When she confesses that she is no longer worthy of his attentions, he rushes from the laundry in a rage. Encountering Funelli in the street, he wounds him and Funelli staggers into Assunta's room to die. The police enter and Assunta allows herself to be led away as the perpetrator of the crime.
2 Brunetta, *Storia del cinema italiano 1895–1945* (Rome: Editori Riuniti, 1979), pp. 81–84.
3 The print studied was a Dutch-language copy in the Desmet Collection of the Eye Institute Netherlands in Amsterdam. A DVD version has been issued by the Cineteca di Bologna, based on the same print.
4 Ben Brewster and Lea Jacobs, *Theatre to Cinema: Stage Pictorialism and the Early Feature Film* (Oxford: Oxford University Press, 1997).
5 Frederick and Lise-Lone Marker, *Ibsen's Lively Art: A Performance Study of the Major Plays* (Cambridge: Cambridge University Press, 1989), p. 105.
6 'Die Freie Bühne in Berlin', *Berliner Tageblatt*, no. 16 (18 October 1909). A similar point was made by Percy Hammond in a review of a performance by the Moscow Arts Theatre troupe during their American tour in 1923: 'A peculiar thing about the Russian actors is that the most important of them can come into a room or leave it without theatrical emphasis. You suddenly discover that they are present or that they are absent.' See Victor Emeljanov, ed., *Chekov: The Critical Heritage* (Boston: Routledge, 1981), p. 238.
7 Our analysis, which was conducted by Ben Brewster as well as myself, is based on the print restored by L'Immagine Ritrovato in 1993, which was screened at a number of venues in the USA in 2000 as part of a 'Silent Divas'

series circulated by the Cineteca del Comune di Bologna. The restoration combined footage from two copies: one in the Milan Cineteca printed from the original negative in the 1960s, the other from a Portuguese-language copy dating from the film's release held by the Cinemateca Brasileira in São Paulo. There is a DVD version of the film issued by Kino Video; according to David Shepard, who produced the DVD, it derives from a print he obtained from the Cineteca in Milan. Unfortunately, this copy lacks several of the scenes in the lobby of the court at Castelcapuano that we discuss below, and many of the titles are different. The titles cited here are English translations of the titles in the L'Immagine Ritrovato print.
8   This scene is missing from the American DVD.
9   Part of this scene is also missing from the American DVD.
10 Jon Burrows, *Legitimate Cinema: Theatre Stars in Silent British Films, 1908–1918* (Exeter: University of Exeter Press, 2003), p. 61.

Chapter 3

1   See Francis Lacassin, 'Les films policiers de Léonce Perret' in Bernard Bastide and Jean A. Gili (eds), *Léonce Perret* (Paris: Association française de recherches sur l'histoire du cinéma, 2003), p. 108.
2   Perret loved to layer high-contrast lighting in depth, activating the background behind a darkened foreground, or perhaps keying the foreground and background at the expense of the midground. The strategy was not only highly visually appealing, but also economical. Ben Brewster and Lea Jacobs accurately describe the underlying sets in many of Perret's films as 'rather perfunctory'. See Ben Brewster and Lea Jacobs, *Theatre to Cinema: Stage Pictorialism and the Early Feature Film* (New York: Oxford University Press, 1997), p. 181; see also Jean A. Gili, 'L'Enfant de Paris' in Bastide and Gili (eds), *Léonce Perret*, p. 178.
3   Gili, 'L'Enfant de Paris', 182. Note that all translations in this paper are mine.
4   Kristin Thompson, 'The Continuity System' in David Bordwell, Janet Staiger and Kristin Thompson, *The Classical Hollywood Cinema* (New York: Columbia University Press, 1985), p. 108.
5   See François de la Bretèque, 'La veine réaliste de Léonce Perret' in Bastide and Gili (eds), *Léonce Perret*; Brewster and Jacobs, *Theatre to Cinema*, pp. 150–57.
6   Of course, there is no reason to choose one or the other, to pigeon-hole Perret as *either* a master of depth-staging *or* an early investigator of editing's potential. Most of the authors cited would, I think, agree with David Bordwell's observation that 'Although analytical cutting and lengthy takes can be seen

as logical alternatives, historically they often functioned as flexible, non-exclusive options'. See David Bordwell, 'Exceptionally Exact Perceptions: On Staging in Depth' in *On the History of Film Style* (Cambridge: Harvard University Press, 1998), p. 199.
7   Cited in Gili, 'L'Enfant de Paris', p. 182.
8   Laurent Le Forestier, 'Les comédies de Léonce Perret, fleurons de la production Gaumont' in Bastide and Gili (eds), *Léonce Perret*, p. 39.
9   Richard Abel, *The Ciné Goes to Town: French Cinema 1896–1914, Updated and Expanded Edition* (Berkeley: University of California Press, 1994), p. 383.
10 Ibid., p. 388.
11 Ben Brewster, 'Deep Staging in French Films' in Thomas Elsaesser (ed.), *Early Cinema: Space, Frame, Narrative* (London: BFI, 1990), p. 52.
12 Moreover, since Brewster published his observations about the 1914 film, Gaumont has released DVD copies that significantly lower the barriers to sustained inspection of Perret's editing (and framing) practice.
13 With early cinema, it is always possible that some footage is missing. It is also possible that the Gaumont publicist miscounted. Perhaps most likely, though, Gaumont staff were using a definition of tableaux that excluded some interior scenes and included others, in a variation that is slightly different from any I've experimented with.
14 Inserts and returns to the master shot within each scene are not counted separately.
15 An additional six shots are recurring pans that I believe probably are unique, but I have not counted them since the camera's movement makes it difficult to judge its precise position.
16 The one exception is a 180 degree cut over Captain de Valens's head when he addresses crowds in the street upon his triumphant return to Paris. It is possible that Perret saw this set-up as analogous to a POV shot. It is also possible that the set-up preceding and following the 180 degree displacement are slightly different. If so, however, the difference is so slight that it cannot be definitively separated from the significant background noise of instability from movement of the film in the camera and the printer's gate in the Gaumont transfer.
17 Brewster, 'Deep Staging in French Films', p. 50.
18 Ibid., p. 53.
19 Bordwell places the bottom line higher, between knee and mid-thigh. See David Bordwell, 'Feuillade, or What Was Mise-en-Scène' in *Figures Traced in Light: On Cinematic Staging* (Berkeley: University of California Press, 2005), p. 46. I think this is too close, but the problems of watching silent film on 16 mm or video transfers, or in 35 mm on a flatbed, make this point

rather tenuous. The salient idea is that the *plan français* entails a slightly larger shot scale than the *plan américain*.
20 Brewster, 'Deep Staging in French Films', p. 52.
21 Bordwell, 'Feuillade, or What Was Mise-en-Scène', pp. 46–47. Interestingly, Salt says scene dissection is *more* characteristic of the European context than the American one until right around 1912, when he clearly thinks the Americans begin to edit much more. See Barry Salt, *Film Style & Technology: History & Analysis*, 2nd expanded edn (London: Starword, 1992), p. 92. Bowser has also observed that American film-makers are changing angles when they cut in by 1912. See Eileen Bowser, *The Transformation of Cinema* (Berkeley: University of California Press, 1990), p. 261.
22 Laurent Le Forestier is particularly enamoured of Perret's analytical editing. Le Forestier, 'Les comedies de Léonce Perret, fleurons de la production Gaumont'.
23 There is some margin of error here (say plus or minus two or three views), since it is ultimately a judgement call when the camera has moved enough to count as a different viewpoint.
24 Cited in Salt, *Film Style & Technology: History & Analysis*, p. 98.
25 I am indebted to Richard Abel's partial description of the reel breaks in *L'Enfant de Paris*. See Abel, *The Ciné Goes to Town*, p. 384.
26 For a detailed description of the bar, and the action preceding this sequence, see Brewster and Jacobs, *Theatre to Cinema*, pp. 195–97.
27 In the first reel of *L'Enfant de Paris*, there is a more ambiguous case. Perret cuts away from the de Valen home to Casablanca, where Captain de Valen is engaged in conflict with rebel insurgents. The sequence is much shorter than the Bachelier/Bosco sequence, numbering only six shots. Perret fades from an inserted photograph of Captain de Valen (gazed at lovingly by Marie-Laure and her mother in long shot) to the Captain himself atop the walls of a fort. In a series of three shots, the Captain is (apparently) killed. A dissolve returns the action to the de Valen salon, where the Captain's brother Jacques reads the paper. Yet, this is far from a clear example of cross-cutting, and it may even strain the definition of parallel editing. The simultaneity in this sequence is rather loose. Moreover, Perret cuts only once to Morocco and finishes the line of action there before returning to the family's Parisian living room.

Chapter 4

1 Richard Koszarski, 'Maurice Tourneur: The First of the Visual Stylists', *Film Comment*, 9.2 (March/April 1973), 24–31; Richard Suchenski, "'Turn

Again, Tourneur": Maurice Tourneur between France and Hollywood', *Studies in French Cinema*, 11.2 (2011), 87–100.
2. Suchenski, '"Turn Again, Tourneur"', 92.
3. Jan-Christopher Horak, 'Good Morning, Babylon: Maurice Tourneur's Battle against the Studio System', *Image*, 31.2 (September 1988), 1–12.
4. Kevin Brownlow, *The Parade's Gone By* (New York: Bonanza Books, 1968), pp. 418–20.
5. Kevin Lewis, 'A World Across from Broadway: The Shuberts and the Movies', *Film History*, 1.1 (1987), 39–51.
6. Owen Davis, *My First Fifty Years in the Theatre: The Plays, the Players, the Theatrical Managers and the Theatre Itself as One Man Saw Them in the Fifty Years between 1897 and 1947* (Boston: Walter H. Baker Company Publishers, 1950), pp. 58–60.
7. 'Davis Forsakes Way of Melodrama', *New York Times*, 21 January 1910, 11.
8. Peter Milne, '*The Wishing Ring*', *Motion Picture News*, 14 November 1914, 41.
9. '*The Wishing Ring*', *Moving Picture World*, 7 November 1914, 793.
10. Ben Singer and Charlie Keil, 'Introduction: Movies and the 1910s' in Charlie Keil and Ben Singer (eds), *American Cinema of the 1910s: Themes and Variations* (New Brunswick, NJ: Rutgers University Press, 2009), p. 14.
11. Kristin Thompson, 'From Primitive to Classical' in David Bordwell, Janet Staiger and Kristin Thompson, *The Classical Hollywood Cinema: Film Style and Mode of Production to 1960* (New York: Columbia University Press, 1985), p. 167; Tom Gunning, 'Systematizing the Electric Message: Narrative Form, Gender, and Modernity in *The Lonedale Operator*' in Charlie Keil and Shelley Stamp (eds), *American Cinema's Transitional Era: Audiences, Institutions, Practices* (Berkeley: University of California Press, 2004), p. 17; Barry Salt, *Film Style & Technology: History & Analysis*, 2nd edn (London: Starword, 1992), pp. 111–13.
12. Thompson, 'From Primitive to Classical', p. 169.
13. Kristin Thompson, 'Narrative Structure in Early Classical Cinema' in John Fullerton (ed.), *Celebrating 1895: The Centenary of Cinema* (Sydney: John Libbey & Company, 1998), p. 236.
14. Louis Reeves Harrison, 'Five Reels', *Moving Picture World*, 7 February 1914, 652.
15. Ben Brewster, '"Traffic in Souls": An Experiment in Feature-Length Narrative Construction', *Cinema Journal*, 31.1 (Fall 1991), 37–56.
16. W. Stephen Bush, 'Weekly Masterpieces', *Moving Picture World*, 31 January 1914, 520.
17. Louis Reeves Harrison, 'When Features are Failures', *Moving Picture World*, 21 March 1914, 1505.

18 Epes Winthrop Sargent, 'The Photoplaywright', *Moving Picture World*, 16 October 1915, 432.
19 See e.g. Epes Winthrop Sargent, 'The Photoplaywright', *Moving Picture World*, 4 December 1915, 1828–29.
20 '*The Wishing Ring*', *Variety*, 31 October 1914, 27.
21 'Davis Forsakes Way of Melodrama', *New York Times*, 21 January 1910, 11.
22 Epes Winthrop Sargent, 'The Photoplaywright', *Moving Picture World*, 4 December 1915, 1829.
23 '*The Wishing Ring*', *New York Dramatic Mirror*, 4 November 1914, 35.
24 Horak, 'Good Morning Babylon', 3.
25 The cutting rate was determined using the copy of *The Wishing Ring* included on the 2003 Image Entertainment DVD, *Before Hollywood, There was Fort Lee, N.J.*
26 Maurice Tourneur, 'Movies Create Art', *Harper's Weekly*, 29 April 1916, 459.

Chapter 5

1 Cinematographer Julius Jaenzon and his team used multiple exposures of the same lengths of film to produce the ghostly transparency of the carriage and its occupants, moving through and within the solidity of the material world. 'The backdrop, the setting, had to remain dark for the spirits to stand out . . . First they shot the background. Then they would run the same strip of film through the camera a second time in order to catch the spirits against a dark, neutral background . . . Jaenzon had to keep detailed notes about film lengths and crank speed . . . An occasional film strip had to be used four times to properly complete a scene. Of course, the spirits were transparent, so the furniture in back of them had to shine through. At the same time, the furniture in front of them needed to obscure them.' Louis Delluc, quoted by Bo Florin, *Regi: Victor Sjöström/Directed by Victor Seastrom* (Stockholm: Cinematek/Svensk Filminstitutet, 2003), p. 75.
2 Tom Gunning, 'A Dangerous Pledge: Victor Sjöström's Unknown Masterpiece, *Masterman*' in John Fullerton and Jan Olsson (eds), *Nordic Explorations: Film Before 1930* (New Barnet: John Libbey Press, 1999), p. 205.
3 Graves quotes from Lagerlöf's letters: 'For years now I've had in my head the plan to write a Christmas story of the kind Dickens used to write'; 'If I could get my Christmas Carol finished and about 90 to 100 pages long I would bring it out as a little book for Christmas'. These are cited in Selma Lagerlöf, *The Phantom Carriage*, trans. by Peter Graves (Stockholm: Norvic Press, 2011), p. 115.
4 As David relates the story of Georges, a flashback takes us to the scene and, as Georges begins to tell David and the other men present about death's

carriage, that in turn is dramatized—our first view of the phantom carriage—with Georges' 'voice' continuing in the intertitles.

5   Where titles are inserted into continuous action from a single set-up we have counted only one shot.

6   Bo Florin notes of these earlier films that 'systematic cuts across the 180 degree line to a completely reversed camera position, thus creating a 360 degree cinematic space' were common in Swedish films of the period but particularly frequent in Sjöström. See Bo Florin, *Transition and Transformation: Victor Sjöström in Hollywood 1923–1930* (Amsterdam: Amsterdam University Press, 2013), pp. 20–21.

7   In a discussion of *Girl from the Marsh Croft* (1916), Gunning notes that Sjöström uses closer shots than those typically found in Swedish film in the mid-1910s, together with an increase in the number and variety of camera angles. See Gunning, 'A Dangerous Pledge', p. 208.

8   Bo Florin's concept of 'lyrical intimacy' evokes significant aspects of the sequences here: 'lyrical intimacy, created through downplayed acting, *mise en scène* and montage privileging a circular space with a clear centre, towards which movements converge'. See Florin, *Transition and Transformation*, 20–21. However, the 'circular' space established here is considerably more complex than those in the films Florin is discussing.

9   Barry Salt, *Film Style and Technology: History and Analysis* (London: Starword, 1992 edition), p. 171, states that the 'basic Griffith style of scene dissection, with cuts into a closer shot made from a frontal direction, continued to be practised by many film-makers into the early 1920s, both in America and particularly in Europe'.

10 Sjöström had made use of mirrors in similar ways in other films, notably *The Girl from the Marsh Croft*.

11 Ben Brewster and Lea Jacobs, *Theatre to Cinema: Stage Pictorialism and the Early Feature Film* (Oxford: Oxford University Press, 1997), pp. 133–34.

12 Charles Barr, 'Sjöström and Seastrom', *Norwich Papers in European Languages, Literatures and Culture*, no. 1 (1994), argues that Sjöström was unique in making the transition fully and successfully from the 'pre-classical' period to the 'classical'. Barr juxtaposes *Ingeborg Holm* (1913) and *The Scarlet Letter*, which was made in Hollywood in 1926. But the transition was made while Sjöström was still working in Sweden.

13 Salt notes in *Film Style and Technology*, p. 125, that the use of arc lights for night scenes was beginning to appear around 1916–17 and cites Sjöström's *The Outlaw and His Wife* (1917).

14 Darragh O'Donaghue, '*The Phantom Carriage*', http://sensesofcinema.com/2010/cteq/the-phantom-carriage/.

15 Unlike many of the films to which Sjöström owed his eminence at this time,

which were celebrated for their use of landscape and the natural world, *The Phantom Carriage* is predominantly set in interiors, and rarely in daylight.

Chapter 6

1. Tom Gunning, *The Films of Fritz Lang: Allegories of Vision and Modernity* (London: BFI, 2000), p. 99, argues that these are not playing cards but *cartes de visites*, 'hand sized photographs introduced in the nineteenth century bearing one's portrait to be exchanged with friends and relatives'. However, as he himself points out, these photographs 'blend two realms of reference, one of which is gambling' (which often involves the playing of cards), the other of which is acting.
2. Ursula Hardt, *From Caligari to California: Eric Pommer's Life in the International Film Wars* (Providence, RI: 1996), pp. 52–53; Klaus Kreimeier, *The Ufa Story: A History of Germany's Greatest Film Company, 1918–1945*. Trans. Robert and Rita Kember (Berkeley: University of California Press, 1966), pp. 88–89. According to Kreimeier, the final instalments were accompanied by stills from the forthcoming film.
3. David Kalat, *The Strange Case of Dr Mabuse: A Study of the Twelve Films and Five Novels* (Jefferson, NC: McFarland, 2001), p. 16.
4. For details on the production process, see Bernard Eisenschitz, *Fritz Lang au Travail* (Paris: Cahiers du Cinéma, 2011), pp. 32–37. A number of books claim incorrectly that the two parts of *Dr Mabuse* were premiered on consecutive evenings (27 and 28 April), among them Kalat, *The Strange Case of Dr Mabuse*, p. 52, and Patrick McGilligan, *Fritz Lang: The Nature of the Beast* (New York: St Martin's Press, 1997), p. 86. The Ufa-Palast am zoo was one of Ufa's flagship cinemas. Ufa and Decla-Bioscop had merged to form a vertically integrated corporation in November 1921, so the Ufa-Palast was an obvious premiere venue.
5. The first act in Part Two is introduced as a 'Prelude', its conclusion as the 'End of Act One'. The fifth act in Part Two concludes with the announcement of a 'Finale' prior to notification of the end of Act Five and the beginning of Act Six.
6. Quoted in Kalat, *The Strange Case of Dr Mabuse*, p. 55.
7. Rudmer Canjels, *Distributing Silent Film Serials: Local Practices, Changing Forms, Cultural Transformation* (New York: Routledge, 2011).
8. Ibid., pp. 83–87.
9. Unlike *Les Vampires*, and with the exception of *Juve Contre Fantômas*, most of the episodes of *Fantômas* were self-contained.
10. For a detailed account of *Die Herrrin der Welt* and its distribution in Germany, see Canjels, *Distributing Silent Film Serials*, pp. 63–75.

11 According to Canjels, *Distributing Silent Film Serials*, p. 122, over forty two-part serial features were released in Germany in the early 1920s. According to Norbert Grob, '"Bringing the Ghostly to Life": Fritz Lang and His Early Mabuse Films' in Dietrich Scheuneman (ed.), *Expressionist Films—New Perspectives* (Rochester, NY: Camden House, 2003), p. 106, note 11, *Die Spinnen* was originally planned to consist of four parts. Whether the vogue for two-part serial features or whether other factors were responsible for the change of plan remains unclear.
12 Gunning, *The Films of Fritz Lang*, pp. 88–94.
13 An extract from this interview is included as an extra on the Transit DVD. I have modified the translation to make it more idiomatic.
14 In German editions of the novel, von Wenk is called a 'Staatsanwalt'. As noted by Lilian A. Clare, the translator of the first edition of the novel in English, 'there is no equivalent to this position in Britain': 'Translator's Note' to *Dr Mabuse, Master of Mystery* (London: George Allen & Unwin, 1923), p. 5. In English-language books and essays, and in English-language intertitles, he is variously identified as a detective or as a State or Public Prosecutor. In Clare's translation he is called a State Attorney.
15 Noel Burch, 'Notes on Fritz Lang's First *Mabuse*', *Ciné-Tracts: A Journal of Film and Cultural Studies*, 4.1 (Spring 1981), 4.
16 As Kalat points out in *The Strange Case of Dr Mabuse*, pp. 10, 11, Gino Starace's famous poster image of Fantômas towering over the rooftops of Paris was evoked in a number of posters for the film version of *Dr Mabuse* too.
17 See Kalat, *The Strange Case of Dr Mabuse*, p. 39.
18 For a detailed description, see Gunning, *The Films of Fritz Lang*, pp. 96–97.
19 Ibid., p. 97.
20 Ibid., pp. 94–95.
21 For a detailed account of the technological and stylistic characteristics of German cinema in the late 1910s and early 1920s, see Kristin Thompson, *Herr Lubitsch Goes to Hollywood: German and American after World War I* (Amsterdam: University of Amsterdam Press, 2005).
22 See Barry Salt, *Moving into Pictures: More on Film History, Film Style, and Analysis* (London: Starword, 2006), pp. 190–96.
23 For a detailed account of this aspect of *Mabuse*, see T. Elsaesser, *Weimar and After: Germany's Historical Imaginary* (London and New York: Routledge, 2000), pp. 168–73.
24 Situational dramaturgy was a hallmark of nineteenth- and early twentieth-century theatre, and has been a hallmark of commercial, feature-length films from the 1910s to the present day. For details and examples, see Ben Brewster and Lea Jacobs, *Theatre to Cinema* (Oxford: Oxford University Press, 1998), esp. pp. 18–32; Scott Higgins, 'Suspenseful Situations: Melo-

dramatic Narrative and the Contemporary Action Film', *Cinema Journal*, 47.2 (Winter 2008), 74–96.
25 Elsaesser, *Weimar and After*, p. 174.
26 Ibid., p. 176.
27 Gunning, *The Films of Fritz Lang*, pp. 104–5.
28 Lotte Eisner, *Fritz Lang*. Trans. Gertrud Mander (NewYork: Oxford University Press, 1977), p. 59.
29 Gunning, *The Films of Fritz Lang*, p. 118. According to Lang, the siege scenes were based on a real-life siege in Paris and Mabuse's exploits were partly inspired by Al Capone, as McGilligan notes in *Fritz Lang*, p. 82. However, while the derivation of the siege may be accurate, most histories of organized crime, among them Herbert Asbury, *The Gangs of Chicago* (London: Arrow Books, 2003) and David E. Ruth, *Inventing the Public Enemy: The Gangster in American Culture, 1918–1934* (Chicago: Chicago University Press, 1996), argue that Capone was more or less unknown outside local criminal circles in New York and Chicago until the mid-1920s.
30 As far as I am aware, Lang was never asked about this, which seems either to be an error in continuity or a deliberate piece of unexplained sensation.
31 As Kalat points out in *The Strange Case of Dr Mabuse*, p. 58, this denouement is entirely different from that in the book, in which von Wenk is captured by Mabuse, and in which the Countess rescues von Wenk by throwing Mabuse from his plane while en route to Brazil. Kalat also points out that the Countess 'is undoubtedly the true hero of Jacques' book', that Lang's filmography is otherwise 'rife with dominant females and ineffectual males', and that her reduced role in the film 'may have something to do with issues of class'.

Chapter 7

1 'A Little Child Leads the Way in This One', *Chicago Daily Tribune*, 9 November 1925, p. 17.
2 Display Ad, *Photoplay* (September 1925), 7.
3 Hervé Dumont, *Frank Borzage*, trans. Jonathan Kaplansky (Jefferson, NC: McFarland, 2006), pp. 13, 16.
4 '*Lazybones*', *Billboard*, 14 February 1925, p. 27.
5 '*Lazybones*', *Daily Variety*, 1 October 1925, p. 15.
6 Ibid.
7 Steve Neale, 'Melodrama and Tears', *Screen*, 27.6 (1986), 6–22.
8 Ibid., 12.
9 These are all melodramatic situations identified in 1897 by Georges Polti: 21c:2 (self sacrifice for kindred); 28d (free union impeded by opposition of

relatives); 33b (false suspicions drawn upon oneself to save a friend). Georges Polti, *The Thirty Six Dramatic Situations* (Boston: The Writer Inc., 1977).
10 Lea Jacobs, *The Decline of Sentiment: American Film in the 1920s* (Berkeley: University of California Press, 2008), pp. 34–36, 37–42.
11 Ibid., 42.
12 Peter Milne, *Motion Picture Directing* (New York: Falk Publishing Company, 1922), p. 112.
13 Ibid., 114.
14 Cecelia Ager, 'That Sentimental Gentleman from H'Wood, Borzage Tells How', *Variety*, 7 March 1933, p. 2.
15 Ibid.
16 Jacobs, *The Decline of Sentiment*, 77.
17 Ibid.
18 'Cowboy Star in Dramatic Role', *Los Angeles Times*, 22 November 1925, section C31; 'Buck Jones in Drama Role', *Los Angeles Times*, 9 August 1925, 26.
19 Ager, 'That Sentimental Gentleman from H'Wood', p. 2.
20 Much of the film is shot with a filter that diffuses and softens the periphery of the frame, leaving clear focus in the centre. It is a pictorial choice that is in line with Borzage's preference for soft focus, and the rural drama's association with nostalgia may motivate it. Though it is a global effect, the device takes on more specific functions in emotionally wrought scenes, such as this.
21 Ager, 'That Sentimental Gentleman from H'Wood', p. 2.
22 Dumont, *Frank Borzage*, p. 106.
23 '*Lazybones*', *Daily Variety*, 9 December 1925, p. 42.
24 'A Little Child Leads the Way in This One', p. 17.
25 'Buck Makes Good in *Lazybones*', *Los Angeles Times*, 23 November 1925, section A9.

Chapter 8

1 Douglas Gomery, *The Hollywood Studio System* (London: BFI, 1986), pp. 102–107. The Lubitsch films were *The Marriage Circle* and *Three Women* (both 1924), *Kiss Me Again* (1925), and *So This is Paris* (1926). As Scott Simmon points out in his 'Program Notes' for *More Treasures from American Archives 1894–1931* (San Francisco, CA: National Film Preservation Foundation, 2004), p. 145, the 1925 version of *Lady Windermere's Fan* was road-shown at premium prices in a number of specially rented legitimate theatres (a practice usually reserved for prestige productions), as well as shown in conventional cinemas.
2 Charles Musser, 'The Hidden and the Unspeakable: On Theatrical Culture,

Oscar Wilde and Ernst Lubitsch's *Lady Windermere's Fan*', *Film Studies*, no. 4 (Summer 2004), 12–47.

3   Ernst Lubitsch, 'The Motion Picture Art is the Youngest of All the Muses' in Laurence A. Hughes (ed.), *The Truth About the Movies by the Stars* (Hollywood, CA: Hollywood Publishers, Inc., 1924), p. 347.

4   Ernst Lubitsch, 'Lubitsch Talks of Epigrams on Screen', *New York Herald Tribune*, 27 December 1925, section 3E. Among the more famous lines in the play are 'Experience is the name everyone gives to their mistakes' and 'We are all in the gutter, but some of us looking at the stars'.

5   The most detailed account of Lubitsch and his films in English can be found in William Paul, *Ernst Lubitsch's American Comedy* (New York: Columbia University Press, 1983). Paul refers to some of his German films in passing, but (presumably because he was unable to locate a print) does not discuss *Lady Windermere's Fan*. The most comprehensive set of essays on Lubitsch and his films (including those he directed in Germany) can be found in Bernard Eisenschitz and Jean Narboni (eds), *Ernst Lubitsch* (Montreuil-sur-Mer: Cahiers du Cinéma/Cinémathèque Française, 1985). In his 'Program Notes', pp. 143–44, Simmon observes that 'Lubitsch often built his slightly risqué comedies around sexually and socially aggressive women ... as played by Pola Negri in *Madame Dubarry* and other of his German films and by Miriam Hopkins in his early sound films', and that in *Lady Windermere's Fan* 'her type is played by Irene Rich'.

6   This is the first point in the play at which we know for sure that Mrs Erlynne is Lady Windermere's mother and that the former abandoned the latter (and her father) in order to pursue an affair. The parallels between them are augmented in the play and the Ideal version (but not the Lubitsch one) by the fact that Lady Windermere has a child. Wilde tinkered with the placing of information about Mrs Erlynne and her past. Initially revealing the truth in the final act (which, it was argued, may have disconcerted audiences and entailed too sudden and too great a shift in understanding and allegiance), he was persuaded by the play's actor manager to reveal the truth earlier on and bit by bit. See Peter Raby, 'Introduction' to Oscar Wilde, *The Importance of Being Earnest and Other Plays* (Oxford: Oxford University Press, 1995), p. ix.

7   As Musser points out in 'The Hidden and the Unspeakable', p. 30, 'Mrs Erlynne has not only changed her last name but has concealed her identity with a different first name—Edith—as well. Here ... Lubitsch's film differs from the James-Paul one and from the play. In the play Mrs Erlynne only reveals her first name—Margaret—in the final act, and it comes as a surprise (but not a revelation) to her daughter, who shares the same name. In the Ideal film, Mrs Erlynne uses this first name throughout, expressing no

concern for what her first name might reveal. Lubitsch, in contrast, assigns her a different first name in the prologue, which enhances her mystery, and the extremes to which she has gone to conceal her identity. Only in the end does she divulge her first name as Margaret.' Thus 'Lubitsch has insisted on the centrality of the secret—of things being hidden. . . . Thus all three of the principal characters are hiding something (and in certain respects so is the fourth—Darlington).'

8   Simmon, 'Program Notes', 144.
9   David Bordwell discusses this sequence in detail in *Narration and the Fiction Film* (London: Methuen, 1985), pp. 181–86. He argues that it deliberately deviates 'from the film's intrinsic spatial norms' by cutting to a shot of the desk drawer from an unexpected angle—an angle that does not correspond to the direction of Lady Windermere's gaze, her previous position in the room or the direction of her movement—then restores these norms when cutting from Windermere's gaze to a perfectly matched shot of the opened drawer later on. However, he does not comment on the causal suppression involved in its opening.
10 Similar garden party scenes, each of them built around amorous scenarios, looks and glances, and layers of inference, occur in *The Marriage Circle* (1924) and *So This is Paris* (1926), both directed by Lubitsch.
11 Bordwell, *Narration and the Fiction Film*, pp. 179–80.
12 Unlike a number of contemporary directors, Lubitsch edited all his films himself. There is an equivalent to this top-hat shot in the Ideal version (which clearly inspired it), but it is filmed from a lower height and angle, and is much less precisely composed.
13 Kristin Thompson, *Herr Lubitsch Goes to Hollywood: German and American Film after World War 1* (Amsterdam: Amsterdam University Press, 2005).
14 See, in particular, Lea Jacobs, *The Decline of Sentiment: American Film in the 1920s* (Berkeley: University of California Press, 2008), pp. 79–126. According to Scott Eyman, *Ernst Lubitsch: Laughter in Paradise* (New York: Simon & Schuster, 1993), p. 104, Lubitsch saw a rough cut of *A Woman of Paris* prior to its release.
15 Musser, 'The Hidden and the Unspeakable', 19.
16 Ibid., 32.
17 Bordwell, *Narration and the Fiction Film*, p. 178.

Chapter 9

1   Lionel Collier, *Picturegoer*, 13.7, no. 8 (June 1927), 16.
2   Harry Langdon, 'The Serious Side of Comedy Making' in Richard Dyer

MacCann, *The Silent Comedians* (Metuchen, NJ: Scarecrow Press, 1993), p. 234.
3 Joanna E. Rapf, 'Doing Nothing: Harry Langdon and the Performance of Absence', *Film Quarterly*, 59, no. 1 (Fall 2005), 30.
4 See Carl Plantinga, 'The Scene of Empathy and the Human Face on Film' in Carl Plantinga and Greg M. Smith, *Passionate Views: Film, Cognition, and Emotion* (Baltimore: Johns Hopkins University Press, 1999), pp. 239–55; Carl Plantinga, *Moving Viewers: American Film and the Spectator's Experience* (Berkeley, CA: University of California Press, 2009), pp. 125–28; Murray Smith, *Engaging Characters: Fiction, Emotion, and the Cinema* (Oxford: Oxford University Press, 1995), pp. 158–60.
5 Tamar Lane, 'That's Out', *Motion Picture Magazine*, no. 28 (October 1924), 9. Emphasis in original.
6 Ibid. For this reading of *The General*, see Noël Carroll, 'Buster Keaton, The General, and Visible Intelligibility' in Peter Lehman (ed.), *Close Viewings: An Anthology of New Film Criticism* (Tallahassee: Florida State University Press, 1990), pp. 125–40.
7 *Motion Picture News*, 34, no.15 (9 October 1926), advertisement.
8 For enthusiastic accounts of Langdon's career, see e.g. Lane, 'That's Out', p. 9; Madeleine Matzen, 'That Funny Little Man', *Motion Picture Magazine*, 32, no. 5 (December 1926), 36–37, 96; Fred Fox, 'The Sad-Eyed Zany', *Hollywood Vagabond*, 1, no. 2 (17 February 1927), 5.
9 Fred Fox, 'The Sad-Eyed Zany', p. 5. For an account of John Grierson's similar view of Langdon, see 'Speaking Editorially', *Motion Picture News*, 34, no. 12 (18 September 1896), 1072.
10 Seth Soulstein, 'Concrete Irrationality: Surrealist Spectators and the Cult of Harry Langdon', *Scope: An Online Journal of Film and Television Studies*, 25 (February 2013), 1–16.
11 Michael J. Hayde et al., *Little Elf: A Celebration of Harry Langdon* (Albany, GA: BearManor Media, 2012), Amazon Kindle e-book.
12 James Agee, *Agee on Film. Vol. 1: Essays and Reviews* (New York: Universal Library, 1969), p. 14.
13 Joyce Rheuban, *Harry Langdon: The Comedian as Metteur-en-Scène* (Rutherford, NJ: Fairleigh Dickinson University Press, 1983). See also Ben Urish, 'The Case for Harry Langdon: How and Why Frank Capra was Wrong', *Journal of Popular Culture*, 41, no. 1 (2008), 141–57; William Schelly, *Harry Langdon: His Life and Films*, 2nd edn (Jefferson, NC: McFarland and Company, 2008); Hayde et al., *Little Elf*. An eminent recent exception is Noël Carroll, who tends to follow Capra's argument that Langdon's contributions were chiefly limited to his brilliant pantomime: Noël Carroll, *Comedy*

Incarnate: Buster Keaton, Physical Humor and Bodily Coping (Oxford: Blackwell, 2009), pp. 143–51.
14. See, especially, Urish, 'The Case for Harry Langdon', pp. 147–48.
15. 'Opinions on Current Short Subjects', *Motion Picture News* (6 February 1926), 699.
16. Laurence Reid, '*The Strong Man:* A Top-Notch Comedy—Amusing all the Way', *Motion Picture News*, 34, no. 12 (18 September 1926), 1101.
17. Ibid.
18. Laurence Reid, '*Long Pants*: Langdon has a Rollicking Number Here', *Motion Picture News* (8 April 1927), 1275.
19. '*Tramp, Tramp, Tramp*', *Motion Picture Magazine*, 32, no. 5 (August 1926), 61.
20. '*The Strong Man*', *Motion Picture Magazine*, 32, no. 5 (December 1926), 63.
21. Collier, *Picturegoer*, p. 16.
22. F.W.F., 'Vagabond Verdicts', *Hollywood Vagabond*, 1, no. 24 (11 August 1927), 5. In the immediate wake of Capra's departure from this film, this magazine proved to be one of Langdon's most staunch defenders. See also 'Wiseacre Critics Hurl Rocks at Langdon as Director Quits', *Hollywood Vagabond*, 1, no. 7 (24 March 1927), 7.
23. Willis Goldbeck, 'Heart Trouble', *Motion Picture Magazine*, 34, no. 5 (December 1928), 61.
24. '*The Chaser*—First National', *Photoplay Magazine*, 33, no. 5 (April 1928), 149.
25. *The Film Spectator*, 4, no. 7 (26 May 1928), 15.
26. Publicity photograph, *Photoplay Magazine*, 30, p. 3.
27. Ibid.
28. Rheuban, *Harry Langdon*, p. 82.
29. Alan Bilton, *Silent Film Comedy and American Culture* (Houndmills: Palgrave Macmillan, 2013), pp. 195–216.
30. Soulstein, 'Concrete Irrationality', pp. 7–9.
31. Carroll, *Comedy Incarnate*, pp. 145, 147, 148.
32. 'Advertising Section', *Photoplay Magazine*, xxx.5 (October 1926), 102.
33. Plantinga, 'The Scene of Empathy and the Human Face on Film', p. 239.
34. Ibid., p. 244.

Chapter 10

1. Ben Singer, *Melodrama and Modernity: Early Sensational Cinema and Its Contexts* (New York: Columbia University Press, 2001), p. 53.
2. Paul Rotha, *The Film Till Now: A Survey of World Cinema*, revised edn (New York: Twayne Publishers, 1963), p. 247.

3 Ibid., 247.
4 Jay Leyda, *Kino: A History of the Russian and Soviet Film*, revised edn (Princeton: Princeton University Press, 1983), p. 212.
5 Denise Youngblood, 'Americanitis: The Amerikanshchina in Soviet Cinema', *Journal of Popular Film & Television*, 19.4 (1992), 148–56.
6 Samuel D. Cioran, 'Introduction' to Marietta Shaginian, *Mess-Mend: Yankees in Petrograd*, trans. by Samuel D. Cioran (Ann Arbor: Ardis, 1991), p. 16.
7 Boris Dralyuk, *Western Crime Fiction Goes East: The Russian Pinkerton Craze, 1907–1934* (Leiden: Brill, 2012), p. 127.
8 Cioran, 'Introduction', p. 14.
9 Shaginian, *Mess-Mend: Yankees in Petrograd*, pp. 27–31.
10 Ibid., p. 30.
11 Ibid., p. 31.
12 Cioran, 'Introduction', p. 8.
13 Shaginian, *Mess-Mend: Yankees in Petrograd*, p. 78.
14 Ibid., p. 93.
15 Nikolai Bukharin, 'Podrastaiushchie rezervy i kommunisticheskoe vospitanie', *Pravda*, 25 November 1921, 2.
16 Dralyuk, *Western Crime Fiction Goes East*, pp. 89–91.
17 Ibid, p. 87.
18 Julia Vaingurt, *Wonderlands of the Avant-Garde: Technology and the Arts in Russia of the 1920s* (Evanston: Northwestern University Press, 2013), p. 184.
19 George N. Dove, *The Reader and the Detective Story* (Bowling Green: Bowling Green State University Popular Press, 1997), p. 37.
20 Michael Walker, 'Melodrama and the American Cinema', *Movie* 29/30 (1982), 16.
21 Ibid., 17.
22 Louise McReynolds and Joan Neuberger, 'Acknowledgements' in *Imitations of Life: Two Centuries of Melodrama in Russia* (Durham: Duke University Press, 2002), p. ix.
23 Louise McReynolds and Joan Neuberger, 'Introduction' to *Imitations of Life*, pp. 1–10.
24 Ibid., pp. 5–6.
25 Julie A. Cassiday, 'Alcohol Is Our Enemy! Soviet Temperance Melodramas of the 1920s' in *Imitations of Life*, p. 152.
26 Ibid., p. 153.
27 '*Miss Mend*' in Olga E. Glagoleva *et al.* (eds), *Sovetskie khudozhestvennye fil'my: Annotirovannyi katalog*, vol. 1 (Moscow: Iskusstvo, 1961), pp. 149–151.
28 Steve Neale, *Genre and Hollywood* (London: Routledge, 2005), p. 196.

29 Ana Olenina and Maxim Pozdorovkin, *'Miss Mend' and Soviet Americanism* (Los Angeles: Flicker Alley, 2009), p. 12.
30 David Bordwell and Kristin Thompson, 'Toward a Scientific Film History?' *Quarterly Review of Film Studies*, 10.3 (1985), 237.
31 Olenina and Pozdorovkin, *'Miss Mend' and Soviet Americanism*, p. 12.
32 Shaginian, *Mess-Mend*, p. 97.
33 Maureen Turim, 'Gentlemen Consume Blondes' in *Movies and Methods*, vol. 2, ed. Bill Nichols (Berkeley: University of California Press, 1985), p. 370.
34 Singer, *Melodrama and Modernity*, p. 46.
35 Olenina and Pozdorovkin, *'Miss Mend' and Soviet Americanism*, p. 12.
36 Advertisement for *Miss Mend*, *Izdatel'stva*, 4 November 1926, p. 6.
37 *'Miss Mend'*, *Sovetskie khudozhestvennye fil'my*, p. 149–51.
38 Details on the various theatres mentioned here come from *Teatral'naia Moskva: Teatr—Muzyka—Estrada—Kino: Putevoditel' Sezon 1926–1927 goda* (Moscow: Izdatel'stvo Moskovskogo Kommunal'nogo Khoziaistva, 1927), pp. 179–90.
39 *'Mat'*, *Sovetskie khudozhestvennye fil'my*, p. 147; advertisement for *Mother* and *Miss Mend*, *Izvestiia*, 23 October 1926, p. 6.
40 Advertisement for *Miss Mend*, *Izvestiia*, 26 November 1926, p. 6.
41 Advertisement for *Miss Mend*, *Pravda*, 3 December 1926, p. 6.
42 Advertisement for *Miss Mend*, *Izvestiia*, 16 December 1926, p. 6.
43 Advertisements for *Miss Mend*, *Pravda*, 15 January 1927, p. 6.
44 Advertisement for *Miss Mend*, *Pravda*, 29 May 1927, p. 6; Advertisement for *Miss Mend*, *Izvestiia*, 29 May 1927, p. 6.
45 Denise Youngblood, *Movies for the Masses: Popular Cinema and Soviet Society in the 1920s* (Cambridge: Cambridge University Press, 1992), p. 173. Youngblood quotes figures reported in a lecture by film historian Maia Turovskaia.
46 Adrian Piotrovsky, '"Ideology" and "Commerce"', trans. by Richard Taylor in Richard Taylor and Ian Christie (eds), *The Film Factory: Russian and Soviet Cinema in Documents 1896–1939* (London: Routledge, 1994), p. 189. Originally published as A. Piotrovskii, 'Ob "ideologii" i "kommertsii"', *Zhizn' iskusstva*, 27 December 1927, p. 5.
47 Boris Gusman, *'Miss Mend'*, *Pravda*, 12 November 1926, p. 6. Boris Dralyuk describes the review as being on the front page, but in fact it was on the last page. Film reviews at this time rarely made the front page of *Pravda*.
48 Dralyuk, *Western Crime Fiction Goes East*, p. 125. Olenina and Pozdorovkin, *'Miss Mend' and Soviet Americanism*, pp. 13–14.
49 Dralyuk, *Western Crime Fiction Goes East*, p. 125.

Chapter 11

1 '"Wings" Record Run at Criterion Ends', *Exhibitor's Review*, 13 October 1928, pp. 1–2.
2 'Wings', *Variety*, 17 August 1927, p. 21.
3 For a discussion of *Wings*' status as a 'superspecial', see Sheldon Hall and Stephen Neale, *Epics, Spectacles, and Blockbusters: A Hollywood History* (Detroit: Wayne State University Press, 2010), pp. 60–61.
4 Hall and Neale *Epics, Spectacles, and Blockbusters*, pp. 60–61.
5 Edwin Schallert, 'Wings', *Motion Picture News*, 10 August 1927, p. 510. The *Motion Picture News* column 'Pictures and People', 26 August 1927, p. 573, similarly said that 'Wings glorifies the airplane's part in war and carries a strong if incidental message for peace'.
6 The trade papers were filled with stories about how well *Wings* performed at the box office. See e.g. 'Reports "Wings" a Sellout', *The Film Daily*, 19 August 1927, p. 1; 'New Specials Click; Broadway Grosses Up', *The Film Daily*, 23 August 1927, p. 1; 'Steadiness of Lowes is Feature of Week', *The Film Daily*, 8 September 1927, p. 9; 'Record Claimed for "Wings" with $30,115', *The Film Daily*, 7 September 1927, p. 1; '"Wings" Showing Strength at B.O., Grey Reports', *The Film Daily*, 30 December 1927, p. 2; 'New "Wings" Record', *Exhibitors Daily Review*, 31 July 1928, p. 3; 'P-F-L "Wings" First Year Celebration Aug. 12', *Exhibitors Daily Review*, 8 August 1928, p. 1; '"Wings" at Regular Prices Doing Big Business', *Exhibitors Daily Review*, 20 September 1928, p. 1; '"Wings" Biggest Money Maker Jumps Highest P-F-L Earnings', *Exhibitors Daily Review*, 30 November 1928, p. 1.
7 'Taglines', *IMDb*, 2 March 2014, www.imdb.com/title/tt0015624/taglines?ref_=tt_stry_tg.
8 See e.g. 'And That's That', *Film Daily*, 15 January 1927, p. 3; 'Famous Players Dedicate "Wings" to Colonel Charles Lindberg', *Photoplay*, 27 August 1927, p. 6.
9 Edwin Schallert, 'Wings', *Motion Picture News*, 10 August 1927, p. 510.
10 George B. Clark, *The American Expeditionary Force in World War I: A Statistical History, 1917–1919* (Jefferson, NC: McFarland, 2013), p. 56.
11 William Wellman Jr, *The Man and His Wings: William A. Wellman and the Making of the First Best Picture* (Westport, CT: Praeger Publishers Inc., 2006), pp. 13, 16, 18, 37.
12 Ibid., p. 14.
13 John Horne, *A Companion to World War I* (Hoboken, NJ: John Wiley & Sons, 2010), p. 163.
14 Wellman, *The Man and His Wings*, pp. 128–30.
15 Ibid., pp. 130–31.

16 'Wings', *The Film Daily*, 21 August 1927, p. 8.
17 Laurence Reid, 'Wings', *Motion Picture News*, 26 August 1927, p. 594.
18 'Wings', *Variety*, 17 August 1927, p. 21.
19 '"Wings" a Truly Great Picture', *Film Spectator*, 3 March 1928, p. 7.
20 Lea Jacobs, *The Decline of Sentiment: American Films in the 1920s* (Berkeley: University of California Press, 2008), p. 136.
21 Ibid., p. 137.
22 Ibid., pp. 152, 169.
23 Peter Brooks, *The Melodramatic Imagination: Balzac, James and the Mode of Excess* (New Haven: Yale University Press, 1995), pp. 15, 20.
24 Linda Williams, *Playing the Race Card: Melodramas of Black and White from Uncle Tom to O.J. Simpson* (Princeton: Princeton University Press, 2001), pp. 16, 19.
25 Ibid., p. 28.
26 Schallert, 'Wings', p. 510.
27 Sara Ross, '"Good Little Bad Girls": Silent Comediennes and the Performance of Girlish Sexuality', *Film History*, 13.4 (2001), 409–23.
28 'Wings', *Variety*, 17 August 1927, p. 21. For a further discussion of *Wings*'s status as a road-show picture, as well as the mechanics of its use of sound, see Hall and Neale, *Epics, Spectacles, and Blockbusters*, pp. 60–61.
29 Ibid., pp. 70–71.
30 John Belton, *Widescreen Cinema* (Cambridge, MA: Harvard University Press, 1992), p. 38.
31 'Wings', *Variety*, 17 August 1927, p. 21.
32 Allison Griffiths, *Cinema, Museum, and the Immersive View* (New York: Columbia University Press, 2008), p. 94.
33 Scott Higgins, '3D in Depth: Coraline, Hugo, and a Sustainable Aesthetic', *Film History*, 24.2 (2012) 198; Pia Tikka, 'Cinema as Externalization of Conciousness' in Robert Pepperell and Michael Punt (eds), *Screen Consciousness: Cinema, Mind, and World* (Amsterdam: Rodolpi B.V., 2006), p. 151.
34 Sara Ross, 'Invitation to the Voyage: The Flight Sequence in Contemporary 3D Cinema', *Film History*, 24.2 (2012), 210–20.
35 It is notable in this context that the most striking point-of-view shots before this sequence provide the perspective of the German Gotha crew as they bomb the French village.

Chapter 12

1 Christine Gledhill, *Reframing British Cinema, 1918–28: Between Restraint and Passion* (London: BFI, 2003), pp. 4, 174–78.
2 Advertisement in *Kinematograph Weekly*, 26 July 1928, pp. 5–7.

3   Elvey made over 300 films in all. See Lawrence Napper's entry on Elvey in Robert Murphy (ed), *Directors in British and Irish Cinema* (London: BFI, 2006), pp. 178–79.
4   Elvey directed *Dombey and Son* (1919), *Bleak House* (1920) and *The Adventures of Sherlock Holmes* (1921), and *The Hound of the Baskervilles*, *The Sign of Four* and *Don Quixote* (all 1923) for Stoll's 'Eminent Author' series. In the USA, he directed *My Husband's Wives*, *Curlytop*, *Folly of Vanity* (all 1924) and *She Wolves* (1925) for the Fox Film Corporation.
5   Rachael Low has noted Maurice Elvey's acute sense of box-office appeal and his tendency to rework successful formulas in *The History of the British Film: 1918–1929* (London: George Allen & Unwin Ltd, 1971), p. 173. However, she is rather dismissive of Elvey here, presenting him as slick, shrewd and technically accomplished, rather than as creative or original. In 1928, prior to the release of *Palais de Danse*, Herbert Thompson, writing in *The Bioscope*, 3 May 1928), p. 41, pointed out that 'Maurice Elvey hopes to achieve . . . even better results [here] than he obtained under similar circumstances at the Tower Ballroom, Blackpool, for "Hindle Wakes"'.
6   Review of *The Constant Nymph*, *The Bioscope*, 23 February 1928, p. 55; Arthur C. Findon, 'A British Mary Pickford', *The Weekly Dispatch*, 26 February 1928.
7   Gledhill, *Reframing British Cinema*, p. 154.
8   Review of *Palais de Danse*, *Kinematograph Weekly*, 2 August 1928, pp. 42–43.
9   Review of *Palais de Danse*, *The Bioscope*, 1 August 1928.
10 Prior to *Palais de Danse*, Hilda Moore had co-starred with one of Britain's most acclaimed actors, Gerald du Maurier, in Elvey's film version of John Galsworthy's play *Justice* (1917). She also appeared as Sappho in one of a series of twelve short films produced by H.B. Parkinson, compiled under the title of *Tense Moments with Great Authors* (1922), in which stage luminaries (including Sybil Thorndike, Phyllis Neilson-Terry and Ethel Irving) appeared in highlights from *Sappho* (by Alphonse Daudet), *Oliver Twist* (Charles Dickens), *Les Misérables* (Victor Hugo) and *Vanity Fair* (William Thackeray). Moore was, however, primarily a stage actress. See John Parker (ed.), *Who Was Who in the Theatre: 1912–1976: A Biographical Dictionary of Actors, Actresses, Directors, Playwrights, and Producers of the English-Speaking Theatre, Volume 3, I–P* (Detroit: Omnigraphics Books, Gale Research Company, 1978), pp. 1740–41.
11 See Lotte H. Eisner, *The Haunted Screen: Expressionism in the German Cinema and the Influence of Max Reinhardt* (Berkeley: University of California Press, 2008 edition), pp. 141–49.
12 In particular, the works of Pre-Raphaelite painters such as William Holman

Hunt, John Everett Millais, Dante Gabriel Rossetti and Ford Madox Brown. See Gledhill, *Reframing British Cinema*, p. 42.
13 Ibid., p. 18.
14 Ibid., p. 43.
15 The terms 'colloquial', 'rhetorical' and 'epic' are derived from actor-manager Henry Neville (1837–1910), who in 1895 elaborated his approach to stage acting in his essay 'Gesture' in H. Campbell, R.F. Brewer and H. Neville (eds), *Voice, Speech and Gesture: Practical Handbook to the Elocutionary Art* (London: Charles William Deacon & Co., 1895). For more details, see Gledhill, *Reframing British Cinema*, p. 43.
16 Christine Gledhill has argued that one of the dominant traits of British cinema of the 1920s is a particular style of acting involving emotional continence, whereby actors in leading roles pitch their performance between restraint and passion. Bound by middle-class codes of decorum, most leading British actors lent their characters greater emotional intensity through *intimations* of feelings that remain largely unexpressed. See Gledhill, *Reframing British Cinema*, pp. 62–64.
17 Poulton's Nettleford films were 'Quota Quickies' (or B-movies) shot at the former Cecil Hepworth Studios at Walton-on-Thames. These consisted of *Troublesome Wives*, *A Daughter in Revolt* (both 1928) and *The Silent House* (1929).
18 Christine Gledhill, 'The Screen Actress from Silence to Sound' in Maggie B. Gale and John Stokes (eds), *The Cambridge Companion to the Actress* (Cambridge: Cambridge University Press, 2007), p. 207.

Chapter 13

1 Sukhdev Sandhu, 'Forgotten Siren of the Silent Age', *Daily Telegraph*, 19 March 2004.
2 Herbert G. Luft, 'E.A. Dupont 1891–1956', *Films in Review*, 28.6 (June–July 1977), 348.
3 Paul Rotha, *The Film Till Now: A Survey of the Cinema* (London: Jonathan Cape, 1930), p. 233.
4 A review by Geoff Brown of the 2004 restoration characterized *Piccadilly* as having 'the sluggish pace of footage shot underwater'; see *The Times*, 30 March 2004, p. 40.
5 Anthony B. Chan, *Perpetually Cool: The Many Lives of Anna May Wong* (Lanham, MD: Scarecrow Press, 2003); Graham Russell Gao Hodges, *Anna May Wong: From Laundryman's Daughter to Hollywood Legend* (New York & Basingstoke: Palgrave Macmillan, 2004); Philip Leibfried and Chei Mi Lane, *Anna May Wong: A Complete Guide to Her Film, Stage, Radio*

and *Television Work* (Jefferson, NC: McFarland, 2010); Karen J. Leong, *The China Mystique: Pearl S. Buck, Anna May Wong, Mayling Soong and the Transformation of American Orientalism* (Berkeley: University of California Press, 2005); Elizabeth Wong, *China Doll (The Imagined Life of an American Actress)* (Woodstock IL: Dramatic Publishing Company, 2005); 'Anna May Wong: From Laundryman's Daughter to Hollywood Legend', Museum of Modern Art, New York, 22–25 January 2004; 'Rediscovering Anna May Wong', University of California at Los Angeles, 9–25 January 2004; 'Anna May Wong', National Portrait Gallery, London, 8 December 2004–15 June 2005; *Anna May Wong—Frosted Yellow Willows: Her Life, Times and Legend* (USA; Dir. Elaine Mae Woo, 2007); *Anna May Wong: In Her Own Words* (USA; Dir. Yunah Hong, 2011).

6 Sandhu, 'Forgotten Siren of the Silent Age'. (It should be noted that what may appear as 'documentary textures' in the film are not literally so: *Piccadilly* was shot entirely in the studio.)
7 'The Editor Mingles', *Picturegoer*, March 1929, p. 15.
8 *Kinematograph Weekly*, 7 February 1929, p. 57.
9 *The Bioscope*, 6 February 1929, p. 27.
10 *The Cinema*, 6 February 1929, p. 9.
11 Rotha, *The Film Till Now*, p. 232.
12 Hugh Castle, 'Some British Films', *Close Up*, 5.1 (July 1929), 45.
13 Peter Wollen, 'Riff-raff Realism', *Sight and Sound*, 8.4 (April 1998), 22.
14 Excluding *Piccadilly* itself, these are: (films): *The Case of a Doped Actress* (UK; 1919), *A Smart Set* (UK; 1919), *Broken Blossoms* (USA; 1919), *The Yellow Claw* (UK; 1920), *Dream Street* (USA; 1921), *Cocaine* (UK; 1922), *Crushing the Drug Traffic* (UK; 1922), *The Sign of Four* (UK; 1923), *Curlytop* (USA; 1924), *A Girl of London* (UK; 1925), *The Blackbird* (USA; 1926), *Blinkeyes* (UK; 1926), *London* (UK; 1926), *While London Sleeps* (USA; 1926), *Twinkletoes* (USA; 1927), *The Alley Cat* (*Nachtgestalten*) (UK–Ger.; 1929), *The Mysterious Dr Fu Manchu* (USA; 1929); serials: *The Mystery of Dr Fu Manchu* (15 episodes) (UK; 1923), *The Further Mysteries of Dr Fu Manchu* (UK; 1924), *The Mysterious Dr Syn Fang* (6 episodes) (UK; 1926); (miscellaneous serial episodes): *The Adventures of Dorcas Deene, Detective: No. 4—A Murder in Limehouse* (UK; 1919), *The Adventures of Sherlock Holmes: The Man with the Twisted Lip* (UK; 1921), *The Ace of Scotland Yard: No. 4—The Depths of Limehouse* (USA; 1929).
15 The seminal work is Andrew Higson and Richard Maltby (eds), *'Film Europe' and 'Film America': Cinema, Commerce and Cultural Exchange 1920–1939* (Exeter: University of Exeter Press, 1999).
16 Gerben Bakker, 'The Decline and Fall of the European Film Industry:

Sunk Costs, Market Size, and Market Structure, 1890–1927', *Economic History Review*, 58.2 (2005), 321.

17 Klaus Kreimeier, *The Ufa Story: A History of Germany's Greatest Film Company, 1918–1945*, trans. by Robert and Rita Kember (Berkeley: University of California Press, 1999), p. 125. Richard W. McCormick, 'The Carnival of Humiliation: Sex, Spectacle, and Self-Reflexivity in E.A. Dupont's *Variety* (1925)' in Randall Halle and Margaret McCarthy (eds), *Light Motives: German Popular Film in Perspective* (Detroit, MI: Wayne State University Press, 2003), p. 44.

18 Felix Hollaender, *The Sins of the Fathers*, trans. by Sarah J.I. Lawson (New York: Payson & Clark, 1927).

19 *Daily Telegraph*, 23 March 1928, p. 8, quoted in Andrew Higson, 'Polyglot Films for an International Market: E.A. Dupont, the British Film Industry, and the Idea of a European Cinema, 1926–1930' in Higson and Maltby, *'Film Europe' and 'Film America'*, p. 281.

20 *Daily Sketch*, 26 March 1928, p. 21, quoted in Higson, 'Polyglot Films for an International Market', p. 282.

21 *Daily Express*, 23 March 1928, p. 11, quoted in Higson, 'Polyglot Films for an International Market', p. 282.

22 Arnold Bennett recorded the precise date—12 April 1928—when he was first approached by BIP in his diary. See Newman Flower (ed.), *The Journals of Arnold Bennett III: 1921–1928* (London: Cassell, 1933), p. 260.

23 Andrew Higson and Richard Maltby, '"Film Europe" and "Film America": An Introduction' in Higson and Maltby, *'Film Europe' and 'Film America'*, p. 18.

24 Tim Bergfelder, 'Negotiating Exoticism: Hollywood, Film Europe and the Cultural Reception of Anna May Wong' in Higson and Maltby, *'Film Europe' and 'Film America'*, p. 307.

25 Ibid., p. 303.

26 Juan Antonio Ramirez, *Architecture for the Screen: A Critical Study of Set Design in Hollywood's Golden Age*, trans. by John F. Moffitt (Jefferson, NC: McFarland, 2004), p. 76.

27 Maria Tatar, *Lustmord: Sexual Murder in Weimar Germany* (Princeton, NJ: Princeton University Press, 1997), pp. 4–6, 22–27.

28 See e.g. 'Chinese Woman Strangled: Husband Arrested', *Manchester Guardian*, 21 June 1928, p. 12; 'Chinaman to Die: Guilty Verdict in Lakes Murder Trial. Passionate Denial from the Dock', *Manchester Guardian*, 25 October 1928, p. 8.

29 Anne Witchard, 'A Threepenny Omnibus Ticket to "Limey-housey-Causeyway": Fictional Sojourns in Chinatown', *Comparative Critical Studies*, 4.2 (2007), 234.

30 Flower, *The Journals of Arnold Bennett III*, pp. 87–88.
31 *Daily Herald*, 6 June 1932, p. 6.
32 This same pub was subsequently recreated for a scene in the 1936 British remake of *Broken Blossoms*, which nods to those in the know by featuring a picture of Charlie Brown on the wall.
33 Paul Matthew St Pierre, *E.A. Dupont and His Contribution to British Film: Variété, Moulin Rouge, Piccadilly, Atlantic, Two Worlds, Cape Forlorn* (Madison, NJ: Farleigh Dickinson University Press, 2010), pp. 29, 64.
34 Hugh Castle, 'The Battle for Wardour Street', *Close Up*, 4.3 (March 1929), 14.
35 Rotha, *The Film Till Now*, p. 279.
36 Castle, 'Some British Films', p. 46.
37 Thomas Brandlmeier, 'Fragmenting the Space: On E.A. Dupont's *Variété*' in Dietrich Scheunemann (ed.), *Expressionist Film: New Perspectives* (New York: Camden House, 2003), p. 212.
38 See Don Fairservice, *Film Editing: History, Theory and Practice* (Manchester: Manchester University Press, 2001), pp. 93–99.
39 *Piccadilly* 'Shooting Script and Breakdown', S10595, held in BFI Reuben Library, Special Collections.
40 '"Piccadilly". New British Film at the Carlton', *The Times*, 2 February 1929, p. 10.
41 Paul Newland, *The Cultural Construction of London's East End: Urban Iconography, Modernity and the Spatialisation of Englishness* (Amsterdam: Rodopi, 2008), p. 127.
42 Jon Burrows, "A Vague Chinese Quarter Elsewhere: Limehouse in the Cinema, 1914–1936', *Journal of British Cinema and Television*, 6.2 (Summer 2009), 282–301.
43 See e.g. Shannon Case, 'Lilied Tongues and Yellow Claws: The Invention of London's Chinatown, 1915–45' in Stella Deen (ed.), *Challenging Modernism: New Readings in Literature and Culture, 1914–45* (Aldershot: Ashgate, 2002), pp. 17–34; John Seed, 'Limehouse Blues: Looking for Chinatown in the London Docks, 1900–40', *History Workshop Journal*, 62 (2006), 58–85.

Chapter 14

1 For a useful summary of Feyder's career, see Alan Williams, *Republic of Images: A History of French Filmmaking* (Cambridge, MA: Harvard University Press, 1992), pp. 186–91. For a discussion of Feyder's time in Hollywood, see Martin Barnier, '*The Kiss, Si L'Empereur savait ça*, Jacques Feyder et la MGM dans le contexte de la généralisation du son à Hollywood' in Jean

Gili and Michel Marie (eds), *Jacques Feyder* (Paris: L'association française de recherche sur l'histoire du cinéma, 1998), pp. 141–50.
2 Lucy Fischer, *Designing Women: Cinema, Art Deco, and the Female Form* (New York: Columbia University Press, 2003), pp. 105–13.
3 Charles Ford reports the friendship between Feyder and Murnau in *Jacques Feyder* (Paris: Édition Seghers, 1973), p. 48.
4 Fischer, *Designing Women*, p. 106.
5 My discussion of narration as a process of organizing the sequence of story events to produce effects in the viewer is influenced both by Meir Sternberg's theory of narrativity and David Bordwell's adaptation of Sternberg's ideas for the cinema. See, among many works, Meir Sternberg, 'Telling in Time (II): Chronology, Teleology, Narrativity', *Poetics Today* 13.3 (1992), 463–541; David Bordwell, 'Three Dimensions of Film Narrative' in *Poetics of Cinema* (New York: Routledge, 2008), pp. 85–133.
6 For a narratological argument concerning different kinds of unreliability in narration, see Tamar Yacobi, 'Package Deals in Fictional Narrative: The Case of the Narrator's (Un)Reliability', *Narrative* 9.2 (2001), 223–29.
7 For images of the publicity photos taken for *The Mysterious Lady*, including the image that appears in Figure 3, see 'The Mysterious Lady: Stills and Portraits', *Garbo Forever*, www.garboforever.com/Film-Pic-10.htm [accessed 4 August 2013]. For an interesting discussion of Ruth Harriet Louise's portraits of Garbo, see Robert Dance and Bruce Robertson, 'Photographing Garbo' in *Ruth Harriet Louise and Hollywood Glamour Photography* (Berkeley: University of California Press, 2002), pp. 157–83.
8 Mary Pickford famously denounced Lubitsch as a 'director of doors'. See the discussion of Lubitsch's use of doors in Barbara Bowman, 'Lubitsch's Film Space: Implying Space to Stimulate the Imagination' in *Master Space: Film Images of Capra, Lubitsch, Sternberg and Wyler* (Westport, CT: Greenwood Press, 1992), pp. 61–82.
9 Richard Abel, 'Realist Films' in *French Cinema: The First Wave, 1915–1929* (Princeton: Princeton University Press, 1984), pp. 94–137.
10 Jacques Feyder, 'The Woman Accused', 16 April 1929, Turner/MGM Scripts Collection, Margaret Herrick Library, Los Angeles.
11 Hans Kraly, 'Jealousy', 8 June 1929, Turner/MGM Scripts Collection, Margaret Herrick Library, Los Angeles.
12 Hans Kraly, 'Jealousy', 3 July 1929, Turner/MGM Scripts Collection, Margaret Herrick Library, Los Angeles.
13 Fischer, *Designing Women*, pp. 106–107. The reference to *The Smiling Madame Beudet* seems perfectly apt. We might add *The Kiss*'s superimposition-heavy tennis sequence as another homage to Dulac's film.
14 Rosay, quoted in Ford, *Jacques Feyder*, p. 46. My translation.

15 Feyder, quoted in Ford, *Jacques Feyder*, p. 51. My translation. See also Feyder's even harsher assessment in Jacques Feyder and Françoise Rosay, *Le Cinéma, Notre Métier* (Geneva: Cailler, 1946).

Chapter 15

1. Huang Yicuo, 'Chuangban Lianhua yingye yuanqi' ('The founding of United Photoplay Service Co. Ltd'), *Yingxi zazhi* (*The Film Magazine*), 1.9 (August 1930), 44.
2. See Anne Kerlan, 'Un nouveau cinéma pour une nation en construction : le "mouvement" de renaissance du cinéma chinois au début des années 1930' in C. Gauthier, A. Kerlan and D. Vezyroglou (eds), *Loin d'Hollywood ? Cinématographies nationales et modèle hollywoodien. France, Allemagne, URSS, Chine, 1925–1935* (Paris: Nouveaux Mondes, 2013), pp. 153–82.
3. According to *Lianhua nianjian* (*UPS Yearbook*), 1933–34, p. 12; *Lianhua nianjian*, 1934–35, p. 23.
4. See Christophe Falin, 'Les réponses techniques à la transition du muet au parlant dans le cinéma chinois' in Gauthier *et al.*, *Loin d'Hollywood*, pp. 37–49.
5. *Yu guo tian qing* (*Blue Skies After Rain*) (1931), produced by the Dazhongguo and Jinan film companies. The film was screened in Shanghai on 1 July 1931. See Falin, 'Les réponses techniques', p. 42.
6. See Huang Yicuo, 'Guopian fuxing ying you de bu zouzou' ('The new direction that must be taken in the Chinese film Renaissance'), *Yingxi zazhi*, 1.9 (August 1930), 30.
7. Huang Yicuo, 'Guopian fuxing ying you de bu zouzou', p. 30.
8. Ibid.
9. See Huang Yicuo, 'Guonei xin yingye: Lianhua jihua jinxing zhong de zhiqu' ('A new national industry: the impact of the development of UPS'), *Yingzi zazhi*, 1.10 (October 1930), p. 30.
10. For a detailed discussion of the production and significance of *Two Stars of the Milky Way*, see Kristine Harris, '*Two Stars* on the Silver Screen: The Metafilm as Chinese Modern' in Christian Henriot and Yeh Wen-hsin (eds), *History in Images: Pictures and Public Spaces in Modern China* (Berkeley: University of California Press, 2012), pp. 191–244. For further discussion of the film's soundtrack, see Andrew F. Jones, *Yellow Music: Media Culture and Colonial Modernity in the Chinese Jazz Age* (Durham, NC: Duke University Press, 2001), pp. 97–99.
11. Advertisement in *Yingxi zazhi*, 1.9 (August 1930), 22.
12. Luo Mingyou, 'Shezhi *Lian'ai yu yiwu* zhi yuanyin' ('Why did we make a film of *Love and Duty*?'), *Yingzi zazhi*, vol. 1, nos 11-12 (April 1931), p.

69. See also Kristine Harris, 'Ombres Chinoises: Split Screens and Parallel Lives in *Love and Duty*' in Carlos Rojas and Eileen Cheng-Yin Chow (eds), *The Oxford Handbook of Chinese Cinemas* (Oxford: Oxford University Press, 2013), which focuses in detail on Ruan Lingyu's performance.
13. S. Horose, *La Symphonie des ombres chinoises* (Paris: Editions de la Madeleine, 1932), p. xiv.
14. In the preface to *La Symphonie des ombres chinoises*, Horose says that she had been living in China for two decades.
15. According to Zhu Shilin, '*Lian'ai yu yiwu* zuozhe Luo Chen nüshi zhi zhushu ji qi baofu' ('The writings and hopes of Miss Luo Chen, the author of *Love and Duty*') in *Yingxi zazhi*, 1.11–12 (April 1931), 69, her Chinese publications include *Nü boshi* (*A PhD Woman*), *Tongguo xuesheng* (*Students from the Same Country*), *Xinwen* (*Writings from the Heart*) and *Ta yu Ta* (*He and She*).
16. Zhu Shilin, '*Lian'ai yu yiwu* zuozhe Luo Chen nüshi zhi zhushu ji qi baofu', p. 69. According Harris, 'Ombres Chinoises', p. 56, a fifth, expanded version was published three years after the film's release.
17. Luo Mingyou, 'Shezhi *Lian'ai yu yiwu* zhi yuanyin', p. 69. The North China Company managed a theatre chain in Northern China and as such needed people like Zhu Shilin to translate publicity booklets and brochures.
18. The names given here are those used in the French edition of the book. In the film, they differ slightly because of transcription: Yang Nei-fan (played by Ruan Lingyu) for Yang Neifan; Li Tsu Yi (played by Jin Yan, a.k.a. Raymon King) for Li Tsoju; Huang Ta Jen (played by Lay Ying) for Hwang Tajen; Ping'er (played by the Young Chen Yanyan) for Pingel.
19. Zhu Shilin, '*Lian'ai yu yiwu* zuozhe Luo Chen nüshi zhi zhushu ji qi baofu', p. 69.
20. Zhu Shilin, '*Lian'ai yu yiwu*' ('*Love and Duty*'), *Yingxi zazhi*, 1.10 (October 1930), 38.
21. Harris, 'Ombres Chinoises', p. 44.
22. Zhu Shilin, '*Lian'ai yu yiwu*', p. 38.
23. Harris, 'Ombres Chinoises', p. 49.
24. Zhu Shilin, '*Lian'ai yu yiwu*', p. 38.
25. Horose, *La Symphonie des ombres*, p. 18.
26. According to Harris, 'Ombres Chinoises', p. 41, the film was shot in the French Concession in Shanghai.
27. 'Un remède étranger ... moderne ... Doux et terrible', Horose, *La Symphonie des ombres*, p. 260.
28. There is no direct evidence that Bu Wancang (or Zhu Shilin or Luo Mingyou) had seen DeMille's marriage comedies. However, films like this were popular with Chinese audiences in the late 1920s and early 1930s, as is evident in *Aiyu zhi zheng* (*The Struggle Between Love and Desire*) (1931), *Fen*

hongse zhi meng (*A Pink Dream*) (1932) and *Qinghai chong wen* (*Kisses Again*) (1928), the last of which, as Zhiwei Xiao points out in an as yet unpublished paper entitled 'For Better or for Worse, *Don't Change Your Husband!*: The Remaking and Appropriation of American Films in Republican China, 1911–1949', was a remake of DeMille's 1919 film.

29 *Shun Pao*, 6 June 1931.
30 *Yingxi zazhi*, 21 (July 1931), 36.
31 *Pour Vous, L'hebdomadaire du cinéma*, no. 133 (4 June 1931), p. 11, 'Progrès du cinéma dans la Chine moderne'. My thanks to Nicolas Schmidt, who helped me to find this article.
32 *Shun Pao*, 16 December 1932.
33 *Shun Pao*, 20 February 1933.
34 Gu Yelu, 'My Five "Firsts"' in *Friends, Sorrows and Joys on Stage and Screen* (Beijing: China Film Press, 1994), quoted by Chinese Mirror, http://www.chinesemirror.com/index/2013/03/wide-ranging-influence-of-love-and-duty.html (accessed on 3 July 2013).
35 I would like to thank Emmanuel Soland for his inspiring reflections on *Love and Duty*.

Chapter 16

1 Freda Frieberg, 'The Transition to Sound in Japan' in Tom O'Regan and Brian Shoesmith (eds), *History on/and/in Film* (Perth: History & Film Association of Australia, 1987), p. 76.
2 Joseph L. Anderson, *The Japanese Film: Art and Industry* (Princeton: Princeton University Press, 1982), p. 442. See also Hideaki Fujiki, '*Benshi* as Stars: The Irony of the Popularity and Respectability of Voice Performers in Japanese Cinema', *Cinema Journal*, 45.2 (Winter 2006), 68–84.
3 Samuel Taylor Coleridge, *The Friend* (London: Edward Moxon, 1863), p. 115.

Chapter 17

1 Scholars attribute Naruse's muted recognition abroad to a range of factors, including his modesty and lack of self-promotion; his dark worldview; the relative invisibility of his mature style; the limited international circulation of his films during his lifetime; the lack of translations of Japanese scholarship on his films; and, apart from occasional retrospectives beginning in the 1980s, the rarity of his films in the West until the 2000s. See Audie Bock, *Japanese Film Directors* (Tokyo: Kodansha International Ltd, 1978), p. 102;

Catherine Russell, *The Cinema of Naruse Mikio: Women and Japanese Modernity* (Durham: Duke University Press, 2008), pp. 1–3.
2 Mitsuyo Wada-Marciano, 'Imaging Modern Girls in the Japanese Woman's Film', *Camera Obscura*, 20.3, 60 (2005), 47.
3 Ibid., pp. 19, 47.
4 Kido Shiro, *Nihon eigaden: Eiga seisakusha no kiroku (Japanese Cinema Tales: A Record of a Film Producer)* (Tokyo: Bungei Shunjusha, 1956), pp. 52–56, quoted in Wada-Marciano, 'Imaging Modern Girls', p. 20.
5 Wada-Marciano, 'Imaging Modern Girls', pp. 19–20, 47.
6 Tadao Sato, *Currents in Japanese Cinema* (Tokyo: Kodansha International, 1982), p. 20.
7 Russell, *The Cinema of Naruse Mikio*, pp. 41–42.
8 Wada-Marciano, 'Imaging Modern Girls', pp. 28–44.
9 Joseph L. Anderson and Donald Richie, *The Japanese Film: Art and Industry*, expanded edition (Princeton: Princeton University Press, 1982), pp. 364–365; Bock, *Japanese Film Directors*, p. 105.
10 Audie Bock interview with Kido Shiro, November 1976, quoted in Bock, *Japanese Film Directors*, p. 102.
11 Kido, *Nihon eigaden*, quoted in Donald Richie, *A Hundred Years of Japanese Film*, revised edition (Tokyo: Kodansha International, 2005), p. 44.
12 Audie Bock interview with Fujimoto Sanezumi, June 1976, quoted in Bock, *Japanese Film Directors*, p. 110; Anderson and Richie, *The Japanese Film*, p. 364.
13 Bock, *Japanese Film Directors*, p. 124.
14 Ibid., p. 103.
15 Russell, *The Cinema of Naruse Mikio*, p. 40.
16 Ibid., p. 77.
17 Wada-Marciano, 'Imaging Modern Girls', p. 28.
18 Bock, *Japanese Film Directors*, p. 121.
19 David Bordwell, 'Visual Style in Japanese Cinema, 1925–1945', *Film History* 7 (1995), 18.
20 Ibid., pp. 21–22.
21 Naruse inserts a cutaway to a street lamp in a scene at the end of *Not Blood Relations* (1932) in order to prolong an emotional beat, but it is an isolated usage; in *Street Without End*, he expands the strategy by incorporating it into a scene-length editing pattern.
22 Bordwell, 'Visual Style in Japanese Cinema', p. 22.

Bibliography

Books

Abel, Richard, *The Ciné Goes to Town: French Cinema 1896–1914* (Berkeley: University of California Press, 1994 edn)
—— *French Cinema: The First Wave, 1915–1929* (Princeton: Princeton University Press, 1984
—— *French Film Criticism and Theory, 1907–1939*, vol. 1 (Princeton: Princeton University Press, 1988)
Abel, Richard (ed.), *Encyclopedia of Early Cinema* (New York: Routledge, 2005)
Agee, James, *Agee on Film*, vol. 1: *Essays and Reviews* (New York: Universal Library, 1969)
Anderson, Joseph L., and Donald Ritchie, *The Japanese Film: Art and Industry* (Princeton: Princeton University Press, 1982 edn)
Asbury, Herbert, *The Gangs of Chicago* (London: Arrow Books, 2003 edn)
Barnouw, Erik, and S. Krishaswani, *Indian Film* (New York: Columbia University Press, 1963)
Bastide, Bernard, and Jean A. Gili (eds), *Léonce Perret* (Paris: Association française de recherches sur l'histoire du cinéma, 2003)
Belton, John, *Widescreen Cinema* (Cambridge, MA: Harvard University Press, 1992)
Bertellini, Giorgio (ed.), *Italian Silent Cinema: A Reader* (New Barnet: John Libbey Publishing, 2013)
Bilton, Alan, *Silent Film Comedy and American Culture* (Houndsmills: Palgrave MacMillan, 2013)
Bock, Audie, *Japanese Film Directors* (Tokyo: Kodansha International, 1978)
Bordwell, David, *Narration and the Fiction Film* (London: Methuen, 1985)
—— *Ozu and the Poetics of Cinema* (London: BFI, 1988)
—— *On the History of Film Style* (Cambridge, MA: Harvard University Press, 1998)
—— *Figures Traced in Light: On Cinematic Staging* (Berkeley: University of California Press, 2005)
—— *Poetics of Cinema* (New York: Routledge, 2008)

Bordwell, David, Janet Staiger and Kristin Thompson, *The Classical Hollywood Cinema* (London: Routledge/New York: Columbia University Press, 1985)

Bowser, Eileen, *The Transformation of Cinema, 1907–1915* (New York: Scribner's/Berkeley: University of California Press)

Brewster, Ben, and Lea Jacobs, *Theatre to Cinema: Stage Pictorialism and the Early Feature Film* (Oxford: Oxford University Press, 1997)

Brooks, Peter, *The Melodramatic Imagination: Balzac, James and the Mode of Excess* (New Haven: Yale University Press)

Brownlow, Kevin, *The Parade's Gone By* (New York: Bonanza Books, 1968)

Brunetta, Gian Piero, *Storia del cinema italiano 1895–1945* (Rome: Editori Riuniti, 1979)

Burrows, Jon, *Legitimate Cinema: Theatre Stars in British Silent Films, 1908–1918* (Exeter: University of Exeter Press, 2003)

Campbell, H., R.F. Brewer and H. Neville (eds), *Voice, Speech and Gesture: Practical Handbook to the Elocutionary Art* (London: Charles William Deacon & Co., 1895)

Canjels, Rudmer, *Distributing Silent Film Serials: Local Practices, Changing Forms, Cultural Transformations* (New York: Routledge, 2011)

Carrol, Noël, *Comedy Incarnate: Buster Keaton, Physical Humor and Bodily Coping* (Oxford: Blackwell, 2009)

Cavendish, Philip, *The Men with the Movie Camera: The Poetics of Visual Style in Soviet Avant-Garde Cinema of the 1920s* (New York: Berghahn Books, 2013)

Chabria, Suresh (ed.), *Light in Asia: Indian Silent Cinema, 1912–1934* (New Delhi: La Giornate de Cinema Muto and the National Archive of India, 1994).

Chan, Anthony B., *Perpetually Cool: The Many Lives of Anna May Wong* (Lanham, MD: Scarecrow Press, 2003)

Christie, Ian, and John Gillet (eds), *Futurism/Formalism/FEKS: 'Eccentrism' and Soviet Cinema, 1918–36* (London: BFI, 1978)

Clark, George B., *The American Expeditionary Forces in World War I: A Statistical History, 1917–1919* (Jefferson, NC: McFarland, 2013)

Crafton, Donald, *The Talkies: American Cinema's Transition to Sound, 1926–1931* (New York: Scribner's/Berkeley: University of California Press, 1997)

D'Amico, Alessandro, and Lino Vito (eds), *Cronache 1914/1955, Primo Volume–Tomo I, 1914–1918* (Palermo: Idola, 2001)

Dance, Robert, and Bruce Robertson, *Ruth Harriet Louise and Hollywood Glamour Photography* (Berkeley: University of California Press, 2002)

Davis, Owen, *My First Fifty Years in the Theatre: The Plays, the Players, the Theatrical Managers and the Theatre Itself as One Man Saw Them in the Fifty Years between 1897 and 1947* (Boston, MA: Walter H. Baker Company Publishers, 1950)

Dove, George N., *The Reader and the Detective Story* (Bowling Green, OH: Popular Press, 1997)

Dralyuk, Boris, *Western Crime Fiction Goes East: The Russian Pinkerton Craze, 1907–1934* (Leiden: Brill, 1991)

Dym, Jeffrey A., *Benshi Japanese Silent Film Narrators and their Forgotten Narrative Art of Setsumei: A History of Japanese Silent Film Narration* (New York: Edwin Mellen Press, 2003)

Eisenschitz, Bernard (ed.), *Fritz Lang au Travail* (Paris: Cahiers du Cinema, 2011)

Eisenschitz, Bernard, and Jean Narboni (eds), *Ernst Lubitsch* (Montreuil-sur-Mer: Cahiers du Cinéma/Cinémathèque Française, 1985)

Eisner, Lotte H., *The Haunted Screen: Expressionism in the German Cinema and the Influence of Max Reinhard* (Berkeley: University of California Press, 2008 edn)

Eisner, Lotte H., *Fritz Lang*, trans. Gertrude Mander (New York: Oxford University Press, 1997)

Elsaesser, Thomas (ed.), *Early Cinema: Space, Frame, Narrative* (London: BFI, 1990)

Elsaesser with Michael Wedel (eds), *A Second Life: German Cinema's First Decades* (Amsterdam: Amsterdam University Press, 1996)

Elsaesser, Thomas, *Weimar and After: Germany's Historical Imaginary* (London: Routledge, 2000)

Eyman, Scott, *Ernst Lubitsch: Laughter in Paradise* (New York: Simon & Schuster, 1993)

Fairservice, Don, *Film Editing: History, Theory and Practice* (Manchester: Manchester University Press, 2001)

Feyder, Jacques, and Françoise Rosay, *Le Cinéma, Notre Metier* (Genève: Cailler, 1946)

Fischer, Lucy, *Designing Women: Cinema, Art Deco, and the Female Form* (New York: Columbia University Press, 2003)

Florin, Bo, *Regi: Victor Sjöström/Directed by Victor Seastrom* (Stockholm: Cinematek/Svensk Filminstitutet, 2003)

—— *Transition and Translation: Victor Sjöström in Hollywood, 1923–1930* (Amsterdam: Amsterdam University Press, 2013)

Flower, Norman (ed.), *The Journals of Arnold Bennett III: 1921–1928* (London: Cassell, 1933)

Ford, Charles, *Jacques Feyder* (Paris: Édition Seghers, 1973)

Fullerton, John (ed.), *Celebrating 1895: The Centenary of Cinema* (Sydney: John Libbey, 1998)

Fullerton, John and Jan Olsson (eds), *Nordic Explorations: Film Before 1930* (New Barnet and Sydney: John Libbey, 1999)

Gauthier, Christopher, Anne Kerlan and Dimitri Vezyroglou (eds), *Loin d'Hollywood? Cinématographies nationales et modèle hollywoodien: France, Allemagne, URSS, Chine, 1925–1935* (Paris: Nouveaux Mondes Editions, 2013)
Gili Jean, and Michel Marie (eds), *Jacques Feyder* (Paris: L'association française de recherche sur l'histoire du cinéma, 1998)
Glagoleva, *et al.*, *Sovetski khudozhestvennye film'my: Annotirovannyi katalog*, vol. 1 (Moscow: Iskusstvo, 1961)
Gledhill, Christine, *Reframing British Cinema, 1918–1928: Between Restraint and Passion* (London: BFI, 2003)
Gomery, Douglas, *The Hollywood Studio System* (London: BFI, 1986)
Griffiths, Alison, *Cinema, Museum, and the Immersive View* (New York: Columbia University Press, 2008)
Gunning, Tom, *The Films of Fritz Lang: Allegories of Vision and Modernity* (London: BFI, 2000)
Hagemann, Carl, *Regie: Die Kunst der szenischen Darstellung*, 3rd edn (Berlin: Schuster & Loeffler, 1912)
—— *Regie: Die Kunst der szenischen Darstellung*, 5th edn (Berlin: Schuster & Loeffler, 1915)
Hall, Randall, and Margaret McCarthy (eds), *Light Motifs: German Popular Film in Perspective* (Detriot: Wayne State University Press, 2003)
Hall, Sheldon, and Steve Neale, *Epics, Spectacles and Blockbusters: A Hollywood History* (Detroit: Wayne State University Press, 2010)
Hardt, Ursula, *From Caligari to California: Eric Pommer's Life in the International Film Industry* (Providence, RI: Berghahn Books, 1996)
Harter, Chuck, and Michael J. Hayde (eds), *Little Elf: A Celebration of Harry Langdon* (Albany, GA: BearManor Media, 2012)
Henriot, Christian, and Yeh Wen-hsin (eds), *History in Images: Pictures and Public Spaces in Modern China* (Berkeley: University of California Press, 2012)
Higson, Andrew, and Richard Maltby (eds), *'Film Europe' and 'Film America': Cinema, Commerce and Cultural Exchange 1920–1939* (Exeter: University of Exeter Press, 1999)
Hodges, Graham Russell Gao, *Anna May Wong: From Laundryman's Daughter to Hollywood Legend* (New York & Basingstoke: Palgrave Macmillan, 2004)
Hollaender, Felix, *The Sins of the Fathers*, trans. by Sarah J.L. Lawson (New York: Payson & Clark, 1927)
Holm, John, *A Companion to World War I* (Hoboken, NJ: John Wiley, 1910)
Horak, Jan-Christopher (ed.), *Lovers of Cinema: The First American Film Avant-Garde, 1919–1945* (Madison: University of Wisconsin Press, 1995)
Horose, S., *La Symphonie des ombres chinoises* (Paris: Editions de la Madeleine, 1932)

Jacobs, Lea, *The Decline of Sentiment: American Film in the 1920s* (Berkeley: University of California Press, 2008)

Jacques, Norbert, *Dr Mabuse, Master of Mystery*, trans. Lilian A. Clare (London: George Allen & Unwin, 1923)

Jones, Andrew W., *Yellow Music: Media Culture and Colonial Modernity in the Chinese Jazz Age* (Durham, NC: Duke University Press, 20011)

Kalat, David, *The Strange Case of Dr Mabuse: A Study of the Twelve Films and Five Novels* (Jefferson, NC: McFarland, 2001)

Keil, Charlie, and Ben Singer (eds), *American Cinema of the 1910s: Themes and Variations* (New Brunswick, NJ: Rutgers University Press, 2009)

Keil Charlie, and Shelley Stamp (eds), *American Cinema's Transitional Era: Audiences, Institutions, Practices* (Berkeley: University of California Press, 2004)

Kido, Shiro, *Nihon eigaden: Eiga seisakusha no kiroku (Japanese Cinema Tales: A Record of a Film Producer)* (Tokyo: Kodansha International, 1982)

Kreimeyer, Klauss, *The Ufa Story: A History of Germany's Greatest Film Company* (Berkeley: University of California Press, 1996)

Lagerlöf, Selma, *The Phantom Carriage* trans. Peter Graves (Stockholm: Norvic Press, 2011)

Larsen, Lisabeth Richter, and Dan Nissen, *100 Years of Nordisk Film* (Copenhagen: Danish Film Institute, 2006)

Lebfried, Philip, and Chei Mi Lane, *Anna May Wong: A Complete Guide to Her Film, Stage, Radio and Television Work* (Jefferson, NC: McFarland, 2010)

Leong, Karen J., *The China Mystique: Pearl S. Buck, Anna May Wong, Mayling Soong and the Transformation of Hollywood Orientalism* (Berkeley: University of California Press, 2005)

Leyda, Jay, *Kino: A History of Russian and Soviet Film* (Princeton: Princeton University Press, 1983 edn)

Low, Rachael, *The History of the British Film*, vol. 3: 1914–1918 (London: George Allen & Unwin, 1950)

—— *The History of the British Film: 1918–1929* (London: George Allen & Unwin, 1971)

MacCann, Richard Dyer, *The Silent Comedians* (Metuchen, NJ: Scarecrow Press, 1993)

Marker, Frederick J. and Lise-Lone Marker, *Ibsen's Lively Art: A Performance Study of the Major Plays* (Cambridge: Cambridge University Press, 1989)

McGilligan, Patrick, *Fritz Lang: The Nature of the Beast* (New York: St Martin's Press, 1997)

McReynolds, Louise, and Joan Neuberger, *Imitations of Life: Two Centuries of Melodrama in Russia* (Durham, NC: Duke University Press, 2002)

Murphy, Robert (ed.), *Directors in British and Irish Cinema* (London: BFI, 2006)

Neale, Steve, *Genre and Hollywood* (London: Routledge, 2005)

Newland, Paul, *The Cultural Construction of London's East End: Urban Iconography, Modernity and the Spatialistion of Englishness* (Amsterdam: Rodolfi, 2008)

Nowell-Smith, Geoffrey, *The Oxford History of World Cinema* (Oxford: Oxford University Press, 1996)

O'Regan, Tom, and Brian Shoesmith (eds), *History on/and/in Film* (Perth: History & Film Association of Australia, 1987)

Olenina, Ana, and Maxim Pozdorovkin, *'Miss Mend' and Soviet Americanism* (Los Angeles: Flicker Alley, 2009)

Parker, John (ed.), *Who Was Who in the Theatre: 1912–1976: A Biographical Dictionary of Actors, Actresses, Directors, Playwrights, and Producers of the English-Speaking Theatre*, vol. 3 (Detroit: Omnigrapics Books, Gale Research Company, 1978)

Paul, William, *Ernst Lubitsch's American Comedy* (New York: Columbia University Press, 1983)

Pearson, Roberta, *Eloquent Gestures: The Transformation of Performance Style in the Griffith Biograph Films* (Berkeley: University of California Press, 1992)

Plantinga, Carl, and Greg M. Smith, *Moving Viewers: American Film and the Spectator's Experience* (Berkeley: University of California Press, 2009

Polti, Georges, *The Thirty Six Dramatic Situations* (Boston, MA: The Writer Inc., 1977 edn)

Ramirez, Juan Antonio, *Architecture for the Screen: A Critical Study of Set Design in Hollywood's Golden Age*, trans. by John F. Moffitt (Jefferson, NC.: McFarland, 2004)

Rheuban, Joyce, *Harry Langdon: The Comedian as Metteur-en-Scène* (Rutherford, NJ: Farleigh Dickinson University Press, 1983)

Rojas, Carlos, and Eileen Cheng-Yin Chow (eds), *The Oxford Handbook of Chinese Cinemas* (Oxford: Oxford University Press, 2013)

Rotha, Paul, *The Film Till Now: A Survey of World Cinema* (London: Jonathan Cape, 1930/New York: Twayne Publishers, 1963)

Russell, Catherine, *The Cinema of Naruse Mikio: Women and Japanese Modernity* (Durham, NC: Duke University Press, 2008)

Ruth, David E., *Inventing the Public Enemy: The Gangster in American Culture, 1918–1934* (Chicago: Chicago University Press, 1996)

Salt, Barry, *Film Style & Technology: History & Analysis* (London: Starword, 1992 edn)

—— *Moving into Pictures: More on Film History, Style, and Analysis* (London: Starword, 2006)

Sato, Tadao, *Currents in Japanese Cinema* (Tokyo: Kodansha International, 1982)

Schelly, William, *Harry Langdon: His Life and Films* (Jefferson, NJ: McFarland, 2008 edn)

Shaginian, Marietta, *Mess-Mend: Yankees in Petrograd*, trans. and intro. by Samuel D. Cioran (Ann Arbor: Ardis, 1991)

Singer, Ben, *Melodrama and Modernity: Early Sensational Cinema and Its Contexts* (New York: Columbia University Press, 2001)

Smith, Murray, *Engaging Characters: Fiction, Emotion, and the Cinema* (Oxford: Oxford University Press, 1995)

St Pierre, Paul Matthew, *E.A. Dupont and His Contribution to British Film: Variété, Moulin Rouge, Piccadilly, Atlantic, Two Worlds, Cape Forlorn* (Madison, WI: Farleigh Dickinson University Press, 2010)

Tatar, Maria, *Lustmord: Sexual Murder in Weimar Germany* (Princeton: Princeton University Press, 1997)

Taylor, Richard, and Ian Christie (eds), *The Film Factory: Russian and Soviet Cinema in Documents, 1896–1939* (Cambridge, MA: Harvard University Press, 1988)

—— *Inside the Film Factory: New Approaches to Russian and Silent Cinema* (New York: Routledge, 1991)

Thompson, Kristin, *Herr Lubitsch Goes to Hollywood: German and American Films after World War One* (Amsterdam: University of Amsterdam Press, 2005)

Thompson, Kristin, and David Bordwell, *Film History: An Introduction* (New York: McGraw-Hill, 2003 edn)

Tsivian, Yuri, *Early Cinema in Russia and Its Cultural Reception* (London: Routledge, 1994)

Tsivian, Yuri, with Paulo Cherchi Usai, Lorenzo Cordelli, Carlo Montato and David Robinson (eds), *Silent Witnesses: Russian Films, 1908–1919* (London: BFI, 1994)

Usai, Paulo Cherchi, and Lorenzo Codelli (eds), *Before Caligari: German Cinema, 1895–1920* (Pordenone: Biblioteca dell'Edizioni dell'Imagine, 1990)

Vaingurt, Julia, *Wonderlands of the Avant-Garde: Technology and the Arts in Russia of the 1920s* (Evanston, IL: Northwestern University Press, 2013)

Wellman, William, *The Man and His Wings: William A. Wellman and the Making of the First Best Picture* (Westport, CT: Praeger Publishers, 2006)

Wilde, Oscar, *The Importance of Being Earnest and Other Plays* (Oxford: Oxford University Press, 1995)

Williams, Alan, *Republic of Images: A History of French Filmmaking* (Cambridge, MA: Harvard University Press, 1992)

Williams, Linda, *Playing the Race Card: Melodramas of Black and White from Uncle Tom to O.J. Simpson* (Princeton: Princeton University Press, 2001)

Wong, Elizabeth, *China Doll (The Imagined Life of an American Actress)* (Woodstock, IL: Dramatic Publishing Company, 2005)

Youngblood, Denise, *Soviet Cinema in the Silent Era, 1918–35* (Austin: University of Texas Press, 1991)

—— Movies for the Masses: Popular Cinema and Society in the 1920s (Cambridge: Cambridge University Press, 1992)
—— *The Magic Mirror: Moviemaking in Russia, 1908–1918* (Madison: University of Wisconsin Press, 1999)

Articles and Book Chapters

Bakker, Gerben, 'The Decline and Fall of the European Film Industry: Sunk Costs, Market Size, and Market Structure, 1890–1927', *Economic History Review*, 58.2 (2005)

Barnier, Martin, '*The Kiss, Si L'Empereur savait ça*, Jacques Feyder et al MGM dans le contexte de la généralisationdu son à Hollywood' in Gili and Marie, *Jacques Feyder*

Barr, Charles, 'Sjöström and Seastrom', Norwich Papers in European Languages, Literatures and Culture, no. 1 (1994)

Bergfelder, Tim, 'Negotiating Exoticism': Hollywood, Film Europe and the Cultural Reception of Anna May Wong' in Higson and Maltby, *'Film Europe' and 'Film America'*

Bertrand, Ina, 'Australia' in Abel (ed.), *Encyclopedia of Early Cinema*

Bloom, Ivo, 'Italy' in Abel (ed.), *Encyclopedia of Early Cinema*

Bordwell, David, 'A Cinema of Flourishes: Japanese Decorative Classicism of the Prewar Era' in Arthur Molletti, Jr and David Desser (eds), *Reframing Japanese Cinema Authorship, Genre, History* (Bloomington: Indiana University Press, 1992)

—— 'Nordisk and the Tableau Aesthetic' in Larsen and Nilssen (eds), *100 Years of Nordisk Film*

—— 'Nordisk and The Tableau Style', http.//www.davidbordwell.net/essays/nordisk.php

—— 'Toward a Scientific Film History?', *Quarterly Review of Film Studies*, 10.3 (1985)

—— 'Visual Style in Japanese Cinema, 1925–1945', *Film History*, 7.1 (1995)

Brewster, Ben, 'Deep Staging in French Films' in Elseasser (ed.), *Early Cinema*

—— 'Mutiple-Reel/Feature Films' in Abel (ed.), *Encyclopedia of Early Cinema*

—— http://uwfilmies.pbworks.com/w/page/4660024/Germinal-1913

Burrows, Jon, 'A Vague Chinese Quarter Elsewhere: Limehouse in the Cinema, 1914–1936', *Journal of British Cinema and Television*, 6.2 (2009)

Carrol, Noël, 'Buster Keaton, *The General*, and Visible Intelligibility' in Lehman (ed.), *Close Viewings*

Case, Shannon, 'Lilied Tongues and Yellow Claws: The Invention of London's Chinatown, 1915–45' in Stella Deen (ed.), *Challenging Modernism: New Readings in Literature and Culture, 1914–45* (Aldershot: Ashgate, 2002)

Cassiday, Julie A., 'Alcohol Is Our Enemy! Soviet Temperance Melodramas of the 1920s' in McReynolds and Neuberger (eds), *Imitations of Life*

Castle, Hugh, 'Some British Films', *Close Up*, 5.1 (1929)

Chabria, Suresh, 'Before Our Eyes: A Short History of India's Silent Cinema' in Chabria (ed.), *Light in Asia*

Christensen, Thomas C., 'Nordisk Films Kompagni and the First World War' in Fullerton and Olsson (eds), *Nordic Explorations*

Cioran, Samuel, 'Introduction' to Shaginian, *Mess-Mend*

D'Amico, Silivio, 'In honore di Lydia Borelli, al Valle', reprinted in D'Amico and Vito (eds), *Cronache 1914/1954*

Dance, Robert and Bruce Robertson, 'Photographing Garbo' in Dance and Robertson, *Ruth Harriet Louise and Hollywood Glamour Photography*

De la Bretèque, François, 'La veine réaliste de Léonce Perret' in Bastide and Gili (eds), *Léonce Perret*

Elsaesser, Thomas, 'Germany: Production' in Abel (ed.), *Encyclopedia of Early Cinema*

—— 'Germany: The Weimar Years' in Nowell-Smith (ed.), *The Oxford Companion to Film History*

Elsaesser, Thomas, and Michael Wedel, 'Germany: Distribution' in Abel (ed.), *Encyclopedia of Early Cinema*

Falin, Christophe, 'Les réponses techniques à la transition du muet au parlant dans le cinema chinois' in Gauthier, Kerlan, Veyzyroglou (eds), *Loin d'Hollywood?*

Frieberg, Freda, 'The Transition to Sound in Japan' in O'Regan and Shoesmith (eds), *History on/and/in Film*

Fujiki, Hideaki, '*Benshi* as Stars: The Irony of the Popularity and Respectability of Voice Performers in Japanese Cinema', *Cinema Journal*, 45.2 (2006)

Fullerton, John, 'Sweden' in Abel (ed.), *Encyclopedia of Early Cinema*

Gili, Jean A., '*L'Enfant de Paris*' in Bastide and Gili, *Léonce Perret*

Glagoleva, *et al.*, 'Miss Mend' in *Sovetski khudozhestvennye film'my*

Gledhill, Christine, 'The Screen Actress from Silence to Sound' in Maggie B. Gale and John Stokes (eds), *The Cambridge Companion to the Actress* (Cambridge: Cambridge University Press, 2007)

Gu, Yelu, 'My Five "Firsts"', in *Friends, Sorrows and Joys on Stage and Screen* (Beijing: China First Press, 1994)

Gunning, Tom, 'A Dangerous Pledge: Victor Sjöström's Unknown Masterpiece, *Masterman*' in Fullerton and Olsson (eds), *Nordic Explorations*

Harris, Kristine, '*Two Stars* on the Silver Screen: The Metafilm as Chinese Modern' in Henriot and Yeh Wen-hsin (eds), *History in Images*

Hawkridge, John, 'British Cinema from Hepworth to Hitchcock' in Nowell-Smith (ed.), *The Oxford History of World Cinema*

Higgins, Scott, 'Suspenseful Situations: Melodramatic Narrative and the Contemporary Action Film', *Cinema Journal*, 47.2 (2008)
Higson, Andrew, 'Polyglot Films for an International Market' in Higson and Maltby, *'Film Europe' and 'Film America'*
Higson, Andrew, and Richard Maltby, 'Introduction' to *'Film Europe' and 'Film America'*
Hiley, Nicolas, 'Great Britain' in Abel (ed.), *Encyclopedia of Early Cinema*
Huang, Yicuo, 'Chuangban Lianhua yingye yuanqi' ('The Founding of United Photoplay Service Co. Ltd'), *Yingxi zazhi* (*The Film Magazine*), 1.9 (1930)
—— 'Guopian fuxing ying you de bu zouzou' ('The New Direction That Must be Taken in the Chinese Film Renaissance'), *Yingxi zazhi*, 1.9 (1930)
—— 'Guonei xin yingye: Lianhua jihua jinxing zhong de zhique' ('A New National Industry: The Impact of the Development of UPS'), *Yingxi zazhi*, 1.10 (1930)
Jacobs, Lea, 'Acting Styles' in Abel (ed.), *Encyclopedia of Early Cinema*
—— http://uwfilmies.pbworks.com/w/page/466017/Bertini
Horak, Jan-Christopher, 'Good Morning, Babylon: Maurice Tourneur's Battle against the Studio System', *Image*, 31.2 (1988)
Jung, Uli, and Martin Loiperdinger, 'World War I' in Abel (ed.), *Encyclopedia of Early Cinema*
Kepley Jr, Vance, 'Federal Cinema: The Soviet Film Industry, 1924–32', *Film History*, 8.3 (1996)
Kerlan, Anne, 'Un nouveau cinéma pour une nation en construction: le "mouvement" de renaissance du cinéma chinois' in Gauthier *et al.* (eds), *Loin d'Hollywood*
Koszarski, Richard, 'Maurice Tourneur: The First of the Visual Stylists', *Film Comment*, 9.2 (1983)
Lacassin, Francis, 'Les Films policiers de Léonce Perret' in Bestide and Gilli (eds), *Léonce Peret*
Langdon, Harry, 'The Serious Side of Comedy Making' in MacCann, *The Silent Comedians*
Le Forestier, Laurent, 'Les comédies de Léonce Perret, fleurons de la production Gaumont' in Bestide and Gilli (eds), *Léonce Perret*
Le Fanu, Mark, 'Revolutionary Road: Boris Barnet's *The House on Trubnaya Street*', http//bfi.or.uk/news/revolutionary-road-boris-barnet-s-house-trubnaya-street
Lewis, Kevin, 'A World Across from Broadway: The Shuberts and the Movies', *Film History*, 1.1 (1987)
Luft, Herbert G., 'E.A. Dupont', *Films in Review*, 28.6 (1977)
Lubitsch, Ernst, 'Lubitsch Talks of Epigrams on Screen' in Laurence A. Hughes

(ed.), *The Truth About the Movies by the Stars* (Hollywood: Hollywood Publishers, 1924)

Luo, Mingyou, 'Shezhi *Lian'ai yu yiwu* zhi yuanyin' ('Why Did We Make a Film of *Love and Duty?*'), *Yinkzi zazhi*, 1.11–12 (1931)

McCormick, Richard W., 'The Carnival of Humiliation: Sex, Spectacle, and Self-Reflexibility in E.A. Dupont's *Variety*' in Halle and McCarthy, *Light Motives*

McReynolds, Louise, and Joan Neuberger, 'Acknowledgements' in McReynolds and Neuberger (eds), *Imitations of Life*

—— 'Introduction' to McReynolds and Neuberger (eds), *Imitations of Life*

Müller, Corinna, 'Germany: Audiences' in Abel (ed.), *Encyclopedia of Early Cinema*

Musser, Charles, 'The Hidden and the Unspeakable: On Theatrical Culture, Oscar Wilde and Ernst Lubitsch's *Lady Windermere's Fan*', *Film Studies*, no. 4 (2004)

'The Mysterious Lady: Stills and Portraits', *Garbo Forever*, http://garboforever.com/Film-Pic-10.htm

Neale, Steve, 'Melodrama and Tears', *Screen*, 27.6 (1986)

Neville, Henry, 'Gesture' in H. Campbell, R.F. Brewer and H. Neville (eds), *Voice, Speech and Gesture*

O'Donaghue, Darragh, '*The Phantom Carriage*', http://sensesofcinema.com/2010/cteq/the-phantom-carriage

Olsson, Jan, 'Exchange and Exhibition Practices: Notes on the Swedish Market in the Transitional Era' in Fullerton and Olsson (eds), *Nordic Explorations*

—— 'Nils Krok's Social Pathos and Paul Garbagni's Style', *Film History*, 22.1 (2010)

Piotrovsky, Adrian, '"Ideology" and "Commerce"' in Taylor and Christie (eds), *The Film Factory*

Plantinga, Carl, 'The Scene of Empathy and the Human Face on Film' in Platinga and Smith, *Passionate Views*

Raby, Peter, 'Introduction' to Oscar Wilde, *The Importance of Being Earnest and Other Plays*

Rapf, Joanna E., 'Doing Nothing: Harry Langdon and the Performance of Absence', *Film Quarterly*, 59.1 (2005)

Ross, Sara, '"Good Little Bad Girls": Silent Comediennes and the Performance of Girlish Sexuality', *Film History*, 13.4 (2001)

—— 'Invitation to the Voyage: The Flight Sequence in Contemporary 3D Cinema', *Film History*, 24.2 (2012)

Sandberg, Mark B., 'Multiple-reel/feature films:Europe' in Abel (ed.), *Encyclopaedia of Early Cinema*

Seed, John, 'Limehouse Blues: Looking for Chinatown in the London Docks, 1900–40', *History Workshop Journal*, no. 62 (2006)
Simmon, Scott, 'Program Notes' to *More Treasures from American Archives 1894–1931* (San Francisco: National Film Preservation, 2004)
Singer, Ben and Charlie Keil, 'Introduction' to Keil and Singer (eds), *American Cinema of the 1910s*
Soulstein, Seth, 'Concrete Irrationality: Surrealist Spectators and the Cult of Harry Langdon', *Scope: An Online Journal of Film and Television Studies*, 25 (2013)
Sternberg, Meir, 'Telling in Time (II): Chronology, Teleology, Narrativity', *Poetics Today*, 13.3 (1992)
Suchenski, Richard, '"Turn Again, Tourneur": Maurice Tourneur between France and Hollywood', *Studies in French Cinema*, 11.2 (2011)
'Taglines', http://imdb.com/title/tt0015624/taglines?ref_=tt_stry-tg
Thompson, Kristin, 'National or International Films? The European Debate during the 1920s', *Film History*, 8.3 (1996)
Turim, Maureen, 'Gentlemen Consume Blondes' in Bill Nichols (ed.), *Movies and Methods*, vol. II (Berkeley: University of California Press, 1985)
Tybjerg, Casper, 'Denmark' in Abel (ed.), *Encyclopedia of Early Cinema*
Urish, Ben, 'The Case for Harry Langdon: How and Why Capra was Wrong', *The Journal of Popular Culture*, 41.1 (2008)
Usai, Paulo Cherchi, 'Italy: Spectacle and Melodrama' in Nowell-Smith (ed.), *The Oxford History of World Cinema*
Vivaldi, Giuliano, http://www.brightlightsfilm.com/73/73barnet_vivaldi.php
Wada-Marciano, Mitsuyo, 'Imaging Modern Girls in the Japanese Woman's Film', *Camera Obscura*, 20.3 60 (2005)
Walker, Michael, 'Melodrama and American Cinema', *Movie*, no. 29/30 (1982)
Widding, Astrid Söderbergh, 'Towards Classical Narration? Georg af Klercker in Context' in Fullerton and Olsson (eds), *Nordic Explorations*
Witchard, Anne, 'A Threepenny Omnibus Ticket to "Limey-housey-Causey-way": Fictional Sojourns in Chinatown', *Comparative Critical Studies*, 4.2 (2007)
Yacobi, Tamar, 'Package Deals in Fictional Narrative: The Case of the Narrator's (Un)reliability', *Narrative*, 9.2 (2001)
Youngblood, Denise, 'Russia' in Abel (ed.), *Encyclopedia of Early Cinema*
Zhu, Shilin, '*Lian'ai yu yiwu* zuozhe Luo Chen nüshi zhi zhushu ji qi baofu' ('The Writings and Hopes of Miss Luo Chen, the Author of *Love and Duty*'), *Yingxi zazhi*, 1.11–12 (1931)

Newspapers, Magazines and Film Industry Journals

The Billboard, 14 February 1925
The Bioscope, 23 February 1928; 3 May 1928; 1 August 1928; 6 February 1929
Chicago Daily Tribune, 9 November 1925
The Cinema, 6 February 1929
Daily Express, 23 March 1928
Daily Herald, 6 June 1932
Daily Sketch, 26 March 1928
Daily Telegraph, 23 March 1928; 19 March 2004
Daily Variety, 9 December 1925
Exhibitors Daily Review, 31 July 1928; 8 August 1927; 20 September 1928; 30 November 1928
Exhibitor's Review, 13 October 1928
Film Daily, 19 August 1927; 21 August 1927; 23 August 1927; 7 September 1927; 8 September 1927; 30 December 1927; 15 January 1927;
Film Spectator, 3 March 1928; 26 May 1928
Harpers Weekly, 29 April 1916
Hollywood Vagabond, 17 February 1927; 24 March 1927
Izdatel'stva, 4 November 1926
Izvestiia, 23 October 1926, 26 November 1926, 16 December 1926, 29 May 1927
Kinematograph Weekly, 26 July 1928, 7 February 1929
Lianhua nianjuan (UPS Yearbook), 1933–34; 1934–35
Los Angeles Times, 9 August 1925; 22 November 1925
Manchester Guardian, 21 June 1928; 25 October 1928
Motion Picture Magazine, October 1924; August 1926; December 1926; December 1928
Motion Picture News, 6 February 1926; 18 September 1926; 9 October 1926; 8 April 1927; 10 August 1927; 21 August 1927; 26 August 1927
Moving Picture World, 31 January 1914; 7 February 1914; 21 March 1914; 4 December 1915
New York Dramatic Mirror, 4 November 1914
New York Herald Tribune, 27 December 1925
New York Times, 21 January 1910
Photoplay Magazine, September 1925; October 1926; August 1927; April 1928
The Picturegoer, June 1927; March 1929
Pour Vous, L'hebdomadaire du cinéma, 4 June 1931
Pravda, 25 November 1921; 3 December 1926; 15 January 1927; 29 May 1927
The Times, 2 February 1929
Variety, 17 August 1927; 31 October 1914; 7 March 1933
The Weekly Dispatch, 26 February 1928

Index

Abel, Alfred, 95, 105
Abel, Richard, 49, 228
acting, 2, 3, 14–17, 30–33, 36–38, 46–47, 82–83, 104–106, 151, 167, 194, 196–204, 238, 287, 288, 301; expressionist acting, 198–199, 202–203; naturalist acting, 2, 14–16, 32–33, 37, 46, 82, 196–199; 202; melodramatic acting, 197–203; pictorial acting, 2, 14–17, 30–31, 32–33, 36–38, 46–47
actuality films, 55, 217
adaptations, 63, 112–113, 168, 235; issues of, 30, 63
Afgrunden (*The Abyss*) (1910), 32–33
Aitken, William Maxwell (Lord Beaverbrook), 211
The Alley Cat (*Nachtgestalten*) (1929), 211
Ame d'Artist (*Heart of an Actress*) (1924), 195
American Telephone & Telegraph Company, 10
Anna Christie (1930), 222
Antoine, André, 14, 61
Apart from You (1933), 253, 266
Arlen, Richard, 179, 182
art deco, 10, 222, 224, 238
L'Assommoir (1909), 15, 279
Assunta Spina (1915), 1, 2, 32–47

Astor, Gertrude, 147, 149, 157
L'Atlantide (1921), 221, 228–229
avant-garde, 206, 228, 254
Avatar (2009), 177
Ayres, Lew, 223

Bacon, Frank, 114
Bai Hong, 241
Bailey, William, 111
Bakker, Gerben, 208
Balfour, Betty, 195
Bard, Ben, 111
Barnet, Boris, 8, 162–163, 165, 168–169, 172–3
Barnett, Chester, 62, 68
Barthes, Roland, 152
Battleship Potemkin (1925), 162–163, 169
Bauer, Evgenii, 167
Beaverbrook, Lord (Max Aitken), 211
Bed and Breakfast (1938), 204
Belgium, 153, 157
Bellamy, Madge, 111, 122
Belton, John, 188
Benedetti, Carlo, 3, 42, 46–47
Bennett, Arnold, 9, 206, 209, 211–212, 216–219
benshi, 12, 244–5
Bergfelder, Tim, 210
Berliner Illustriete Zeitung, 92

Bernhardt, Sarah, 33
Bertini, Francesca, 2–3, 32–36, 38–39, 42–44, 46
The Big Parade (1925), 8, 114, 178, 181
The Billboard, 112, 114
Biograph Studios, 16
The Bioscope, 196, 300
Blackmail (1929), 204
Bock, Audie, 255, 257
bolshevism, 168, 170
Bonnard, Mario, 47
Bonner, Priscilla, 157
Bordwell, David, 5, 10, 11, 13, 54, 136, 142, 169, 259, 270, 278, 282, 283, 293
Borelli, Lyda, 33, 46–47
Borgström, Hilda, 82
Borzage, Frank, 6, 110–111, 113–121, 123–130, 291
Bow, Clara, 9, 182, 186–187
Bradin, Jean, 209
Brady, William, 61
Brahm, Otto, 37, 46, 275
Brandes, Werner, 215
Brandlmeier, Thomas, 215
Brewster, Ben, 2, 4, 33, 36, 49, 53, 63, 82, 275, 281, 282, 283
British Film Institute (BFI), 205
British International Pictures (BIP), 9, 208, 210–211
Brody, Estelle, 195
Broken Blossoms (1919), 210–211, 216–217
Brooks, Peter, 182
Brown, Clarence, 222
Brunel, Adrian, 195
Bu Wancang, 235, 239, 241–242, 307
Bukharin, Nikolai, 165, 167
Buñuel, Luis, 149
Burch, Noel, 95

Burke, Thomas, 210–211
Bush, W. Stephen, 64

The Cabinet of Dr Caligari (*Das Kabinett des Dr Caligari*) (1919), 5
Cabiria (1914), 32, 47
Caesar Film, 33
Canada, 140, 241
Canjels, Rudmer, 93, 289
Capellani, Albert, 14–15, 61, 279
capitalism, 165
Capra, Frank, 149–152, 294, 295
Carmen (1926), 221, 228
Carné, Marcel, 222, 230
Carroll, Madeleine, 143
Carroll, Noël, 153
Castle, Hugh, 206, 215
Cassiday, Julie, 167
Cavalcanti, Alberto, 207
Celio (film company), 33
Chaplin, Charles, 7, 115, 140, 144, 146, 148–9, 151, 157–158, 161
Chapman, Edythe, 111
The Chaser (1928), 149, 151, 159–161
Chautard, Emile, 61
Cheirel, Jeanne, 17, 21
Cherrill, Virginia, 157
Chevalier, Maurice, 256
Chiang Kai-shek, 233
Chicago Daily Tribune, 110, 129
Chicago International Trade Fair, 241
China; culture, 11, 207, 211–212, 216, 232–235, 237; film production, 2, 11, 232–234, 241; literature, 235
China Sun Motion Picture Company (Minxin yingpian gongsi), 233
A Christmas Carol, 74
Cinderella, 193–194

cinematography, 83, 89, 120, 126, 176–177, 189, 214–215; aerial cinematography, 8, 176–177, 187, 189–191
Cioran, Samuel D., 164, 165
The Circus (1928), 7
City Lights (1931), 157–158
Clarke, Frank, 183
Close Up, 206
Coleman, Ronald, 133
Coleridge, Samuel Taylor, 245
Comédie française, 20, 59
The Constant Nymph (1928), 195, 202–204
continuity filming/shooting, 52, 54, 59
Cooper, Gary, 179, 183
Cormon, Eugene, 15
A Couple in Trouble (1913), 2
Le Courrier de Lyon (1911), 15
communism, 8, 165
Crainquebille (1926), 221, 228–229
Craven, Frank, 114
Crown v. Stevens (1936), 204

Daily Express (London), 209, 211
Dali, Salvador, 149
Daniels, Williams, 226
Daumery, Carrie, 135
Davis, Owen 4, 62, 110, 112–113
Daybreak (1931), 222
Days of Love, Blood and Tears (*Quin tian xue lei*) (1938), 241
Dean, Basil, 204
DeMille, Cecil B., 239, 307
Denmark, 2, 4; film market, 32
detective genre; films, 55, 166, 174; literature, 166
deus ex machina, 171, 173
Les Deux orphélines (1909), 15
Dickens, Charles, 74

'diva films', 32–33, 37–38, 46–47
Dr Mabuse, der Spieler (1922), 5–6, 91–109
Don't Change Your Husband! (1919), 239
Dove, George N., 166
Dralyuk, Boris, 164, 165–6, 174
Dulac, Germaine, 195, 230
Dumont, Hervé, 110
Dupont, Ewald André, 9–10, 205–209, 211, 213–219
Duse, Eleanora, 33
Duval, Henri, 50

Eagels, Jeanne, 204
editing, 36, 49, 51, 54, 68–70, 82, 118–119, 123, 126, 133, 173, 215, 253, 256, 259–260, 267, 269–271; analytical editing, 10, 49, 54, 214, 262–264, 282; continuity editing, 49, 80, 89, 140, 252, 254; cross-cutting, 56, 59, 67, 96, 101, 111, 120, 126–127, 173; shot-reverse-shot technique, 3, 40, 49, 70, 81, 83–84, 116, 121, 154, 251, 262, 263, 268
Eisner, Lotte, 106
Elsaesser, Thomas, 101, 102, 103
Elstree studios, 9, 206, 208
Elvey, Maurice, 9, 194–196, 202–203, 300
Emelka (studio), 9, 208
L'Empire du diamant (1922), 56
The End of Saint Petersburg (1927), 163
L'Enfant de Paris (1913), 3, 48–59
d'Ennery, Adolphe, 15
Escape (1930), 203
Evening Standard, (London), 211
Every Night Dreams (1933), 253, 258, 266

expressionism; cinema, 5–6, 198, 276. See also acting
The Extraordinary Adventures of Mr West in the Land of the Bolsheviks (1924), 163, 169

Faces of Children (*Visages d'enfants*) (1925), 228–229
Fairbanks, Douglas, 239
Falkenstein, Julius, 98
Famous Players-Lasky Corporation, 188
The Fan (1949), 143
Fantômas (1913–14), 8, 48, 93–96, 99
Farnum, William, 280
Farrell, Charles, 110–111, 120
fascism, 165
Fenton, Leslie, 111
Feuillade, Louis, 50, 53
Feyder, Jacques, 10, 221–222, 225–231, 304, 305
Film d'Art, 14, 20, 32
Film d'Arte Italiana, 32
film colouring techniques, 1, 176, 187
The Film Daily, 180
'Film Europa', 9, 207–208, 210, 212
The Film Spectator, 151, 181
First National Pictures, 148, 150
The First Year (1926), 114
Fischer, Lucy, 222, 230
Fitzroy, Emily, 111
flapper, 186–187, 257
Flesh and the Devil (1926), 113
The Flight Commander (1927), 195
Florence Nightingale (1915), 195
The Flying Squad (1929), 204
Fogel, Vladimir, 165
Forbidden Paradise (1924), 6
Ford, John, 114–115
Fox Film Corporation, 110, 114–115, 300

Forster-Larringa, Robert, 91, 105
France, 1–3, 5, 50, 61, 112, 178, 183–184, 221–222, 235, 241; actors/acting, 20; film production, 16, 32, 48, 49, 53, 55, 94; *plan français*, 53
Francis, Alec B., 62
Frozen Alive (1964), 204

Gad, Urban, 32
Gainsborough Pictures, 203
Gallina, Angelo, 34
Galsworthy, John, 203
Garbo, Greta, 10, 221–222, 226–227, 230
Garry, Claude, 16
Gaumont, 3, 5, 48–50, 53–55, 194–195, 204, 283
Gaynor, Janet, 110–111, 120
Genuine (1920), 5
Gérard, Marc, 17, 50
Germany, 2, 4–6; culture, 94, 106, 140, 211; film market, 32, 93; film production, 5, 32, 92–94, 98, 132
Germinal (1913), 2–3, 14–31, 48
The Ghosts of Berkeley Square (1947), 204
Giacomo, Salvatore di, 2, 33
Gili, Jean A, 48
A Girl in London (1925), 217
Gish, Dorothy, 210–211
Gish, Lillian, 211
The Glad Eye (1927), 195
Glan, Natalya, 165
Glass, Gaston, 111
Gledhill, Christine, 9, 194, 195. 201, 203–4, 301
Gloria-Film (studio), 9, 208
The Goddess (1934), 242
Goetzke, Bernard, 97, 105–106

INDEX

The Gold Rush (1925), 7
Gordon, Robert, 239
Gorky, Maxim, 167
Gosho Heinosuke, 255
Gray, Eve, 209
Gray, Gilda, 213
Great China and Lily Film Company (Dazhonghua baihe yingpian), 233
Greed (1925), 114–115
Gribiche (1926), 228
Griffith, David Wark, 16, 49, 210–211, 287
Griffiths, Allison, 188
Gu Yelu, 242
Gunning, Tom, 63, 73–4, 95, 101, 103, 106, 287, 288

Hall, Sheldon, 188
Hall-Davis, Lillian, 195
The Hands of Orlac (1924), 198
Harbou, Thea von, 6, 92, 94
Harris, Kristine, 237, 238, 307
Harrison, Louis Reeves, 63–4
Hayward, Helen, 160
The Hazards of Helen (1914–1917), 93
The Heart of Humanity (1918), 185
Heart Trouble (1929), 149, 151
Hearts of the World (1918), 185
Hernani, 15
hero (character type), 182–183, 191
heroine (character type), 33
Die Herrin der Welt (The Mistress of the World) (1919–1920), 93–94
Higgins, Scott, 6, 188
Higson, Andrew, 209
Hindle Wakes (1927), 194–195
His First Flame (1927), 149
History is Made at Night (1937), 111
Hitchcock, Alfred, 204, 205, 222
Ho-Chang, King, 213

Hollaender, Felix, 208
Holland; film market, 93
Hollywood, 5, 8, 9, 10, 110, 114, 177, 181, 195, 203, 204, 208, 210, 221–3, 241, 256, 276, 278; Classical Hollywood cinema, 3, 6, 11, 60, 63, 66, 130, 140, 223, 227–8, 230–1, 233–4, 238–9
Hollywood Vagabond, 151
Holm, Astrid, 4, 75, 82
Hopkins, Miriam, 257
Hopper, Victoria, 204
Horak, Jan-Christopher, 60, 68
Horose, S., 11, 235, 241
Hugo, Victor, 14–15, 17
Humoresque (1920), 110–111

I Was Born, But… (*Umarete wa mita keredo*) (1932), 11–12, 243–252
Ibsen, Henrik, 15, 37; *Ghosts*, 37
Ideal Films, 7, 131, 133–134, 136, 140, 142, 292, 293
Ilyinsky, Igor, 165, 171–172
Imitation of Life (1959), 113, 120
L'Immagine Ritrovata, 42
Das indische Grabmal (The Indian Tomb) (1921), 94
Ingeborg Holm (1913), 4, 83
Ingmarssönerna (1919), 16
Irvine, Robin, 193
Italy; culture, 38–39; film market, 32; film production, 1, 2, 5, 32–33, 38, 47

J'Accuse (1919), 94
Jacobs, Lea, 2–3, 4, 6, 15, 49, 82, 114–5, 168, 181, 282
Jaenzon, Henrik, 83
Jaenzon, Julius, 83, 286
Jamison, Bud, 160

327

Jannings, Emil, 208
Japan; culture, 253–254, 264; film production, 2, 11–13, 244–245; *gendai-geki* genre, 12, 254; *jidai-geki* genre, 12; *josei-eiga* genre, 254; *shomin-geki* genre, 254
Jacques, Norbert, 6, 92
Jacquinet, Jean, 21, 30–31
James, Benedict, 131
Jealousy (1929), 204
Jin Yan, 237, 242
Jofa (studio), 92
John, Georg, 96
Jones, Buck, 6, 110–111, 115, 129
Jones, Hannah, 218
Josephson, Julien, 131, 133
Juno and the Paycock (1929), 204
Just Pals (1920), 115

Kalat, David, 92, 289, 290
Katori Chiyoku, 13
Keaton, Buster, 7, 144, 148, 151, 239
Keppens, Émile, 50
Kholodnaia, Vera, 167
The Kid (1921), 7, 115
Kido Shiro, 13, 254–255, 272
Kinematograph Weekly, 196
The Kiss (1929), 10, 221–231
Klein-Rogge, Rudolph, 91, 104
Komarov, Sergei, 165, 167
Koszarsky, Richard, 60
Koval-Samborsky, Ivan, 165
Kraly, Hans, 227, 229
Krauss, Henry, 2, 16–17, 19, 21, 31, 280
Kuleshov, Lev, 8, 163
Kurosawa Akira, 253

Lady Windermere's Fan (1925), 6–7, 131–143, 291, 292

Lagerlöff, Selma, 4, 74–75, 84, 286
Lagrénée, Maurice, 50
Lang, Fritz, 6, 92–96, 98, 101, 106–108
Langdon, Harry, 7, 144–153, 155–161, 294, 295
Lay Ying, 238
Lazybones (1925), 6–7, 110–130
Le Forestier, Laurent, 49, 284
Letter from an Unknown Woman (1948), 113
Leubas, Louis, 50
Leyda, Jay, 163
Li Minwei, 233, 235
The Life Story of David Lloyd George (1918), 195
Lightnin' (1925), 114–115
Lindbergh, Charles, 178
Lianhua Film Company (Lianhua yingye gongsi), 11, 232
lighting, 61, 80, 83–84, 98, 120–121, 140, 226; chiaroscuro lighting, 198
Limehouse (London), 10, 207, 210
Lloyd, Harold, 7, 144, 148, 151, 256
London (1926), 210-2, 214, 216–20, 302
Long Pants (1927), 149–150, 152
Long takes, 61, 68, 70–1, 83, 160
Longden, John, 193–200, 202–204
Los Angeles Times, 115, 129
Losey, Joseph, 207
Louise, Ruth Harriet, 227
Love and Duty (*Lian 'ai yu yiwu*) (1931), 1, 11, 232–242
The Love Parade (1929) 241
Lubitsch, Ernst, 5, 6–7, 131, 133–134, 136–137, 140, 142–143, 228, 256, 291, 292, 293, 305
Lucky Star (1929), 111, 115
Luft, Herbert, 205

INDEX

Lunacharsky, Anatoly, 167
Lundholm, Lisa, 76
Luo Mingyou, 233, 235, 241, 307
Lydell, Burt, 133

Ma l'amor mio non muore! (1913), 46–47
Mademoiselle Parley Voo (1928), 195
MacWilliams, Glen, 120
Magnascope, 176, 188
Malone, Dorothy, 167
Man's Castle (1933), 111
March, Fredric, 204
Marie, Michel, 2, 14–5, 16, 30, 31
Marie-Laurent, Jeanne, 50
Marion, Frances, 111–114, 117, 120, 124, 126–127, 129
Marker, Frederick, 37
Marker, Lise-Lone, 37
The Marriage Circle (1924), 6
Martin, Vivian, 62
Marxism, 168
Mästerman (1920), 73–74
matte shot, 141–143
May, Joe, 93
May, Karl, 93
Mayer, Louis B., 60
McAvoy, May, 133
McConnell, Gladys, 159
melodrama, 2, 6–7, 12, 15, 62, 110, 112–114, 117, 122, 124, 129–130, 163, 166–168, 170, 176–177, 182, 185–186, 191, 194, 196, 200–203, 290. See also acting
Metro-Goldwyn-Mayer Studios (MGM), 10, 110, 143, 221, 227, 229–231
Mévisto, 22
Mezhrabpom (film studio), 8, 174
miming, 19–20

mise-en-scène, 53, 84, 145, 148, 167, 222, 262, 271. See also staging
Les Misérables (1912), 14, 278
Miss Mend (*Мисс Менд*) (1926), 8, 162–175
Miss Lulu Bett (1922), 114
Mizoguchi Kenji, 253
modernism, 228, 253
modernity, 95, 223, 255–256, 272
The Monastery of Sendomir (1920), 80
'monopoly film', 32
Moore, Hilda, 9, 193–194, 196, 199–204, 300
Moreau, Louis-Mathurin, 15
Moscow Arts Theatre, 281
Moulin Rouge (1928), 208–209, 215, 218
Mother (1926), 163, 168, 173–174
Motion Picture News, 150, 178, 181, 186, 298
Murder on the Second Floor (1932), 204
Murnau, Friedrich, Wilhelm, 222, 305
Museum of Modern Art (MOMA), 205
musical accompaniment, 187
Musser, Charles, 131, 140, 292
Les Mystères de Paris (1912), 15
The Mysterious Lady (1928), 227

Nagel, Conrad, 221
Napierkowska, Stacia, 16
Naruse Mikio, 11–12, 253–259, 262–267, 269–273, 278, 308, 309
narration, 10, 54, 61, 62–7, 70, 72, 119–20, 127, 130, 133, 142, 152, 166, 172–3, 221, 223–8, 231, 245, 270, 293, 305
National Portrait Gallery, 205

329

naturalism, 2, 16, 30, 33, 36–38, 40, 82, 86–7, 110, 113–115, 124, 129, 196; literary naturalism, 2, 15; naturalist theatre, 6, 15, 37. See also acting
Navarre, René, 95
Navaro, Ramon, 222
Neale, Steve, 112–3, 120, 122, 168, 188
Nelson (1918), 195
Nettleford Studios, 203
The New Woman (1935), 242
New York Dramatic Mirror, 68
New York Times, 62
Die Nibelungen (The Nibelungs) (1924), 94
Nielsen, Asta, 32–33
Nikkatsu (film studio), 2, 12, 278
Nissen, Egeda, 97, 105–106
No Greater Glory (1934), 111
North China Film Company (Huabei dianying gongsi), 233, 235, 307
Not Blood Relations (1932), 266, 309
Nothing Else Matters (1920), 195
Notre Dame, 56
Notre Dame de Paris (1911), 14–15
Novak, Jane, 111
Novello, Ivor, 202–203
Now Don't Get Excited (1931), 257

O'Donoghue, Darragh, 86
The Old Curiosity Shop (1921), 195
Olenina, Ana, 169, 172, 174
Old Ironsides (1926), 188
The Old Swimmin' Hole (1920), 114–115
Otsep, Fedor, 8, 162–163
out-of-sequence filming/shooting, 53–54, 59

Ozu Yasujiro, 11–12, 244, 253, 255, 278

Palais de Danse (1928), 1, 9, 193–204
Paramount Pictures, 143, 176, 178, 188, 204, 208, 210; 'Magnascope' projection, 176, 188
parody, 164, 169, 171, 173–174
Passion Play productions, 1
Pathé, 5, 14, 20, 32, 53, 55, 234; cameras, 20
Paul, Fred, 131
Pearson, Roberta, 15, 16, 278
The Perils of Pauline (1914), 93
Perret, Léonce, 3, 48–50, 52–59, 282, 283
Phantom (1922), 92
The Phantom Carriage (Körkarlen) (1921), 4, 73–90
Piccadilly (1929), 9–10, 205–220
Pickford, Mary, 195, 239, 305
pictorialism (acting style), 33, 38, 46–47
Pitts, Zasu, 111, 120
Plain français, 53, 284
Pleasures of the Dance Hall (Ge chang chunse) (1931), 234
Point-of-view shot (POV), 51, 54, 117–118, 126, 128, 140, 189–191, 218, 225, 248–249
Polanski, Roman, 207
Pommer, Erich, 92
Pool of London (1951), 204
Poulton, Mabel, 9, 193–197, 202–204
Pour Vous, 241
Powell, Michael, 204
Pozdorovkin, Maxim, 169, 172, 174
Preminger, Otto, 143
Pravda, 165, 174

Die Prinzessin Suwarin (*Princess Suwarin*) (1922), 92
Privat, Suzanne, 49
propaganda, 164, 169–170, 173
psychoanalysis, 97, 101, 113
Putti, Lya De, 208

Quatre-vingt-treize (1921), 14
Quinneys (1927), 195
Quo Vadis? (1913), 32

Raja Harischandra (1913), 2
Ralston, Jobyna, 182
Randolf, Anders, 223
Raskolnikov (1923), 5
Ray, Charles, 115
Renoir, Louis, 204
The Return of the Rat (1929), 203
Rich, Irene, 134
Richter, Paul, 97
Rickenbacker, Eddie, 178
Ritchard, Cyril, 213
Rittner, Rudolph, 37
RKO Pictures, 10
road-show exhibition, 8, 187, 291
Robertshaw, Jerrold, 193
Rodchenko, Aleksandr, 164
Rogers, Charles, 179, 182
Le Roman d'un mousse (1914), 49
romance (genre/narrative), 30, 180–181
Rosay, Françoise, 222, 230
Rotha, Paul, 163, 205, 206, 214
La Roue (1923), 94
Royal Danish Theatre, 32
Rozen-Sanin, Mikhail, 165
Rosenel, Natalya, 165, 167
Roses of Picardy (1927), 195
Ruan Lingyu, 11, 237, 240, 242
Rubens, Alma, 111
Russell, Catherine, 254, 256

Russia, 2, 5, 8; film production, 162–164; literature, 164, 166–167

Sadoul, Georges, 49
St Pierre, Paul Matthew, 213
Salt, Barry, 63, 276, 284, 287
Sandhu, Sukhdev, 205–7
Sangue bleu (1914), 2–3, 33, 36, 38, 46
Sargent, Epes W., 64, 67
Saturday Afternoon (1926), 150
Saunders, John Monk, 178
Schettlow, Hans Adalbart, 96, 106
Schneiderman, George, 120
Seiichi Kato, 250
Sennett, Mack, 148
Serena, Gustavo, 33
serials, 6, 8, 50, 92–94, 166, 171, 207, 289
Seven Chances (1925), 239
Seventh Heaven (1927), 110–111, 114, 126
Shaginian, Marietta, 8, 164
Shakespeare, William, 72
Shallert, Edwin, 178, 186
shell shock, 153, 156
Shimazu Yaujiro, 255
Shimizu Hiroshi, 255
Shinobu Setsuko, 13, 164
The Ship That Died of Shame (1955), 204
Shochiku (studio), 11–13, 253–259, 266, 278
Shubert Productions, 61–62
Shun Pao (Shanghai), 241
The Silver Fleet (1943), 204
Singer, Ben, 163
The Singing Beauty (*Yu Meiren*) (1931), 241
The Sins of the Fathers (1928), 208
Siraudin, Paul, 15

Sirk, Douglas, 113, 167
Sjöström, Victor, 4–5, 16, 73–76, 80–84, 86–87, 89–90, 287
The Skin Game (1931), 204
The Smiling Lieutenant (1931), 256
The Smiling Madame Beudet (1923), 230
Smith, Winchell, 114
So This is Paris (1926), 7, 143
Société Cinématographique des Artistes et des Gens de Lettres (Artists' and Writers' Film Company), 14, 20
Son of India (1931), 222, 231
Songstress Red Peony (*Genü hong mudan*) (1931), 234, 241
sound cinema, 40; technology, 10; transition to the 'talkies'/sound era, 10–12, 203, 244–245
Spaak, Charles, 222
Specht, Georges, 3, 48–50, 52
special effects, 73, 83, 89
Die Spinnen (*The Spiders*) (1919–1920), 94, 289
Spione (*Spies*) (1928), 106
The Spoilers (1914), 280
Stage Fright (1950), 222
Staging, 4, 33, 37, 38, 46, 49, 71, 80, 83–6, 96, 98, 101, 120, 133, 146, 189, 250, 259, 267–9, 282–3. See also *mise-en-scène*
Stanislavsky, Konstantin, 15, 37
Star Film Company (Mingxing yingpian gongsi), 11, 234
Star Wars (1977), 177
Stella Dallas (1937), 113, 120
Stepanova, Varvara, 164
Stiller, Maruice, 5
Stoll Picture Productions, 195
Strange to Relate (1943), 204
Street Angel (1928), 110, 114

Street Without End (*Kagiri naki hodo*) (1934), 11, 13, 253–273
Steinhoff, Hans, 211
Stroheim, Erich von, 114
The Strong Man (1926), 7, 144–161
Suchenski, Richard, 60
Sue, Eugène, 15
Sugawara Hideo, 12, 243
'superspecials', 8, 176, 187
Svennberg, Tore, 76
Svenska Film, 4–5
Sweden, 4; film production, 2, 4–5, 73
Sylvie, Louise, 21, 25, 30–31, 280
synchronized sound, 221, 234–235, 241, 244, 246

tableau (shot type), 7, 15, 24, 50–51, 54–55, 117
Takeshi Sakamoto, 243
Tatar, Maria, 211
Tatsuo Saito, 12, 243
Taxi for Two (1929), 203
Terror on Tiptoe (1936), 204
Das Testament des Dr Mabuse (*The Testament of Dr Mabuse*) (1933), 108
Thalasso, Arthur, 145
Thomas, Jameson, 212
Thompson, Kristin, 5, 10, 63–4, 140, 169, 278
The 1000 Eyes of Dr Mabuse (*Die 1000 Augen des Dr Mabuse*) (1960), 108
Three Comrades (1938), 111
Three's a Crowd, (1927), 149, 151
Thurston, Charles, 160
Tie-ins, 6, 92–3
The Times (London), 219
Toho Studio, 253, 255
Tokkan Kozo, 243

Tourneur, Maurice, 3, 60–62, 66, 68, 69–70, 72
Traffic in Souls (1913), 63
Tramp, Tramp, Tramp (1926), 144, 149, 152
Triangle Distributing Corporation, 131
Tschechowa, Olga, 208
Turim, Maureen, 171
Two Stars of the Milky Way (*Yin han shuang Xing*) (1931), 235
Tybjerg, Casper, 83, 87

Uclo-Decla-Bioscop (studio), 92, 94
Ullstein Publishing Company, 92
Unique Film Company (Tianyi yingpian gongsi), 11, 234
United Kingdom; culture, 206; film production, 2, 5, 9, 47, 203, 206–207, 245
United Photoplay Service (UPS), 11, 232–5, 239
United States of America, 1, 170; film production, 4, 5, 32, 47, 48–49, 59, 60, 93, 95, 140, 163, 177, 203, 208, 221, 230–231, 233, 238–239, 245; critical response to American films, 64, 163
University of California, Los Angeles (UCLA), 205
Universum Film Aktiengesellschaft (Ufa), 5, 92, 104, 108, 176

Les Vampires (1915–16), 8, 93, 95
Variété (1925), 208, 213–215, 218
Variety, 65, 112, 114, 129, 176, 177, 181, 187, 188–9, 208
variety performance, 1, 147
vaudeville, 1, 152, 208
Veidt, Conrad, 198

verismo, 38
Verneuil, Louis, 204

Wada-Marciano, Mitsuyo, 254
Walker, Michael, 166–7
Wallace, Edgar, 204
Ward, Warwick, 208, 213
Warner Bros., 10, 131, 143, 204
Warning Shadows (*Schatten*) (1922), 5
Waxworks (*Wachsfigurenkabinett*) (1924), 5
Weijden, Tor, 88
Welcker, Gertrud, 95, 105
Wellman, William, 9, 177–180, 191
western (genre), 115
Western Electric, 10,
What Price Glory (1926), 181
Whitechapel (1920), 211
Why Change Your Wife? (1920), 239
wide-screen films, 188
Wife! Be Like a Rose! (1935), 253
Wilcox, Herbert, 210
Wild Flowers (*Ye cao xian hua*) (1930), 234
Wilde, Oscar, 7, 131–132, 292
Williams, Linda, 182, 186
Wings (1927), 8, 176–192
The Wishing Ring: An Idyll of Old England (1914), 3–4, 60–72
Witchard, Anne, 211
Wollen, Peter, 207
A Woman of Paris (1923), 7, 140
The Woman Tempted (1926), 195
Wong, Anna May, 9, 205, 210, 212
World War I (1914–1918), 5, 48, 94, 178–179, 186–187; impact on film production, 4, 5; films/scenes set during, 8, 111–113, 124, 153, 157, 176–192; representations of, 9, 177
World Film Corporation, 3, 61

Xinhua Company, 241

Yankee Doodle in Berlin (1919), 185
Yingxi zazhi (The Film Magazine), 232–5, 241
Young and Innocent (1937), 204
Youngblood, Denise, 163, 174
Yuan Meiyun, 242

Zhang Shankun, 241
Zhu Shilin, 11, 235–238, 307
Zola, Emile, 2, 14–15, 17, 20, 30
Zukor, Adolph, 188

www.ingramcontent.com/pod-product-compliance
Lightning Source LLC
Chambersburg PA
CBHW020639300426
44112CB00007B/165